THE CIVILIZATION OF THE AMERICAN INDIAN SERIES

THE CREEK FRONTIER, 1540–1783

The Creek
Frontier
1540-1783

by David H. Corkran

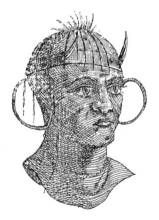

UNIVERSITY OF OKLAHOMA PRESS : NORMAN

BY DAVID H. CORKRAN

The Cherokee Frontier: Conflict and Survival, 1740–62 (Norman, 1962)
The Creek Frontier, 1540–1783 (Norman, 1967)

LIBRARY OF CONGRESS CATALOG CARD NUMBER: 67–10143

TO HARRIET

Foreword

With the number of excellent studies of the southern Indians already available, another work on the Creeks perhaps may seem redundant. But so far as I know there has as yet been no attempt to piece together the entire available history of the Creeks in the colonial period. Nor has there been an effort to study the southern frontier from the Indian point of view; that is, from the point of view of the primarily Indian factors which operated to influence events. Indeed, the entire American frontier needs to be restudied from the Indian point of view, not only to recapture the essential Indian but to cast a fresh new light on factors operating in the Indian nations which influenced history. From such a study it is clear that estimates of the colonial governors' handling of Indian affairs must be revised; for frequently they are credited with triumphs of diplomacy which were mere ratifications of decisions already made by the Indians in council based on Indian factors. In crisis the Indian leadership was often intelligent, astute, and canny in taking advantage of the conflicting forces which swelled around them. The Creeks, though deficient in great leadership, were wise in council, and managed, despite bitter factionalism, for the most part to steer through the shoals which threatened their independence in the period under consideration. In this respect they were perhaps the most successful Indians on the English colonial frontier. Certainly no group of Indian headmen worked more conscientiously for their national good. Their success was a triumph of their well-developed system of council and consensus—republican rather than democratic, a congeries of semi-representative and hereditary oligarchs which functioned in a rude parliamentarianism.

Although the overriding importance of the deerskin trade to the Creeks demonstrates anew the importance of economic determinism, yet the key to much of Creek history lies in such institutional factors as the iron-clad character of the clan tie, the prestigial influence of the elders, and the tribal expectation that the young men conduct themselves with boldness. There is, moreover, an individualistic factor—the behavior or decision of any one man at a given moment may and does turn the tide of history. These factors justify the emphasis upon episode and individuals which characterizes this presentation of Creek history.

DAVID H. CORKRAN

Chicago, Illinois
December 1, 1966

Acknowledgments

THE RESEARCH NECESSARY for this study was made possible by a grant from the American Philosophical Society which enabled me to visit the Clements Library, Ann Arbor, Michigan; the Library of Congress; the South Carolina Historical Society, Charleston, S.C.; and the Department of Archives and History, Columbia, S.C. Much of the work was also done at The Newberry Library, Chicago, Illinois. Chief Librarian Lawrence Towner, Fred Hall, Joseph Wolf, and Colton Storm of that institution have rendered me invaluable assistance. At the Clements Library, William Ewing's helpful hand guided me through the intricacies of that manuscript collection. In South Carolina Mrs. Marjorie Prior, librarian of the South Carolina Historical Society at Charleston, and Francis Lee and William L. McDowell, Jr., of the Department of Archives and History at Columbia placed the resources of their collections at my disposal and pointed the way to significant materials. Maps were adapted by Denison B. Hull from eighteenth-century maps.

D. H. C.

Contents

Illustrations

xv

THE CREEK FRONTIER, 1540–1783

Introduction: The Creeks

THE CREEK OR MUSKOGEE INDIANS of the sixteenth, seventeenth, and eighteenth centuries lived in what is now central and northern Alabama and Georgia. The derivations of the names are uncertain. The name "Creek" seems to have been given them by the English. According to the eighteenth-century writer James Adair, who as a trader traveled their country, the English called them "Creeks" after the many streams and rivers of their country. The twentieth-century historian Verner Crane derives the name "Creek" from Ochise Creek or the Ocmulgee River, on which they lived when the English began to have heavy trading contacts with them. "Muskhoge," Adair says, means "dwellers in the swamps," but if this is the true original name, it probably has some other meaning, for the Muskogees came out of the arid trans-Mississippi west, and even in their eastern home the land they occupied is not swampy. From their name, "Muskhoge," anthropologists have classified as Muskogeans a large group of Indian tribes who speak related languages. Lately it has been suggested that the Muskogeans are related to the northern Algonkians.

3

Creek legends state that the tribe came to the Southeast by way of the Red River. When they came is obscure, but it is possible that they were part of the great intrusion of northern Indians which entered the southwest by way of the eastern Rockies in the period A.D. 800–1000. Archaeologists classify prehistoric Creek culture late Mississippian, or late temple mound, as distinguished from the early Mississippian or early temple mound which characterizes the builders of the great mound near Macon, Georgia. The early mound builders belong to the period A.D. 800–1200. Whether they were destroyed, dispersed, or incorporated by the invading Creeks is not known. The last is a distinct possibility, for Indian tribes tended to increase their numbers by incorporating the survivors of the conquered, and the Creeks had a genius for taking fragments of other tribes under their wing. When history opened on the Creeks, they had already accepted into their confederacy the Alabama, Koasati, and Hitchiti Indians. In historic times they incorporated elements of the Apalachee, Shawnee, Yuchi, Yamasee, Natchez, and Chickasaw tribes.

Though of disparate tribes, the Creeks considered themselves a nation distinct from the Cherokees in the mountains to the north, the coastal tribes to the east, the Timucas and Mobiles to the south, and Choctaws and Chickasaws to the west. Theirs was a loose confederacy, built around the original Muskogee towns of Coweta, Cussita, Tuckabatchee, and Coosa. It was held together by ties of language—the incorporated tribes having the Creek as well as their ancestral languages—intermarriage of clans, and the annual national meetings and frequent regional meetings of village headmen, presided over by a principal headman of either the Upper or the Lower Towns, as the accidents of heredity and prestige dictated at various periods. In historic times the Creeks numbered from seven thousand to nine thousand people, capable of mustering from twenty-five hundred to thirty-five hundred fighting men. They lived in approximately sixty towns, some forty of which including those of the Alabamas and Koasatis, constituted the Upper Towns on the Coosa and Tallapoosa rivers of Alabama. The Upper Towns fell into three divisions: the Alabamas, the Tallapooses, and the

4

Abeikas. Principal towns of the Tallapooses were Muccolossus, Tuckabatchee, and Tallassee. Those of the Abeikas were Coosa in the earlier period, Okchai and Okfuskee in the later. The twenty Lower Towns, originally ten, situated at various times on the Ocmulgee, Flint, and Chattahoochee rivers of Georgia, had as their chief towns Coweta and Cussita. The national capital, in so far as one existed, was usually at whichever of the above-named towns was the home of the presiding chief of the national meeting. Other towns sporadically held the distinction, notably Little Tallassee during the American Revolution. During the historic period, the primary chieftainship was held most often by the Cowetas in the Lower Towns and by the Abeikas in the Upper Towns. Towns were divided into two categories: war or red towns, and white or peace towns. This distinction had nothing to do with the temperament of the towns, but was a traditional designation and probably related to ritualistic functions in the making of war and the making of peace. It would seem that Okmulgee in the Lower and Okchai in the Upper Towns were the primary white towns, and Coweta and Cussita in the Lower and Okfuskee in the Upper were the primary red towns.[1]

The Creek Country: Early reporters represented the natural beauties of the Creek country as almost idyllic. James Adair, who traveled the region between 1745 and 1765, wrote: "The Upper part of the Muskohge country is very hilly—the middle—less so—the lower towns level. . . . Most of their towns are very commodiously and pleasantly situated on large beautiful creeks, or rivers where the lands are fertile, the water clean and well tasted, and the air extremely pure. As the streams have a quick descent, the climate of a most happy temperature, free from disagreeable heat or cold, unless for the space of a few days in summer or

---

[1] John R. Swanton, the historian of the early Creeks, is explicit in stating that Cussita was a white or peace town (*Early History of the Creeks and Their Neighbors*, 218, 225). However, at the meeting at Picolata in Florida in November, 1765, Captain Allick, a headman of Cussita, said that "Tallachea [of Okmulgee] spoke for the peace towns, that he [Allick] was from a war town, Cussita, and would speak for the war towns" (Stuart to Gage, Jan. 21, 1766, Papers of General Thomas Gage relating to his command in North America, 1762–76 [hereinafter referred to as Gage Papers], Vol. XLVII).

winter .... In their country are four bold rivers which spring from the Apalache mountains and interlock with the eastern branches of the Mississippi. The Koosa river . . . is two hundred yards broad . . . Okwhuske [Tallapoosa] lies seventy miles from the former, which taking a considerable southern sweep, runs westward and joins the aforesaid great stream. . . . seventy miles eastward from Okwhuskee . . . Chattahoochee river near the old trading path . . . a great limpid stream is 200 yards broad and lower down it passes by the Apalache into Florida. . . . this nation extends 140 miles in breadth from east to west, according to the course of the trading path."[2] The British officer Thomas Campbell, who visited the Upper Creek Towns in 1764, spoke of "a most delightful country . . . villages and plantations always near running water." Besides the "great many small creeks that run across the country," he mentioned the Tallapoosa and Coosa rivers, the banks of which are "high and steep," and those parts which are low are "mostly thick cane swamps." Near the towns on the flat lands were "fields large, even, and open." But the country was dominated by forests of oak, hickory, poplar, tupelo, sweet gum, and pine.[3]

The Creek Villages: Francis Ogilvie in the summer of 1764[4] reported fifty-nine Creek villages, thirty-nine in the Upper Towns and twenty in the Lower Towns, with a total of 3,683 gunmen— the term used to describe those capable of bearing arms. The Upper Creeks he divided into three groups: the Alabamas, about or below the junction of the Coosa and Tallapoosa rivers; the Tallapooses, curving around the great westward bend of the Tallapoosa River; and the Abeikas, up the Coosa from the forks and on the Tallapoosa somewhat above the Tallapoose towns. Ogilvie listed the Alabama towns, six in number, as Puckna, Little Oachoys, Weetmhees, Little Cussauties, Fushegies, and Cussawaties. The Tallapoose list contained thirteen towns: Muckelasses, Conohachie, Fushatchies, Cullamies, Cleonothies, Oakfushutchies, Otassies,

---

[2] James Adair, *The History of the American Indians*, 275.

[3] Thomas Campbell, "Narrative of a Visit to Creek Nation 1764–1765," Athell Papers.

[4] Gage Papers, Vol. XXI, July 8, 1764.

Sowcahatchies, Swaglees, Tuckabatchees, Eutchies, Talassees, and Nosaties. The largest group consisted of the twenty Abeika towns: Little Tallassee, Hatchesoufke, Weokas, Hatchecupe, Kaulegies, Ochehoy, Eufales, Oakfuskees, Hatchahatchie, Soukechoupege, Ottasies, Hillaby, Hillapoushe, Ouakekeys, Puckatalahassie, Patlake, Abekutchies, Notchees, Nanahumgies, and Tallasathachies. In listing the Lower Towns, mostly on Chattahoochee River, Ogilvie included the Seminole villages of Letchawie and New Ocony which were but eighty miles from St. Augustine in Florida. The other Lower Towns were Coweta, Swaglaws, Cussitas, Euthchies, Ousutchies, Chihaws, Hitchitas, Pallachicolas, Okonies, Hatchicapa, Oakfenulgues, Osswaygle, Little Ofswagle, Youfalas, Chewallies, Oyallies, Weuopkies, and Puconawheedla.

The villages each had from twenty-five or thirty houses to a hundred or more, radiating in little square compounds from the central village government and ceremonial square and chunky yard or play field. The earliest account of a Creek village, that of the Gentleman of Elvas, one of the De Soto chroniclers (1540), describes Toalli, a presumably Hitchiti town which does not appear in the 1764 list: "The houses of this town were different from those behind [in the march from Florida] which were covered with dry grass; then upward they are roofed with cane after the fashion of tiles. They are kept very clean: some have their sides so made of clay as to look like tapia. . . . Throughout the cold country every Indian has a winter house, plastered inside and out, with a very small opening, which is closed at dark and a fire being made within, it remains heated like an oven, so that clothing is not needed during the night. He has likewise a house for summer and near it a kitchen, where fire is made and bread baked. Maize is kept in barbacoas, which is a house with wooden sides like a room, or raised aloft on four posts and has a floor of canes. The difference between the houses of the masters or principal men and those of the common people is beside being larger than the others, they have deep balconies on the front side, with cane seats like benches; and about are many barbacoas in which they bring together the

7

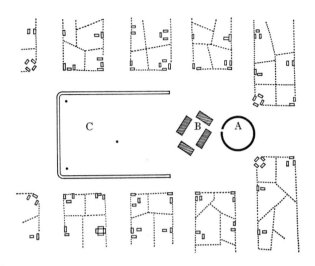

CREEK TOWNS AND DWELLINGS

(After Bartram, last quarter of eighteenth century)

The general position of the Chunk-Yard and Public Buildings of the Creeks, in respect to the dwellings of the Indians themselves is shown in the following engraved plan:

A, is the Rotunda; B, the Public Square; C, the grand area or Chunky-Yard. The habitations of the people are placed with considerable regularity in streets or ranges, as indicated in the plan.

tribute their people give them of maize, skins of deer, and blankets of the country."[5]

The account of William Bartram, who was in the Creek country in 1775, helps us to visualize a family compound: "The dwellings of the Upper Creeks consist of little squares, or rather of four dwelling houses inclosing a square area, exactly on the plan of the public square. Every family, however, has not four of these houses; some have but three, others not more than two, and some but one, according to the circumstances of the individual, or number of his family. Those who have four buildings have a particular use for each building. One serves as a cook room and winter lodging house,

5 Edward Gaylord Bourne, *Narratives of the Career of Hernando de Soto*, I, 53.

another as a summer lodging house and hall for receiving visitors, and a third for a granary or provision house, etc. The last is commonly two stories high, and divided into two apartments, transversely, the lower story of one end being a potato house, for keeping such other roots as require to be kept close and defended from cold in winter. The chamber above it is the council. At the other end of this building, both upper and lower stories are open on their sides; the lower story serves for their shed for their saddles, pack saddles, and gears and other lumber; the loft over it is a very spacious, airy, pleasant pavilion, where the chief of the family reposes in the hot seasons, and receives his guests, etc. The fourth house (which completes the square) is a skin or warehouse, if the proprietor is a wealthy man and engaged in trade or traffic, where he keeps his deerskins, furs, merchandise, etc., and treats his customers. Smaller or less wealthy families make one, two, or three houses serve all their purposes as well as they can."[6]

Agriculture and Food: Besides being hunters of the abundant deer, woods buffalo, bear, and wild turkey, the Creeks were agriculturalists. Campbell reported in 1764: "They begin to plant corn, beans, and sweet potatoes the beginning of April and the end of March, all the men and women go into the field together without distinction and hoe and inclose for the use of the village, which is distributed when ripe to the different families in proportion to their number. Their grounds are very rich as they seldom change and never manure them and have generally good crops, and they depend so much upon it, as to plant no more than just serves from one year to another. When they have a bad crop they must be in great distress, as Indian corn is their chief food all summer which they use in many different ways; by beating to a fine flower in a large wooden mortar they make bread of it; by parching before it is made into flower they make homeny or potage; and by preparing it not quite so small, and boiling it with oak or hickory ashes, they make their drink, which is mostly used all summer, the

---

[6] William Bartram, "Observations on the Creek and Cherokee Indians," Transactions of the American Ethnological Society [hereinafter referred to as "Observations"], III, Pt. 1, pp. 55–56.

salts which is in the ashes makes it ferment after boiling which gives it an agreeable taste, makes it cool, refreshing, wholesome and fitt for that hott season."[7]

Appearance and Dress: In appearance, the Creeks, according to LeClerc Milfort (1776–1783) were "of medium stature, of copper-red colour; they are very strong and robust and easily bear fatigue."[8] According to Campbell, "The men are in general middle size well lim'd and clean, made woth features serious, manly, agreeable. The women are short, thick and strong in proportion, and some of them very handsome."[9]

The ancient dress of the Creeks was comprised of short "blankets" and skins of beasts. The Gentleman of Elvas described the blankets and their use, saying, "these are like shawls, some of them made from the inner bark of trees, and others of grass resembling nettles, which, by treading out, becomes flax. The women use them for covering, wearing one about the body from the waist downward and another over the shoulder with the right arm left free after the manner of the gypsies: the men wear but one, which they carry over the shoulder in the same way, the loins being covered with a braguerire of deer-skin, after the fashion of the woolen breech cloth that was the custom of Spain. The skins are well dressed the colour being given them that is wished, and is such perfection, that when of vermillion, they look like very fine red broad cloth, and when black, the sort in use for shoes, they are of the purest. The same hues are given to blankets."[10]

Adair noticed in 1775, after the Creeks had long been accustomed to European clothes, a certain degree of preference for the older forms of dress with some admixture of the new: "Their chief dress is very simple . . . of choice many of their old men wear a long wide frock, made of skins of wild beasts. . . . They formerly wore shirts, made of dresst deerskins, for their summer visiting

---

[7] Campbell, "Visit to Creek Nation."

[8] LeClerc Milfort, *Memoirs or a Quick Glance at My Various Travels and My Sojourn in the Creek Nation* (ed. and trans. by Ben C. McCary), 134. Permission to use material from Milfort's *Memoirs* has been granted by the translator.

[9] Campbell, "Visit to Creek Nation."

[10] Bourne, *De Soto Narratives*, I, 58.

dress; but their winter hunting clothes were long and shaggy, made of skins of panthers, bucks, bears, beavers and others; the fleshy sides outward, sometimes doubled, and always softened like velvet cloth, though they retained their fur and hair. . . . The women's dress consists only of a broad softened skin, or several soft skins sewn together, which they wrap and tye round their waist, reaching a little below their knees: in cold weather they wrap themselves in softened skins of buffalo calves, with the wintry shaggy wool inward, never forgetting to anoint and tye their hair except in time of mourning. The men wear for ornaments, and the conveniencies of their hunting, their deerskin boots, well smoked, that reach so high up their thighs as with their jackets to secure them from brambles and brachy thickets. They sew them about five inches from the edges which are formed into tassels, to which they fasten fawn's trotters (hooves) and small pieces of tinkling metal, or wild turkey cockspurs. The beaus used to fasten the like to their war pipes, with the addition of a piece of an enemy's scalp with a tuft of long hair hanging down from the middle of the stem, each of them painted red; and they still observe that old custom, only they choose bell buttons to give a greater sound. The young Indian men and women through a fondness for their antient dress, wrap a piece of cloth around them, that has a near resemblance to the old Roman toga. . . . 'Tis about a fathom square bordered seven or eight quarters deep to make a shining cavalier of the beau monde and to keep out both heat and cold. With this frantic apparel the red heroes swaddle themselves, when they are waddling, whooping and prancing it away in their sweltering town houses . . . around the reputed holy fire.

"They have a great aversion to wearing breeches . . . the men wear a slip of cloth about a quarter of an ell wide and an ell and a half long in lieu of breeches, which they put between their legs, and tye round their haunches, with a convenient broad band . . . .

"The women since the time we first traded with them wrap a fathom of the breadth of stroud cloth round their waist, and tye it with an leathern belt, which is commonly covered with brass runners or buckles; but this sort of loose petticoat reaches only to their knees, in order to show their extremely fine proportioned limbs.

"They make their shoes for common use, out of the skins of the bear and elk, well dressed and smoked, to prevent hardening; but they chiefly go barefooted, and always bare-headed. The men fastened several different sorts of beautiful feathers, frequently in tufts, or the wing of a red bird, or the skin of a small hawk, to a lock of hair on the crown of their heads. And every Indian nation when at war, trims the hair after a different manner, through contempt of each other."[11]

A 1739 ranger's report of a dance at Coweta includes a description of dress: "They dance round a large fire by beating of small drums and six men singing; their dress is very wild and frightful, their faces painted with several sorts of colours, their hair cut short (except three locks, one of which hangs over their forehead like a horses fore-top), they paint the short hair and stick it full of feathers, they have balls and rattles about their waists and several things in their hands. Their dancing is of divers gestures and turnings of their bodies in a great many frightful postures. The women are mostly naked to the waist wearing only one short petticoat which reaches from their waist a little below their knees, they are very neat in smoothing and putting up their hair, it is so very long when untied that it reaches to the calves of their legs."[12]

Creek Government: Of Creek government, Governor Wright of Georgia wrote in 1764 that "they have no form of government or any coercive power among them." This was only partially true. General Oglethorpe earlier had perceived somewhat the same situation; he saw the role of the headmen as advisory and persuasive rather than coercive: "the weakness of the executive power is such, that there is no other way of punishment but by revenge of blood . . . for there is no coercive power . . . Their kings can do no more than persuade. All the power they have is no more than to call their old men and captains and to propound to them the measures they think proper. After they have done speaking, all the others

[11] Adair, *History of the American Indians,* 8–9.
[12] Newton D. Mereness, *Travels in the American Colonies,* 220–221.

have liberty to give their opinions also; and they reason together with great temper and modesty, till they have brought each other into some unanimous resolution, then they call in the young men and recommend the putting in execution the resolution with their strongest and most lively eloquence. In speaking to their young men they generally address to the passions; in speaking to their old men they apply to reason only."[13]

John Wesley said, "They have often three or four micos (kings) in a town; but without so much as a shadow of authority only to give advice, which everyone is at liberty to take or leave."[14] Some headmen, he noted, rose to more eminence and prestige than others: "But age and reputation for valor have given Chicali, a micko of Coweta town, a more than ordinary influence in the nation." Governor Johnstone of West Florida mentions the rise to influence of certain headmen: "The nature of Indian government, which is so many united republics, leaves a vast competition for power amongst them and produces a number of leading men, who, each has his weight in the direction of affairs."[15]

William Bartram (1789) gave a more explicit picture: "The mico is considered the first man in dignity and power and is the supreme civil magistrate; yet he is in fact no more than president of the national council of his own tribe and town, and has no executive power independent of the council, which is convened every day in the forenoon, and held in the public square."[16] But he notes, "It sometimes happens that the king (mico) is war-chief and high priest, and then his power is very formidable and sometimes dangerous to the liberty of citizens and he must be a very cunning man if the tomahawk or rifle do not cut him short." Hawkins (1799) gives the powers of the mico and the origins of his power: "The mico of the town superintends all public and domestic concerns, receives all public characters, hears their talks, lays them before

[13] Georgia Historical Society, *Collections* [hereinafter referred to as Ga. Hist. Soc., *Coll.*], II, 60.

[14] John Wesley, *The Journal of the Rev. John Wesley, A.M.*, I, 65.

[15] Dunbar Rowland (ed.), *Mississippi Provincial Archives, English Dominion, 1763–67*, p. 186.

[16] Bartram, "Observations," 23.

the town, and delivers the talks of his town. The mico of the town is always chosen from some one family, the mico of Tuckabatchee is of the eagle tribe (clan). After he is chosen and put on his seat, he remains for life. On his death, if his nephews are fit for the office, one of them takes his place as his successor; if they are unfit one is chosen of the next of kin, the descent always being in the female line. . . . When a mico from age, infirmity, or any other cause, wants an assistant, he selects a man who appears to him to be best qualified and proposes him to the counsellors and great men of the town; and if he is approved by them, they appoint him as an assistant . . . and he takes his seat in the cabbin accordingly. The mico of the town generally bears the name of the town, as Cussitah mico. He is what is called by the traders the Cussitah king."[17]

Next to the mico in prestige and influence was the head warrior of each town, the Tastanage. According to Benjamin Hawkins, a United States agent to the Creeks in the eighteenth century, "The Great warrior . . . is appointed by the mico and counsellors from the greatest war characters. When a young man is trained up and appears well qualified for the fatigues and hardships of war . . . the mico appoints him a governor, or, as the name imports, a leader . . . and if he distinguishes himself repeatedly in warlike enterprises arrives to the rank of Great Leader. This title though greatly coveted is seldom attained; as it requires a long course of years and great or numerous successes in war."[18]

"Surrounding the mico were two classes of councillors: the Micnggee and the Enchau ulgea. The Micnggee were a type of secondary councillor (the origin of which is unknown). The Enchau ulgee [henihi] or people second in command, the head of whom was called by the traders, second man. These had the direction of public works appertaining to the towns, such as public buildings, building houses in the town for new settlers, or working the fields. They were particularly charged with the ceremony of a-cee—the black drink, under the direction of the mico."[19] They were akin in function to the Cherokee peace or white chiefs.

The great warrior was surrounded by younger war leaders of

[17] *Ibid.*, 62.   [18] *Ibid.*, 63.   [19] *Ibid.*, 62.

the second class, and a third class of councilors was the "Iste-chaque" or, beloved men, the patriarchal former great warriors of renown, retired Micnggee, and others, who had attained distinction.[20] One gathers from the record that these men seldom spoke in council, but when they did, they were listened to with great respect and were very influential in the course of events. They held the beads giving the history of the nation, having memorized the beads from the accounts of the past elders who handed them down.

The evidence, then, points to a rulership by an assembly of great men, some of whom reached councilor position by age and service, some by heredity, and some by achievement. The colonial record, however, indicates that heredity was a strong factor. Micos tended to hand on the office to their sons (rather than to nephews as Bartram states) whom they trained up to follow in their footsteps. Mico and great warrior were often brothers or brothers-in-law, and sometimes one man was simultaneously mico and great warrior. Thus strong men arose by heredity, and it would seem from the record that when a strong man of one of the great towns or one of the four traditionally prestigious founding towns of Coweta and Cussita in the Lower and ancient Coosa (and its descendant Okchai) and Tuckabatchee in the Upper Towns achieved ascendancy, he was likely to be "emperor" or supreme mico, having a voice of considerable dimension in regional and sometimes national affairs. Thus in the Lower Towns arose the ascendancy of the mico of Coweta in the extended period from 1670 to 1763 where the line Brims-Chigelley-Malatchi-Togulki held sway. The ascendancy of the Gun Merchant of Upper Towns Okchai, about 1750–74, seems to relate to distinction attained through the white or peace phalanx of the henihi, for the Gun Merchant's official name was Enochtonachee, apparently meaning a chief henihi or second man who by personal force overshadowed the mico and himself became mico, by what routes of heredity and achievement the record does not suggest. Whatever the means by which a headman rose, the Creeks expected from him good sense and moderation. A Frenchman named Hubert reported of the head-

[20] *Ibid.*

men he had met: "The Indians are savage only in name. They have as much discernment and shrewdness as can be expected of a people without education. They talk little but very much to the point. They have a regular government among themselves after their own fashion, no injustice, no quarrels, a very exact subordination and great respect, whom they obey spiritedly."[21]

What the sentimental and romantic Hubert did not perceive was that in the councilor type of government, where freedom of speech characterized the councilors and ambition for high office spurred on the younger men, division of sentiment was inevitable. This was further stimulated by the factor of unswerving clan loyalty. A clan headman served the interests of his clan, and councilor agreement was impossible unless all the clans were satisfied. Such satisfaction was sometimes difficult to achieve, and the mico developed devices of circumventing clan obstruction by means of secret personal negotiation. Moreover, personal politicking by headmen or ambitious characters was a feature of Creek life, and more often than not Creek public action was determined by a successful *bund*, a clique of talents and family—with a bow to tradition and prestiges. An unsuccessful minority voice had either to get along as best it could by the devices of individual action which would be supported by clan loyalty until it could raise up a majority around itself or else by desperate deed precipitate the nation into an unsalvageable crisis. Too often Creek political life presents the picture of bitter division which prevents the councils from taking any stand at all while a species of anarchy exists. However, it is true that by and large the daily life of personal social relationships went along smoothly.

The Creek Square: The meeting places of the Creek governing councils were the square and the town house, the former for the daily public meetings in clement weather, the latter for ceremonial and winter meetings and also for meetings of a less public character. Bartram's is the classic description of the square: "The great or public square generally stands alone in the center and highest part

21 Dunbar Rowland and A. G. Saunders (eds.), *Mississippi Provincial Archives,* II, 249.

of the towns; it consists of four square or cubical buildings or houses of one story, uniform and of the same dimensions, so situated as to form an exact tetragon, encompassing an area of half an acre of ground; more or less according to the strength and largeness of the town, or will of its inhabitants; there is a passage or avenue at each corner of equal width; each building is constructed of a wooden frame fixed strongly in the earth, the walls filled in and neatly plastered with clay mortar; closed on three sides, that is, the back and two ends, except within about two feet of the wall plate or eves, which is left open for the purpose of a window and to admit a free passage of the air; the front or side next the square is quite open like a piazza."[22] David Taitt (1772) gives a description of the Tuckabatchee square: "The square is formed by four houses about forty feet in length and ten wide. Open in front and divided into three different cabins each. The seats are made of canes split and worked together and raised three feet off the ground and half the width of the house, the back half being raised above the other about one foot."[23]

For the purposes of council, the headmen and councilors occupied the houses and benches by specific rank and function. The first house, that of the mico, occupied the west side with its open front facing east. The mico sat in the center. To the right, or south, of him sat the Micnggee and councilors; to the left, or north, sat the Enchau ulgea. The second house was that of the warriors and was on the north side of the square, its opening facing south. The head warrior sat at the west end, nearest the cabin of the mico, and beside him sat the other war leaders. In the second division of the warriors' cabin sat those next in rank below the war leaders; and in the third division, the young warriors. The third house, that on the south side with its open front facing north, was that of the beloved men. This, however, was seldom full, for most of the great beloved men sat in the mico's cabin as councilors on his right. The fourth and lowest grade of cabin was on the east side with its open

[22] William Bartram, *Travels through North and South Carolina, Georgia, East and West Florida*, 451.

[23] Mereness, *Travels*, 503.

17

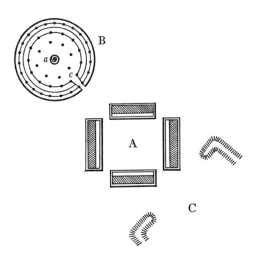

ARRANGEMENT OF THE PUBLIC BUILDINGS

(After Bartram, last quarter of eighteenth century)

This is the most common plan or arrangement of the Chunky-Yard, Public Square, and Rotunda of the modern Creek towns. A, the Public Square or area. B, the Rotunda; *c*, the door opening towards the square; the three circular lines show the two rows of seats, sofas, or cabins; the punctures show the pillars or columns which support the building; *a*, the great central pillar, or column, surrounded by the spiral fire, which gives light to the house. C, part of the Chunky-Yard.

front facing the mico's cabin on the west. It was occupied by the young people and their associates.[24] Thus presumably the daily morning meetings of the headmen were held in full view of all the responsible males of the town, seldom more than two hundred when all could be gathered, which was relatively infrequently, most of the beloved men being too old to leave their hot houses, many of the young people being busy about their hunting or other excursions, and some of the headmen absent on hunts or missions. Women or children were not allowed in the square. Usually the leading headmen had the square pretty much to themselves. White

24 Bartram, "Observations," 61–63.

men such as traders and visiting colony or crown officials were admitted to the square and seated with the micos.

However, much of the public business was transacted in the mico's private home and some in secret sessions in the town house or rotunda which was generally built at the northwest corner of the square with its door facing the southeast. Taitt depicted the rotunda at Tuckabatchee as being "a square building about thirty feet in diameter rounded a little at the corners; the walls are about four feet high; from these walls the roof rises about twelve feet, terminating in a point at the top. The door is the only opening in this house; for they have no window or funnel for the smoke . . . there is a small entry about ten feet long built at the outside of the door and turned a little round the side of the house to keep out the cold and prevent the wind blowing the fire about the house."[25] This house also served as a dancing and ceremonial center for certain religious rites.

From Bartram comes a picture of a ceremonial meeting of greeting and friendship for visiting whites at Upper Town Otassee in 1776: "In the first place the governor or officer who has the management of this business with his servants attending orders the black drink to be brewed which is a decoction or infusion of the leaves and tender shoots of the cassine; this is done under an open shed or pavilion at twenty or thirty yards distant, directly opposite the door of the council house. Next he orders bundles of dry canes to be brought in. These are previously split and broken in pieces to about the length of two feet, and then placed obliquely crossing one another on the floor, forming a special circle round about the great center pillar, rising to a foot or eighteen inches from the ground; and this circle spreading as it proceeds round and round, often repeated from right to left, every revolution increases its diameter, and at length spreads to a distance of ten or twelve feet from the center, more or less, according to the length of time the meeting or assembly is to continue. By the time these preparations are accomplished it is night and the assembly have taken their seats in order. The exterior or outer end of the special circle takes

[25] Mereness, *Travels*, 503.

fire and immediately rises into bright flame (but how this is effected I did not plainly apprehend, I saw no person set fire to it; there might have been fire in the earth, however, I neither saw nor smelt fire or smoke until the blaze instantly ascended upward) which gradually and slowly creeps round the center pillar with the course of the sun, feeding on dry canes, and affords a cheerful gentle, and sufficient light until the circle is consumed and the council breaks up. Soon after this illumination takes place the aged chiefs are seated in their cabins or sophas on the side of the house opposite to the door, in three classes or ranks, rising a little one above or behind the other; and the white people and red people of confederate towns in like order on the left hand; a transverse range of pillars supporting a thin clay wall about breast high separating them: the king's cabin or seat is in front; the next to the back of it the head warrior's; and a third or last accommodates the young warriors, etc. The Great War chief's seat or place in the cabin with and immediately to the left of the mico or king; and next to the white people; and to the right hand of the mico or king the most venerable headmen and warriors are seated. The assembly now being seated in order and the house illuminated, two middle aged men who perform the office of slaves or servants, pro tempore, come in together at the door, each having very large conch shells full of black drink, and advance with slow, uniform and steady steps, their eyes or countenance lifted up, singing very low but sweetly; they come within six or eight paces of the king's and white people's cabins, when they stop and each rests his shell on a tripos or little table, but presently takes it up again and, bowing very low, advances obsequiously crossing or intersecting each other about midway; he who rested his shell before the white people, now stands before the king, and the other who stopped before the white people; when each presents his shell, one to the king and the other to the chief of the white people, and as soon as he raises it to his mouth, the slave utters or sings two notes, each of which continues as long as he has breath; and as long as these notes continue, so long must the person drink or at least keep the shell to his mouth. These two long notes are very solemn and at once

20

strike the imagination with religious awe or homage to the supreme, sounding somewhat like a-hee-ejah and a-lu-yah. After this manner the whole assembly are treated, as long as the drink and light hold out, and as soon as the drinking begins, tobacco and pipes are brought. The skin of a wild cat or young tyger stuffed with tobacco is brought, and laid at the king's feet, with a great or royal pipe, beautifully adorned; the skin is usually of the animal of the king's family or tribe [clan], as wildcat, otter, bear, rattlesnake, etc. A skin of tobacco is likewise brought and cast at the feet of the white chief of the town, and from him it passes from one to another to fill their pipes from, though each person has besides his own peculiar skin of tobacco. The king or chief smokes first in the great pipe a few whiffs, blowing it off ceremoniously, first towards the sun, or as it is generally supposed toward the great spirit, for it is puffed upwards, next toward the four cardinal points, then towards the white people in the house; then the great pipe is taken from the hand of the mico by a slave and presented to the chief white man, and then to the great war chief, whence it circulates through the rank of headmen and warriors and then returns to the king. After this each one fills his pipe from his own or his neighbor's skin."[26]

This was evidently a ceremony to pledge peace and harmony during a white official's visit. It centered on three ancient symbols of the creator—the slant cross, the circle, and the fire, and symbolizes union in the white peace of the creator's blessing. Black drink and pipe symbolized cleansing and peace in the presence of the creator or "master of breath." Strikingly, the ceremony was in the nature of a communion service.

All meetings and daily morning conferences of the headmen were preceded by the drinking of the a-cee or black drink—a brew of the leaves of the cassine yupon—an oleaceous broad-leaved evergreen bush. Its evergreen presumably symbolized life eternal and was a water symbol of the creator. Milfort said the drink was immediately vomited and spit out. The purpose of the drink, he said, was to assure the chief of the assembly that each of the mem-

[26] Bartram, *Travels*, 450–52.

bers who composed it had a stomach free from food and consequently a clear head and that all deliberations would take place dispassionately.

Also held in the squares of the leading towns were annual regional meetings of the headmen of the various towns and sometimes whole nation meetings of headmen. Milfort asserted that the annual meeting was held in May: "The chiefs of the nation must assemble every year in the month of May to consider everything which can be of importance to the nation both internally and externally. When they are all at the place of meeting, called the grand cabin . . . the assembly is formed; and when it is formed none of those who compose it can leave its compass until all the public business is concluded. The president alone can absent himself for a few moments; but as all the others, he is obliged to spend the days and nights in the assembly and to be present at all deliberations.

"During the session of the assembly, no one can go nearer than twenty paces to the grand cabin. Only the chiefs of the warriors are admitted there; the subordinate chiefs who are present are intended to serve the others but have no voice in the deliberations. The women have the duty of preparing the necessary food and drink for the assembly; they bring and place everything at the distance marked out; the subordinate chiefs go get the provisions and place them in the grand cabin for the members of the assembly. In the center of the square formed by the cabin, a fire is lighted which burns continuously. At sunset the young people of both sexes assemble and come and dance round this fire until the appointed time; during this time the assembly breaks up and each member goes if it suits him to the cabin which is assigned to the rank he has attained; or he remains in the grand cabin and there enjoys the dance and amusements of the young people; but without being able to go outside the compass of the square so long as business is not entirely completed. When the dances which are to last only a limited time, are over, if the business of the assembly is not too urgent, each of the members rests in the cabin which belongs to his class; but as soon as the sun appears above the horizon, a drum calls all the chiefs to the assembly, which remains in session until the sun goes down."[27]

Bossu, who visited the Creeks in 1759, stated of the annual assembly: "They have an annual general assembly in the principal village of the nation. They build a large cabin for the occasion and each one takes his place according to rank. Each one speaks in turn, depending upon his age, his ability, his wisdom, and the services he has rendered the nation. The great chief of the tribe opens the meeting with a speech on the history and traditions of their land. He tells of the military exploits of his ancestors who distinguished themselves defending the nation, and urges his subjects to imitate the virtues of these men by bearing hardships and misery without muttering against the great spirit, who is the master of all living beings. He advises them to face adversity courageously and to sacrifice everything for the love of nation and liberty."[28]

Creek government thus appeared to express in the geometrical forms beloved of the Indian—the square, the circle, and the pyramid of office and prestige—the Creeks' essential love of orderliness under the white peace of the master of breath.

Hospitality and Courtesy: Hospitality was one of the outstanding characteristics of the Creeks. Campbell, having noted the ferocity of their warfare and treatment of prisoners, stated: "This seems not, however, to be their natural disposition; for they are compationate and asist each other when in distress and are hospitable to strangers where they have no suspition of their having designs against them."[29]

White visitors to the Creeks commented enthusiastically on Creek courtesy. Their fine feeling for the ritual of first meeting always surprised and pleased the whites. The ranger who reported General Oglethorpe's reception at Coweta in 1739 gave the following account: "Aug. 7th. We set forward on our way, we found several strings of cakes and bags of flower etc., which the Indians

[27] Milfort, *Memoirs*, 130.

[28] Jean-Bernard Bossu, *Travels in the Interior of North America, 1751–62*, 154.

[29] Campbell, "Visit to Creek Nation."

had hung up in the trees for our refreshm't—Aug. 8th. We encamped about two miles from the Indian town, the Indians sent boys and girls out of their towns with fowls, venison, pompions [squash or pumpkins], potatoes, watermelons and sundry other things. About ten of the clock we set forward and were met by the Indian king and some of their chiefs, the king had English colours in his hand. We saluted them and they returned our salute, and then shaking hands with the general and company, the king very gracefully taking him by the arm led him towards the town and when we came there they brought us two logs which they had placed for that purpose covered with bearskins and desired us to sit down which when we had done the head warriors of the Indians brought us black drink in conkshells which they presented to us and as we were drinking they kept whooping and haloowing as a token of gladness to see us."[30]

Bossu (1759) referring to his reception among the Abeikas wrote: "These Indians and their beautiful wives are very friendly. Upon landing among them you are greeted with a handshake and the peace pipe. After you have smoked, they ask you the reason for your trip, the length of time you have been travelling, if you intend to stay a long time, and whether you have a wife and children."[31]

Campbell (1764) said of his visit to the Tallapoosas, "Upon our arrival at the Muckliasseh, the Wolf King's village, they had up the English colours and he and the old men came to the trader's house we put up at. . . . After the chief first and the rest in turn had taken us by the hand, we all sat down, and after remaining silent for some minutes in order to rest and recollect, a custom they never neglect, the Wolf told us as we had travelled and must be fatigued, he would ask no questions that night to trouble us but would go home and send us some refreshment. He took his leave and the rest followed and immediately sent us some very fine boiled corned beef with sweet potatoes roasted."[32]

[30] Mereness, *Travels*, 220.
[31] Bossu, *Travels*, 131.
[32] Campbell, "Visit to Creek Nation."

Taitt (1772), making his debut as representative of the crown, wrote: "When I went in [to the hot house-rotunda] the men present came and shook hands with me and offered me their tobacco to smoke, afterwards they presented me with a calabash filled with black drink made from leaves of cassine."[33]

Creek Young Men: It is to be presumed that the undistinguished young men did not speak at all in the councils of town, region, and nation, unless called upon by the mico to make a statement. Youth was not generally regarded as a fount of wisdom as it is in our society and was expected to be silent in meeting. However, if the young would not follow the leadership of the elders, as appears to have been increasingly the case as white contacts became more frequent, the elders held their peace, merely refusing promotion to those whose hotheadedness involved harsh consequences for the nation. Actually, reckless rashness was expected of young warriors, and a young man could get nowhere without a display of spirit. Then at some time in his career a young man being groomed for a micoship was expected to break out of rashness into the moderation which entitled him to public trust. In a society where boasting of one's prowess in war was one of the anticipated experiences of the young men, boldness and bravery in battle which led to the taking of enemy scalps caused public note. This fact caused many of the young men to be forever in a fever for war, and the last thing a mico wished to do was to dampen the ardor of youth. But an ambitious young man had early to develop a feel for situation and learn how to temper his actions accordingly. Indeed there is reason to believe there was a class of young beloved men who even in the rigors of war were entrusted with the less strenuous duties, such as guarding horses, while the wilder spirits went to battle. Whether these quiet youths were hereditarily destined for the role of henihi is not clear, but the concept of a "pecking order" whereby the biggest bullies won the prizes, favored by some anthropologists, does not quite fit the Creek scene. Heredity played an important part even in the war phalanx. True, most of the rising young men of the mico class were expected to show

[33] Mereness, *Travels*, 502.

bravery in war and to win promotion on the battlefield. But if they were to move to the micoship, they must at some point in their careers show moderation and impress with wisdom. The height of Indian ambition seems to have been that of the micos to train their sons up to the bravery and moderation which would make them eligible to take their fathers' places. If a father failed in this, the leadership passed to a collateral line.

Clans: The Creeks were divided into matrilineal clans, i.e. groupings according to the mother's lineage. How many of these clans existed in colonial times is nowhere indicated, but there were at least seven and, judging from Swanton's listing for later periods and from the absorption of minor tribes, probably a great many more. Records for the colonial period name but four: the Wind, the "Tyger," the Bear, and the Eagle. Some members of each clan lived in almost every village. Marriages presumably were exogenous, i.e., into some other clan than that into which one was born. All children belonged to the mother's clan. Of clan chiefs, other than war chiefs, there is no mention; nor is there mention of clan matriarchs, though presumably these existed. Going to war was apparently by clan, and wars sometimes had the character of vendettas by particular clans; for the duty of blood vengeance for death or injury to any clan member lay upon all members of the clan. What the women's influence was here is not clear, but the violent death of a clansman was an injury to the mother's blood, and it seems likely that the women stirred up any sluggish members of the clan to vengeance. It appears that clan loyalty was greater than town or tribal loyalty. Punishment of a wrong doer had to be done by clan members or with the consent of the guilty man's clan. This led to frequent national division and caused a very serious strain on the tact and prestige of the headman. On this subject the Wolf of the Muccolossus informed Governor Wright of Georgia in 1766 that "our nation is all in tribes [clans] and the murderers have some of their tribes in every town, whenever there is any satisfaction demanded the whole tribe joins together and say when they are killed let the talk be made strait, so that we few headmen

26

cannot withstand those tribes or attempt to take satisfaction by force."[34]

Creek Warfare: Although the Creeks appear always to have been at war with one neighbor or another and although success in warfare was traditionally the primary means of gratifying the young men's egos, the coming of the white man intensified their war activity even more, not so much against the whites as against their neighbor Indians, who were all used in the power politics of the competing Europeans. The accentuation of war in the Creek polity led to a great increase in the influence of the war chiefs. Milfort wrote in 1802 of his experience (1776–84) that "the Tastanagey or great war chief had, at first, no part in the domestic administration. His authority lasted only as long as the war; but, today, he is the head chief of the nation with respect to civil as well as military affairs."[35] The war chief did not always have such universal power in the eighteenth century, but it is apparent in the Brims-Chigelley-Malatchi line of the Lower Creeks. When this line lost out, however, the ascendancy in the Lower Creeks passed to a peace chief, Tallachea of Okmulgee, for a while. In the Upper Creeks the peace chiefs, Hobohatchey and the Gun Merchant, retained a strong ascendancy during the period 1720–74. One of the factors leading to the rise of the war chiefs was the English practice of commissioning war chiefs to act as their agents in the towns; and, in the nature of the situation with conflict between Spain and France on the one hand and England on the other, the Europeans tended to cultivate the war chiefs with attention and gifts. Large beneficiaries of this tendency in the Upper Creeks were the Wolf King of the Muccolossus and Emisteseguo of Little Tallassee in the period 1763–83. Both apparently were notable warriors. English recognition practically gave Emisteseguo his position, and English support was also an important factor in the rise of Alexander McGillivray to be the "king" of the Creeks.

[34] Allen D. Candler (ed.), *Colonial Records of the State of Georgia* [hereinafter referred to as *Ga. Col. Rec.*], XXXVII, 157.

[35] Milfort, *Memoirs*, 147.

Creek warfare, with some marked exceptions in the earlier colonial period, was largely a matter of sporadic forays of small parties to take a few scalps and prisoners. Campbell (1764) wrote: "When at war they are generally in parties of twenty or thirty, sometimes fewer. They never ask any but their own family or clan to go with them and these they only acquaint they are going against such a nation and will remain at such a creek or hill where those who have a mind will find them. Their prisoners they often kill in a very cruel manner, and the wenches assist and are worse than the men."[36]

Milfort gave elaborate detail of the functioning of the war chief and the battle preparations of the warriors: "He was responsible for watching continually over the public safety, and for informing the peace chiefs of the wrongs done the nation or of matters which would disturb its tranquillity. When he had made known the need of assembling the warriors, a club, part of which was painted red, was immediately exhibited in public; that signified that a part of the nation, that is to say the young men, must hold themselves in readiness to march; for if the club had been painted red all over, the entire nation should have had to keep ready, which happened in most unusual cases. The manner of painting this club red, even today informs each particular chief, how many men he is to bring with him to the appointed meeting place."[37]

"When this club has arrived, each band chief has the drum beaten in front of the grand cabin of the town . . . all the inhabitants go there immediately; he informs them of the day and place where he must light his fire; he goes to this place before dawn and lights the fire by rubbing two pieces of wood together; he places it in the middle of a square formed by four stakes, and which is only large enough to hold the number of warriors he wants to assemble.

"As soon as daylight appears, the chief places himself between the two stakes which face the rising sun; he holds a bundle of sticks in his hand. When a warrior enters the enclosure, which is open only on this side, he throws away a stick and continues thus until the

36 Campbell, "Visit to Creek Nation."
37 Milfort, *Memoirs*, 147.

last one, which corresponds to the number of soldiers he needs. All those who present themselves afterwards can no longer be admitted, and turn back to their homes to take up their hunting arms, while indicating the place where they are going to hunt so that they can be found if needed. Those who have thus presented themselves too late, are ill received when they return to their families who reproach them for lack of eagerness to defend the native land."[38]

Each war chief carried a "medicine" or charm bag which assured good luck on his campaign. Milfort said that this included portions of the garments of a successful war chief: "When a war campaign is over, and the army returns, all the band chiefs accompany the Tastenagi or head war chief to the door of his house; and there the two oldest chiefs take him off his horse and then begin to undress him completely; during this time two other chiefs present him with a piece of bark and tree leaves which he uses to make a waist band. As soon as he is stripped, the two old men who took off his clothes, tear them into small pieces and distribute them among all the band chiefs who have engaged in the expedition and each one places his portion in the little medicine bag. . . . The army attributes such great value to this little bag that any chief who had forgotten it would not be able to command. When this distribution is completed, they sing a war song, each discharges his gun, and they separate to their respective habitations,"[39] where the warriors underwent a period of several days of purgation by physic to rid them of blood pollution.

Highest honors went to those taking scalps. Because of the limited nature of warfare, relatively few attained these honors. There was therefore a premium on taking scalps and almost any means was used down to assaults on innocents, anything to enable a warrior to brandish the hair of an enemy and sing of his own triumphs.

Traditionally, the Creek warrior painted his face for battle and stripped before he went into action. These preparations required time and the unawareness of the enemy. Therefore con-

[38] *Ibid.*, 149–50.
[39] *Ibid.*, 197.

cealment and deliberation were necessary with the result that the carefully laid trap on a small and unsuspecting group of enemy was usual. Impetuosity in action was not the rule, and it was recognized that the actual storming into an enemy was an act of signal bravery. Survival to celebrate victory was the objective, and at no time in the colonial period was the Creek nation decimated by war. A little loss was the occasion of great mourning, a small success the occasion of great rejoicing. The object of Creek life was to live it and savour it to its full. Most Creeks were totally undistinguished and lived out their lives in "the simple annals of the poor," and one gets the impression that the worship of war was a species of Indian rhodomontade, designed to scare the would-be aggressor and give the ambitious an avenue of advancement. Save for the ritualistic color and noise, the Creeks didn't like war. Indeed Adair stated that they were "timorous," "cautious," and "crafty."[40] Despite all the noise about war, woman stealing and horse stealing had much more appeal to the young men. The elaborate ritual of war points back to a day before the more settled life in Georgia and Alabama, and to the need for self preservation which called for a fierce national image.

Creek Women, Marriage, and Family: As seen through the military and trade reports, Creek society seems dominated by males with women taking the roles of mistresses, wives, mothers, helpmates, cooks, and housekeepers. Yet Creek society was matriarchal in that all belonged to clans determined by the mother's line. There were *prestigial* clan matriarchs who apparently had political influence. In 1774 during talk of the possibility of a Creek war with the English, the Cherokee Beloved Woman of Sugartown sent a message to "the Creek Beloved Woman of Coweta" advising peace.[41] Since this is the only reference to a Creek beloved woman except Mary Bosomworth in records, it is difficult to ascertain just who the Creek "beloved" women were, but because the term "beloved" as it relates to men or women in

[40] Adair, *History of the American Indians*, 6.

[41] Cameron to Stuart, Mar. 1, 1774, British Public Records Office C.O.5/75 [hereinafter referred to as B.P.R.O., C.O.5].

the southern Indian tribes refers to "white" or "peace" officials, i.e., civil authorities as opposed to war authorities, it is to be assumed that the eighteenth century Creeks had a category of influential female civil officials. Occasionally other women exercised authority. The half-blood Mary Bosomworth, Emperor Brim's niece, addressed councils in the nation, whether in the squares or in the micos' homes is not clear. In the 1750's the wife of the Gun Merchant of the Okchais, "King" of the Abeikas, exercised a strong behind-the-scenes influence on her husband's policies and attitudes. The women's opinions certainly affected high policy, for on one occasion the women's objection to the punishment of a murderer prevented it, and on another occasion when a group of young warriors seemed bent on provoking war by plundering a traders' convoy, the women took the traders' goods and hid them until the danger passed. "Regal women," the sisters, daughters, and nieces of micos, were given in marriage to aliens as a form of sealing alliances. Influential traders made a practice of "marrying" high to attach the headmen to them, and ambitious Indians sought marriage alliance with the micos. The loyalty of Indian women to their trader husbands in the trader massacre of 1760 saved the lives of many. It therefore seems that, though barred from the square, the petticoat influence seeped through into high councils from the home and clan organizations. In lesser quarters it was felt in other ways; for instance, the hunter stocking up with traders' goods certainly bought with the needs of his women and children in mind.

As has been pointed out, many of the Creek women were pretty, and much has been written about their looseness. A Jesuit writing from the southern Indian country in the 1740's opposed Frenchmen's marrying Indian women on the grounds that "the Indian women are accustomed to a loose life and leave their husbands when they are not pleased."[42] Milfort gave a colorfully Gallic account of four Creek women who cornered him in a loft and forced him to demonstrate his manhood.[43] Bossu wrote that "when

---

[42] Rowland and Saunders, *Miss. Provincial Archives*, II, 218.
[43] Milfort, *Memoirs*, 200–201.

an unmarried brave passes through a village, he hires a girl for the night, and her parents find nothing wrong in this."[44] Campbell stated that "the women before marriage have a right to act with men as they please."[45]

However, both Bossu and Campbell pointed out that this sort of freedom generally ceased with marriage. Bossu said the Indians have "one wife of whom they are very jealous. . . . The Indian girls do not abuse their freedom, since they find it to their interest to appear modest if they want to be sought in marriage. The married women, however, say that they sell their freedom when they become wives and must be faithful to their husbands. The men reserve the right to have several women and are free to leave their wives, though that happens rarely. If a woman is found guilty of adultery, the least that can happen is that she will be repudiated. Her husband leaves the cabin; if there are children, he takes the sons with him, leaving the daughters with his wife. The woman must remain unmarried for one year, but the man can take a wife immediately."[46] Campbell said that if women transgress after marriage, "the parties concerned have their ears and hair cut off" and "are beat often till left for dead."[47]

Marriage was a matter of barter and contract. Said Bossu: "Marriage among the Indians . . . is completely natural and takes no form other than the mutual agreement of the parties involved. The future groom gives gifts of furs and food to his bride's family. After the presents have been accepted, there is a feast to which the whole village is invited. When the meal is over the guests dance and sing of the battle exploits of the groom's ancestors. The next day the oldest man in the village presents the bride to her husband's parents. . . . All the Indians trace their ancestry from their mother's family, since they are sure that they are her children but cannot be certain of the male parent. The good hunters and warriors choose the prettiest girls; the others take the rejected and ugliest ones. The girls, knowing that they will not be free in matters of the

---

44 Bossu, *Travels*, 131.
45 Campbell, "Visit to Creek Nation."
46 Bossu, *Travels*, 131.
47 Campbell, "Visit to Creek Nation."

heart once they are married, try to make the best matches possible. Once they have husbands there are no more love affairs. The woman's job in the household is to prepare meals, dress skins, make shoes, spin buffalo wool, and weave little baskets, a job at which Indian women are quite skilful. . . . Women switch women who seduce someone else's husband—much to the amusement of the young men, who finally snatch the sticks away to keep them from killing the poor wretch."[48]

Adair's account shows the Creek men as very zealous to put their women under obligation. He said, "The Muskohge men, if newly married, are obliged by antient custom to get their own relations to hoe out the corn fields of each of their wives, that their marriage may be confirmed: and the more jealous repeat the custom every year, to make their wives subject to the laws against adultery."[49]

It is apparent that the giving of presents to a girl in a liaison and to her parents in a marriage was essential. The coming of the traders probably complicated this practice, for the girls and their parents came to demand expensive trade goods which could only be had at the expense of laborious hunting expeditions to provide the deerskins with which the trade goods could be bought. In this respect the traders, seeking personal satisfaction, could bid the market up. The Creeks of the later colonial period made many complaints of trader competition for the women, married and unmarried. The girls' and women's avidity for ornamentation and dress made the whites attractive. There were many half-bloods in the nation. The rise of the goods and property economy with the coming of the white man also gave propertied Indians an advantage over their fellows.

Plural marriages, despite the men's right to them, were rare. The only recorded one is that of "Emperor" Brims, who had at least two wives and probably more. The relative poverty of the Indian society worked against the practice. In the meager agricultural and hunting economy, a man had all he could do to provide

[48] Bossu, *Travels*, 132–33.
[49] Adair, *History of the American Indians*, 147.

33

for a few mouths. This same factor probably tended to keep families small. John Wesley reported abortion to have been a common practice,[50] and Chigelley is quoted as saying that the women murdered their children. Yet love of children was characteristic. Lachlan McGillivray, the Scot trader, commented on a French officer's seeking popularity with the Creeks by kissing babies in the presence of fond parents; and fathers, especially micos, showed great attachment to their sons. Campbell noted that Creeks "gave their children great indulgence."[51] Yet, although the treatment of children was permissive, there came a time in a boy's life when he underwent rigorous training to become a good Indian. According to Campbell, "Their sons they teach to bear with patience cold, heat, hunger, and to despise all fatigue, to live without fire or any other food except a little parched Indian corn for several days."[52]

Superstition and Religion: Campbell spoke of widespread superstition among the Creeks. Adair, writing of the southern Indians in general, said, "There are no greater bigots in Europe, nor persons more superstitious than the Indians (especially the women) concerning the power of witches, wizards, and evil spirits. It is the chief subject of their idle winter night's chat. . . . They will affirm that they have seen, and distinctly, most surprising apparitions, and heard horrid shrieking noises."[53] Bartram mentioned the Creeks' abandoning a town because of fear of ghosts. Ill success in war was laid to overriding bad luck which cursed the leader. No warrior would go to war without his medicine or charm bag. The Creeks were a ghost- and spirit-ridden people who did a great deal of conjuring and repetition of magic formulas to ward off evil.

Bartram wrote of "priests or doctors, who make the people believe by their cunning, that they have supernatural spiritual communication with invisible spirits of good and evil, and that they have the power of invoking the elements and dispensing all their attributes good or bad. They make the people believe that by

---

[50] Wesley, *Journal*, I, 63.
[51] Campbell, "Visit to Creek Nation."
[52] *Ibid.*
[53] Adair, *History of the American Indians*, 39.
[54] Bartram, "Observations," III, Pt. 1, p. 23.

conjuration, they can bring rain, fine weather, heat, cooling breezes, thunder and lightning, bring on or expel and cure sickness."[54] Although in the records priests do not appear as obviously influential factors in high decisions, Bartram stated, "They have a high priest with juniors in every town and tribe [clan?]. The high priest is a person of great power and consequence in the state. He always sits in council and his advice in affairs of war is of great weight and importance and he or one of his disciples always attends a war party. It sometimes happens that a king is war-chief and high priest and then his power is very formidable."[55]

In religion the Creeks belong to the tradition of fire and water as manifestations of the great creator above. Every morning the whole village plunged into the stream flowing by, and in their festival rites "going to the water was essentual to the ritual." Adair observed that "the Muskohge Indians sacrifice [to the fire] a piece of every deer they kill at their hunting camps or near home."[56] He mentioned a drunken warrior who fell into the fire and cursed it, and thereafter was regarded by his fellow townsmen as forever accursed.[57] Bartram noted that "they venerate fire and have some mysterious rites and ceremonies which I could never perfectly comprehend. They seem to keep the eternal fire in the great rotunda, where it is guarded by the priests."[58] The Green Corn Dance or Bosketau centered about the making of new fire under the auspices of a priest. In Bartram, Efau Hanjo, great medal chief of Tuckabatchee, says in answer to Bartram's question, "What is the origin of the new fire and of the Bosketau?" that "I have always been taught from my infancy that there is an Esaugetu Emissee [Master of Breath] who gave these customs to the Indians as necessary to the Indians and suited to them; and that to follow them entitles the red people to his care and protection in war and difficulties. It is our opinion that the origin of the Bosketau and our physic, proceeds from the goodness of Esaugetu Emissee; that he communicated them in old times to the red people and im-

[55] *Ibid.*
[56] Adair, *History of the American Indians*, 117.
[57] *Ibid.*, 116.
[58] Bartram, "Observations," III, Pt. 1, p. 26.

pressed it upon them to follow and adhere to them, and they would be of service to them."[59]

Concerning the nature of Esaugetu Emissee, Bartram identifies him with the great spirit "the giver and taker away of the breath of life."[60] He notes, however, "homage to the sun, moon, and planets as mediators or ministers of the Great Spirit."[61]

The central religious ceremonial of the Creeks was the annual busk or dance of the Green Corn, usually held at the end of July or beginning of August. One of the best accounts of the Creek busk is that which appears in the early nineteenth-century John Howard Payne manuscripts: "The Creeks seemed to unite all their feasts as far as practicable into one . . . and in order to do this they made their year commence with the moon which had its first appearance about the time of Green Corn . . . which was about the first of August. The feast was commenced a little before the new moon. . . . The First Fruits being grown, the priest sent his messenger to enquire through the town and country, whether the first fruits were fully grown. The messenger receiving affirmative answer returned. The priest then dispatched a runner to notify the people to meet at the town house on the morning of the sixth day. He then sent another runner to pluck seven ears of corn from seven different fields belonging to seven different clans.

"On the morning of the sixth day all assembled and spent the day in feasting.

"Towards night each woman was directed to repair to her house, extinguish all the old fire,—throw out all the brands and ashes and cleanse her whole house, and all her household furniture. Men were also appointed to cleanse the council house and the sacred square in every part. These men also took up the hearth (of three stones) on which sacrifices were offered, cleansed the stones from all pollutions, and the ground beneath, and replaced them. After cleansing the council house, they white washed anew the white seats and such other parts as were kept white.

59 *Ibid.*, 71.
60 *Ibid.*, 21.
61 *Ibid.*

"The night was kept as a vigil though not in dancing. On the first appearance of daylight, the next morning, the priest appointed men to make new fire. This was done as follows, viz. Three stones were placed on the ground. On these were placed two or three pieces of dry poplar wood, and on them were placed certain dry weeds, and a piece of skunk [punk]. The two men with another piece of poplar, rubbed the tinder wood, weeds and skunk till fatigued, and were relieved by others; and so on until fire appeared. The priest then took the fire, and kindled it on the hearth in the sacred square. He kindled and made fire of the following kinds of wood, dry and sound, without worms or [k]nots, hickory, black oak, red oak, willow oak, post oak, white oak and dogwood.

"Immediately on the fire being kindled, the priest offered the sacrifice, that is, he took seven kernels of corn from the seven ears above mentioned, marked them, and threw them into the fire, together with a small piece of meat, praying etc. This being done, the women and children might partake of the new fruits. The women, not being permitted to enter the sacred square, sent the boys to get the new fires and were admonished by the priest to take the new fire to their house, and feed it with sound wood of seven kinds of trees (the same with which it was first kindled) and to keep it burning with those kinds of wood four days, not suffering it to go out. He also gave them various other instructions. After four days they might burn any kind of wood they pleased. This direction was strictly obeyed. But women being in any kind of uncleanness could not work nor warm by the new fire, nor partake of the green fruit; but used the old fruit and the old food out in the woods or in a tent for the purpose until the time of their separation was ended. Then they washed their flesh,—their clothes, their utensils, etc., and partook of the fruits of the new year and the benefits of the new fires. The uncleanness attending the common courses of women continued seven days, but that after childbirth one moon or one month.

"Before the women retired with the new fire, they were told when to return for the purpose of being purified with the water of purification. . . . It was made of the roots of a small kind of willow.

37

These were pounded and put into two large pots, which were then filled with water. One of these was for the men, and one for the women and children. All drank of the water above mentioned, and washed more or less with it and were then considered clean from the pollutions of the past year. The men made use of this water occasionally for their cleansing during the whole festival. At twelve o'clock on this day the priest appointed two singers for the men and two for the women, and selected two women to lead the female dance. These carried each in his [her] hand a fan made of swan feathers, and had a certain picture fastened on her head. The women danced in a place by themselves, and the two men appointed to sing for them were seated on a bench near them. The men danced in the sacred square. . . . Each man carried in his right hand a bush or stick with swan's feathers tied to the end. This he held up when dancing thus giving the whole company a graceful appearance. . . . The musicians for the dancers were not seated, but moved from place to place. The dancers advanced toward them, and when they stopped moved round them. Thus the dance of both parties continued till night. The men then repaired to a river and washed. They then returned and ate of old fruit having fasted all day, except as they drank of the water above mentioned or the black drink which was made of button snake root. They then spent the night dancing. This part they continued thus four days. During this time they must not go to their houses, nor have any intercourse with their wives. Each day was spent in dancing, and drinking the purifying water and black drink, till near night when they repaired to the water, washed and returned and partook of food of old corn, and again spent the night in dancing. Thus they not only denied themselves of food during the day, but also of sleep during the night, for four nights successively. On the morning after the fourth night of the fast and the fifth of the festival, the women brought the new corn etc. cooked and set down near the sacred square. The men then for the last time repaired to the water and washed. Being now considered clean from all impurities they partook of the new fruits and the feast closed."[62] After such a sweating out, a man, when he had rested, must have felt clean indeed and pretty well drained of any bad temper. Milfort reports that the time of the busk was a time of forgiveness in all old quarrels: "A savage, who, after the festival would recall an old quarrel, would be blamed by all the others."[63] In this ceremony the Creek men certainly had the hell danced out of them. If modern priests could achieve any such purification of mankind, the Creek Green Corn busk would be worth trying.

Amusements: The two primary amusements of the young men and women were dancing and playing ball. Besides dancing for ceremonial occasions, the young people danced in the town house of evenings for entertainment. The dances were in formal traditional patterns, generally circular and in procession, sometimes in single file and sometimes in double. Men and women danced separately and usually in dances assigned to each sex. Although the dances enacted traditional drama in limited form and used traditional steps, individual freedom of gesture was sometimes allowed. Dressing and painting for the dance was part of the fun, and both beaus and belles exhibited themselves at the dances in their finest.

The ball play was generally that enjoyed by all the southern Indians, a lacrosse-like stick-and-ball game with thirteen or more to the side and no holds barred. The object was to score by getting the golf-ball-sized ball between two upright sticks at either end of the playing field, which was a hundred yards or more in length. The ball was passed from player to player by means of a short web-ended stick with which each player was equipped. A player could run with the ball or even carry it in his mouth. The result was a whacking bruising game, characterized by much wrestling, running, and piling on. Players wore no padding and generally, save for a breechcloth, were stripped. Teams representing the different towns played each other for stakes—usually all the personal property of the players. There is record of women's teams

[63] Milfort, *Memoirs*, 135.

playing each other. The game was probably preceded by shamanistic rites for the cleansing and strengthening of the players. It was a wild sport which the Indians loved.

Older men played at chunkey, a sort of lawn bowling. Quieter gambling games, such as the one in which players drew from the hand small sticks of varied lengths or tossed different-colored beans, pieces of bone or stones, also flourished.

Boredom seems never to have characterized Creek life. If an Indian was not hunting, working the fields or household, or going to war, ritualizing, trading, visiting relatives or far-off nations, or gaming or dancing, he could always find someone with whom to gossip, for gossip was a main feature of Indian life. Finally, lacking anything else to do, one could sit and smoke and meditate on the fact that barring bad luck, war, famine, or disease, the Indian life was good, as they all seemed to think it was and as many white men who drifted into the nation to stay seemed also to think.

The coming of the white man, for all its distresses, and they were many, added new and satisfying dimensions to Indian life. It accented hunting, trading, ceremonial diplomacy, and the accumulation of ornament and personal property. And finally it gave more efficient tools: steel knives, guns, iron hoes, steel needles, iron axes, metal pots, scissors, ready-woven cloth and garments, and ready-made paints and dyes. It expanded the Indian's mobility with the horse, and his food resources with cattle, pigs, and chickens. The Creek felt enriched by the contact, and he exhibited extraordinary strength in retaining his Indianness while reaching out for the new world of abundance.

1

Facing the Conquistadors
1540-60

Iₙ MARCH OF 1540 when Hernando De Soto's six hundred gold-seeking European adventurers marched out of the pines and ponds of northwest Florida into southwest Georgia, the Lower Creeks were well east of the Chattahootchee River, occupying an area on the Ocmulgee and Flint rivers south and west of present-day Macon. The names of the towns given by the Spanish chroniclers are difficult to identify with the towns known later to the English. Nevertheless, the towns appear to have been a conglomerate of Hitchiti and Muskogee, the principal one being Ocute on the Ocmulgee just above modern Hawkinsville. Other towns of size and importance were Ichisis, Altamaca, and Patofa, the first on the Flint River north of Albany, the second on the Ocmulgee below Abbeville, and the third on the Ocmulgee near Hawkinsville. The populous clean villages of square plastered and peaked-roofed houses sat in a country "strong and fertile," of "open forests" and "good fields along the margin of the rivers."[1] In each village were ceremonial mounds and a balconied chief's house. The red-skinned

[1] Bourne, *De Soto Narratives*, 271.

and black-haired inhabitants were neatly dressed in cloth or skin mantles and short skirts or breechcloths. They were abundantly supplied with game and maize, products of their agriculture and hunting, and dogs abounded in the villages. The confederacy already existed, for the villages were at peace one with another, and there seemed to be a hierarchy of prestiges with the headman of Ocute as the foremost. At this time the Lower Creeks were at war with a distant princess who ruled Cofitachique on the Savannah River to the northeast.

On the morning of March 24, 1540, the Spaniards, in a burst of monstrous horses, helmeted harquebusmen, and musketeers, surprised the Hitchiti village of Toa, twenty-five miles west of present-day Albany, Georgia. The terrified inhabitants fled, but were rounded up and required to provide a train of bearers for the packs and bundles of the invaders and to escort them to the next town, Ichisi, on the Flint River. Although Ichisi panicked, De Soto captured a few strays and, through an interpreter he had acquired in Florida, required them to summon the headman. Before the over-awed headman, De Soto proclaimed himself a child of the sun come to seek rich provinces and a great princess. The headman, eager to be rid of the invaders, replied that all that sort of thing lay to the northeast in the province of Ocute and furnished De Soto with guides, bearers and an interpreter for his journey. Piously erecting a cross on the village mound and paying honors to it before his kneeling army, the Spanish captain glinted the light of Roman Catholic Christianity over the pagan village. Then, craving the meat of which the village could not supply enough, his men decimated the dog population for roasts and moved on.

In four days, De Soto came to the Ocmulgee River opposite the town of Altamaca. Comomo, headman of Altamaca, the first Creek headman whose name is known to history, having been advised by runners of the Spanish approach, held his people steady. He advised De Soto, who had no boats, to billet himself in the houses on the west bank and in the morning sent dugout canoes to ferry the army across, but failed to come himself to meet the stranger. Sending for him, De Soto encountered a delicate nuance of Indian protocol. The Indian protested that, being at war with Cofitachique, he always went armed and could not in that condition welcome De Soto with the emblems of friendship the situation required. De Soto sent back word for the headman to come as he was. Thereupon Comomo presented himself, armed, and De Soto in a felicitous display of diplomacy offered him a large plume, probably white, adorned with silver. The amazed headman, to whom a feather presented in diplomacy was a powerful medicine, grasped the feather, saying, "You are from heaven and this plume which you have given me I shall eat with it; I shall go to war with it; I shall sleep with my wife with it." Comomo even hinted that he would gladly become De Soto's vassal; he asked him to whom he should now pay tribute, De Soto or the headman of Ocute. The Spaniard, with his eyes on riches to be had to the northward, had no intention of lingering at Altamaca or collecting impoverished Indian vassals and told him to pay to Ocute until he heard otherwise. De Soto then sent for the headman of Ocute, who came down to him and received as presents a plume and a shirt and cap of yellow satin, the first European clothing to be worn by a Creek. Having set up a cross on the mound of Altamaca and celebrated it before kneeling soldiers and Indians, De Soto set out on April 8 for Ocute (Coweta?) to the north. At Ocute he was given bearers and sent on to Patofa. In this region he was first informed of the powerful lord of Coosa far to the northwest, probably the foremost of all Creek settlements, but he elected to continue his search for Cofitachique to the northeast. At Patofa he requisitioned four hundred bearers and plunged into the wilderness to fumble his way toward the mysterious princess.

Deserted by his Creek bearers, De Soto finally found the Lady of Cofitachique whose realm turned out to be a disillusionment. Seizing her as hostage, De Soto set out northwestward toward the mountains and possible gold mines. After three months of rigorous and fruitless marching toward the north and west, during which the Indian princess escaped and many other Indians were enslaved to bear the Spanish soldiers' burdens, the expedition found itself on the westward-flowing river now called the Tennessee with the

lure of the wealthy and populous town of Coosa beckoning southward. Coosa, the leading town of the Abeika Upper Creeks, was
then in northern Alabama, about thirty miles east of present-day
Birmingham on the Coosa River, the great southward-flowing
stream of central Alabama. It was the center of a cluster of Abeika
towns, which, by the eighteenth century, appear to have moved
some forty miles southeastward to establish themselves on Tallapoosa River. First called to De Soto's attention in the Lower Creek
Towns on the Ockmulge in April, 1540, Coosa apparently had a
primacy among all Creek towns as the seat of a great and influential headman and as one of the founding towns of the confederacy.
The sway of the headman of Coosa, whose name is not given in the
records, appears to have extended south to the junction of the
Coosa and Tallapoosa rivers. He met De Soto on July 16, 1540,
just outside his town with more pomp than the Spaniard was to
see among the Indians in all the rest of his travels through the
country. As the Gentleman of Elvas reports it, "The cacique came
out to receive him at the distance of two crossbow shots from the
towns, borne in a litter on the shoulders of his principal men, seated
on a cushion, and covered with a mantle of marten skins, of the
size and shape of a woman's shawl: on his head he wore a diadem
of plumes, and he was surrounded by many attendants playing
upon flutes and singing. Coming to where the governor was, he
made his obeisance and followed it by these words: 'Powerful lord,
superior to every other on earth: Although I come but now to meet
you, it is a long time since I have received you in my heart. That
was done the first day I heard of you, with so great desire to serve,
please and give you contentment!' "[2]

Although the Gentleman's rendition of this speech is probably
romanticized, its spirit is true to the inherent courtesy of a Creek
headman's official greeting of peace to an important stranger.
De Soto is credited with an equally gracious reply. The Spanish
captain then accompanied his host into the town and there boldly
seized him to hold him as hostage for the good behaviour of the
populace which had immediately fled into the woods. Desperately

[2] *Ibid.*, 81–82.

hungry from the spring scarcity of food in the mountain towns, the Spaniards plundered the now full corn houses of Coosa and feasted themselves in plenty. Quartering themselves in the town, they rounded up and put in chains a number of the inhabitants, among them the sister of the cacique and some of the headmen. After twenty-five days in Coosa, in which the Spaniards consumed all the town's old and new corn, they moved southward. They carried with them the cacique in order to compel to peace all the Creek towns through which the army passed and a long train of chained Indian bearers. The headmen were to be released, but De Soto held the cacique's sister and carried her southward out of the Creek country along with many of the townsmen and women who were to be the slaves and concubines of their captors.

Passing through several deserted towns early in September, the Spaniards came before the palisaded town of Ulibahali on the great westward bend of the Tallapoosa River. It was a frontier town of the Creek nation, fortified against the Mobilians to the southward with whom the Creeks were or recently had been at war. The Ulibahali headmen had prepared to rescue the cacique of Coosa if he should give the sign. They came out of their town to meet De Soto, bearing peace signs of bunches of feathers but armed. But the cacique, fearing the great power of the Spaniards, would not give the sign to attack, and De Soto entered the village unharmed. The headman was sent for, and, overawed, gave De Soto thirty women and some of his villagers as bearers. The conqueror then set out southward toward Mobile, collecting women in the Creek towns on the way. His last stop in the Creek country was at a town called Telassie, a large fortified village which stood on the Alabama River somewhat below its beginning in the junction of Coosa and Tallapoosa rivers and a considerable distance westward of the eighteenth-century village of the same name. This town was described as having ambivalent loyalties, being overawed by the Mobilians. There the son of the cacique of Mobile awaited De Soto to guide him to their towns. De Soto now released the cacique of Coosa who left him in tears of rage because the conquistadors would not free his sister.

Besides starvation and bereft homes, the Spaniards left behind in the Creek country two or three deserters and strays, one of them a Negro.[3] One of the soldiers, a Levantine, and the Negro settled down to Creek life and probably fathered, as did many of the army, Creek children. Thus the main contribution of this first incursion of Europeans into the Creek country was a stream of Spanish genes, tinged with Negro and Levantine. Besides these, De Soto left behind a depopulated Coosa region from which he had carried off several hundred people. The rest of the inhabitants had fled terrorized into the hills to subsist on wild game and perhaps to succumb to strange diseases left behind by the invaders. Weakened, the Coosas became subject to attack by former vassal Indians. Tristan de Luna, marching into the region in 1559, discovered that Coosa and its surrounding villages had been reduced to small hamlets and that the fields were uncultivated: "the arrival of the Spaniards in former years had driven the Indians up into the forests."[4] It may have been as a result of this disaster that the Coosas began to settle in the Tallapoosa country above the falls of Tallapoosa River where they were to be so strong in the eighteenth century.

The 1559 incursion of De Luna, who sought another golden Mexico on the Gulf Coast between the sites of Pensacola and Mobile, was not as disastrous to the Creeks as the De Soto invasion was. Short of provisions on the coast, De Luna remembered the De Soto accounts of the wealth of corn at Coosa and marched his men inland the necessary two hundred miles to locate the region. The move was a disappointment, for he found the country devastated and subsistence relatively meager. The Creeks had been much harassed by their neighbors, former tribute payers who had thrown off the Creek yoke. The new cacique of Coosa welcomed the Spaniards as possible allies against his enemies. De Luna obliged with twenty-five horse soldiers and twenty-five foot soldiers who went with three hundred bow-and-arrow warriors against the enemy. The Spanish captain was much impressed by the

---

[3] *Ibid.*, 114.

[4] John R. Swanton, *Early History of the Creek Indians and Their Neighbors,* 231–32.

manner in which the Indians marched to war. The three hundred divided into eight companies, each led by a war captain who carried aloft a pole to the tip of which was tied a bundle of white feathers. The eight companies formed into two groups, each of which marched in a cross form—one company on the north, one on the east, one on the south, and one on the west. In the brief skirmish which ensued, the Spanish guns were decisive. The enemy yielded and returned to Creek vassalage.[5] Thus did the Spaniards rectify the injury done the Creeks by De Soto's devastation.

[5] *Ibid.,* 233–39.

2

The Rise of the Creeks to Power
1670-1715

THE CREEK STORY in the last quarter of the seventeenth century is that of the rise of an obscure and loosely integrated Indian confederacy to become the most formidable and aggressive warriors in the southeast. When the period opened, they were under attack by hostile Indians on almost all sides. From the east the Westo Indians on the Savannah River, armed with English guns which they had obtained by trading with Virginia, terrorized the Creeks, while from the west the numerically-superior Choctaws on the Tombigbe River harassed the Upper Creek Towns, which at the same time took a pounding from the populous Mobilian Indians to the south. From the southeast, Spanish Florida, which by its mission system had subdued the Atlantic and Gulf Coast Indians, cast covetous eyes upon the Creeks as a field for future expansion of the mission system. Thus surrounded and isolated, the Creeks seemed doomed to wilt as a nation either under the attrition of too many wars or under the blessings of the friars. If they had not found a resource for successfully opposing their enemies, they might have called in the friars out of necessity and turned in their

Indian heritage for the peace of the missions and the security of Spanish protection.

The way out of the box seemed to beckon in 1670 when the English settled Charlestown on the seacoast of South Carolina. Perhaps stimulated by the Carolina forest explorer Henry Woodward, the Emperor of Tachequiha—which Swanton and Verner Crane believe to have been Cussita, but which was more probably Lower Town Coweta—sent deputies to Charlestown to suggest an alliance against the Westos. Accepting the proffered friendship, the English colony eschewed military alliance. It was unwilling while still in its infancy to undertake a major Indian war. Thereafter small bands of Creeks appeared at Charlestown to trade, and a few brave and individualistic traders may have made their way to Coweta. English influence soon became so great with the Lower Creeks that a few Creek bands joined other Indians in raids on the Spanish Atlantic coastal missions and forced their abandonment by 1685. The destruction of the Spanish missions caused many of the Indian converts either to flee to St. Augustine or to join the Creek nation.

Nevertheless, by 1685, vassalage to Spain was a genuine threat to the Lower Creeks. In 1674, some of the Lower Creeks—doubtless those of the town of Apalachicola, by which name the Spaniards called all Creeks—sent for Spanish missionaries. The call was not answered until 1679 when Fray Juan Ocun and two assistants set up a cross at "Sabacola"—probably Apalachicola. The "Emperor" of Coweta—the record specifically states Coweta—not having been consulted, ordered the Spaniards to leave, and they withdrew.[1] In 1681, the Spaniards tried again. Two Franciscans with seven Spanish soldiers came to Sabacola. So successful were they that they even began to make an impression on the "Emperor" himself; in a few months' time, however, the Indians once again became hostile and the Spaniards withdrew. Governor Cabrera of St. Augustine suspected English influence and threatened military action. The threat enabled him to draw the Christianized Indians

[1] Herbert E. Bolton, *Arrendo's Historical Proof of Spain's Title to Georgia,* 46–47.

49

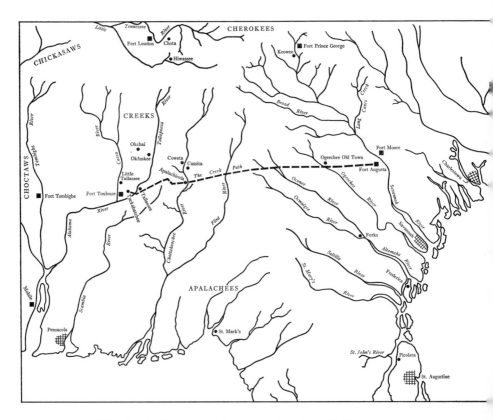

The Creek Country. Adapted by Denison Hull from a map
in the Clements Library.

of Sabacola off to a mission established at the junction of the Flint
and Chattahoochee rivers, far down toward the thriving Spanish
missions of Apalachee in northwest Florida.

In 1685, Henry Woodward with a large convoy of traders and
English goods arrived at Coweta near the falls of Chattahoochee
and had the Indians build him a trading stockade. Alarmed at this
English invasion of territory claimed by Spain, Antonio Matheo,
Spanish commander of Apalachee, marched toward Coweta with
250 men. The first of the Creek towns in his path welcomed him,
but Coweta, Cussita, and two other of the northernmost towns re-

sisted, and Matheo burned them to the ground. Protected by Indians, the English traders hid out, and as soon as the Spaniards had left, renewed the trade. The trade was a great success, for Woodward led a train of 150 Indian burdeners laden with packs of deerskins back to Charlestown. This event is generally regarded as the formal opening of the profitable Creek-English deerskin trade.[2] Although finally all the Lower Creeks swore allegiance to the Spanish Crown, the English traders kept coming and the next year, 1686, penetrated as far west as Tuckabatchee among the Upper Creeks on Tallapoosa River. The Spaniards made several campaigns to halt the English infiltration, but the Indians always protected their traders. Finally in 1689 the Spaniards under Primo de Rivera established a garrison at Apalachicola, and in 1690 a council at Coweta promised to keep the English out. Fear of the Spaniards probably forced the concession, which was so unpalatable to the northern Lower Creeks that Coweta and several other towns moved eighty miles eastward to the Ocmulgee River at the site of the mounds at present-day Macon, Georgia, where they could enjoy an uninterrupted English trade. With the Lower Creeks now becoming armed with English guns, the Spaniards found the fort at Apalachicola untenable and withdrew. The Apalachicolas and other Creeks began a decade of harassment of the Spanish Apalachee missions.

In 1686–87 a Spanish expedition under Del Gado, searching for the intruding La Salle's lost colony of Frenchmen, which was five hundred miles away on the Texas coast, was among the Upper Creeks on the Tallapoosa and Coosa rivers. Del Gado found the Upper Creeks at war with the Choctaws to the west and the Mobilians to the south. He also found towns among them relatively recently settled by the Alabamas, Shawnees, and other Indians who had fled from wars with the Choctaws, Chichamacas, Yuchis, and English, and many Apalachees who had run away from the Spanish missions to the south and had gone native by marrying Creek women. These last gave ill reports of the Spaniards, and the Upper Towns were pervaded with anti-Spanish feeling. The

[2] *Ibid.*, 52.

Upper Creeks had also begun to perceive the advantages of English trade. Del Gado, however, made friends, brought about a peace between the Mobilians and the Upper Creeks, which was cemented by a curious ceremony of the former hostiles' hooking little fingers together, and persuaded many of the recusant Apalachees to return to their mission towns.[3] When Del Gado left the Upper Creeks, they exhibited great friendliness towards the Spaniards. But St. Augustine made no move to send in Spanish missionaries. The intermittent war of the Lower Creeks with the Apalachees and the steady growth of the English trade among them ended whatever possibility Del Gado's expedition had opened of Upper Creek submission to the Spaniards.

The primary Spanish contribution to the Creeks in the period 1690–1700 was the horse. Lower Creek warfare on the Apalachee missions may have taken the form of horse-stealing raids. Certainly in the intervals of peace the Lower Creeks traded corn, furs, deerskins, and artifacts for Apalachee horses. Most, if not all, horses so obtained were traded by the Creeks to the English traders for English manufactures. Horses were scarce in Carolina, and the traders needed horses for the long trek between Charlestown and the Creek towns, and the Apalachees seem to have been the principal source of supply. It is probable that the Creeks themselves retained few, if any, horses, for the practice of transporting deerskins and trade goods to and from the Atlantic seaboard on the backs of walking Indian burdeners remained in vogue at least until the Yamasee war in 1715. The horse trade brought on the fiercest phase of the Apalachee war. Spanish officials urged the Apalachees to raise the price of horses by demanding English trade goods, particularly guns. The higher prices would have eliminated the Creek profits. In 1701, angered by the Apalachee demands, the Creeks murdered the Apalachee negotiators on the subject and raided the Apalachee missions. Spanish forces put up a vigorous defense, and the Apalachee war became a Spanish war. In May of 1702, the

3 Mark F. Boyd, "Expedition of Marcus Delgado from Apalache to the Upper Creek Country in 1686," *The Florida Historical Quarterly*, Vols. XVI–XVII, No. I (July, 1937), 8–26.

Lower Creeks, abetted by English traders, stormed up to the walls of the Spanish mission of Santa Fe of Apalachee, burned the mission town, and took many captives which they sold to the English as slaves. Thus when Queen Anne's War, involving the English, French, and Spaniards, broke out in 1702, the Creeks were already aggressors against Spanish Florida.

Between 1687 and 1701, the Upper Creeks, plentifully supplied with English weapons, had gone on the offensive against the Choctaws and had confined them in terror to their towns, which were subject to constant Creek slaving raids. Regular coffles of Choctaw captives flowed to the Charlestown slave mart, from which some went to Carolina plantations and others were shipped north or to the West Indies. For the Creeks, Indian slaves were probably the most profitable item in the trade, and all their neighboring tribes felt the scourge of their lust for profits. These profits took the form not only of knives, guns, pots and kettles, but of English clothing—woolen mantles, calico dresses, shirts, hats, etc.—and such items of ostentatious display as silver gorgets, metal nose bobs, and huge brass earrings. Through the media of intensified warfare, hunting, and trading, the Creeks became, comparatively speaking, a fiercely acquisitive and affluent Indian society. They lost many of their old manual arts and became abjectly dependent upon the English trading system; nevertheless, in the process they had raised themselves to be a potent factor in the dynamics of the conflicting European imperialisms which developed around them and taught their headmen new doctrines of international behavior.

In 1701, the establishment of the French settlements in the Biloxi-Mobile area on the Gulf had immediate repercussions in the Creek country. English traders who carried Creek hunters and warriors on credit had grown arrogant toward their debtors during the fifteen years of their monopoly. While no accounts have been uncovered to indicate what their practices were in this period, a few years later their injustices in repossessing goods, seizure of the property and often the relatives of Indian debtors, beating of debtors, systematic overcharges, and cheating on weights and measures were reported as common. These abuses were frequently connived at, or at least tolerated, by headmen, themselves favored debtors, recipients of presents, and often relatives by marriage to the traders, who politicly took the influential daughters and sisters of headmen as concubines or wives. As soon as the Carolina Assembly learned of the arrival of the Gulf Coast French with threats of war and rivalry in the trade, it sent word to the traders that abuses in the trade would be investigated.[4] Traders suddenly began to court their customers and to use all their influence to incite hostility toward the French. They succeeded with a notable assist from the French themselves: Governor Bienville, looking for Indian allies to cover the new Louisiana settlements and to serve as buffer against hostiles—Indians, English, or Spaniards—perceived the English to be entrenched among the Creeks and speedily entered into an alliance with the Choctaws and armed them against their Creek predators. By early 1702 the Choctaws had turned on the Creeks and had carried successful war to the Tallapoosa towns. The Creeks did not need the English to tell them who their enemies were. Along with their Apalachee and Choctaw wars they took on a French war.[5]

Bienville had not sought a Creek war. Hoping by his power play with the Choctaws to bring the Creeks into negotiation, he had sent a French mission to the Creeks. The mission brought eight Alabamas—the French in this period called all Creeks Alabamas—to Mobile for a talk on their making peace with the Chickasaws and Mobilians who were subject to their slave raids. Frenchmen returned to the Creek towns with the Alabama deputies and were encouraged to believe that a friendly intercourse could be established. Two Alabama headmen went down to Mobile to escort up to their nation a French party intent on obtaining corn for Bienville's garrison. But the Alabamas, probably incensed at the French help to the Choctaws, had prepared a trap in which four Frenchmen were killed. With diplomacy a failure, Bienville resorted to force and terror. Leading fifty Frenchmen and eighteen hundred Choctaws

---

[4] W. S. Jenkins (ed.), South Carolina Journals of the Commons House of Assembly, Aug. 11, 1701.

[5] Ibid., Apr. 2, 1702.

and Mobilians, he marched against the Creeks. But his allies deserted him, and the Frenchmen, after making a surprise attack on a small party of Alabamas, retreated. That winter, Bienville harassed Alabama hunting parties, killing men and taking women and children to be sold as slaves.[6] For seven years the French and Creeks were intermittently at each others' throats, while the Choctaws bored in on the Creek flank, much to the profit of the English traders.

In 1702 with the outbreak of Queen Anne's War against the French and Spaniards, the English traders engaged the Lower Creeks to move against Spanish Apalachee. The Spaniards had meanwhile organized an expedition of nine hundred Apalachees to attack Carolina. Having been warned, English traders and Lower Creeks numbering five hundred trapped the enemy on Flint River. With the Apalachees approaching them, the Creeks made camp as for the night, then left their blankets rolled as if they were sleeping and crept into the woods. At dawn the Apalachees poured in on the pseudo-encampment, and the surrounding Creeks emerged from concealment in the underbrush mowing them down and routing the survivors.[7]

The English took advantage of the Creeks' facing enemies of the English on two fronts and entered into alliance with them. One objective of the alliance was to move the Creeks nearer to Carolina so that Creek forces would be immediately available to resist French or Spanish seaborne attacks on the Carolina coast. The Creek headmen refused to move but accepted English colors to hoist in the squares, English drums to rouse the war spirit, and English guns and ammunition with which to assault the French and Spaniards.[8] Soon the Lower Creeks were so hotly engaged with the Apalachees that they requested English troops. Joint Creek and Carolina forces attacked St. Augustine in mid-1703; and in 1704, Colonel James Moore with fifty Carolinians went to the Lower Towns and raised over one thousand Creeks to attack

[6] André Pénicault, *Fleur de Lys and Caeumlet*, 65–67.
[7] W. S. Jenkins (ed.), South Carolina Journal of the Upper House of Assembly, Vol. VII, 422; Journal of the Commons House of Assembly, 1741–42, p. 80.
[8] Jenkins, S.C. Commons House Journals, Apr. 17, 1702, p. 75.

the Apalachee missions. The assault captured Spanish Fort St. Lewis, destroyed several Apalachee towns, killed several hundred Apalachees, and took over one thousand prisoners. The missions were wiped out, and the Apalachee survivors were carried away to be sold as slaves in the Carolina slave mart for the profit of Moore, his men, and the Creeks.[9] Several hundred of the Apalachees were also moved from their homeland and forced to settle as an English protectorate on the Savannah River. The Upper Creeks under trader inspiration made an alliance with the Chickasaws against the French-allied Choctaw and Tunica Indians.[10] In 1707, Tallapooses stormed into Pensacola, burned the town, and laid the Spainsh fort under siege.[11] Failing to capture the place, they returned again in October, 1708, killed many Indians and several Spaniards, but were unable to take the fort.[12] In May of 1709 when the Creeks were so bold as to attack Mobile, a wild sortie of French soldiers repulsed them with loss.[13] Theophilius Hastings of Carolina led thirteen hundred Lower Creeks under "Emperor" Brims against the Choctaws in 1711.[14]

The war had given the Creeks fighting and scalp glory such as they had never known before. They had destroyed the Apalachees, ruined the Spanish Apalachee missions, penned the French into Mobile and the Spaniards into St. Augustine and Pensacola, and had given the Choctaws a severe thrashing. From their own point of view they were a great success; from the English point of view they had formed a massive wall which dammed the French and Spanish advance into regions toward which England's rising empire was flowing.

Then suddenly in 1711–12 a crack appeared in the western front of the dike. The Creeks on their own initiative made a peace with the French. The probable cause was a Carolina trader's gross abuse of an Alabama headman. The trader, one Gower, took sev-

[9] Jenkins, S.C. Upper House Journals, Vol. VII, 422.

[10] Bernard de la Harpe, *Historical Journal of the Establishment of the French in Louisiana*, 35.

[11] *Ibid.*, 36.

[12] Rowland and Saunders, *Miss. Provincial Archives*, II, 41.

[13] *Ibid.*, 136.

[14] Verner W. Crane, *The Southern Frontier*, 96.

eral captives away from him in payment of a debt owed by another Indian.[15] Such abuses, though appearing slight and merely to an individual, were of the stuff which governed tribal conduct, for they made for bad talk and roused the enmity of the entire clan of the injured Indian. Combined with war weariness and heavy battle losses, this seemingly unimportant incident had the power to precipitate cessation of hostility toward an enemy as a rebuke to the ally. Bienville confirmed the peace in 1712, and it was to remain permanent as long as the French occupied the Gulf Coast.[16] By-products of peace with the French were peace with the French-allied Choctaws and a cessation of war against Spanish Apalachee, to which the Alabamas returned seventy captive Spaniards.[17] The Alabama tribe, as distinct from the Creek nation, received Frenchmen among them and began to go to Mobile to trade. In 1713 with the end of Queen Anne's War overseas, the Carolinians sought to counter the Alabama defection to the French by building a large trading warehouse among the Upper Creeks and to win the Choctaws over through the medium of the Creek-Choctaw peace to an English alliance based on trade. Bienville looked with alarm upon this vigorous act of expansionism, which threatened to strip Louisiana of her Choctaw bulwark. With France at peace with England he needed a Creek-English war. His devices were conspiratorial, his allies the Alabamas, and the *casus belli* the abuses which had crept back into the trade once Queen Anne's War had subsided. In April, 1715, the devastating Yamasee-Carolina war broke out with the Creeks as *agents provocateurs* and allies of the Yamasees. The Yamasees, related to the Creeks, had moved north from the neighborhood of St. Augustine to be near the English trade. With the consent of Carolina, which was glad to have them out of the Spanish orbit, they established a dozen or more towns in the back country between the Savannah River and Beaufort Sound. They had prospered in trade, but they had also accumulated a huge debt as a result of the overzealous extension of credit

[15] W. L. McDowell, Jr. (ed.), *Journals of the Commissioners of the Indian Trade,* 1710-18, 49.

[16] Rowland, *Miss. Provincial Archives,* III, 161.

[17] *Ibid.,* II, 173.

by the Carolina traders. Finally, hard pressed by their own creditors, the traders had begun forcibly to collect the Indian debt by the seizure of Yamasee wives and children to be sold as slaves. The Yamasees revolted, and in their first onslaughts almost ruined the Carolina colony.

The war, at the time believed to have been inspired by the Spaniards, seems to have developed out of a widely ramifying intertribal plot developed by the Creeks to remedy abuses in the trade and fanned by the French at Mobile. In early April of 1715, word had reached Charlestown of Creek dissatisfaction with their traders, that "they had made several complaints without redress" and "upon the first affront of any of the traders they would done with them and so go on with itt," along with a report from Yamasee trader William Bray that "a Yamasee came to his wife and told her—that the Creek Indians had a design to cut of[f] the traders first and then to fall on the settlements and thatt itt was very near."[18] The extent to which Bienville was involved in this situation, though he stayed in Mobile, is suggested by his 1726 statement in which, referring to the English trading warehouse at the junction of the Coosa and Tallapoosa rivers, he said, "In 1715 I induced the Indians to drive them away from it."[19] Since the post was in the immediate neighborhood of the Alabama towns and the French had developed close relations with those towns, it is reasonable to suppose that he operated through the Alabamas to work up Creek determination to take arms against the trading tyrants. It would seem therefore that the Yamasee war was as much Bienville's dark work as anybody's. Certainly Bienville had proposed to his home government in 1714 that a French fort be built near or on the site of the obnoxious English trading post among the Alabamas, for in the summer of 1715 he received orders from Pontchartrain, the minister of marine, to put a garrison in the Creek country.[20] In June of 1715, before he had received word of the Yamasee outbreak and after he had received orders in

[18] McDowell, *Journals of the Commissioners of the Indian Trade, 1710–18*, 65.
[19] Rowland, *Miss. Provincial Archives*, III, 512.
[20] *Ibid.*, III, 185.

April from Cadillac, he wrote of the English, "I am making every effort to thwart them in their enterprises."[21] It is true that the records do not give the dates on which the Creeks attacked the Carolina traders in their towns, but presumably it was not until after the Yamasees had struck. In both Upper and Lower Towns the massacre was general. When, in July, Bienville learned that the Creek break with the English had occurred, he sent a Frenchman to the Upper and Lower Towns to bring Indians down to Mobile to make a treaty of alliance and trade.[22]

The extent of the Creek participation in the actual warfare in Carolina is not clear. It would appear that after their massacre of the Carolina traders they sent war parties to join the Yamasees. In August, 1715, in the last great push of the hostiles into Carolina, Chigelley, who was Brims's brother and the head warrior of Coweta, led several hundred Apalachees and Creeks almost to Charlestown, only to be thrown back. With the rout of the Yamasees the war became openly a Creek war. The Creeks made a bold effort to induce the Cherokees, some of whom had tentatively joined the war only to draw back, to commit themselves in force to the all-Indian cause. This possibility was dreaded in Carolina, which in the late fall of 1715 sent three hundred men under Colonels Moore and Chicken into the Cherokee country to keep the Cherokees at least neutral and if possible to win them over to the English cause. While the Carolinians were billeted in the Cherokee towns, undercover negotiations were going on between the Cherokees and the Creeks, the purport of which was that the two nations should combine in a surprise massacre of Moore's soldiers. In January of 1716, large forces of Creeks hovered in the woods outside the Lower Cherokee Towns awaiting the signal to strike. However, Colonel Moore's diplomacy prevailed. Cherokees murdered the secret Creek envoys in their villages, roused the Carolinians, and went out with them to attack the Creek forces in the woods. The Creeks fled.[23] For the Creeks, the Cherokee commit-

21 *Ibid.*, III, 182–83.
22 *Ibid.*, III, 187–88.
23 McDowell (ed.), *Records in the British Public Records Office Relating to South Carolina, 1663–1762* [hereinafter referred to as *S.C. B.P.R.O. Records*].

ment to war against them was a disaster because their northern flank was exposed to Cherokee attack. The Creeks made three major decisions. The first was for the Lower Towns on the Ocmulgee to withdraw westward to their old sites on the Chattahoochee. The second was to grant the French permission to erect Fort Toulouse in the Upper Creek country near the Alabama towns at the junction of the Coosa and Tallapoosa rivers. The third was to seek an alliance with the Spaniards in Florida. This last was achieved in the summer and fall of 1716 when Upper and Lower Creek deputies and warriors visited Pensacola, where they took an oath of allegiance to Spain. Several Upper Towns headmen were sent to Mexico City to become vassals of the Viceroy.[24]

[24] Yearbook of the City of Charleston, 1894, pp. 340–45.

3

Aftermath of the Yamasee War
1716-33

T HE DECADE after the Yamasee war is the great period of "Emperor" Brims of Lower Towns Coweta. Having learned the lesson of overcommitment to the English and having experimented with Spanish overlordship, he developed the doctrine of neutrality in struggles among the Europeans, which was to be the most clearly defined and influential Creek national diplomatic policy during the remainder of the colonial period. It was not always pleasing to all parties in the nation, nor was it rigidly adhered to, but it was to develop the sanctity of tradition, and to be a potent force in any councils seeking partisan commitment, and was always available to be thrown as a cloak over any double dealing. It was a positive policy rather than a negative one. The Creeks were to seek benefits from and to give promises to the French, the Spanish, and the English, and as far as possible to avoid hostilities with any of them. They were to utilize each nation's fears of the other two, to extract concessions, and to protect their independent position.

Early in 1716, after the withdrawal of the Lower Towns to the Chattahoochee, with a Cherokee war on their northern flank and a

threat of English attack from the east, Emperor Brims sought protection from the Florida Spaniards. To wipe out the stain of a
dozen years of war with the Spaniards he appointed as head of
his mission to St. Augustine his son, Sepeycoffee, whose mother was
a Christianized Apalachee woman. Sepeycoffee took along with
him three Spanish captives who had not been released at the cessation of hostilities three years before. He was instructed to seek the
establishment of a Spanish fort at Coweta. Such a fort would not
only serve as a brake on the English, but would be an effective
countercheck to the French Upper Creek fort. Sepeycoffee was received with fanfare at St. Augustine and his proposal taken under
delighted advisement.

The Upper Towns co-operated with Brims's diplomacy by
sending deputies under Tejane of Tallassee to Pensacola in July accompanied by Lower Townsmen. These overtures culminated on
September 30, when at Pensacola the whole Creek nation through
its deputies swore allegiance to the crown of Spain. Pleased with
the prospect, the cumbersome Spanish imperial machine got under-
way to incorporate the new territory into the Spanish empire by
outfitting an expedition in 1717 to build a fort at Coweta and by
inviting Creek deputies to Mexico to swear allegiance before the
Viceroy and to accept Christianity. In February, Tejane with six
other Upper Creeks embarked for Vera Cruz where they were
given a ceremonial welcome by the Viceroy and taken to Mexico
City. Tejane swore allegiance, was baptized as a Christian, and
was sent home with splendid gifts and a commission as commander
of the Creek nation. He arrived at Tallassee on Tallapoosa River
in February, 1718, where he was welcomed by Brims and Sepeycoffee who had come up expressly for the occasion.

But by then the great Spanish opportunity had evaporated.
The Creeks had slipped from under the Spanish yoke and had
found refuge in the doctrine of neutrality. This turn of events had
its genesis in the mind of Hobohatchey, mico of the Abeikas, and
primary mico of the Upper Creeks. By early 1716 it had become
apparent that from the Creek point of view the Yamasee war had
failed, since the effort to win the Cherokees into the Indian alliance

had resulted disastrously in an English-Cherokee alliance against the Creeks. The Abeikas suffered from repeated Cherokee attacks, their English trade had been destroyed, and the French had been unable to supply them either with goods or munitions. About the time Brims and Tejane sought a Spanish alliance, peace talk began among the Abeikas. A minority voice in June, as the summer unrolled and neither Spanish nor French goods came into the nation, the English peace party gained strength. In January, 1717, two Upper Creeks appeared at Carolina Fort More on the Savannah River to announce that peace could be had. The overture found receptive listeners in Charlestown where sentiment was torn between a desire to have vengeance upon the Creeks for causing the war and the need for peace to restore the colony's shattered economy. As other messages to the same effect came from the Creek country, the Carolina assembly resolved to send Colonels Theophilus Hastings and John Musgrove under escort with a pack train of presents to Coweta.

In August, 1717, Sepeycoffee, returning from St. Augustine with the Spanish Captain De Pena, who came to mark out a fort site, was shocked to find at Coweta a party of twelve Englishmen with whom Brims was seriously discussing the advisability of sending emissaries to Charlestown to seal the peace. Sentiment was divided. The Spanish venture was full blown, but the English, actively sponsored by Brims's wife, Goa, were on the ground talking peace and trade. Brims, seeing the way out of the Spanish protectorate and into the old time peace and plenty with the English, embraced the opportunity to complete the now assured English negotiation. He gave his niece, Coosaponakeesa, daughter of his sister, to be married to Johnny, the half-breed son of Colonel Musgrove. Said by some to be the daughter of Henry Woodward, Coosaponakeesa had been educated as a Christian at Pon Pon in South Carolina well before the Yamasee war, and later was to become famous in Creek and Georgia history as Mary Musgrove or Mary Bosomworth. In 1717 she was a regal pledge between Brims and the English. At that time she must have been thirty.

Sepeycoffee, after some delay, ushered De Pena into Brims's

presence. The Spanish captain boldly taxed the emperor with violating the Spanish alliance which the Creeks had sought. If De
Pena's account is to be believed, Brims in tears and with bowed
head, stated that the English were there of their own free will, and
that he himself esteemed the Spaniards. But the damage was done.
Factionalism flared around the Spaniards. While Sepeycoffee
talked to De Pena of seizing the English, and the Spaniard entertained headmen with wine and presents, other Creeks talked of
burning the house where De Pena stayed and killing him. De Pena,
fearing for his life, withdrew down the Chattahoochee and advised
the governor of East Florida that a Spanish fort could only be
built among the Apalachees, who, having fled the English frontier
in the Yamasee war, had returned to the lower Chattahoochee.

Leaving Hastings at Coweta as a hostage for the peace, Musgrove with Lower Creek deputies went down to Charlestown where
Upper Creek deputies under Hobohatchey joined him. In late October or early November they concluded a peace for all the Creeks.
This is the first Creek treaty with the English the details of which
are known. By article one the English agreed to set up trade with
the Creek towns at fixed rates. Article two provided that Englishmen who robbed or murdered Creeks or damaged Creek crops and
horses would be punished by the English and satisfaction given.
By the third article the English guaranteed ammunition for the
Creeks against their enemies provided those enemies were not at
peace with the English. Under the fourth article the Creeks were
made to understand that, if they did not behave well toward the
English, trade would be withdrawn. Corollary to this was the fifth
article by which Creeks agreed not to injure the persons or goods
of the traders and to protect the traders from their common
enemies. By the sixth article Creeks agreed to deliver up any of
their people who in the future were guilty of any crimes against the
English; the Creeks were to avoid coming into English settlements
without permission of the governor of South Carolina, and they
were to protect traders who passed through their country on the
way to other Indian nations. Under the seventh article they agreed
to apprehend and deliver runaway slaves. Finally the Creeks were

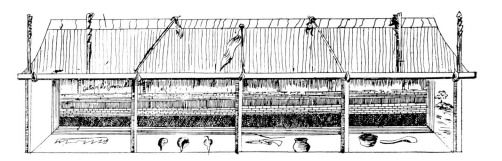

Council house of the Alabamas

Courtesy of Smithsonian Office of Anthropology, B.A.E. Collection

James Edward Oglethorpe. Founder of the Georgia colony,
sketched at the age of eighty-eight. From the pen-and-ink
sketch by S. Ireland, 1785.

not to encourage any but English to settle among them and were not to have further correspondence with the Spaniards.[1] The treaty was signed by Oloyhathey (Hobohatchey), King of the Abeikas; Youholomico, the Coosa King; Fannemiche, King of the Oakfuskees; and Tickhonobey; all of the Upper Creeks. Lower Creeks signing were Tomeechy and Tuccaftanogee, mico of the Pallachicolas; King Hott of the Eusitchees; and King Hubblebubble of the Cheehaws. Apparently in the treaty talks Carolina gave verbal assurance that the English would not settle south and west of the Savannah River.[2] On the face of it the treaty made the Creek nation an English trading fief and eliminated the French and Spanish from influence in the Creek country. Actually it did no such thing. In late 1716 or early 1717 the French built Fort Toulouse at the junction of the Coosa and Tallapoosa rivers and stayed there for nearly half a century. Spanish agents continued to come into the Creek towns where there was always a faction to welcome and protect them. The Creek attitude seems to have been that of acquiescing in whatever terms were necessary for re-establishing the trade and trusting that they would not be called on to deliver the full bill of particulars.

With the treaty signed, Governor Robert Johnson ordered trade to be reopened. This time, since private enterprise had been guilty of the malpractices which led to the Yamasee war, trade was declared a state monopoly. At the old Shawnee town below modern Augusta, Georgia, called Savanno town by the colonials, Colonel Charlesworth Glover was permitted to trade with Creeks who came to him, and a convoy of twenty-three packhorses was dispatched to the Creek country. In June of 1718, Creek headmen came to Charlestown to settle a fixed scale of prices for the trade.

When in September, 1717, Brims assured De Pena that he esteemed the Spanish, he spoke from a sentiment that remained with him for the rest of his life. He felt that true Creek policy was to remain on friendly terms with the English, French, and Spanish. In February, 1718, not yet having heard of the success of negotia-

---

[1] Jenkins, S.C. Commons House Journals, 1736–39.
[2] Candler, *Ga. Col. Rec.*, XXXVI, 316.

65

tions at Charlestown and perceiving the value of continued diplomacy with the Spaniards, he went over to Ulibahali on the Tallapoosa River to welcome Tejane's return from Mexico City. Tejane arrived with Don Juan de Orta, Fernandez, and other Spaniards. On October 27, Brims confirmed Creek and Spanish friendship with appropriate ceremonies and declared that Sepeycoffee would be his successor as emperor at Coweta. He confirmed Tejane as the Spanish-appointed commander-in-chief of the Tallapooses. But that was as far as the Creeks were willing to go. When Don Juan proposed to the Tallapooses that they remove to settle near Pensacola, they refused, saying they loved their land and would not leave it for any reason.

Then news came that Colonel Musgrove with thirty Englishmen and a pack train of goods had arrived at Cussita, neighbor to Coweta. Sepeycoffee suggested to De Orta that they plunder and kill the English, but Fernandez, foreseeing complications with England, with whom Spain was at peace, declined. Brims and his entourage returned to the Lower Towns to welcome Musgrove, who had brought back Creek prisoners taken by the English in the war and was accompanied by the eleven Creek deputies who had set their marks to the treaty at Charlestown. Brims ratified the peace and the Carolina trade was immediately reopened—interestingly under the direction of Sepeycoffee, who did his father's bidding. He was primarily his father's hand toward the Spaniards just as another of Brims's sons, Ouletta, was to become his father's hand toward the English. Brims himself was also to bow in a friendly fashion toward the French whose invitation to Mobile for ceremonies and presents he readily accepted.

With the completion of the Carolina-Creek peace and the reduction of the Creek-Spanish relationship to one of mere friendship, the Spaniards withdrew from Coweta to the Apalachee towns below the junction of the Flint and Chattahoochee rivers. There they made an unsuccessful attempt to win the Apalachees to move to the neighborhood of the Spanish forts on the gulf. They did, however, obtain the friendship of Cherokeeleechee, the anti-

English principal headman of the Apalachees. Large numbers of Apalachees went with them to St. Augustine to cement an alliance with the Spaniards, under whose protection they were to become a nuisance on the Carolina frontier.

Although the Carolina-sponsored traders pushed into the Upper Creek country to the very neighborhood of newly established Fort Toulouse, two awkward residues of the Yamasee war plagued the English for the decade to come. These were the Creek-Cherokee war and the anti-English inveteracy of the Yamasees. In 1717 when Hastings and Musgrove had suggested that a Cherokee peace be included in the Creek-English negotiation, Brims had bluntly rejected it. Not only had the Senecas of New York, with whom Brims had entered into an alliance against the Cherokees, refused to allow him to make a separate peace, but the Creeks were determined that the war should go on until they had full vengeance on the Cherokees for the murder of the Creek ambassadors in January of 1716. Carolina could only obtain a Creek promise not to molest Carolina trading pack trains to the Cherokee country and to avoid injury to the Carolina traders in the Cherokee towns.

The Yamasees, sheltered under the guns of the fort at St. Augustine, hotly rejected English overtures for peace and, abetted by the Spaniards who hoped to prevent English expansion west and south of the Savannah River, carried on a prolonged quarrel with Carolina. They raided the frontier and occasional trading pack trains. Cherokeeleechee's Apalachees joined in some of these forays. It was difficult for the Creeks to avoid implication. Both Yamasees and Apalachees were related to the Creeks by ties of marriage and blood. Yamasee and Apalachee parties lingered in or near Creek towns. As long as the Cherokee war persisted the Lower Creeks would do nothing to force the Yamasees to make an English peace; for they resented Carolina's supplying munitions to the Cherokees and they suspected that Carolina used the Cherokees as a club against them, as indeed was the case. Carolina, distrustful of Brims's friendship for the Spaniards and his close ties with the

Yamasees and Apalachees, abetted the Cherokees while she laboured to force Brims into an outright break with the Yamasees and the Spanish.

The Carolina trade with the Creeks, returned to private enterprise in 1721 under the pressure of Charlestown merchants, prospered; but for a few years Creek and Carolina relations were on a dubious footing. Governor Nicolson, taking office in Carolina in 1721, inaugurated vigorous efforts to induce the Creeks to force the Yamassees to come to Charlestown to make a peace. Failing in that, he attempted to bring about a Creek break with the Yamasees. When he was unable to move Brims in this direction, he set about bribing individual Creek warriors to break the Creek-Yamasee alliance by leading small parties against the Yamasees. When, in 1721, Nicholson invited Brims down to pay him a visit of ceremonial welcome, Brims remained aloof. He sent his son Ouletta, his English arm. Nicholson protested that unless the emperor himself came he would regard him as unfriendly to the English; for, said he, the Creeks had allowed the French to build a fort among them.[3] Ouletta's mission returned to Coweta to negotiate some sort of agreement, the nature of which the records do not disclose,[4] but it was undoubtedly anticipatory to the treaty executed the next May. Meanwhile, Colonel Theophilius Hastings had been in the nation attempting to induce some of the Creeks to move down to the Altamaha River where the English intended a fort as protection against the Spaniards and Yamasee. Hastings, or a Carolina agent among the Creek traders, got the Creek warrior Ochio, probably an Upper Townsman, to go out and take a few Yamasee scalps, and Ochio was invited to Charlestown to receive a reward.[5]

About the same time, Governor Nicolson issued a proclamation which declared Carolina settlements out of bounds for uninvited Creeks, who, coming to the settlements under color of seeking trade, destroyed cattle and encouraged Negro slaves to run away

[3] Jenkins, S.C. Commons House Journals, 1736–39, pp. 111–12.

[4] South Carolina Department of Archives and History. Council Journal [hereinafter referred to as S.C. Council Journal], Aug. 25, 1761.

[5] W. S. Jenkins, Journals of His Majesty's Honorable Council [hereinafter referred to as S.C.H.C.], Feb. 28, 1722, p. 198; Jan. 5, 1722–23, p. 145.

with them. It was sometimes difficult to tell whether the visitors were Creeks or marauding Apalachees and Yamasees. It developed that the principal offenders were a party of Creeks who wandered the islands near Port Royal. But for a time Johnny Musgrove's Indian uncle, Willimico, who had settled with him and Coosaponakeesa on Musgrove lands at Pon Pon, was suspected of harboring trouble makers. Actually, Willimico's relatives came frequently to visit him and share in the plantation prosperity of his nephew. Indians were great family people, great exacters and sharers of hospitality. Willimico, to retain his comforts and prosperity at Pon Pon, had to forego visits from his relatives.[6]

On May 25 and 26, 1722, Ouletta headed a delegation in Charlestown for treaty talks. Nicolson delivered himself at length on the subjects of peace and friendship and then demanded that the Creeks call home the vagabonds on Port Royal Island and either force the Yamasees to come in and make a peace or go to war against them. He reminded Ouletta of how the English had made great warriors of the Creeks and promised that the English would support them against their enemies. Then he brought out a parchment commission for Brims "to act as headman of the Creek nation" and another for Ouletta to act in that capacity under his father. He also gave Ouletta commissions to be carried to the Tuckabatchee headman and the Captain of the Okfuskees.[7] Ouletta answered enthusiastically that the peace agreement would be welcome, and that he would haul up the English flag in Coweta square, saying "I shall take care to have everything delivered and see your orders puncually obeyed."[8] He seems, though the record does not state it, to have promised to take a strong stand in his father's councils against the Yamasees. The Carolina assembly, not content with Ouletta's promises, sent Colonel Hastings up to the Lower Towns to make known Carolina's wishes on the Yamasees and to lead parties of Creeks against them.[9]

Hastings, arriving in the nation in the fall, found no disposition there to carry out Ouletta's treaty. Indeed, the Yamasees, far from

[6] *Ibid.*, Jan. 5, 1722–23, p. 144; Mar. 8, 1722, pp. 209–210; May 4, 1722, p. 6.
[7] *Ibid.*, May 25, 1722, p. 9.   [8] *Ibid.*, 10.   [9] *Ibid.*, 11, 16.

being brought to a peace, were rumored to be preparing to send a large force against the newly built Altamaha outpost.[10] Hastings discovered that Spanish propaganda had countered Carolina diplomacy with a tale that the presents Nicolson had sent up with Ouletta were actually from St. Augustine, sent by the Spaniards to Charlestown to be forwarded to the Creeks. One can credit Creek gullibility, but it was true that the Creeks would allege anything as a cover for inaction due to tribal disagreement. While the Carolina assembly discussed an embargo on the Lower Towns to enforce its will, Hastings stayed on in the nation to keep an eye on Creek affairs. The situation was not quite as anti-English as Nicolson feared. It is true Upper Creek warriors under the Mortar aided Marchand, the commander of Fort Toulouse and reputed grandfather of the later great Alexander McGillivray, to capture a large party of French deserters. Nevertheless the Upper Creeks did all their trading with the English traders at the Okfuskees; for the French had no goods. Stray Creek parties looking for plunder raided among the Spanish settlers and herds in Florida. Though Hastings complained that Ouletta and Brims "stifled talk among the Lower Creeks," the town of Cussita inclined to cooperate with the English.[11] Hastings seems to have induced some of the Upper Creeks—Oulatche of Tuckabatchee and the Captain of the Okfuskees—to visit Charlestown and listen to Nicolson's anti-Yamasee talk. They raised war parties and took Yamasee scalps, but this did not cause a break between Brims and the Yamasees.

Finally, to force the Lower Creeks into a definitive break with the Yamasees, South Carolina embargoed the Lower Creek trade.[12] Brims's apparent response to this was to go down to Mobile to see Bienville (Crane says Sepeycoffee went). The embargo and its purpose were hotly debated in the Lower Towns, with Cussita standing for the English position. On news that Tallapooses had brought Yamasee scalps into Charlestown and that Cherokeeleechee's marauding village of Apalachees had been broken up, Co-

10 *Ibid.*, Dec. 3, 1722, pp. 111–12.
11 Crane, *Southern Frontier*, 265.
12 Jenkins, S.C.H.C., June 10, 1724, p. 274.

weta began to waver and talked of sending war parties against the Yamasees. Ouletta went down to Charlestown where, after facing a severe lecture from Nicolson, he said that the Lower Creeks were too divided to act. The division turned on Brims's firm support of the Yamasees. Early in 1724, when an Upper Creek war party under Tickonoby along with some Cussitas went against the Yamasees, Brims threatened to have Tickonoby killed. He also threatened to kill an English trader, John Bee, who from the Altamaha was attempting to lure the Yamasees to Charlestown. Cussita blocked these threats, and as a reward Carolina lifted the embargo on that town but kept it on the other Lower Creeks.[13] Pressured by Carolina and grimly divided, the Creeks seemed headed toward civil war in 1724 when two episodes occurred which seriously altered the situation: Yamasees killed Brims's pro-English son, Ouletta, who had apparently lifted a strong voice in council against them; and a Tallapoose head warrior, Steyamasiechie or Gogel Eyes, in attacking the Cherokee town of Toogaloo, robbed trader John Sharp's store, wounded Sharp, and carried off goods and a Negro slave woman and her two children.

Indignant, Carolina in the summer of 1725 sent Colonel Tobias Fitch to the nation with orders to close out the Creek-Cherokee war, detach the Creeks from the Yamasees, and obtain reparation for Sharp's injuries and the return of his goods and slaves.[14] Implicit in Fitch's mission was the suggestion that unless the Creeks yielded on all three points, the English would join the Cherokees against the Creeks. The ensuing negotiation was many faceted, revealing in its nuances Creek attitudes and methods of handling difficult situations.

On July 9, the King of Upper Towns Okfuskee cordially received the Carolina emissary. Wrote Fitch: "The king of the town takeing me by the hand led me to a house where were sitting all the headmen of the several towns thereabouts; and after passing some compliments there was some fowls brought in and set before me; and before I was suffered to eat the king made the following speech:

[13] *Ibid.*, 274–75.
[14] *Ibid.*, Mar. 17, June 3, 1725.

'I am glad to see you here in my towns but I am sorry that I cannot entertain you with such as I am entertained when I go down to your great town; but I hope you will except of such as I have and you are very welcome to it.' "[15] Though the house was a thatched native hut and the hosts breech-clouted and mantled red men, the hospitality was as courteous as anything a European could offer. The headmen agreed to summon a meeting of the headmen of the Abeikas and Tallapooses at Okchai on July 20. Diplomatic cordiality of the chiefs was one thing, the attitude of the young warriors another. These latter, on news that Fitch sought satisfaction for Gogel Eyes' misbehavior, glowered, for they knew that Gogel Eyes' attack upon Sharp reflected the sentiment of most Creeks that English traders who warned Cherokees of Creek attacks ought to suffer. They talked of beating up Fitch. But word got around that Fitch would be defended by the headmen, and the angry talk subsided.[16]

On July 20 in Okchai square, sixty headmen representing twenty towns of the Abeikas and Tallapooses heard Fitch accuse Gogel Eyes and demand reparation. Gogel Eyes, who had ordered the assault on Sharp, disingenuously disclaimed responsibility, saying he had been absent at the time his men had made the attack. The headmen, who knew the truth, discredited the disclaimer, and forced the warrior to agree to return what he could of the loot, to surrender the slave woman and child, and to pay in deerskins for the goods he had destroyed. The headmen agreed to help him gather the necessary deerskins, but pointed out to Fitch that it was the wrong time of year for deer hunting and that reparation would be delayed till autumn. At Fitch's suggestion, Hobeyhatchey, King of the Abeikas, was appointed to receive the deerskins and to see that they were forwarded to Carolina. When Fitch took up peace with the Cherokees, the headmen demurred, saying they still had vengeance to exact for the death of some of their men and must send out one more war party. When this returned, they said, they would send to Carolina to begin peace negotiations.

15 Mereness, *Travels*, 176.
16 Jenkins, S.C.H.C., Vol. III, 53–59.

In order to restore himself to Carolina favor, Gogel Eyes determined to go to war against the Yamasees, hoping to take some Yamasee prisoners to give to Fitch to be sold as slaves in part payment of his obligations.

Fitch then went down to Coweta to force Brims to break with the Yamasees and to enlist him in the move for a Cherokee peace. On August 2 at Coweta, Brims was grim. His son Ouletta had recently been killed, by Cherokees he thought. Though a vengeance party against the Cherokees brought in fifty scalps and thirty prisoners, nothing less than annihilation of the Cherokees would satisfy the emperor. He told Fitch that the Upper Creeks could make peace with the Cherokees if they would, but he would never join it. He was bitter against the Upper Creeks for having gone to war against the Yamasees. Fitch boldly told him that the Upper Creeks warred on the Yamasees by English orders, and that if he wished to avenge attacks on the Yamasees he should attack the English. Knowing also the truth of Ouletta's death, he told him that the Yamasees were guilty. At this news Brims did an abrupt about face. If it were so that the Yamasees had killed Ouletta, he would go to war against the Yamasees, and his son, Sepeycoffee, would give up his friendship for the French and Spaniards and take over Ouletta's English commission to be his father's successor.

Yet when a Spanish delegation with a runaway Carolina Negro as interpreter came into Coweta bringing four Yamasees to apologize for the death of Ouletta, Brims received them, accepted their presents and drank their rum. Fitch feared for his newly patched up peace. He went to Cussita, which at this period strongly espoused the English, raised up a hundred warriors, and returned to Coweta square where he confronted the Spaniards and seized the Negro for return to bondage in Carolina. There was consternation in Coweta, and Brims even tolerated a dressing down from Fitch; but the Spaniards and Yamasees were allowed to depart. Brims later explained that his friendly reception of the visitors was intended to conceal his warlike plans. There appears to have been some truth in this, for shortly after the Spaniards and Yamasees had left the town, Sepeycoffee led a war party against the Yamasees

73

at St. Augustine. Cussita, making the most of English friendship, assured Fitch that the Creeks were not impressed with the French at Fort Toulouse because they were constantly weakened by desertions and could not provide trade goods. The Cussitas, with a catholic taste in jealousies of their own kind, accused the Tallapooses of being determined to use all Europeans in their own interests.

The Coweta line toward the English softened. This was in part due to the return of Creek deputies to the Six Nations in New York. The deputies were accompanied by Seneca ambassadors who stated that it was the Six Nations' will that the Creeks remain friends with the English. The Senecas, however, urged continuance of the war with the Cherokees.

Fitch now heard that five hundred Choctaws were to rendezvous with the Upper Creeks in the autumn to go against the Cherokees. He sent word to Governor Nicolson, who in turn relayed the news to his agent, Colonel Chicken, among the Cherokees. Fitch also heard that there was bad talk among the Upper Creeks by those who resented the disciplining of Gogel Eyes and that the Creek-Choctaw war party against the Cherokees was assembling in the remote town of Lichouya in the Abeikas. He hurried off to frustrate the war party if he could. In the Abeikas, Hobohatchey reassured him of his and Abeika friendship. The war party, fearful of Fitch's intentions, had already assembled in hopes of getting off before he arrived. Fitch let out word that dire consequences would follow any injury to English traders among the Cherokees; thereupon all but forty of the assembled warriors went home. The forty went off only to learn that, as they had feared, the Cherokees had been warned.

Carolina policy at this period forbade the Cherokees from making peace with the Creeks until the Creeks gave assurance of a break with the Yamasees. Brims, well aware that Carolina supplied the Cherokees with munitions of war and hearing rumors that Colonel Chicken had promised the Cherokees three hundred white men to aid them against the Creeks, held his communications

74

with St. Augustine open. The Spaniards, anxious to prevent Brims's desire for revenge upon the Yamasees from involving them in war with the Creeks, sent a peace mission to Brims with the heads of three Yamasees guilty of murdering Ouletta. Appeased, Brims sent deputies to St. Augustine who heard Governor Benevides accuse the English of fomenting Cherokee attacks upon the Creeks.

In March, 1726, Benevides' accusations seemed confirmed when five hundred Cherokees and Chickasaws bearing English colors marched into the Lower Creek country. Forty Cussitas caught them in ambush, killed sixty and captured the English flag, and Brims sent runners to Tuckabatchee to propose war on the English. He gathered up the Yamasee prisoners Sepeycoffee had taken the year before and sent them off to St. Augustine to be followed by deputies from all the Creek towns who proposed an alliance with the Spanish and Yamasees. But not wishing to plunge lightly into so great an undertaking, Brims proposed to send deputies to Charlestown to ask if Carolina had set the Cherokees upon them. He sent his brother, Chigelley, head warrior of Coweta, to the Upper Towns to sound out sentiment for war. There the first reaction to the flag incident had been to halt the collection of deerskins for the Gogel Eyes reparation and to talk of joining an attack upon the English if the Cussitas would make the first move. By the time Chigelley had arrived, cooler heads had prevailed. That winter the Upper Creeks had been severely dealt with by the Cherokees and desperately felt the need of English ammunition to hold their own in the long struggle. The headmen rejected the proposed conference with the Spaniards, saying that the Spaniards were never able to supply the nation with goods and that they therefore preferred to stand by the English. Nevertheless they sent deputies to the Lower Towns to discuss the situation. These found that Brims's deputies had returned from St. Augustine with proposals for a Spanish alliance, but that King Hott of Cussita was strongly opposed. They returned to the Upper Towns and called a meeting of Tallapoose and Abeika headmen which rejected the alliance. With it now clear that a large majority of Upper and Lower Creeks opposed a Spanish alliance, the Upper Towns headmen decided to go ahead with the payment of Gogel Eyes' reparation—thus assuring the continuance of the English trade.

Meanwhile in Carolina it had been decided that the Creek-Cherokee war must be closed out. The Cherokee use of English colors in the March raid coupled with a Cherokee attack upon a Carolina trader, one McIntosh, bound for the Creek country, indicated that the war was getting out of hand. The assembly decided again to send Fitch and Chicken as agents to the two nations. But by then Upper and Lower Creek deputies were on their way to Charlestown to inquire into the flag episode. In May, Carolina officials, relieved to learn that the dominant Creek sentiment favored peace with Carolina and that the Gogel Eyes reparation would be met, disavowed the flag episode. Fitch and Chicken then proceeded on their respective missions to the Creeks and Cherokees to launch the peace overtures between the two nations.

Brims and Chigelley, having failed in their anti-English program, agreed to send deputies to Charlestown in the fall to make peace with the Cherokees. While Fitch was in Coweta, Sepeycoffee died in a fit of drunkenness and Fitch presented Chigelley with Sepeycoffee's English commission to become Brims's successor on the Emperor's death. This was probably done on Creek advice that, for lack of a male heir of proper age, the headship moved to the first man's brother of most respected age and authority. In the Cherokee country, Chicken, reproving the Cherokees for the use of the British flag by war parties and the murder of McIntosh, threatened a trade embargo if the Cherokees did not make peace with the Creeks. The Cherokees agreed to send deputies to Charlestown to meet the Creeks.

The peace meeting took place in Charlestown in January, 1727. Twenty Cherokee headmen under the Long Warrior of Tanase met Hobohatchey, King of the Abeikas, and Chigelley, head warrior of Coweta, and agreed to exchange peace deputies in the two nations during the spring and summer. As a by-product of the peace, Hobohatchey and Chigelley agreed to a complete break with the Yamasees. Thus ten years of Carolina frontier troubles seemed about to be terminated.[17]

But the Carolinians had reckoned without the Spaniards. While the deputies were in Charlestown, Spanish overtures were being received by Brims. Chigelley returned to find Brims unenthusiastic about the Cherokee peace and unwilling to break with the Spaniards and Yamasees. Both Lower and Upper Creek individuals went to St. Augustine, where the Spaniards, still hoping to forestall English movement southward, were spiriting the Yamasees to further border depredations. In July, 1727, errant Creeks joined a Yamasee raid against trader Smallwood's store at the forks of Altamaha, well south of the Savannah River. They killed Smallwood and five of his men and took several whites prisoner. Certainty of Creek participation in this raid did not reach Carolina till January, 1728. Meanwhile, Yamasees had raided in the neighborhood of Pon Pon, South Carolina, and killed several Carolinians. Brims and Chigelley failed to ratify the Cherokee peace, but Hobohatchey faithfully carried out his bargain for the Upper Creeks and sent deputies to the Cherokees.

Carolina decided that a bold step must be taken to put an end to the Lower Towns' refusal to co-operate. At first the assembly considered sending to Coweta a force of three hundred men to collect reparations for the Smallwood murder, but since this might have brought on a general Creek war, prudence prevailed. Instead an embargo of Lower Towns trade was determined upon, and Charlesworth Glover was sent to the Upper Creeks to make them exert pressure on the Lower Creeks to give the required satisfaction and to break with the Yamasees. Hobohatchey sent down to Charlestown a specific disclaimer of Upper Creek involvement in the Smallwood affair and a strong assertion of Upper Creek friendship for the English.

In the struggle which ensued during the winter of 1727–28, Brims fought a losing battle for independence of action. Glover held aces against him in the threat of renewed Cherokee war, the

[17] B.P.R.O., C.O.5/387, No. 70.

actuality of Carolina embargo, and the determination of Hobo-hatchey to permit no break with the English. When Brims and Chigelley stalled on breaking with the Yamasees and encouraged Spanish overtures, Glover sent out Upper Creek war parties, at first under half-blood Johnny Musgrove and later under Hobo-hatchey, to take Yamasee scalps. By maneuvering through friendly King Hott of Cussita, he obtained from the relatives of an Upper Townsman who had participated in the Smallwood raid consent to the marauder's assassination, the first such tribal punishment the English exacted from the Creeks. Glover confronted French and Spanish emissaries in Coweta and forced them to advise Brims to be friends with all white men. Finally through the pressure of the developing pro-English party in the Lower Towns, he persuaded the Apalachicolas to bring in Cherokeeleechee, one of their chiefs who had participated in Yamasee raids on Carolina. Cherokeelee-chee was forced to settle down in a pro-English Lower Creek Town where he could be prevented from going on any more raids. In December of 1728, Carolina sent an expedition which destroyed the Yamasee towns under the guns of St. Augustine. Brims, con-vinced the Spaniards no longer were able to protect the Yamasees, consented to a final break with the Yamasees and Spaniards. Caro-lina sent him presents and lifted the trade embargo, and from then on until his death Brims was quiet. However, though he had been defeated by circumstances, he believed to the end that the true policy of the Creeks should be independence with freedom to treat with all comers. On his deathbed he bequeathed this policy to his twin sons, Essabo and Malatchi, who in their minority under the guardianships of Youhowlakee and Chigelley were to be his suc-cessors.

Thus the Yamasee war was ended, leaving the Creeks undis-putably a trading fief of the English. But there remained a vein of admiration, especially at Coweta, for Brims's strong personal effort to maintain independence and freedom of diplomatic maneuver.

The exact nature of the "emperorship" of Coweta is difficult to define. As the foregoing events reveal, it was not an absolute overlordship of the Creeks; nevertheless, it was strongly influential. It apparently was a prestigial primacy hereditary in the micoship of Coweta, one of the four founding towns of the Creek confederacy. What was its relationship to the primacy of the headman of "Ocute" in De Soto's time, is difficult to say, for though it seems to have been hereditary from father to son, when in the late colonial period the Brims's line failed to turn up a masterful man, the primacy seems to have passed from Coweta to the head beloved man of another town. The "emperorship" was strengthened by the English and French practice of issuing commissions to it to be "head of the Creeks." One must regard it as a "first voice," maintained through high hereditary prestige, which when wielded by a strong personality became as close to a true monarch as the Creek political organization was capable of sustaining.

Old Brims died between 1730 and 1733.[18] Sepeycoffee, his eldest son, nominated by both English and Spaniards to be his successor, had died of drunkenness in 1726. The English commissioned Chigelley, Brims's brother and head warrior of the Cowetas, to be Brims's successor. This nomination accorded with Creek usages to the extent that it granted Chigelley his brother's primacy. Yet in Creek tradition, Chigelley was merely an interim first man by the fact that the Indians had appointed him guardian of the Young Twin, Brims's underage son, Malatchi, who on reaching maturity was to become "Emperor" or "First Man."[19] Nor did Chigelley immediately succeed to power. There was another interim headship by Youhowlakee, who was guardian of the other twin, Essabo, described as "young head warrior of Coweta." Youhowlakee and Essabo set their marks to James Oglethorpe's 1733 treaty with the Creeks.[20] Chigelley's voice as the first power does not rise until after Youhowlakee's death in 1733–34.[21] With the death of Essabo in 1735, young Malatchi comes forward as the regal heir. Patrick McKay in 1735 describes him as a "worthless

[18] Force, Transcripts of Georgia Records, Vol. I, 9.
[19] Candler, *Ga. Col. Rec.*, III, 297.
[20] Force, Transcripts, Vol. I, 10.
[21] Candler, *Ga. Col. Rec.*, XXXI, 71.

drunken fellow and intirely in the French interest."[22] Chigelley as his guardian was in effect "Emperor" until 1746.

It is to be noted that the patterns of power at Coweta present a tightly knit ruling family which absorbs to itself by heredity both the micoship and the head warriorship. This pattern suggests that of the Cherokee Ukuship, the relationship among the Powhatans of Virginia where Powhatan is succeeded by his brother Itspatin,[23] and the regal inter-relationships in the Pequot-Mohican-Narragansett complex of New England, and may be presumed to be the normal pattern of the eastern woodland Indians where "royalty" tended to marry "royalty" and "royalty" to succeed "royalty." The prestige and power of the Coweta regal line reached even to the female members and is to be seen in the prestige and influence of Brims's niece on his sister's side, Coosaponakeesa or Mary Musgrove-Bosomworth, who in 1732 with her husband, Johnny Musgrove, set up a trading establishment at Yamacraw Bluff, near the future site of the English settlement of Savannah, Georgia.

In 1729, so strong was the English influence at Coweta that French Governor Bienville of Mobile considered sending a Jesuit in disguise to develop a pro-French party. The outcome of this project is obscure. But so attractive was the English trading pull that visiting Creeks became a nuisance on the Carolina frontier. Despite the agreements of the decade before, straggling bands drifted into the Pon Pon area of South Carolina and unscrupulously feasted upon the settlers' stray cattle. Other bands of Creeks were drawn to settle near the Musgrove store at Yamacraw bluff on the Savannah River. From 1730 to 1734 the Creeks intermittently fought with the Cherokees and preyed on the Yuchi Indian settlement near the Carolina Apalachicola garrison on the Savannah River. These disturbances and the murder of two Carolina traders on the Creek path led in 1733 to a brief Carolina suspension of the trade. Suspicion for the murders rested on dissolute young Malatchi, who was sighted near the scene; but trader investigation in the Upper and Lower Towns failed to produce sound evidence. Since

---

[22] *Ibid.*, XX, 323.
[23] L. G. Tyler, Narratives of Early Virginia, 334.

The Georgia Council. Tomochichi's party in London. From a copy of W. Verelst's painting, now hanging in Rhodes Memorial Hall, Atlanta, Georgia.

Tomochichi and his nephew Tooanabey. From an engraving by
John Faber after a portrait by William Verelst, 1734.

no one seemed to know who the guilty parties were, the murders were finally ascribed to the Yuchis or Yamasees, and the trade ban was lifted. By 1733, when James Oglethorpe appeared to found Savannahtown in Georgia, harmony prevailed between the Creeks and Carolina. It is likely that since the Creeks needed ammunition for their war with the Cherokees and since they appear to have shared the disillusionment of most of the southern Indians with the French for their destruction of the Natchez Indians in 1729, they were in no mood to protest the English invasion into Creek territory south of the Savannah River. Indeed the new English trading center was not unwelcome.[24]

[24] Candler, *Ga. Col. Rec.*, XXXII, 297.

4

Oglethorpe's Friends
1733-39

I N January of 1733, John and Mary Musgrove were settled at
their trading post and plantation near Pipemaker's Creek a
mile or two west of Yamacraw Bluff on the Savannah River. Much
visited by Mary's Creek relatives and friends, they had one of
Carolina's most prosperous trading establishments; they did an
annual business of twelve thousand deerskins, about a sixth of
Charlestown's annual take. Nearby stood chief Tomochichi's
Yamacraw village with a population of forty or fifty hunters and
perhaps two hundred Indians all together. Drawn to this location
by the proximity of the Musgroves and the mounded tombs of
Tomochichi's ancestors, the Yamacraws were outlaw Creeks
banished from the Creek nation several years before. Just who
these banished Creeks were is the subject of differing opinions.
Although Swanton, the authority on the early Creeks, gives Tomochichi's first appearance in history as at "Palla-chucola" on the
Savannah River, thus suggesting that he was an Apalachee, Harris,
an early nineteenth-century biographer of General James Oglethorpe, the humanitarian founder of Georgia, says the Yamacraws

were Yamasees. Yet the Creeks regarded Tomochichi as one of themselves; and it is probable that he had a Yamasee father and a Creek mother, nationality being determined by the mother's line. Certainly the Yamacraw region was pre-Carolina Yamasee country and the ancestral tombs of Tomochichi must have been Yamasee. It is likely that Tomochichi's banishment from the Creeks occurred as late as 1728 when the Creeks made their definitive break with the Yamasee, for the records show that one "Tamachi" accompanied Chigelley in 1728 to St. Augustine in Chigelley's unsuccessful attempt to obtain a Yamasee break with the Spaniards. It seems probable that this failure and Glover's Carolinian diplomacy of that year resulted in the banishment of the band of mixed Yamasees and Creeks at Coweta who had formed the core of opposition to the Creek-Yamasee break. There being no Spanish deerskin trade, the banished had wandered in the woods near the Carolina frontier, trading where they could, until in 1732 Carolina gave them permission to settle at Yamacraw near the Musgroves. Whatever his origins, Tomochichi became an important figure in the settlement of Georgia and with Mary Musgrove was instrumental in Oglethorpe's success.

Late in 1732, with Oglethorpe at Charlestown on his way to found the colony of Georgia, the South Carolina assembly sent word to Johnny Musgrove to give the colonists every assistance. Therefore, when in the latter part of January the colonists, much to the distress of Tomochichi and his people, landed at Yamacraw Bluff, Mary Musgrove calmed the Indians and brought them to a meeting with Oglethorpe. With Mary as interpreter, Tomochichi and Oglethorpe entered into a treaty by which the Yamacraws, in return for a guarantee of their own holdings, agreed to permit the English to lay out a townsite.[1] However, Oglethorpe's settlement was a violation of South Carolina's agreement at the conclusion of the Yamasee war to refrain from settlement beyond the Savannah River, and it was necessary to obtain the consent of the major Creek headmen. Much impressed by Oglethorpe's kindness, Tomochichi and Mary forwarded to Coweta Oglethorpe's invitation to the Creek headmen to come down and treat with him.

[1] Force Transcripts, Vol. I, 13.

The Lower Towns headmen, moved by the prospect of a new trading center to undercut Carolina's monopoly, responded favorably, and in May the headmen of eight towns, led by Youhowlakee, the "mico of Coweta," and his ward, Essabo, Brims's son and Mary's close kin, came down to Savannah. In the reassuring presence of Mary and Tomochichi and with Johnny Musgrove as interpreter, amenities were exchanged and on May 21 a treaty of land cession, trade, and friendship was made. In return for Georgia's sending traders to their towns, the Creeks agreed to permit the English to settle on all lands the Indians did not need, provided that in each new town the English would preserve a place of rest for visiting Indians. Oglethorpe promised to punish all English subjects who caused injury or death to Indians, and the headmen undertook to punish Indians who injured English subjects or damaged English goods, or if they could not, to surrender the offenders to Georgia justice. The Creeks agreed to surrender fugitive slaves who sought asylum in their territory and to restrain nationals of countries other than England from settling among them. A list of prices to be charged in the deerskin trade was appended to the treaty.[2]

This first treaty is vague in the matter of territorial cession and seems to have covered oral understandings that the English would make no new settlements without the consent of the Indians, that they could establish a fort on the upper Savannah River, and that otherwise their settlements must be confined to the tidewater area.

With the founding of Savannah, the Musgroves achieved a major position. Not only were they acknowledged by Oglethorpe to be an important liaison in negotiations with the Indians, but from their beef herd and corn cribs they furnished a major food supply to the settlers during their first hard year. Through Oglethorpe's benevolent interest Tomochichi also rose to an importance he never before had held and showed himself equal to his new stature as a headman of consequence. An episode early in the history of the colony revealed his sterling quality. When in despond over some personal matter, a Yamacraw committed suicide and his

2 *Ibid.*, 9–13.

kinsmen believing the English had murdered him vowed vengeance, Tomochichi confronted the avengers and told them that before they could take an English life they must take his. The planned attack upon the English collapsed.[3]

Oglethorpe was so impressed with the old man, who showed all the sweetness and dignity expected of a patriarchal headman, that he invited him to go to England with him for a formal ratification of the treaties. Tomochichi obtained the consent of the Lower Towns headmen, who sent down to him the proper tokens and authorities. The official party numbered nine Indians, including Tomochichi, his wife Senauki, his nephew Tooanabey, an Apalachicola headman by name Umpyche, and a warrior, Hillispulli. Johnny Musgrove accompanied as interpreter. En route in April, 1734, they stopped at Charlestown to await a ship for London; there, ever good showmen, they entertained the Carolinians with a lively ball game gotten up with some Natchez Indians also visiting the Carolina capital, and in the evening put on a wild war dance before the governor's palace.

On June 19, Tomochichi's party arrived at Gravesend aboard the H.M.S. *Aldborough*.[4] The Georgia Trustees, informed of their arrival, sent a sleek many-oared barge manned by liveried boatmen down the Thames to pick them up and bring them to London where they were lodged in comfortable quarters.[5] On July 4 the formal reception by the Trustees took place in the Trustees' offices in Old Palace Yard with the Earl of Egmont presiding. Unafraid and manifesting a kindly disposition and great modesty, Tomochichi instantly won the Earl and his friends. The old warrior began his formal speech by "excusing himself if he did not speak to right purpose; for, he said, when he was young he neglected the advice of the wise men and therefore was ignorant." He was now old, he said, "and could not live long wherefore he desired to see his nation settled before he died. That the English were good men and that he desired to live with them as good neighbors, for which reason he

---

[3] *South Carolina Gazette*, June 30–July 7, 1733.

[4] *Gentleman's Magazine*, Vol. IV (1734), 329.

[5] *London Magazine*, Vol. III (1734), 384.

came over to talk with us, but he would not have done it were it not for Mr. Oglethorpe's sake whom he could trust and who had used him and his people kindly. That he thanked the Great Spirit (at which he pointed and looked upward) that had brought him safe hither and he hoped would carry him safe back."[6] The Earl, deeply moved, gave an equally gracious reply and then ordered wine and tobacco brought in.

The Indians were shown about London and attracted great crowds wherever they went. Meanwhile, as an introduction to what the Trustees expected to do for the Indians in Georgia, Tooanabey was taught to read and write and instructed in Christianity.

On August 1 the formal ratification of the treaty by King George II took place. This was a ceremony for which the Creeks had prepared by sending a bundle of eagle feathers from town to town that all the towns might register the treaty and then sending the feathers to Tomochichi to be delivered to the English sovereign. The Indians desired to appear before King George in their native array, that is, naked, save for a breech clout, painted and be-feathered, but Oglethorpe, somewhat scandalized, prevailed on them to go clothed in the garments given them since their arrival in England. These were for Tomochichi and his wife, Senauki, scarlet cloaks trimmed with gold and fur, and for the others, similar cloaks in yellow and blue. However, they did paint, some their faces half black and half red, and some with triangles and bearded arrows on their chins in place of whiskers. They wore their native moccasins,[7] and they stuck feathers in their hair. Thus splendidly arrayed, they were carried to Kensington Palace in three coaches-and-six, and were escorted by the Trustees through the labyrin-thine halls to the royal presence. The seated monarch and his queen, surrounded by the royal court, formally welcomed them. Then Tomochichi, in the dignity of age and office, holding the eagles' feathers from the forested banks of the Chattahoochee, spoke to the monarchs in the elevated tone and strange accents of

---

[6] The Earl of Egmont, *Journal of the Earl of Egmont* (ed. by Robert McPherson), 58.

[7] *London Magazine*, Vol. III (1734), 447.

an Indian orator. As translated by Johnny Musgrove, once half-blood warrior in the swamps of Florida and now prosperous trader among the live oaks of Yamacraw, the speech ran: "This day I see the majesty of your face, the greatness of your house and the number of your people. I am come for the good of the whole nation called the Creeks to renew the peace which long ago was had with the English. I am come in my old days though I cannot live to see any advantage to myself; I am come for the good of all the children of all the nation of the Upper and of the Lower Creeks, that they may be instructed in the knowledge of the English." Then holding forward the bundled spray of eagles' feathers, he said: "These are the feathers of the eagle which is the swiftest of birds. These feathers are a sign of peace in our land and have been carried from town to town there and we have brought them over to leave with you, O Great King, as a sign of everlasting peace." Handing the feathers to the monarch he concluded: "O Great King, whatever words you shall say to me, I shall tell them faithfully to all the kings of the Creek nation."[8] King George, who was no orator, replied briefly, accepting the eagles' feathers on behalf of himself and the English people and assuring the Creeks of English friendship.

Tomochichi then turned to her majesty and said, "I am glad to see this day and to have the opportunity of seeing the mother of this great people. As our people are joined with your majesty's, we do humbly hope to find you the common mother and protectress of us and all our children."

Her majesty gave a gracious reply and the interview was terminated without further ceremony, much to the regret of Tomochichi, who wished to do a war dance for their majesties. Egmont, eager to know what impression the splendor of the palace and the reception made on Tomochichi, learned that the Indian was much impressed by the size of the palace. However, stout primitive that he was, he remarked that while the English knew many things that his countrymen did not, he doubted that the English were happier than the Indians; anticipating Rousseau, he said that "the English lived worse than the Creeks who were a more innocent people."

8 *Gentleman's Magazine*, Vol. IV, 449.

Having been received at court, the Indians were now welcome in the great houses of the land. On August 17, the Archbishop of Canterbury sent his elaborate barge down the Thames to pick them up and carry them to Putney to dine with Lady Dutry, one of the benefactors of the Georgia settlement. The lady entertained them in a very handsome manner and, on taking his leave, Tomochichi said through his interpreter, "could he but speak English he could tell her the thoughts of his heart and how sensibly he was touched with the noble reception she had given him; and was much more pleased with being able to see and thank her for having assisted in sending the white people to Georgia."

The Indians were then taken to Lambeth Palace to meet the Archbishop of Canterbury. They had some qualms, because they feared the Archbishop was a conjurer.[9] Egmont and the old prelate soon put them at their ease. However, the Archbishop failed in his attempt to induce Tomochichi to talk about the Creek religion. Tomochichi did not wish to discuss it; he said he had already offended the spirits by talking too much about it aboard ship and one of his company had died. The Archbishop expressed a hope that something could be done to teach the Indians Christianity, but the conversation was brief, for the Archbishop was in bad health.[10]

The next day, dining at Charlton, Egmont's seat, the Indians impressed all with their mannerly deportment. "They," wrote Egmont, "had the respect not to eat until my wife and I had taken the first mouthful. They had learned the way of drinking (healths) and bowing to the company and behaved with such decency making no noise or interrupting anyone that spoke." Egmont presented Tomochichi with a gilt cased tobacco box, entertained him with music and dancing, and took him for a walk in the woods about the palace "which much delighted them as it put them in mind of their own country."[11]

In mid-September the Indians visited Eton College and Windsor Castle. Taken into the classrooms at Eton to observe the

[9] Egmont, *Journal*, 61.

[10] *Gentleman's Magazine*, Vol. IV, 174.

[11] Egmont, *Journal*, 61–62.

boys at work, Tomochichi instantly won the boys' favor by proposing to the headmaster that they be given a holiday. When his request was translated, the boys raised a loud "huzza."[12] Later the Indians went to see young Prince William perform on his trained horse, and the famed horse guards were passed in review before them. Prince William gave Tooanabey a gold watch and piously adjured him to say the name of Christ every morning when he first looked at it.

In the intervals between dinners and ceremonial visits, Tomochichi was closeted with the Trustees to discuss the Indian trade. The Indian described the evils of the rum trade and requested its prohibition. He also protested the price of trade goods, which he said were unfair. Johnny Musgrove explained to the Trustees that in the Indian country the measuring weight which passed for a pound of deerskins was actually a pound and a half, with the result that the Indians paid higher than the agreed-upon prices.[13] These and others matters induced the Trustees to venture upon a Georgia regulation of the trade, which, put into practice, caused trouble in the Creek country and a violent dispute between monopolistic Carolina and fledgling Georgia.

Finally on October 31, after several months of entertainment such as no other visiting Indians had ever received in England, Tomochichi and his company were driven down to Gravesend in the royal coaches and put aboard H.M.S. *Prince of Wales* for their return journey. In December they reached Savannah in good health, and the old warrior dispatched runners in the nation to announce their return and to invite the micos of the towns down to Savannah to receive their share of the gifts the Trustees had sent over. For his services as interpreter, the Trustees awarded Johnny Musgrove one hundred pounds in cash and five hundred acres of land, making him, with his trading business, Georgia's most prosperous citizen.

But during Johnny's absence, his trading business had suffered, and his Indian princess, Mary, loomed on the scene as a fighting

---

[12] *London Magazine*, Vol. III (1734), 494.
[13] Egmont, *Journal*, 62, 64.

women. Watson, Musgrove's partner, who had charge of the trade during Johnny's eight months' absence, had taken advantage of the situation to siphon off profits into his own pocket. He had quarreled with Mary and with the neighboring Indians. He further had developed into a belligerent drunken lout. In the process he boasted of having drunk to death his boon companion, the Indian Skee, and accused Mary of being a witch. It is difficult to see at this distance what charms the chunky middle-aged Creek woman had, but she probably turned a beady Indian eye on Watson's performances. In seeking revenge on Watson she did not resort to magic, but to the Georgia court where she won a suit for slander against her husband's partner. Wild with rage, Watson assaulted her with a gun, but the sturdy princess overpowered him and won another suit against him, this time for assault. The Yamacraws were upset over the death of Skee, and to appease them, Georgia authorities tried Watson on charges of defrauding and killing an Indian. Punishment was a fine and an order to pay damages to Skee's relatives. Watson was scared, and, when friendly Indians came to the store to trade, he raised his gun against them and drove them off. Mary advised him to clear out, but he locked himself in the store with Mary's Negro servant, Justice. Angry Indians under Isteche battered down the door, and in the fracas killed Justice who had tried to protect Watson. Watson fled out the back door and took refuge in Savannah where he reeled about, roaring drunk, boasting of his feats against Indians. The Yamacraws threatened to kill him. Georgia authorities ordered him to leave town and appointed the merchant Sam Eveleigh to take over Musgrove's store. Watson refused to leave, whereupon to protect him the council declared him insane and took him into protective custody. Held without trial, Watson raised up a party of friends which was to become the core of the anti-Trustee party in the colony. Colony Secretary Causton labored to calm the Yamacraws and finally appeased them. To Mary, on the Trustees' order, he paid a sum for the loss of her servant Justice. Johnny's return from England restored order in his affairs. Because of his increased stature as a favorite of Oglethorpe and a prosperous citizen, he was made a constable of the colony, but died toward the end of 1735. His death left Mary a widow with substantial property and reputed great influence among the Creek Indians. She was speedily wooed and won by one of the indentured servants about her place, Jacob Matthews, who immediately put on airs, became a noisome character about the colony, and soon associated himself with Watson's anti-Trustee party. But through his incapacity and dissoluteness Mary's fortune began to suffer, though her influence with the Indians by birthright remained unimpaired.

In 1735 the peace that Tomochichi and Mary set up between Georgia and the Creeks prospered. Heeding Tomochichi's invitation, which was seconded by Patrick McKay, Georgia Indian agent who in March had been at Coweta, Lower Towns headmen came in June to Savannah to receive presents and to negotiate a definitive boundary settlement. They were led by Chigelley and Malatchi, who on Essabo's death had replaced Youhowlakee and Essabo as the influential Cowetas. In conference with Georgia officials and with Mary as interpreter, they defined the Georgia limits as including all that territory south and west of the Savannah River up to two hours' walk above tide water and as far south as the St. John's River—only excepting the sea islands of Ossabow, St. Catherines and Sapelo, which they retained for sea-side hunting and fishing.[14] This conference may also have taken up the granting of the site of Augusta at the falls of the Savannah River for a Georgia fort.

Patrick McKay's mission to the Creeks, which began in March, also took up at Coweta the matter of the Augusta site and apparently prepared the way for the Savannah deliberations. But McKay's visit created more confusion than good will. The Georgia Trustees had ruled that all traders in the territory they claimed under their Crown grant, which ran from the headwaters of the Savannah and Altamaha rivers to the Pacific, must take out Georgia licenses. The Trustees had also decided to limit the number of traders and to prohibit rum sales in the area. McKay had begun by telling the Carolina traders who could trade and who

14 Ga. Hist. Soc. *Coll.*, I, 121.

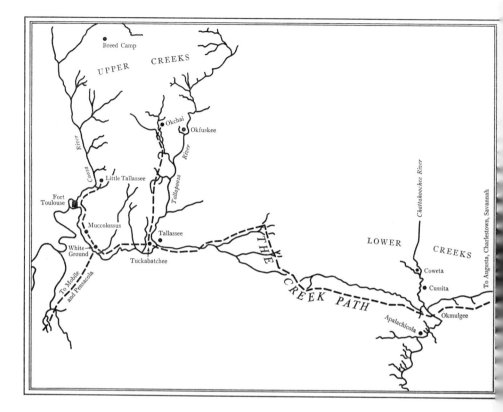

Major Creek Towns in 1773. Adapted by Denison Hull from
David Taitt's map in the Clements Library.

could not. The Carolina traders were angry. Many refused to go
down to Savannah and take out Georgia licenses in addition to their
Carolina licenses.[15] Others, whom McKay had enjoined from trading, hastened to Charlestown to complain. There ensued a juris-
dictional quarrel between Georgia and South Carolina which lasted
several years, finally to be resolved by the Crown in an agreement
to permit joint licensing and occupancy of the trading country. But
McKay's immediate activities in the Creek nation threw the Indians into an uproar. The Upper Townsmen in particular saw Mc-

---

[15] Candler, *Ga. Col. Rec.*, XX, 441–42.

Kay confiscating the goods of long established traders and putting them out of business. These activities were a threat to the Indian economy, for they reduced the flow of trade goods. The prohibition on rum sales, though sought in England and theoretically approved by many of the Creeks, cut into the headmen's social prerogatives and long-nurtured Creek habits. Some headmen threatened McKay and threw the mantle of their protection over the outlawed traders. Though McKay was recalled, the Creek agitation was brought to a head in 1736 by similar activities of one Tanner, a zealous Georgia agent. Hobohatchey of the Abeikas asserted his headship of the Upper Creeks by calling a halt to Georgia seizures and set off to Charlestown to urge the Carolina government to resist the Georgians.

In July of 1736 at Charlestown, Hobohatchey threatened Georgia's territorial claims on the grounds that McKay had overreached him in obtaining a cession of land for a fort in the Upper Creek country. He asserted that the Georgia coastal settlements were violations of the agreement of 1717 in which Carolina had promised not to settle south and west of the Savannah River. For himself he said that in the future he would deal only with Carolina. The Indian's indignation lent fuel to Carolina anger at Georgia and did much to strengthen Carolina's refusal to permit Georgia unilateral control of the Creek trade.[16] Hobohatchey returned to the Upper Towns to declare that he would permit no more Georgia seizures of Carolina traders' goods.[17] Although Georgia built Fort Augusta on the Upper Savannah in 1735, for years the main line of Upper Creek trade was to run to Charlestown where it traditionally had been.

McKay's 1735 mission also had international repercussions. McKay construed his instructions as ordering him to obtain a cession from the Upper Creeks upon which to build a fort to counter French Fort Toulouse. Although England and Spain were at peace, he also believed he should block Spanish attempts at building a fort in the old Creek-claimed Apalachee lands toward the gulf coast

[16] *S.C. Gazette*, July 5–10, 1736.
[17] Jenkins, S.C. Commons House Journals, 1736–39, p. 140.

and continued Creek intercourse with St. Augustine by stimulating Creek attacks on Florida.

At Okfuskee he demanded that the Upper Creeks pull down Fort Toulouse, or failing in that, permit the English to build a fort nearby. These were long-desired Carolina objectives and Carolina had agreed to help pay for the English fort. The time was ripe, for the French in 1735 were in difficulties with the Upper Creeks. One of the Fort Toulouse soldiers had killed a Creek woman. A horde of angry Creeks demanding satisfaction had surrounded the fort. The murderer had been thrust out to them and they had burned him at the stake before the eyes of the horrified garrison.[18] Furthermore, Abeikas, egged on by English traders, had talked to the French-allied Choctaws about opening a trade with the English.[19] But the Upper Creeks were not inclined to an open break with the French. In a week of debate their headmen rejected the destruction of Fort Toulouse, but finally gave their consent to McKay's building an English fort nearby.

McKay muffed his advantage by mixing Georgia's commercial motives with a military project. He recruited traders agreeable to Georgia control of the trade to build the fort as a base for a Georgia licensed trading company. In the process he aroused the enmity of the Carolina traders. Edwards, one of these, became particularly obnoxious to McKay, and the captain disqualified him from trading, and had him stripped and tied to the chunkey pole in the Okfuskee chunkey yard in order to be whipped. At this point Edwards' friend, the One Handed King of the Okfuskees, intervened by flinging his arms about the bound man and declaring he would be whipped with him. Not daring to outrage the mico and his kinsmen, McKay released Edwards who went down to Carolina to complain. The Okfuskees now looked upon the projected Georgia fort as a device to restrain the trade and became hostile to it.[20] Yet the French effort to destroy the trading house, for such the fort actually was, failed, for the Indians desired whatever trade could be had

[18] Candler, *Ga. Col. Rec.*, XX, 582–83.

[19] *Ibid.*, 539.

[20] Jenkins, S.C. Commons House Journals, 1736–39, p. 79.

despite restrictions. The trading house never amounted to an effective fortified position; finally, with the Georgia failure to monopolize the Upper Creek trade and the Carolina refusal to bear any of the expense, it fell into decay.

Against the Spaniards, McKay enjoyed greater success. In March, 1735, at the Apalachicola village among the Lower Creeks, in talks with Cherokeeleechee, the old anti-English leader, he obtained assertions of friendship for the English and promises to go no more to St. Augustine.[21] He also heard Licka, an anti-Spanish headman, say that to prevent Creeks from going to St. Augustine for presents the path must be made bloody. Licka asserted that he desired vengeance on the Spaniards for killing his brother and drinking wine from his skull. McKay discreetly told Licka that the English could not take sides in his quarrel but that he ought to follow the dictates of his heart.[22] McKay's interpreter Barten, moved by no such scruples, told Licka the English would welcome Spanish blood.[23] Licka took a war party to Florida and killed a Spaniard and several Yamasees. When Spanish protests materialized in Carolina, Georgia, and the English court, English officials disavowed the act.

Creek warfare with Florida had been incipient for a year or more. In 1734, while Tomochichi was in England, a Spanish and Yamasee party had attacked a Yamacraw hunting party and had killed the brother of Umpechy who was with Tomochichi. Then in the spring of 1735, the Spanish reaction to Licka's raid had been an attack upon another party of Yamacraws. Georgia, under necessity of keeping the peace, could not sanction Creek or Yamacraw retaliation. In June of 1735, when Licka appeared at the conference in Savannah for the distribution of presents, Georgia authorities were much embarrassed. Licka, of course, should be rewarded for effecting a break in Spanish-Creek relations but to do so officially would cause international complications. The Georgians ostentatiously ignored him, but gave gifts to other headmen who saw

---

[21] Candler, *Ga. Col. Rec.*, XX, 534–44.
[22] *Ibid.*
[23] *Ibid.*, 432.

that Licka obtained his share.[24] That summer McKay went south of the Altamaha to probe Spanish intentions, and Tomochichi and his nephew Tooanabey scouted down toward the St. Johns. Sporadic Creek war parties operated against the Florida frontier amid Spanish cries that the English were fomenting an Indian war.[25] The English, though happy at the turn of events, denied complicity. However, the Creeks were too divided to launch full scale war against Spanish Florida. A faction continued to send deputies to St. Augustine for presents and to declare that peace could be had.

When in the early spring of 1736, Oglethorpe went south of the Altamaha to found Fort Frederica on St. Simon's Island as an outpost against the Spaniards, Tomochichi, Tooanabey, and Hillispilli led a party of Yamacraws as scouts. They sent word to the Lower Creeks to send down a substantial force to guard the new fort site, and themselves accompanied Oglethorpe toward the St. Johns River to spy out the Spanish disposition. They very much hoped for vengeance on the Spaniards for the death of Umpechy's brother and other Yamacraws. Oglethorpe, who had sent an advance party under Captain Richards, had no other objective than to delineate the southern boundary of Georgia. On the way, Tooanabey, enamoured of the gold watch given him in England by Prince William, Duke of Cumberland, gave the name Cumberland to Wesso Island in honor of his benefactor. At the mouth of St. Johns, Tomochichi, pointing to the Spanish post on the far side, declared his determination to attack. Oglethorpe restrained him and, to put the Yamacraws out of temptation's way, sent them back a few miles, while he went forward into Spanish territory to inquire after Captain Richards' party. In the night he was hailed by a breathless messenger from Tomochichi reporting that the Indians had a party of Spaniards surrounded and would attack at daylight. Oglethorpe hastened back to prevent the affray and arrived in time to discover that in the dark Tomochichi had mistaken Richards' party for Spaniards. Once back among the live oaks of Frederica, the Yamacraws entertained their allies with a lively war dance. Then, learn-

24 *Ibid.*, 517–25.
25 *Ibid.*, 438.

ing that the Spanish Indians seemed about to attack the half-completed works, they sent messages to the Creeks to hurry down warriors. A formidable concentration of Creek warriors soon ringed Frederica, but the report of impending attack proved groundless.[26] To prevent unauthorized Creek raids upon Florida, Oglethorpe set up a boat patrol on the St. John's River.

For one brief moment in July of 1736, the Georgia authorities under the spell of missionary John Wesley dreamed of extending the blessings of Christianity to the Creeks. Chigelley and Malatchi, now the dominant leaders at Coweta and of the Lower Creeks, escorted into Savannah Chickasaws and Choctaws seeking an English alliance and trade. The two headmen basked for a few days in the hospitality of their niece-cousin Mary, now Mary Matthews. They both showed great enthusiasm for the new school in Savannah. Chigelley remarked that perhaps the time had now come when the Creek children could be educated in the English way. Observing the children conning their lessons, he said that the English children behaved like men while Creek men behaved like dogs. Malatchi, reaching for the gravity of headman stature, said that if he had twenty children, he would want them all in school.[27] Wesley, who had already been told by Tomochichi that the conflicting stories of French, Spanish, and English on the subject of Christianity had confused the Creeks, tried fervently, with Mary as interpreter, for an opening with Chigelley. Chigelley admitted that the whites knew more than the Indians, but he pointed out the vanity of the whites, who built big houses as if they were to live forever. He also admitted that the Indians lived in sin and stated that he did not believe God would "teach us while our hearts are not white, and our men do what they know is not good: they kill their own children. And our women do what they know is not good; they kill the child before it is born. Therefore he that is above does not send us the good book."[28] Moreover, Wesley, witnessing the drunkenness of the headmen, concluded that the Creeks were

---

[26] Ga. Hist. Soc., *Coll.*, I, 121–27.

[27] Candler, *Ga. Col. Rec.*, XXI, 222.

[28] Wesley, *Journal*, I, 38–39.

too corrupted by the white man's way to be open to conversion. Schoolmaster Benjamin Ingham was either more intellectually curious or more optimistic. He joined the traders on their annual return to the Creek nation to live several months there and compile a Creek-English lexicon and grammar for use when the time was ripe, which it never was.[29] Ingham's work seems to have been the first of its kind for the Creeks in English and, perhaps, in any European language. By October, 1737, Wesley, believing there was "no possibility as yet" of instructing the Indians, decided that God called him to return to England.[30]

In 1737, the Creeks viewed the French and Spaniards with suspicion and tended to look to the English for support. Although some Creeks went to St. Augustine for Spanish presents, among them a few who had offered to serve as English spies,[31] clashes occurred. A party of Upper Creeks, hunting south of the Altamaha, encountered a party of Spaniards and Yamasees whom they suspected of robbing Creeks, and killed them all, leading their horses to Savannah for sale.[32] Creeks in the Upper Towns, apprehensively observing the great French attack on the Chickasaws in 1737, received fleeing Chickasaws into their country and worried about future French designs upon themselves.[33] Yet the French labored to achieve a Creek-Cherokee alliance against the Chickasaws.[34] The move did little more than to engender peace talks between the Creeks and Cherokees who for some time had been distrustful of each other.[35] No doubt hedging against possible French successes in the west, in July, 1737, Creek deputies visited Charlestown to brighten the chain of friendship.[36] Carolina sought to use this advantage to employ Creek agents in an effort to penetrate the Choctaws with trade in order to wean them from the French and get them to make peace with the Chickasaws.[37] Bienville, to hold the

---

[29] Thaddeus Mason Harris, *Biographical Memorials of James Oglethorpe*, 176–77.
[30] Wesley, *Journal*, I, 56.
[31] Candler, *Ga. Col. Rec.*, XXI, 314.
[32] S.C. Gazette, Feb. 26–Mar. 5, 1737.
[33] John P. Corry, *Indian Affairs in Georgia 1732–1756*, p. 97.
[34] S.C. Council Journal, June 29, 1737.
[35] B.P.R.O., C.O.5/438, p. 66.
[36] *S.C. Gazette*, July 9–16, 1737.

friendship of the Creeks, desperately countered English rum with French brandy.[38]

In December, 1737, Georgia found itself confronted for the first time with the murky issue of Indian land titles. In the treaties of 1733 and 1735, Oglethorpe and his associates had recognized the validity of Creek headmen's right to transfer lands from Indian nations to the Crown; now they were displeased to discover that a headman could take it upon himself to transfer lands to private persons. Tomochichi transferred all the Yamacraw holdings, which had been recognized in the treaties of 1733 and 1735, to Mary Musgrove—now Mary Matthews. Though Mary by birthright was an Indian and a royal Indian, her husband, Matthews, was a British subject. The upstart Matthews by this transfer loomed on the Georgia scene as a considerable land holder without the blessing of Georgia or Crown authority.[39] The situation was too delicate for Georgia action. Mary supplied large stocks of beef to the colony, frequently took from colony shoulders the burden of entertaining visiting Indians, and was a vital link to the Coweta micos. Oglethorpe esteemed her and used her on all occasions as official interpreter. But the issues raised by Tomochichi's cession were to torture the colony for a quarter of a century.

In the summer of 1738, the French and Spaniards became more aggressively successful with the Creeks. In June, to forward the Carolina-sponsored Choctaw-Chickasaw alliance aimed at the heart of French Louisiana, the Abeika king Hobohatchey, who for twenty years had espoused the English cause, brought Chickasaw and Choctaw deputies to Charlestown. There he received handsome presents and was told that the French had proposed to the English that the two unite to destroy the Creeks, and that the French after destroying the Chickasaws would turn against the Creeks. This was the vilest of propoganda, but on his return to the nation Hobohatchey called a meeting of Upper Towns headmen to hear it. The Alabamas, stout friends of the French and near neigh-

[37] Jenkins, S.C. Commons House Journals, 1736–39, p. 285.

[38] Rowland and Saunders, *Miss. Provincial Archives*, III, 698.

[39] Candler, *Ga. Col. Rec.*, IV, 50.

bors to Fort Toulouse, refuted the story. They even sent deputies to the Choctaws to counter the Abeikas' overtures on behalf of Carolina.[40] Hobohatchey's grip on Upper Creek policy slipped. The French line gained so much momentum that for a time rumors that the French-inspired partisans would kill the English traders flew about the nation. The Spaniards at about the same time renewed their activity in the Apalachee Old Fields, south of the forks of the Apalachicola.[41] As part of the drive to make Spaniards more attractive to the Creeks, the governor of East Florida invited several official Creeks to St. Augustine, ostensibly to greet Oglethorpe, who they said was visiting there. On discovering the hoax and learning that they had been summoned to hear anti-English talk, they downed their rum, swept in their presents, and went off to Savannah to assure Georgia of their firm friendship.[42] The headmen urged Oglethorpe to visit the nation, and with war between England and Spain impending, he promised that he would.

Oglethorpe, preparing for the inevitable Spanish war, persuaded Mary to establish a trading post up the Altamaha at Mount Venture, to act as a magnet to draw Creeks down to protect the land flank of Frederica.[43] From this position Mary would also be available as liaison between Oglethorpe and the Creeks. Oglethorpe had delayed fulfilling his promise to go to Coweta in 1738, but in the summer of 1739 the journey became imperative. In the first place, a Creek-Choctaw war then raging, the French inspired threats to the English traders. A Creek-English break seemed imminent.[44] In the second place, odd as it may seem in the light of the foregoing, there was talk that the Creeks intended to attack the French. Both had to be thwarted if the Creeks were to be useful to the English in a war against Spain.[45] Chigelley sent messages to Oglethorpe to come up immediately.

On July 17, with several English officers and a force of rangers,

---

[40] Rowland and Saunders, *Miss. Provincial Archives*, III, 319–20.
[41] McDowell, *S.C. B.P.R.O. Records*, XIX, 104–106.
[42] Candler, *Ga. Col. Rec.*, XXXV, 168.
[43] *Ibid.*, IV, 511; XXVII, Oct. 3, 1740.
[44] *Ibid.*, XX, Pt. 2, 208.
[45] *Ibid.*, XXXV, 218.

Oglethorpe set out for Coweta. Chigelley, bearing an English flag and accompanied by numerous headmen, came down the path to meet him. On perceiving him, the English fired a salute which the Indians enthusiastically returned. Then the Creeks escorted Oglethorpe into Coweta square where they gave him the black drink in the ceremony of purification, exchanged amenities, fed him a great dinner, and in the evening danced for him. The General was at Coweta until August 21, holding many talks with many of the headmen of the nation. In the process he heard complaints raised against the traders and promised reform. So great was Creek-English amity that all previous treaties were renewed including those which granted lands west of the Savannah and south to St. Johns, and inland as far as the tide flowed with the exception of the Sea Islands Ossabo, Sapelo, and St. Catherine's. To counter French and Spanish rumors that the English intended to take more lands, Oglethorpe promised that the English "shall not enlarge or take any other lands except those granted as above" and would punish any person intruding upon the lands. To lend force to this clause Oglethorpe issued a proclamation of warning to the Georgia inhabitants not to trespass on Indian lands.[46] How he averted the Creek-French war, if any threatened, is not recorded. The Creeks pledged loyalty to the English, and believing that he had a Creek alliance—though Bienville at Mobile said it was only a pledge of neutrality—Oglethorpe returned to Frederica to receive news that the Spanish-English war was on. He sent to the Creeks and Cherokees for Indian allies and directed Tomochichi's nephew Tooanabey to lead two hundred of the Lower Creeks into the St. John's country.

As Oglethorpe rallied his forces, Tomochichi lay at Yamacraw in his last illness. On October 5, as he neared his end, he lamented that he could not go against the Spaniards, exhorted his Indians to persevere in friendship for the English, and asked that he be buried among the English in Savannah. His body was brought by water down to Savannah and received with full military honors

---

[46] Hugh McCall, *The History of Georgia*, I, 366–67; Candler, *Ga. Col. Rec.*, XXVI, 489.

with the firing of minute guns from the battery. Oglethorpe and the colony officials bore it in a long procession to Percival square in the heart of the town, where it was buried to the firing of volleys by the militia. A pyramid of stone was raised over the grave.[47]

Tomochichi was said to be ninety-seven years old at his death, but this is improbable. He had been much too active on the war path in the Georgia years for a man of that age. More likely he was considerably under seventy-seven.

[47] *Gentleman's Magazine*, Vol. X (1740), 129.

5

The Spanish Border War
1739-48

CREEK PARTICIPATION in the English war with Spain, 1739–48, never reached the proportions Oglethorpe had a right to expect from his reception at Coweta in the summer of 1739. Many factors contributed to this failure: French and Spanish machinations, division in the nation, Choctaw and Cherokee wars, and perhaps, as Bienville thought, a genuine desire for neutrality. Most of the Creek commitment centered around Tooanabey's Yamacraws and such parties of Lower Creeks as Mary Matthews and Tooanabey were able to induce to join them. These served as scouting parties and sometimes to the number of forty or fifty took a valiant part in the English operations on the southern frontier.

In 1740, Chigelley was not ready to assume the burden of an English alliance, for strong voices in the Lower Towns insisted that he listen again to the French who sought to counter Oglethorpe's visit to Coweta and to aid the Spaniards by inciting the Creeks to drive the English traders from their country. Conditioned to follow Brims's style of neutrality, Chigelley cordially received French overtures which came into the Lower Towns in the winter

of 1739–40. The Indians who responded immediately to Oglethorpe's call were Savannah River Yuchis and Chickasaws, and
Yamacraws under Santouchy and Hillispilli, who had been in
England. In December these scouted toward the St. Johns River.
In January they accompanied Oglethorpe in an attack upon the
Spanish post of St. Francis on the north bank of the St. Johns River,
regarded by the Creeks as a trespass upon their territory. Oglethorpe captured the post and, leaving an English garrison, retired
with his Indians to Frederica. There he awaited re-enforcements
from Carolina, the main body of Creeks, and a large force of Cherokees who had promised to join him in an assault on St. Augustine.[1]

Chigelley, having committed himself to a council with the
French in late April, refused to authorize Creek help to the English. Only a few warriors of the Wind clan under Hallachey, who
opposed the French negotiation, set off to join Oglethorpe.[2] In
May, the General with several hundred Cherokees, a small assort-
ment of Yamacraws, miscellaneous Creeks and other Indians, his
regulars, and the Carolina regiment set out to take St. Augustine.
The Yamacraw miscellany participated in the capture of Picolata
on the St. Johns River, and in the ill-fated occupation of Fort
Moosa north of St. Augustine. In the latter affair, a Carolina and
Indian force of 135 men camped in the deserted Spanish outpost
and were surprised in the night by a Spanish attack in which the
English were massacred. The Yamacraws lost a number of warriors, but most escaped into the woods to report the disaster to
Oglethorpe. This setback and impatience with the protracted siege
operations which ran on into the heat of July discouraged the Indians, who determined to go home.[3] Though a sudden change of
heart by Chigelley and Malatchi sent a few more Creeks to join
the English, the fortunes of war frowned on Oglethorpe, and in
July he lifted the siege and returned to Frederica.[4]

Chigelley's about-face had resulted from his disappointment at

[1] Candler, *Ga. Col. Rec.*, XXXV, 238, 242.
[2] McDowell, *S.C. B.P.R.O. Records*, XX, 282.
[3] Jenkins, S.C.H.C., Vol. VII, 436.
[4] Candler, *Ga. Col. Rec.*, XXXV, 275–76; Jenkins, S.C. Commons House
Journals, 1741–42, p. 30.

Fort Toulouse. There in May he had found that the French would give him nothing substantial unless he made a complete break with the English. Prevented in this by Upper Creek opposition, he had burned his new outfit of French clothing and had sent word to Oglethorpe that he was now ready to help the English.

English and French intrigue and counterintrigue in the Upper Creeks in 1739–40 succeeded in practically nullifying each other, though in the long run the French profited when the Creeks became absorbed in a war with the Cherokees.

The road to a Cherokee war was a devious one. French policy, though aimed at frustrating an English-Creek alliance, was dominated by a decade-long attempt to exterminate the Chickasaws. This valiant tribe, living just below modern Memphis, Tennessee, enjoyed a great English trade and lay athwart the French line of communication between New Orleans and the Illinois French settlements. In 1729, with some taint of English trader instigation, the Chickasaws had roused up the Natchez Indians on the lower Mississippi to slaughter the French settlers among them. Brutal French retaliation upon the Natchez had destroyed them as a nation and many had fled to the Chickasaws. When the Chickasaws refused to yield them up to French vengeance, the French with their Choctaw allies attacked. Supplied by Carolina with guns and ammunition and stoutly assisted by Carolina traders, in 1736 the Chickasaws repulsed or destroyed the large French forces sent against them. Unwilling to risk more troops in that dangerous country, the French used the Choctaws under French leadership in an attempt by a war of attrition to annihilate the Chickasaws. The Creeks remained neutral in this struggle, because the English line of supply to the Chickasaws ran through the Abeika country, and the Abeikas themselves for forty years had been dependent upon the English. French intrigue had long attempted to lure the Abeikas into attacking the English Chickasaw-bound convoys, but the Abeikas well knew that a break with the English would end their necessary Carolina trade. Under the leadership of Hobohatchey they remained strongly pro-English. From their base in the Abeikas the English sought by means of opening a trade to lure the Choctaws out of their French alliance and thus put an end to the attacks upon the Chickasaws. The Choctaws could see for themselves that the Abeikas fared better with the English than they did with the French; English prices were lower and the volume of English goods much greater. But by bribery and artful maneuver, the French always succeeded in frustrating the English-Choctaw overtures and the Choctaw-Chickasaw war dragged on. In 1739 the Chickasaw assaults on French Mississippi River convoys seriously threatened communications between New Orleans and Illinois and forced the French to make a specious peace with the Chickasaws.[5] But they quietly egged the Choctaws on to complete the destruction they had failed to achieve.

In the fall of 1739, French objectives were seriously threatened by the prospect of a Creek-Choctaw war which would strengthen the Chickasaws. Abeikas had killed a Choctaw headman, and Choctaws had retaliated by taking Abeika scalps. Though the Abeikas protested that the murder of the Choctaw headman was an accident, Bienville, knowing that a Creek-Choctaw war would benefit the Chickasaw-English alliance and the Creek-English rapport, blamed English intrigue. He determined on countermeasures. He would give the Choctaws armed French aid unless the Creeks speedily made a peace on Choctaw terms, and he would use his connections among the Alabamas to intrigue among the Upper Creeks to foment a Creek-English break. This determination, which also arose from the necessity of preventing the Creeks from going to war against the Spaniards, resulted in the overture to Chigelley in the winter of 1739–40 which had kept Chigelley from sending aid to Oglethorpe.

In April of 1740, D'Arneville, commander at Fort Toulouse, summoned all the Creek headmen for a peace conference with the Choctaws. The Creeks hesitated, but finally in early May, Chigelley, intent on at least collecting as large a present as the occasion warranted, came to Fort Toulouse with two hundred of his fellow Lower Creeks. A great many Upper Creek headmen also attended. D'Arneville designed to have the Creeks and Choctaws seal their

[5] McDowell, *S.C. B.P.R.O. Records*, XX, 277.

peace by destroying the English trading houses in the Upper Creek country. Most immediately he plotted against John Spencer's trading house at the Muccolossus on the Tallapoosa River, seven miles east of Fort Toulouse. In return for the sack of Spencer's place, the Frenchman promised the assembled headmen a huge present of rum and goods which he displayed in barrels and bales before them. Chigelley became enthusiastic, and two hundred anti-English Tallapooses, Alabamas, Stinking Linguas, and Lower Townsmen swarmed from Fort Toulouse to put the torch to Spencer's.

D'Arneville had reckoned without the counterconspiracy. The English traders had loaded the Fort Toulouse meeting with pro-English headmen who sped a warning to the Wolf of the Muccolossus, Spencer's host and "landlord." The Wolf, strongly pro-English, determined to defend his trader. When the painted and howling hostiles burst out of the woods into Spencer's clearing, they came to an abrupt halt. Before them, seated on Spencer's porch, was the Wolf, painted, befeathered and gun in hand. Leveling his gun at the wild crowd, the Wolf grimly shouted he would shoot the first man who invaded the premises. The mob shrank back and after staring a moment in astonishment at the bold figure, retired precipitately on Fort Toulouse. Angry and disappointed, D'Arneville rolled away his rum barrels and bales of goods. The meeting broke up in disgust. Chigelley, his thirst unslaked, his train of bearers empty backed, stalked off to Coweta where he looked in a much more kindly mood upon Oglethorpe. The Creek-Choctaw peace did not materialize. The pro-English party among the Upper Creeks gained strength, and the Wolf of Muccolossus rose strongly in prestige among a people who admired individual valor.[6]

Desperate, D'Arneville and Bienville increased their pressure on the Upper Creeks. They encouraged strong Choctaw war parties to demostrate against them and to attack English convoys to the Chickasaws. The Upper Creeks soon perceived that they either must make peace with the Choctaws or fight a combined French-Choctaw force, with the possibility of civil war. The Alabama

[6] *Ibid.*, 257–63.

members of the confederacy and their relatives among the Upper Creeks opposed a French war. But peace with the Choctaws was also difficult, for the Choctaws demanded the heads of the Creek murderers who had precipitated the war.[7] This was an impossible price since a Creek headman was involved and his clan would not permit his assassination. Circumstances finally offered a way out. In the autumn of 1740, the Cherokees, who supported the Chickasaws against the Choctaws and had raided French convoys on the Mississippi, sent war parties out against the Choctaws. Counting on Creek-Choctaw hostility, one of the Cherokee parties ventured to travel by way of the Creek country. The Abeikas, by now eager not to give the Choctaws further offence, sought to appease them by attacking the marching Cherokees. Abeika and Tallapoose headmen then went to Fort Toulouse and reported what they had done and D'Arneville made a Choctaw peace for them.[8] The Cherokee-Creek war blossomed into a vigor which not only dispelled the possibility of a Creek-Choctaw war, but prevented any large numbers of Creeks from participating in the English war with Spain. It also prevented Oglethorpe's receiving further help from the Cherokees. Indeed, it was only by Mary Matthews' intervention at the request of President Stevens of Georgia that the Cherokees with Oglethorpe were able to get home without an assault by the Creeks.[9]

Chigelley, affronted at Fort Toulouse in 1740, perforce kept his relations with Carolina and Georgia clean, and English agents frequented Coweta in the spring of 1741. Some of these, among them the fantastic globe-trotting English dandy Sir Richard Everard, did the English cause little good. Everard had heard luscious tales of the possibilities of amorous adventure among the Creek girls and had come up from Augusta to sample the wild sweets. Waggish traders presented him to Chigelley, in gold laced hat, powdered wig, and brocaded coat, as a "beloved man" or

---

[7] *Ibid.*, 285.

[8] Jenkins, S.C. Commons House Journals, 1739–41, p. 434; Paris Archives Nationales Colonies [hereinafter referred to as Paris Arch. Nat. Col.], C13 A28, pp. 114–35.

[9] Candler, *Ga. Col. Rec.*, IV, 87–88.

peace emissary of the English. On Chigelley's inquiring his business, Sir Richard, with the artless confidence of the British, informed the old head warrior he had come "to lye with" the Creek women. Unless a marriage was intended, such propositions were made directly to the girls themselves. Chigelley, rising majestically from his seat, reached over and lifted the fine hat from the fervid Englishman's head, clapped it on his own head, and snatching a battered old trading hat from the head of one of his warriors, clapped it on the knight's powdered wig, saying as he did so, "when any of his daughters wanted husbands he would send for him." He suggested that Everard must have escaped from "a strong house" in England and protested indignantly to the traders for their introducing to him so impressive a figure on so frivolous an errand. Humbled and unrequited, the court fop withdrew from the nation to become the laughing stock of provincial Charlestown and Savannah.[10] This entertaining episode, though frowned on by the more serious minded traders as tending to upset Creek-English relations, did not prevent Chigelley's going down to Frederica in June of 1741 and promising co-operation in the Spanish war.[11]

Nevertheless relatively little Creek help was forthcoming when Oglethorpe in June and July of 1742 faced the Spanish assault on Frederica. Yamacraws under Tooanabey and a few Creeks sent down from Mount Venture by Mary did serve importantly in the battle of St. Simon's Island. Oglethorpe gave credit to the Indians and Highlanders for the successful ambuscade of the attacking Spanish column on July 7 in which the tide of battle was turned, and he himself at the head of Indians and Highlanders carried a counterattack to the Spanish beachhead. Tooanabey in the forefront of the assault distinguished himself in a hand-to-hand encounter with a Spanish captain. Though wounded in the arm, he shot the captain through the head.[12] Such boldness was his undoing in the end; in a 1743 foray near St. Augustine in which his Indians ambushed a party of Spanish horsemen, he was killed, the

[10] *Ibid.*, XXIII, 123–24, 128.
[11] *Ibid.*, XXXV, 351.
[12] *Ibid.*, XXV, 490–91; *S.C. Gazette*, July 12–19, 1742.

only fatality in one of the more successful Creek exploits in Florida.

Mary meanwhile encountered new troubles. Her husband, Jacob Matthews, having been appointed captain of twenty men at Mount Venture by Oglethorpe, went down to Savannah, made himself a great nuisance as a member of the anti-Trustee party, became involved in a paternity suit which he lost, and died in May, 1742. In the fall, Spanish Yamasees surprised, looted, and burned the trading post at Mount Venture, killing a number of Creeks.[13] Mary lost heavily in buildings and trade goods; nevertheless, at Oglethorpe's call she went down to Frederica to act as interpreter. So important did Oglethorpe consider her services that upon his departure for England in 1743 he gave her a diamond ring, two hundred pounds, and the right to draw drafts on him for two thousand pounds.[14] Possibly at Frederica she first met Thomas Bosomworth, an adventurer who had come over from England, applied for the position of Georgia agent for Indian affairs, and then returned to England to obtain ordination that he might occupy the church-offered living at Savannah.[15] The conjunction of these two stars, the half-blood widow with wealth and high connections, and the ambitious English adventurer, boded ill for Georgia and was to become a major factor in Creek affairs for a decade and more to come.

Late in 1742 the Lower Creeks had begun to succumb to Spanish efforts to turn them against the English. The Spanish opportunity had come when Stichey, mico of Apalachicola on the Lower Chattahoochee, having murdered English trader Elliott, arrived in St. Augustine. Elliot had stolen a watch given Stichey when he was in England with Tomochichi, and then had seduced Stichey's wife. In a drunken brawl at Elliot's trading house, Stichey had beaten the trader to death.[16] Then Governor Bull of South Carolina had, as he was entitled to do under treaty, demanded that the Creeks send him Stichey's head. Stichey fled to St. Augustine while

[13] Candler, *Ga. Col. Rec.*, XXXVIII, Pt. I-A, 400–401.
[14] *Ibid.*, XXVII, Pt. 1-A, 406.
[15] *Ibid.*, V, 630, 645.
[16] *Ibid.*, XXXVI, 182.

many of the Lower Creeks resented the demand that his life should be forfeit for that of such a character as Elliot.[17] The Spaniards loaded Stichey with gifts and used his dissident kinsmen as go-betweens to the Lower Creeks. These brought overtures to Coweta with offers of great presents if the Creeks would join the Spaniards against the English. In the excited state of the towns, Chigelley listened, but before decision could be made in November, 1742, English Lieutenant Francis arrived with news of the sack of Mount Venture and the killing of Creeks who had relatives in the Lower Towns. Mourning their slain, the kinsmen demanded vengeance on the Spaniards, and Chigelley ordered large parties to go to Frederica to join Oglethorpe's 1743 attempt against St. Augustine.[18]

In a few weeks, when a threat arrived from Fort Toulouse or Mobile that if the Lower Creeks did not end their war with the Spaniards, the French would come with their allies the Choctaws against the Lower Towns, Chigelley dispatched a runner to Frederica for a large supply of ammunition. Feeling the need to resolve all differences with the English, Lower Creeks killed Stichey's sister as satisfaction for the murder of Elliot, and sent Malatchi down to Charlestown with the news.[19]

However, Spanish agents continued to infiltrate the divided nation. Stichey, who was now unwelcome in many of the towns, stayed on in St. Augustine, where early in 1743 he induced a Creek raiding party to come into the town to listen to Governor Montiano. The Governor fed them with stories, re-enforced by the presence of English merchant ships trading in contraband of war, that the English had made peace with the Spaniards and that Oglethorpe acted belligerently for private ends. He offered large rewards for scalps of Oglethorpe's men.[20] Owehuskey, a head warrior of Oconee, defended Oglethorpe, saying the General had given him the clothes from his back, and he would be his friend. A fracas ensued in which Owehuskey was wounded but managed to escape

[17] *Ibid.*, 122.
[18] *Ibid.*, 123–24, 181.
[19] S.C. Council Journal, No. 14, p. 246.
[20] Candler, *Ga. Col. Rec.*, XXXVI, 176–79.

to Frederica where he gave his Spanish presents to Oglethorpe and informed him of the contraband trade and the presence of Creek emissaries at St. Augustine.[21]

French threats of war on the Creeks to aid the Spaniards were bluster; the French were preoccupied with a renewal of the Choctaw-Chickasaw war and with English intrigue among the Abeikas and Tallapooses. To counter the Choctaw-Chickasaw war, the English traders schemed to force the Creeks into war with the Choctaws. In the winter of 1742–43 they succeeded in causing Abeikas to murder two Choctaw hunters.[22] French-backed Choctaw demands for the heads of the murderers only increased the strength of anti-French feeling among the Abeikas. Finally the Alabamas, as always seeking to avert a Creek break with the French mediated a three months' truce with the Choctaws, which the Abeikas for reasons of their own used to attack the Cherokees. Meanwhile, Lieutenant Governor Bull of South Carolina had sent an agent, Captain Wood, to negotiate for the building of an English fort among the Upper Creeks. The overture resulted in a large delegation of Creeks going down to Charlestown in October, where they consented to having a fort built at Okfuskee and to the opening of negotiations for a Cherokee peace. This good will toward the English was a typically Creek move to counter French support of the Choctaws. When the agreement was reported in the Upper Towns, sentiment divided, and some of the Upper Creeks went to Fort Toulouse to profess friendship.[23] Nevertheless, the Choctaw truce having expired, the Abeikas failed to give the Choctaws the desired satisfaction, and Choctaws began to take Creek scalps. Carolina agent Wood, hoping to precipitate a Creek-French war, offered bounties for French and Choctaw scalps,[24] a scandalous measure since France and England, though on the verge of war, were still at peace. In this crisis, Vaudreuil, now governor of Louisiana, sought to mediate the Creek-Choctaw quarrel and to prevent the building of the projected English fort by threatening to

[21] *Ibid.*, 122.
[22] Paris Arch. Nat. Col., C13 A28, pp. 49–54, 97–98, 140–41.
[23] *Ibid.*, 325–28.
[24] S.C. Council Journal, No. 11, Pt. 1, pp. 222–23.

march in and destroy it.[25] The Carolina assembly refused the necessary appropriations, and the fort was never built.[26] The Carolina-sponsored peace with the Cherokees was concluded by April, 1744,[27] but honors were even, for by June 1 a French-sponsored Creek-Choctaw peace had been made.[28] With French influence thus strengthened, when, in May of 1744, Lieutenant Colonel Horton, now in command at Frederica, appealed to Chigelley for Creek help, French threats of retaliation restrained the Coweta warrior's hand.[29] Horton called in Mary to counteract the French, and she succeeded in inducing forty Lower Creeks to join the British forces.[30]

In the summer of 1744, France declared war on England, and James Glen, new royal governor of South Carolina, determined to use the Abeikas against Fort Toulouse.[31] On July 28 at Charlestown, in a secret session with the Okchai king and Mad Turkey of the Alabamas, he enlisted their aid.[32] The conspirators returned to the Upper Towns and called a council on the project. The council, however, elected neutrality, stating that they "would not suffer their land to be stained by the blood of the French." The Okchai king, having accepted an English commission, dissented and declared that if the English would send two hundred men to oppose the Alabamas, who would resist, he would attack Fort Toulouse. However, the king drank himself to death before the proposition could be given effect.[33] Soon the Upper Creeks were again too busy at war with the Cherokees to concern themselves with the French and English. The new outbreak arose directly from the Cherokee efforts to make peace with the northern Indians whom they now allowed to use their towns as bases for attacks upon the Creeks.

[25] Paris Arch. Nat. Col., C13 A28, pp. 199–211.
[26] S.C. Council Journal, No. 10, Dec. 16, 1743.
[27] *Ibid.*, No. 11, Pt. 1, pp. 226–27.
[28] Paris Arch. Nat. Col., C13 A28, pp. 257–59.
[29] S.C. Council Journal, No. 11, Pt. 1, p. 270.
[30] Candler, *Ga. Col. Rec.*, XXVII, 249.
[31] Jenkins, S.C.H.C., Vol. XII, 1067.
[32] *S.C. Gazette*, Aug. 13, 1744.
[33] Paris Arch. Nat. Col., C13 A28, pp. 263–66.

Glen undertook to halt the war, but his peace did not stand up.[34]

By 1744 a number of changes in population and economy had taken place in the Creek country. Several score Chickasaws, faltering under the pounding that nation had taken from the French and Choctaws, had settled in the upper reaches of the Abeika country at a town to be known as the Breed Camp and had become part of the Creek confederacy. As early as 1735, Shawnees had joined Tomochichi's Yamacraws,[35] and in 1744 a village of Shawnees from the Ohio country came to settle among the Upper Creeks.[36] A few years earlier some of the Abeikas of Okchai had removed to settle nearer the French. These in 1745 were induced by the Wolf of the Muccolossus to remove from the French and join his town.[37] The Creeks, too, were becoming more sedentary. An anonymous report from Louisiana in 1746 stated "they are not as wandering as they were formerly. They are beginning to accumulate property, have horses, cattle, hogs and fowls."[38] As early as 1736 Patrick McKay reported from the Lower Creeks that "the Indians . . . have plenty of hogs and I believe 100 cows or steers could be bought up among them."[39] In 1737, Effa Mico of Eufalees in the Lower Creeks complained of trader Alexander Wood's killing his cattle. Cattle, like horses, seem to have come to the Creeks from the Spaniards: McKay said there were "thousands of cattle" in the Apalachee fields.[40] However, though the Creeks began to have beef in pastures near their towns, because of the profitable deerskin trade with the English, they were now more intensive hunters than ever before.

The greatest Creek property-holder was Mary, who, though a half-blood and a baptized Christian, was nevertheless regarded both by herself and the Creeks—especially her cousin Malatchi of

---

34 W. S. Jenkins (ed.), South Carolina Journals of the Upper House of Assembly, 1721–83 [hereinafter referred to as S.C. Upper House Journals], Vol. XVI, Unit 4, p. 151.

35 Candler, Ga. Col. Rec., XX, 246–47.

36 Paris Arch. Nat. Col., C13 A28, pp. 263–66.

37 Candler, Ga. Col. Rec., XXIV, 433.

38 "Memoir pour Louisiane," Paris Arch. Nat. Col., 1746.

39 Candler, Ga. Col. Rec., XX, 537.

40 Ibid.

Coweta—as a Creek. She was no ordinary Creek, but the niece of Emperor Brims and sometimes spoken of by Malatchi, Brims's son and heir, as "sister." As a Creek and a "royal" Creek she was accepted by her kinsmen as having fully as much title to the Creek lands as any headman. In 1744, when she had married the adventurer Thomas Bosomworth, who had returned from England an ordained minister but had given over his living to become full time manager of Mary's property, Mary held the original Johnny Musgrove plantation, the five hundred acres given Johnny by the Trustees for his services in England as interpreter, the Yamacraw lands given her by Tomochichi, the Mount Venture lands on Alta- maha given her by Chigelley and Malatchi, and under the tutelage of her husband was reaching out to occupy and possess under her right as an Indian the islands of Ossabow, Sapelo, and St. Cath- erine's. Guided by Thomas she sought Georgia validation of her Indian titles, which she had made over to him, much to the indigna- tion of the Georgia authorities.[41] To meet the debts incurred on her property by the deceased Matthews and by the Yamasee destruc- tion of Mount Venture, she pressed claims against Georgia for twelve hundred pounds, allegedly for services as colony interpreter for the past twelve years.[42] The ex-preacher was expansively de- veloping Creek-owned St. Catherine's Island as a cattle ranch. To promote his projects Thomas drew large drafts on the now- bankrupt Oglethorpe. They bounced, and in 1745 he went to Eng- land to see Oglethorpe and to press Mary's claims on the Georgia Trustees.[43] The name of Bosomworth had become a byword and a hissing in Savannah, subject to accusations ranging from illegiti- macy to high treason. In their own minds and in those of their Indian relatives they operated legally and justly. Mary's Creek kin, beholding Georgia's refusal to grant their claims, regarded the Georgia attitude as just an instance of white men bilking an In- dian—indeed bilking an important Indian, the niece of Brims and the cousin of Malatchi, whose title to anything Creek was as good as that of the most prestigious headman. Resentment toward Georgia built up at Coweta.

[41] *Ibid.*, XXXI, 85.   [42] *Ibid.*   [43] *Ibid.*, XXXVI, 290.

6

The French Conspiracy
1746-49

CREEK BEHAVIOR in the period 1745–48 was largely motivated by the French-English conflict for the allegiance of the southeastern Indians and by the Bosomworths' quarrel with Georgia. The former saw Louisiana and Carolina pitted in an intense struggle to dominate the Choctaws and a widely ramifying effort of the northern Shawnees to raise up an all-Indian coalition to preserve the peace of the Mississippi Valley. The latter raised the bitter question of Indian land titles and the extent to which the English were to be allowed to encroach upon Creek lands. At times the various issues in the struggles coalesced and gave a strongly anti-English complexion to Lower Creek attitudes, while the Upper Creeks, deeply involved in the Choctaw defection from the French, were fervently pro-English.

In 1745 the Choctaws had begun to feel the pinch which British sea power put on French trade. The French, main suppliers to the Choctaws, were unable to provide them with trade goods. Choctaw feelers toward the possibility of an English trade reached the Upper Creeks that year and induced Abeika trader Lachlan Mc-

Gillivray to petition the Carolina Assembly for a monopoly of a possible Choctaw trade.[1] The venture began to come to a head late in 1745 when the Blind King of the Chickasaws sent a woman emissary to the Choctaws to propose peace and trade between the Choctaws and the English. In January of 1746, Red Shoes, mico of the eastern Choctaws, responded by sending deputies to the Blind King to invite English traders to come into the Choctaw country.[2] Since the Choctaws were allied to the French, with whom the English were at war, the English traders in the Chickasaw country, primarily John Campbell and James Adair, felt the venture too risky unless the Choctaws made an open break with the French. To meet this condition, early in May, Red Shoes' confederates killed three Frenchmen near the French fort on Tombigbe River in the Choctaw country and sent their scalps to the Blind King.[3]

Perhaps as part of the McGillivray scheme, the Upper Creek Abeikas had been urging an English-Choctaw alliance. The Blind King of the Chickasaws sent the three French scalps to the Abeikas as an open challenge for the Abeikas to break with the French in order that the path to the Choctaws might be clear of French interruption. The pro-English headmen were willing, but in the councils of the Upper Creeks they met strong opposition from the French-oriented Alabamas. In the heated debate which ensued, the pro-French and neutralist parties prevailed. A strong argument for their position was the fear that if the Choctaws and English ever got together, the importance of the Creeks to the English might decline. There was also fear that the English trade would strengthen a traditional enemy. Though these jealous arguments seem superficial in light of the strangle hold the Creeks had on the English-Choctaw line of communication, they prevailed and the Frenchmen's scalps were reverently wrapped in a white deerskin and delivered at Fort Toulouse with a declaration that the Creeks

---

[1] Jenkins, S.C. Commons House Journals, 1744–45, p. 349; Upper House Journals, Vol. XVI, 52.

[2] Jenkins, S.C. Upper House Journals, Vol. XVI, Unit 5, pp. 147–49.

[3] *Ibid.*, 104–105.

would go to war against the Choctaws to avenge the Frenchmen.[4] The French perceived a favorable opportunity to press anti-English talk and at Fort Toulouse on August 14 held a meeting of Upper Creek headmen, many of whom now accepted French commissions. Yet the majority of Creek sentiment opposed a break with the English, because the French could not supply the nation with goods. Red Shoes and the English continued their intrigue with the Creeks looking jealously on.

Simultaneously with the beginning of the English overtures to the Choctaws, the Ohio River Shawnees attempted to league all the Mississippi Valley and southern Indians into an all-Indian coalition.[5] In February, 1746, Shawnee emissaries accompanied by Weas and Twightwees from the Wabash River country visited the Alabamas, Tallapooses, Abeikas, and Cowetas,[6] in what seems to have been the first of a long and historic series of efforts of the Shawnees to spread and strengthen the doctrine of Indian country for the Indians. Governor Vaudreuil of Louisiana, well aware of the English machinations among the Choctaws, sought to use the Shawnee venture to French advantage. Apprised of what was going on, he made it a condition of French countenancing of the coalition that the Shawnees and their confederates plunder the English traders and drive them from their midst. Governor Glen of South Carolina looked apprehensively at Indian disturbances on the Carolina frontier as a French-Shawnee attempt to bring all the Indians down on the English.[7] However, seen in its true light, the Shawnee project must be regarded as fundamentally anti-European. The Shawnee visit to Coweta coincided with the rise of Creek anti-English sentiment from other sources. This had its inception in the situation at Frederica in February, 1746, when Upper and Lower Creeks visited the fortress to collect presents and offer their services against the Spaniards.[8] Lieutenant Colonel Horton, short

[4] Paris Arch. Nat. Col., C13 A30, pp. 76–84; Jenkins, S.C. Upper House Journals, Vol. XVI, Unit 4, pp. 11–12, Unit 5, p. 145.
[5] Paris Arch. Nat. Col., B33, p. 335.
[6] *Ibid.* and C13 A30, pp. 28–33.
[7] Jenkins, S.C. Commons House Journals, 1745–46, p. 90; Upper House Journals, Vol. XIII, Unit 3, p. 54.
[8] Candler, *Ga. Col. Rec.*, XXXVI, 212.

of Indian presents and not planning excursions into Florida, gave no presents and refused to employ his visitors. Disappointed, the Creeks went home to peddle the suspicion that possibly the English had made peace with the Spaniards and intended now to neglect the Creeks.[9] This, coupled with the sentiment engendered in connection with the Shawnee proposals and the French suggestion that they be linked with the expulsion of the traders, led to bad talks. All the old sores in the trade chafed with a result that a party of belligerent Creeks visited the Savannah River Chickasaw town, aired their grievances, behaved insolently toward the frontier settlers, and assaulted the nearby English-allied Yuchis.[10] They then went to Captain Kent at Augusta and demanded ammunition. The Captain, advised of the bad talk and the general frontier alarm, bluntly refused the demand, saying he'd give the Creeks powder from the muzzles of his guns. The angry Creeks returned to the nation with their Yuchi prisoners, talked big of their war exploits, and behaved insolently toward the traders.

Governor Glen, alarmed by reports from the Creek country, unrest among the Cherokees, and attacks by the Savannah River Chickasaws upon the Catawbas, planned a tour of the frontier to reassure the settlers, to compose the numerous Indian troubles, and in a grand sweep of diplomacy with the border tribes to confound what he thought was a great French intrigue. He sent up to Coweta for Chigelley and some of the headmen to come down to meet him in May at New Windsor in Carolina just below Augusta.

At the time of the New Windsor meeting, Malatchi was in Savannah on a social visit to Mary Bosomworth, who informed him that Georgia had rebuffed Yamacraw complaints of settlers' trespasses on their lands.[11] The whites had been cutting timber. When Senauki, Tomochichi's widow, had protested and demanded several casks of wine and rum as compensation, Georgia President Stephens had replied that Indian testimony was not enough, and, anyway, the lands had been ceded by Tomochichi when he was in

9 *Ibid.*, 319.
10 *Ibid.*
11 *Ibid.*

England in 1734.[12] Senauki and Santeechey, now a Yamacraw headman, who had been in England with Tomochichi, asserted that this was false. Tomochichi had ceded no lands when he was in England.[13] Malatchi carried the news of this disturbing development back to Coweta.

Chigelley, Captain Allick of Cussita, and other headmen met Glen at New Windsor on May 8. The Carolina governor talked in disapproval of the Creek attack upon the Yuchis and reminded Chigelley that the Creeks depended on the English for trade.[14] Chigelley, defensive, excused the Creeks on the grounds that the Yuchis acted badly toward the English—that the Yuchis had stolen English slaves and carried them to the nation. He also accused the English traders of misbehavior and unfairness in the matter of prices and weights and measures. Some Georgia officials also thought the traders much at fault for the troubles in the nation.[15] The talks closed on a seemingly amicable note, with Horton, who was present, inviting Chigelley to come down to see him at Frederica in the summer, and Glen heaping presents on the headmen. But Chigelley went back to Coweta in an uneasy frame of mind, for Santeechey, who had been at the meeting, had told him of the Georgia claim to the Yamacraw lands.[16]

Arrived at Coweta, Chigelley compared notes with Malatchi, who had just returned from Savannah, and the two had dug up from their storage box a paper on the subject of land cessions which Oglethorpe had given them in 1739. They called in George Galphin, trader at Coweta, to interpret it for them. Galphin told them that the paper supported the Georgia contention in the land cession. Chigelley and Malatchi now believed that Oglethorpe had deceived them. It is true that the Oglethorpe description of the Georgia limits contained no mention of the Yamacraw lands as an exception to the Georgia claim; but it is unlikely that Oglethorpe intended to deceive. It is possible that Galphin, unwilling to court trouble

[12] *Ibid.*, XXVII, 539.
[13] *Ibid.*, 427–29.
[14] *S.C. Gazette*, June 30, 1746.
[15] Candler, *Ga. Col. Rec.*, XXV, 44.
[16] *Ibid.*, XXXVII, 428–31; XXXVI, 300.

with Georgia, interpreted the paper to support the Georgia claim. Suspicion of the English ran high. Chigelley sent Malatchi down to Savannah to ask Mary Bosomworth if she had ceded the disputed lands to Georgia, and Chigelley himself held aloof from going down to Frederica.[17]

The coolness which had developed between Georgia and the Bosomworths on money and land claims was now reflected back to Coweta. From their new trading post at the forks of Altamaha, the Bosomworths circulated stories of their rebuff by Georgia and their financial distress. Malatchi and Chigelley, partisan to their kinswoman, sympathized and refused to deal with Savannah and Frederica. With the leading family at Coweta estranged from the English cause, a disposition arose among the Lower Creeks to treat with the Spaniards and the French who were reaching for any hold to obstruct the English overture to the Choctaws.

Made aware by the traders of the rising pro-French sentiment, Glen in the summer of 1746 invited Chigelley and the Upper Creeks to come down to Charlestown to receive presents and to listen to him. Glen had determined to make an effort through the pro-English among the Abeikas and Tallapooses to win Creek consent to the destruction of Fort Toulouse.[18] Late in October a number of Creek headmen went down to Charlestown led by a new figure, Enochtanachee or the Gun Merchant of the Okchais, who had become the leading Upper Creek; the Wolf of the Muccolossus; and Malatchi of Coweta, who was beginning to take over from Chigelley. In private conversations Glen found that the Wolf would support an English attack on Fort Toulouse but that the Gun Merchant feared a civil war if the attempt were made. The Wolf, therefore, much to the distress of the Gun Merchant, consented to the proposition that the English be allowed to build a fort in the Muccolossus territory, provided the English would make a present of ammunition to the Upper Creeks for nine years to come.[19] Malatchi rejected both propositions. Glen attempted to browbeat

[17] *Ibid.*, XXVII, 428–31.
[18] McDowell, *S.C. B.P.R.O. Records*, 1745–47, XXII, 202.
[19] S.C. Council Journal, No. 3.

him by threatening to withdraw the traders, but to no avail. Malatchi asserted that his father, Brims, had enjoined him never to let the whites—French, Spanish, and English—come to blows in the Creek country.[20]

Showered with presents, the headmen returned to the nation. There the Wolf presented the English proposal to built a fort; the Gun Merchant opposed, and Malatchi, resentful of the ominous talk he had received from Glen, spread stories that the English would withdraw the traders and send military forces into the country, and that Georgia threatened the life of his cousin Mary for making land claims under Indian titles.[21] While Malatchi sent runners off to Fort Toulouse and St. Augustine to inform of Glen's proposals, the Upper Towns talked in bitter debate. The final consensus was presented by Old Brisket of Tuckabatchee, a greatly respected retired mico, who said that while the English were welcome as traders, they were unwelcome as fort builders.[22] Malatchi himself finally went to Fort Toulouse, reported Glen's talk, and received presents.[23]

At this juncture, Red Shoes' anti-French faction won the Choctaw nation to make peace with the English. On November 12, Choctaw deputies arrived in the Chickasaw towns to conclude a peace which included the English traders, and Red Shoes' brother prepared to go to Charlestown by way of the Abeikas to make a formal trade treaty with Carolina. Vaudreuil acted quickly to capitalize on Creek factionalism and the rumors of an intended English invasion to create a rupture with Carolina which would block the English road to the Choctaws. In December, Lasseur, now commander of Fort Toulouse, held a meeting of Creek headmen, among them Malatchi. He told them that the French had always predicted the English would take the Creek country and now they were moving to do so.[24] In the Lower Towns, Malatchi

[20] Jenkins, S.C. Upper House Journals, Vol. XVI, Unit 4, p. 13.
[21] *Ibid.*, 14.
[22] *Ibid.*
[23] *Ibid.*, 15.
[24] Candler, *Ga. Col. Rec.*, XXXVI, 294.

was heard to say that if the English came into the Creek woods he would meet them with bows and arrows if necessary.[25]

But suddenly the conspiracy collapsed; the Cherokees broke out war against the Creeks.[26] Demonstrating a complete lack of co-ordination between French Canada and Louisiana, a French-inspired party of northern Indians with Cherokees concealed in their midst invaded the Creek country. The Creeks now needed English trade more than ever. Headmen who had been insolent toward English traders went about sheepishly courting those whose lives had been threatened, while reports of their former bad intentions reached the seaboard.

Exposure of the conspiracy did not end anti-English feeling. Fear of the English reaction gripped many, and a consciousness of guilt caused others to desire French and Spanish support. Malatchi, who knew that few of the matters really troubling him had been settled, encouraged French and Spanish agents to continue their overtures, and himself went down to St. Augustine.[27]

Colonel Horton at Frederica, alarmed at what he considered a narrow escape from war with the Creeks and desperate to frustrate the French momentum, took countermeasures. He was on excellent terms with the Bosomworths, on whose behalf he had promised to use the military's powerful influence with Georgia, Carolina and British authorities. In the spring of 1747 he sent up to Mary at her trading post on the forks of the Altamaha, asking her to use her influence with Malatchi and Chigelley to get them to drop the French and Spanish.[28] Mary and Thomas, eager to serve so potent an ally, sent a message to Coweta which effectually halted preparations to receive the French.

Mary intimated that one of the causes of the headmen's anti-English feeling had been the failure of Georgia, after Oglethorpe's departure in 1743, to continue annual presents to the Creeks. She apparently informed Horton that an agent should be sent with a present and assurances that in the future presents would be forth-

[25] *Ibid.*, 249.
[26] *Ibid.*
[27] Corry, *Georgia Indian Affairs*, 131.
[28] Candler, *Ga. Col. Rec.*, XXVII, 257.

coming each year. Colonel Heron, who after Horton's death in July succeeded to the command at Frederica, wisely chose as his agent Abraham Bosomworth, brother of Thomas. Abraham had been at Frederica since 1743 and had studiously cultivated the visiting Creeks, learning their language and accompanying their war parties to Florida, making a reputation with the warriors as a great fighter. Since Heron lacked funds for an immediate present but promised to write the Crown for an annual subsidy for the Creeks, Mary outfitted Abraham with horses and presents to the value of three hundred pounds, which she expected the British eventually to pay for. Toward the end of July, Abraham rode off for the nation.[29]

Abraham Bosomworth's mission was a great success. Arriving at Coweta just before the busk, he found strong sentiment in favor of the French. Bearing gifts, news of Heron's commitments on behalf of Mary, and of Mary's renewed good will toward the English, he gave speeches to the Lower Towns headmen which dispelled anti-English feeling in high places. Malatchi, who at this busk was installed as mico to succeed his uncle Chigelley,[30] consented to go down to Frederica to see Heron.[31] The Bosomworths were very much appreciated at Frederica, whence in September Colonel Heron wrote to the Duke of Newcastle: "it will be impossible for me to establish a strict friendship with the Creek Indians without the friendship of Mrs. Bosomworth . . . she is a most useful person and if properly applied to may be of infinite service to the Crown of Great Britain."[32] Heron forwarded to Newcastle Mary's petition for redress of grievances while the authorities at Savannah, hostile to Bosomworthism with its baronial pretentions to lands under Indian titles and demands for large money payments on accounts due, were outraged. They accused Colonel Heron of having corruptly entered into the Bosomworths' land-grabbing schemes.

29 *Ibid.*, 533; XXVI, 483.
30 *Ibid.*, XXXVI, 324.
31 McDowell, *S.C. B.P.R.O. Records*, 1750–51, XXIV, 295–99; Jenkins, S.C. Commons House Journal, 1749–50, pp. 264–66; Candler, *Ga. Col. Rec.*, XXVI, 249.
32 Candler, *Ga. Col. Rec.*, XXXVI, 252–54.

Despite his renewed good will toward the English, Malatchi had not given up the Spaniards. The Spaniards had enlisted a captive Creek to invite Creek deputies to receive gifts, a move which brought an end to Creek raids on Florida.[33]

Early in December, 1747, Malatchi, true to his promise, arrived at Frederica. Officially he represented the Lower Creek answer to the Georgia questioning of Lower Creek land titles. Privately he came as a tool of his kinswoman, Mary Bosomworth, who echoed her husband's clamors for land. Malatchi made the business of his mission the forcing of English recognition of Creek rights to lands and their disposition south and west of the Savannah River according to the treaties of 1717 at Charlestown, 1733 and 1735 at Savannah, and 1739 at Coweta. Such recognition would, of course, validate all Creek grants to the Bosomworths. Thomas Bosomworth's hand was apparent in the logic of the proceedings. On December 7, Malatchi spoke formally of the history of Creek land titles, the Georgia trespasses upon them, and the falsity of the Georgia claim that Tomochichi had surrendered to Georgia the Yamacraw lands. He alleged that his distress in these matters, his fears that Oglethorpe had deceived him, the rumors that his kinswoman Mary would be sent in irons to England, and the South Carolina move to build a fort in the nation, had caused his intercourse with the French. He proclaimed himself head of all the Creek nation and the individual in whom all land title rights lay and asserted his kinswoman's rights to all lands near Savannah, at the forks of Altamaha, and on the islands of Ossabo, Sapelo, and St. Catherine's. He concluded by saying that if the great king of England would send him a talk and annual presents, he would consent to the English occupation of Georgia and would live in good faith with the English.[34] Heron agreed to send Abraham Bosomworth to England to present the Creek case on land titles and the need for annual presents in which the Bosomworths should participate to generous proportions in recognition of their services as intermediaries with the Creek nation.[35]

33 Corry, *Georgia Indian Affairs*, 132.
34 Candler, *Ga. Col. Rec.*, XXXVI, 316–24.
35 *Ibid.*, 310–14, 323–24.

On report of these proceedings, Savannah authorities were greatly perturbed. They heard that the Bosomworths had told Malatchi that the Indians had the right of killing or taking away all cattle they found on lands claimed by the Indians "so that no man is safe in his possessions."[36] In January, 1748, tension was heightened when Thomas and Mary returned to Savannah with Malatchi, who raised the question of Georgia's title to any land whatsoever and asserted Mary's birthright as a member of the imperial family to all the lands she claimed. Malatchi was treated coldly, and Mary and Thomas were regarded as seditious persons for claiming land by Creek titles rather than by the processes of colony grant required of British subjects. Matters were not helped by the fact that whatever Malatchi's pledge to the Bosomworths he had the right of it. The Creek title to land west and south of the Savannah River had been recognized as valid in every treaty of cession, and Georgia had violated the treaties by permitting settlers to cut timber on the Yamacraw lands, and by establishing settlements, notably Ebenezer, well beyond the stipulated tidewater limit. Mary had as much right to Creek land as any Creek headman, either as "royalty" or simply as a member of the nation. The issue was clouded by the fact that her husband as a British subject had no right to accept lands without colony consent. For the colony to validate the claims of Thomas Bosomworth would permit every Georgia adventurer either to marry a Creek "princess" or go to the headmen for a grant of land. Georgia was confronted with a problem which could not be resolved as long as Mary and Thomas were disposed to assert Mary's Creek heritage while Georgia was dependent upon Creek good will, and this assertion was bound to go on as long as their creditors assailed them and Georgia refused Mary further compensation for her services to the colony. Mary held Malatchi in ties of "regal" kinship and Malatchi held an important segment of Lower Creek opinion. As long as his clan was aggrieved by Mary's troubles, there could be no assurance in Georgia of Creek friendship and co-operation.

During the late winter of 1747–48, Creek intercourse with the

[36] *Ibid.*, XXV, 243.

Spaniards continued. In April, 1748, the Spaniards sent a sizable present into the Creek country and many Creeks were entertained at St. Augustine.[37] The happy relationship terminated in August when Colonel Heron prevailed upon Secolachee (the One Eyed King) to go against Florida where he killed the Yamasee Chickillalee, a captain in Spanish pay who had raided English settlements. In retaliation, the Spaniards joined the Yamasee and killed fifteen Creeks. So many clans lost kinsmen in this affray that the Lower Creeks almost unanimously became hostile to the Spaniards. Large war parties went against Florida.

Throughout the latter half of 1747 the Upper Creeks, in the throes of a Cherokee war, had little disposition for hostilities against the English. They needed both English and French ammunition. The Carolina-Choctaw *rapprochement* proceeded unchallenged. Red Shoes' Choctaw emissaries had been received in Charlestown in the early spring of 1747 and had sealed a peace with the English. Carolina traders from the Chickasaws had entered their country while Governor Glen himself embarked upon an ill-fated scheme through the Phoenix Company to serve the needs of the whole Choctaw country. Convoys of goods and presents moved unmolested through the Abeika country to the banks of the Tombigbe.[38] Choctaw war parties immobilized the French with raids to the very gates of Mobile. The Abeikas themselves were prevented from joining the Choctaws by division in the nation. Even Malatchi opposed them.[39]

By mid-1748 the Creeks were asking Governor Glen of South Carolina to intervene to bring a peace in the Cherokee war; but Glen, who by then had a problem of Cherokee intransigence on his hands, wished to use the Creek war as a lever to bring the Cherokees to heel and informed Chigelley that he did not choose to intermeddle.[40] Meanwhile he had threatened an embargo on the Cherokees to force them to accede to his demands, and the Cherokees,

---

[37] *S.C. Gazette*, Mar. 28–Apr. 4, 1748; Jenkins, S.C. Commons House Journals, 1748, p. 18.
[38] Paris Arch. Nat. Col., C13 A22, pp. 121–22.
[39] S.C. Council Journal, No. 15, pp. 353–54.
[40] *Ibid.*

fearful of being deprived of ammunition, had accepted his conditions, which included Cherokee war on the French with attacks on Fort Toulouse and French Mississippi River convoys.[41] However, news of the overseas truce between warring England and France and the pending peace of Aix-la-Chapelle, led Glen to halt the projected Cherokee-French war, which, if it had persisted, would have led to a Creek-French alliance against the English.

In the winter of 1748–49, the Creek-Cherokee war seemed about to die out. Both nations needed to hunt for deerskins to trade for goods and ammunition. Their headmen sent to Glen to arrange for a peace. Knowing that the war played into French hands—for the Creeks were angry that the English supplied the Cherokees with ammunition—Glen acted promptly. At the end of January, 1749, he informed each of the other's overtures. Sometime in February the Upper Creeks, in a meeting at Okfuskee under the leadership of the Gun Merchant of the Okchais, sent ambassadors to Cherokee Great Tellico. Between the departure and return of their deputies the Okfuskees received another peace message from Glen and called a council at Okchai. It was an uneasy meeting, since their deputies to the Cherokees were long overdue and the Creeks feared foul play. Fortunately, the very day of the meeting the ambassadors returned with Cherokee deputies. With this reassurance, the Okchai meeting sent word to Glen that no more war parties would go out against the Cherokees but that to ensure a lasting peace the Cherokees must kill or expel all northern Indians who came among them.[42]

Fort Toulouse Frenchmen attempted to block the peace. When Glen asked the tribes to send deputies to Charlestown, the French asserted that he intended to destroy the Indians with sickness. When the Upper Creeks, undeterred, decided to go ahead, the French bribed Acorn Whistler, a headman, to reopen the war. Acorn Whistler went against the Cherokee town of Hiwassee and took two scalps, which prevented the Creek deputies from going to Charlestown.[43] Nevertheless, peace tokens continued to be ex-

[41] David H. Corkran, *The Cherokee Frontier*, 21–22.

[42] Jenkins, S.C. Commons House Journals, 1749–51, p. 194.

changed between Okfuskee and the Cherokee towns of Hiwassee and Great Tellico. The Cherokees agreed not to allow the northern Indians to base on or pass through their towns to attack the Creeks. They also proposed a fixed line between the hunting grounds of the two peoples across which neither side would trespass, thus making it clear that any foreign parties moving across the line were northerners. Promising not to avenge the deaths of their people killed by the Acorn Whistler, they sent the Creeks 160 fathoms of white beads. They invited Creek emissaries to Great Tellico for the Green Corn dance of August, 1749, at which time Creek and Cherokee would eat in peace together the fruits of the corn and squash seeds the Creeks had sent early in the spring as tokens of good will.

Once again Glen urged a meeting of Creeks and Cherokees in Charlestown at the end of August. The Cherokees accepted the new date, but few Creek headmen of the first rank would come. Malatchi, sending word that he would abide by the decisions made at Charlestown, went off to Savannah on Bosomworth business.[44] The Gun Merchant, alleging the necessity of staying home to make repairs at his farm, also had to keep an eye on the French. The French were indignant that in May some adventurous Abeika youths had joined a Chickasaw war party which had attacked a French post on the Arkansas River, killed Frenchmen, and taken prisoners. They were determined to attack any Chickasaws who came into the Abeikas.[45] The Wolf of the Muccolossus, always ready to manifest his good will toward the English, and the half-blood Captain Allick of Cussita headed the Creek delegation to Charlestown. Early in September under Glen's aegis, the Creek and Cherokee headmen met in the seaboard town. The Cherokees promised, even at the risk of a northern war, to prevent northern Indians coming into the Cherokee country to attack Creeks. Both parties agreed that Carolina should punish with a trade embargo the violator of the peace and that the aggrieved party should take

[43] W. L. McDowell, Jr. (ed.), *Documents Relating to Indian Affairs*, May 21, 1750–Aug. 7, 1754, I, 399.

[44] Candler, *Ga. Col. Rec.*, XXVI, 64–65.

[45] Paris Arch. Nat. Col., C13 A33, pp. 79–88; McDowell, *S.C. B.P.R.O. Records*, 1748–49, XXIII, 390.

his complaint to the governor of Carolina before he took vengeance. But the peace bid fair to backfire when on the homeward path many Creek and Cherokee headmen died, as the French had predicted, of fever contracted in the heat and pestilence of unsanitary tidewater Charlestown. Then, too, upon the road to the Upper Towns, the Wolf and other Upper Towns headmen were pursued by a northern Indian war party, which, according to James Adair, included some young Cherokee warriors.

7

Bosomworth Rampant: Savannah 1749

I N THE SUMMER OF 1749, the Bosomworths, deeply in debt and harassed by their creditors, had high hopes of resolving their difficulties. They expected Abraham Bosomworth's return from England to bring presents for the Creeks in which they would share and Crown answers to their petitions of September and December, 1747, validating their land claims. But Abraham had arrived in Charlestown in April without certainty of the hoped-for relief. The Crown had allotted three thousand pounds for annual presents to the southern Indians, but recompense for the Bosomworths was dubiously provided for in the condition that Georgia would consent.[1] Moreover, Abraham had failed to obtain recognition of Malatchi's sovereignty over the Creeks or of the Malatchi-Bosomworth theory of land titles being vested in the Brims-Malatchi line. Nor had Abraham brought a reply to Malatchi's talk. These circumstances moved the Bosomworths to plan to go to England to press their own case.[2] Yet they expected Abraham

[1] Candler, *Ga. Col. Rec.*, XXXI, 342.
[2] *Ibid.*, XXVII, 516.

would be in Savannah to distribute the Indian presents before they left.[3] Whatever chances they had of receiving anything would be settled by Georgia authority.

For the previous two years talk had permeated the Lower Towns that Mary would be sent in irons to England for her debts and for treason.[4] Malatchi had sworn enmity to Georgia if that occurred. Furthermore Malatchi had built great hopes on the King's reply to his message. With these things in mind Thomas Bosomworth went up to the nation to bring Malatchi down to hear Abraham Bosomworth, to receive presents, and to see Mary go off to England of her own free will.[5] It seems that Thomas also felt the necessity of causing Malatchi to remain beholden to the Bosomworths for favors received. Certainly the arrival of Malatchi in Savannah under Bosomworth auspices might force Georgia authorities to hesitate before again affronting the Bosomworths by rejecting their land claims and denying them a portion of the Indian presents. Already the Georgians had notified the Creek headmen that presents would be available and had asked them to be ready to come down when the presents arrived. But the immediate inspiration to bring Malatchi down in July, 1749, to greet Abraham Bosomworth was Thomas'.[6] Thus it was that the way was prepared for a showdown between the Bosomworths and Georgia.

Early in July, Malatchi with two headmen of the Cussitas and some attendants set out with Thomas Bosomworth for Savannah, leaving word for the other Creek headmen to follow in a few days.[7] Malatchi and his attendants instead of going directly into town to see President Stephens stopped outside at the Bosomworth plantation to await developments. President Stephens and his assistants were surprised and alarmed: surprised because they had expected the Creeks to await a specific official invitation before coming, and alarmed because they feared the Bosomworths would

[3] *Ibid.*
[4] *Ibid.*, VI, 253.
[5] *Ibid.*, XXVI, 492.
[6] *Ibid.*
[7] *Ibid.*, VI, 256.

use Malatchi to question much of the Georgia land claim.[8] Perceiving that a crisis loomed, they chose to ignore Malatchi's presence and probe around to learn the Bosomworths' motives.

However, the Bosomworth plans for a grand festival of presents with a flouting of local authority and a triumphal departure for England were thrown awry. Abraham had not arrived from Charlestown, and the ship in which they were to sail had departed in Thomas' absence. Malatchi was on their hands and full of expectation. Nothing remained but to hope for Abraham's speedy arrival and somehow to bring President Stephens to treat with themselves and Malatchi on the pressing problems. Mary twice sent messages to Stephens that Malatchi, who expected to be treated as visiting royalty by Georgia, was upset that his presence was ignored, and that his distress boded ill for the colony.[9] Stephens finally invited Malatchi and the Cussita headmen to dinner, but was unable to ascertain what was on their minds. Still Abraham did not appear and Malatchi lingered, ominously so Stephens thought, while the President and council became convinced that the Bosomworths were determined to have a showdown on their land claims with Creek good or ill will as the pawn in the game. They determined, if necessary, to resist, but if they could, to detach Malatchi from the Bosomworths.[10]

While Stephens and his council apprehensively debated and awaited a Bosomworth move, the crisis was unexpectedly precipitated. On August 10 in the early dawn, shots mingled with wild cries sounded from the river. Convinced that an Indian attack had begun, the President caused the alarm guns to be beat. Armed citizens poured into the streets prepared to defend the town. The episode expressed the great nervousness of President, council and citizenry, for no attack was planned and none occurred. Sixty or seventy armed Indians merely landed on the old Yamacraw lands just west of town, now claimed by the Bosomworths. These were the Lower Towns headmen and their attendants who had followed

[8] *Ibid.*, XXVII, 519–20.
[9] *Ibid.*, VI, 256.
[10] *Ibid.*, 257–59.

Malatchi's orders to come to Savannah a few days after his arrival. Hungry, for they had expected to be fed by the whites, and anticipating presents in such abundance as Creeks had never seen before, they had been brought down the river in the huge Bosomworth trading boat from their upriver campsite and had exuberantly announced their arrival by firing their guns after the fashion of Indians making a major celebration.[11] Somewhat reassured, Stephens sent word to them that they would be ceremonially received later in the day, but that they must come into town peacefully and unarmed; meanwhile, they were to remain where they had landed, which was an area set aside in the treaty of 1735 for the encampments of visiting Indians and had not been used for the purpose for a number of years. These lands had been ceded to Mary by Tomochichi in 1738.

An immediate clash with the Bosomworths resulted when later that morning the president and assistants, disregarding both Indian title and Bosomworth title, sent a gang of men into the land to clear a path to town that the Indians might be ceremonially escorted to the president's house.[12] No sooner had the men begun work with ax and grub hoe than Thomas Bosomworth appeared and ordered them off his land. The workmen ignored him. Thereupon Mary rushed onto the scene with a band of Indians, seized the workmen's tools, carried them to the boundary line, and threw them back into Savannah.[13]

Thus repulsed, the Georgia authorities decided again to try divisive tactics. Inviting Malatchi and some of the headmen to dinner, they told them that the lands were not Bosomworth's but were Indian lands reserved for Indian use,[14] and that the Indians were being used by the Bosomworths. The Georgia recorder of this affair reports Malatchi to have said that since the Georgians acknowledged the lands as belonging to the Indians he would regard Thomas Bosomworth as a liar and would no longer be his mouth. Round one, therefore, appeared to have ended in Georgia

11 *Ibid.*, XXVII, 548.
12 *Ibid.*, VI, 260.
13 *Ibid.*
14 *Ibid.*, 261.

victory, though at the price of recognizing Indian sovereignty over lands which the colony dearly desired to possess.

Of what transpired in the Bosomworth household that night there is no record, but the next day the president and assistants found themselves confronted with the epitome of Bosomworthism. In the morning the Indians laid down their arms at the edge of town and bearing eagles' tails, pipes and other peace tokens, were escorted by the armed citizenry, horse and foot, to President Stephens' house. At the head of the Indian procession marched Thomas Bosomworth, his younger brother, Adam, who had come from England to participate in Thomas and Mary's land bonanza, Malatchi, and Mary. At the president's house Malatchi was invited in with Mary for formal talks. But it speedily developed that Malatchi had no formal talk to give. He said he had merely come down to untie Mary if the Georgians attempted to tie her, that Mary would give all the talks. Stephens, angry at Malatchi's reversal of position from the previous day's talks, declaimed that if Georgia wanted to tie Mary up, Georgia would, and Malatchi couldn't stop it. Then Mary heatedly declared herself queen of all the Creeks, whose command every Creek would follow. Stephens demanded to know if she, as the child of an Englishman, was not a British subject. Mary said that she was not a British subject, that since she was a sovereign in her own right, she owed no allegiance to the Crown of England.[15]

This was Mary's first declaration of queenship, and how she arrived at it has never been made clear. As far as is known, there never was a queen of the Creeks unless the woman ruler of the Cofitachiques of De Soto's time was a Creek. The queenship would appear to have been the creation of Thomas Bosomworth's logic. Since Brims was "emperor" and Malatchi, his son, had succeeded to the office, Mary as a first cousin on the maternal side occupied an elder sister's position in a matriarchal society, and in so doing had a certain prestige and authority with Malatchi, a younger person than she, who had been declared head of the Lower Creeks in the statement of December 14, 1747. It appears possible

15 *Ibid.*, 262–63.

that at the present juncture, Mary had become the eldest living woman in the female line of the regal family from which Brims and Malatchi descended. Thomas Bosomworth's logic saw this as a queenly position, as it certainly was the most prestigious position in Malatchi's clan.[16] Possibly, she was a "beloved woman."

Be that as it may, the president and assistants saw their problem again knotted, and, hoping to soothe everyone's feelings with food and drink, they invited Mary and the headmen to sit down with them to dinner. But hardly had they been seated when Mary got up and left the house. Malatchi and five Indians rose and followed her. Six other headmen stayed. Apparently Mary had authority, but there was division in the ranks. Very likely those who remained and who were said by the Georgians to be of "equal esteem and authority with Malatchi," were of other clans than Mary's and Malatchi's.[17]

The colony Board that evening concluded that the Bosomworths were a menace whom nothing would satisfy but "a dangerous and unallowable sovereignty; a right to far the greatest part of the lands of this colony and a moiety of those goods that His Majesty's generosity sent over [as] presents to the Indians."[18] They feared a hostile demonstration and that night perceived what they thought was one. In the dark the town was awakened by a hullabaloo of drumming, singing, and marching Indians led by Adam Bosomworth toward the president's house. Thomas Bosomworth afterwards asserted that it was not an attack but was occasioned by Malatchi's drunkenness. It appears that when Malatchi, on leaving the dinner with Mary, arrived at the Bosomworth's house, he had decided to drink off the irritations of the incidents and then had become so mellow that he felt he ought to pay his respects to President Stephens and had summoned up his host to follow. Mary and Thomas had refused to join the drinking and had gone to bed, but Adam, in his new-found fellowship with Indians, had placed himself, wine glass in hand, at the head of the proces-

[16] McDowell, *Indian Affairs Documents*, I, 264.

[17] Candler, *Ga. Col. Rec.*, VI, 263.

[18] *Ibid.*

sion and marched along singing also. The convivial procession ran into a shock when it was confronted by armed citizens, horse and foot, and constables, who commanded the barbarians to retire, and hurried Adam off to jail. Confusion of voices ensued, tempers flared, and someone ran off to summon Mary. Roused, Mary rushed screaming in Creek like a "mad and frantick woman" into the square. What she said no Englishman knew, but Thomas Bosomworth, writing after the event, says that one of the officials had begged her to calm the Indians. The Board in its report of the incident to the Trustees in London said that "she rose to such a pitch of insolence as repeatedly to threaten the lives of some of the magistrates and threaten the destruction of the colony." They quoted her as screeching, "You talk of your white [peace] towns, your General [Oglethorpe] and his treaties. A fig for your general. You have not a foot of land in the colony." Stamping her foot on the ground she declaimed "that very earth was hers."[19]

It was the high imperial moment. Conscious of the wrongs Georgia had inflicted on her and her mother's people and convinced that she was the most regal of the Creeks and the one to whom all ceded lands had reverted on the violation of treaties, she dispossessed all Georgia in a few angry words. Then a stern voice reduced her to meekness. Patrick Graham, a Board member, threatened her with confinement if she did not keep quiet, and the guns of the citizenry were leveled on the turbulent crowd of Indians. Mary calmed at once and suggested that they all go into the president's house to talk it over. Inside the house, President Stephens, perceiving the advantage he held with Adam in jail and Mary subdued, delivered a sharp lecture, and Malatchi, sobered, asked that the matter be dropped and Adam released.[20]

Thomas Bosomworth now appeared, and an acrimonious debate followed as to whether Mary was an Indian or a subject of the Crown. Graham, stoutly fortified with rum, asked "Whether Mrs. Bosomworth had been baptised? Whether she had received the sacrament? Whether she had stood godmother to children?"

[19] *Ibid.*, 263–64.
[20] *Ibid.*, 264–65.

Bosomworth answered that she certainly had received these spiritual benefits. Then Graham declared that in so doing she had been de-Indianized and had lost her Indian rights. Bosomworth, in good voice, replied that she had not: that she was both Christian and Indian. Graham turned to the Indians and asked if Mary was an Indian or a white woman. They answered that she was an Indian. He then asked Mary the same question, and she said she was an Indian. Thereupon Graham snarled, "Madam, if I had told you so, you would have spit in my face."[21] At this juncture Bosomworth's remarks reached a pitch the assembled Board described as "insolent." They faced him down with bold assertions that they could not be frightened and threatened to imprison him and his entire family. Bosomworth, outnumbered and powerless, quieted and promised that if Mary and Adam were released to his recognizance they would appear in the morning to answer for their conduct. The Board agreed. The Indians went back to their camp to drink up the ameliorating present of rum the Board had given them, and the Bosomworths returned with Malatchi and the Cussita headmen to the plantation, where they drowned their woes.

The next morning everyone was too drunk to respond immediately to the summons of the Board; finally, on threat of an arrest, Malatchi went before the Board to speak for the Bosomworths. Meanwhile the Board's emissaries had approached the other Indian chiefs with overtures to convince them that the Bosomworths had led them astray. Now they went to work on Malatchi, using the Crown presents as bait. Malatchi, informed that the Bosomworths expected a third of the presents for their own use in paying their creditors, was asked if he would be content with two blankets while the Bosomworths received the third. The Coweta headman demurred. The Board went on to inform him that they felt it their duty to protect the Indians in their rights to their lands which the Bosomworths were bent on taking. They acknowledged the Indian right to the lands adjacent to Savannah and to the islands of Ossabo, St. Catherines, and Sapelo, the first as a place to camp when the Indians came to town and the others as

21 *Ibid.*, XXXVII, 559–60.

places for the Indians to hunt and fish when they came down to the ocean. No white men, they said, should have these lands. Malatchi, warmed by the Georgia acknowledgment of Creek titles, was understood by the Board to say that he thought the Bosomworths had deceived him on this point.

The Board, finding the Indian in a mellow mood, proceeded to attempt to undermine Mary's imperial claim by asking Malatchi what he meant by allowing that Mary ruled the Creeks when they all knew that he himself was head of the Creeks. Malatchi said that he did not intend to be ranked by an old woman and that he indeed was the chief. The Board then informed him that henceforth they would do business with him and not with Mary. Malatchi, presumably satisfied, left the president's house.[22]

The Board now decided to complete the overthrow of the Bosomworths by distributing part of the Crown presents before Abraham Bosomworth arrived. On August 17, Malatchi and seventy Indians were summoned to the president's house. Pipes and wine glasses were had, and in a gesture of friendship Malatchi asked that all stand, cross arms, and clasp the hands of the men on both sides. But Malatchi in the interval between meetings had been in consultation with Mary and Thomas and had once again perceived the logic of their point of view. In his thinking it was quite true that if the land belonged to the Creeks, as indeed it did, Mary's titles received in her Indian right and by grant from Tomochichi, Chigelley, himself, and other headmen were also good. He had memorized a speech on the subject prepared by Thomas, and, frowning, he rose with paper in hand and delivered from memory the speech which supported Mary's claims in every particular. "It was by Mary's permission," he began, that the English lived at Savannah, for she had lived there before General Oglethorpe had brought any of the white people. Since she had given Oglethorpe permission to settle, the lands the English now occupied were held under her title. Indeed all the lands the whites settled on should be held from her; she was queen and head of the nation; her talk was their talk and they would stand by what she said.[23] Saying that he

[22] *Ibid.*, VI, 267–68.   [23] *Ibid.*, 270–71.

meant no harm and that his heart was still good, he presented the paper to President Stephens. Written in Thomas' hand and style, it announced in the names of several headmen of the Upper and Lower Creeks, including Malatchi, that Mary was "rightful and lawful princess and chief" of the Creek nation. It vested her with sole power to transact all causes and matters relating to lands and other cases with the great king over the water as well as his beloved men on this side. It stated that whatever she should do or say was the same as done and said by themselves.[24] The Board broke into loud anger.

Malatchi again said he meant no harm, that he did not know that the paper was a bad talk, and demanded it back. It was returned to him along with a vigorous talk in which the president by every device he could think of sought to belittle Mary. Said he, "the great squire [Oglethorpe] on his first arrival here with his people, found Mary (then wife of John Musgrove) settled in a small trading house on this bluff by license of the Governor of South Carolina. She then appeared to be in mean and low circumstances with a red stroud petticoat and osnaburg shift. The squire, understanding that she could speak the Creek as well as the English tongue, made use of her as an interpreter first to Tomochichi's small party of Indians found on this spot and afterwards to other parties of Indians invited from the Creek nation. By this means she became generally known among the Indians of that nation. The squire always paid her well, besides making her very extra-ordinary presents for her trouble and made her the woman she now appears to be. The squire and the white people always respected her till she married Bosomworth but she has since been found a lyar. If she was a relative of yours [speaking to Malatchi], she would be looked upon as such, but we well know that she is not of your family, being the daughter of a woman of Tuckabatchee town [in the Upper Creeks] of no note or family by a white man. The squire could not treat with Mary for these lands, she having none of her own. The squire sent soon after he came for all the headmen and old men of the nation, who came down; that it was from them that

24 *Ibid.*, 271.

he had these lands. He had liberty to settle white people when and where he pleased. They [the Creeks] had then said they were glad the white people came to settle among them and that they did not want these lands, having enough for their own use where they lived, which was a great way off."[25]

The crux of the Board's case lay in its assertion that Mary was a pretender and entirely a creature of English manufacture, which was not true, and that the Creek headmen had ceded certain lands to Oglethorpe, which was true. Mary had been given by Brims as a member of the regal family to Johnny Musgrove in 1717 to seal the peace that had ended the Yamasee war. Malatchi knew this. The weak link in Mary's case was that she was not a signatory to any of the treaties ceding lands, though, if she was as important at an early date as she later appears to have become, her presence as interpreter at the treaties and her approval of them—she had urged the headmen to set their marks to them—played a powerful role in the adoption of the treaties.

Malatchi wanted peace with the English; he wanted presents; he wanted Indian titles recognized. He also wanted Mary recognized in the rights she claimed. With three of these objectives achieved he was not disposed to do battle for the fourth, at least not before he had had his dinner. He sat down to dinner with the Board. Apparently informed of the tenor of the discussion, Mary now rushed into the room. She was politely or impolitely told to retire. She shouted that those Creeks present were her people and that they would follow her where she commanded them. Some one shouted back to her to get out and go to bed. That roused Mary to her most frenzied pitch. In an "outrageous and insulting manner" she declared she was empress and queen of the Upper and Lower Creeks. Yes—even king—and could command every man in the nation to follow her "as the whites would soon know to their cost."[26]

The Board's spokesman bluntly told her to be quiet or she would be arrested. Turning to Malatchi, Mary repeated the spokesman's threat coupled with a few incendiary additions in vivid

---

25 *Ibid.*, 272.
26 *Ibid.*, 275–76.

Creek. Malatchi, foaming with rage, sprang to his feet and summoned the Indians to free her if she were seized. A constable laid hands on her and all the Indians rose; not one intervened, however, for none could risk a fight in closed quarters and without arms. Mary was dragged away to confinement. All then sat down quietly as men knowing not what to do, except Malatchi, who displayed the greatest and most outspoken distress of mind. It was a tense situation, for none of the Indians knew the lengths to which the Board was prepared to go, and they were helpless at a dinner which appeared to be a betrayal.

Somehow the situation had to be composed. All the headmen but Malatchi, who was apparently declaiming against the Board, withdrew to talk among themselves. Shortly they let the Board know where they were and blandly informed it that they were ashamed of Malatchi. Meanwhile one of the chiefs had slipped off to the Indian camp and warned the Creeks there to paint and arm. The Indians poured into the square. Alarms sounded in the town, and militia stormed onto the scene.[27] Outnumbered, the Indians laid down their arms on command while officers dragged Mary off toward the prison. Now Thomas Bosomworth ran into the square shouting imprecations and insults at the arresting officers. While soothing his wife he trumpeted "that no man's title to his lands was worth the snap of his fingers." But the Board, with the weight of power on its side, placed Mary in confinement while Thomas went home distracted. An Indian raced off to the nation with the bad news.

In the president's house, Stephens now told the headmen that Bosomworth was under arrest for debts and wanted to pay his debts with the Indian presents. Malatchi foamed at the mouth and commanded all the Indians to leave. The young men went out, but some of the headmen said that they did not want Bosomworth to have their presents. Thereupon Stephens said he would divide the presents, but that they must not allow Bosomworth to fill their heads with nonsense. They professed satisfaction and friendship. Even Malatchi calmed, professed friendship and said he was sorry

[27] *Ibid.*, 276–77.

to see the white people angry.[28] And so the day ended with Malatchi appearing tractable, Mary in jail, and Thomas crestfallen and discredited.

On the morning of the eighteenth, Thomas appeared before the Board as a suppliant begging the release of Mary. Finally, on condition that Thomas tell the Indians that in the future they must have no regard for what Mary said, the Board released Mary. The Indians declared they were satisfied. Malatchi apologized for his wild conduct the night before, Stephens distributed the presents, and the Indians departed town. The colony had weathered its crisis, thwarted the Bosomworths, and mollified the Indians. However, the Board sent frantic accounts of impending Indian war to the Trustees in England. Thomas Bosomworth later declared that they had magnified the dangers for the purpose of alarming the Trustees into reactivating the colony rangers in order to bring cash into Savannah to replace that lost when the regular troops were withdrawn at the end of the French and Spanish wars.[29]

Abraham Bosomworth's arrival on the twentieth or twenty-first of August was an anti-climax. He lacked the expected messages, the Crown presents had been given out, and the Indians had gone. Thomas humbly apologized to the Board for Mary's behavior and begged that the Board give Mary a portion of the presents that she might reopen her trading house at the forks of the Altamaha. Triumphant, the Board would give the Bosomworths nothing unless they would resign their claims, a thing they refused to do. A Savannah mob threatened Thomas' life and to escape them and his creditors he fled with Mary to Charlestown. There, with quickly reviving spirits, he began to prepare new devices for asserting his and Mary's claims.

Malatchi, whose showing at Savannah had been less than brilliant, left town outwardly calm but deeply offended. Snorting anger on the path to Coweta, he told all parties of Indians he met to avoid Savannah where the white people prepared for war.[30] At Coweta,

28 *Ibid.*, 273.
29 *Ibid.*, XXVII, 577–78.
30 *Ibid.*, VI, 289.

on arrival of the runner with news of the confrontation of Indians and militia and Mary's arrest, talk boiled of killing all the traders.[31] Remembering his raids on Carolina during the Yamasee war, old Chigelley said he could see Savannah in flames.[32] Runners carried the news to the Upper Towns, and traders all over the nation feared for their lives.[33] Malatchi's arrival in a distraught frame of mind added to the fever. When a Georgia agent entered the Lower Towns to invite more headmen down to Savannah for presents, Malatchi obstructed him by saying Georgia intended war.[34] Everyone hesitated, but finally cooler heads prevailed. Present-hungry headmen went down to receive more of the Crown's largess. Captain Allick of Cussita, who had been at Glen's meeting in Charlestown in September and knew there was no preparation for war there, went down and spoke lightly to the Georgians of Malatchi's authority in the nation, and Weoffki, the Long Warrior, assured Stephens the Creeks wanted only peace. They both asserted that Malatchi had no power to grant lands, that lands were the property of the whole nation.[35] All this talk was reassuring to Georgia and blandly suited to the occasion of present-receiving. Nevertheless, Coweta under Malatchi's leadership decided the time had come to talk to the French who offered the unctions of flattery to a bruised spirit, promises of presents, and a fruitful alliance. Georgia, if endangered—Bosomworth always asserted that she had not been— had been saved, but at the price of alienating the most prestigious Lower Creek, Malatchi.

31 *Ibid.*, 296.
32 *Ibid.*, XXVII, 486.
33 *Ibid.*, 467.
34 *Ibid.*, XXV, 460–62.
35 *Ibid.*, XXVI, 18–20.

8

Fighting the Cherokees
1750-52

IN THE AUTUMN OF 1749, many Creeks were unhappy with the English. French prophecies of an English trap in the Charlestown meeting of September had seemed fulfilled when some of the Upper Towns headmen had died of disease on the homeward path. From the Lower Towns came Malatchi's account of the evil disposition at Savannah and the possibility of war with Georgia. Talks were exchanged between the towns and Fort Toulouse. When the French, engaged in healing their break with the Choctaws and desiring to prevent the English traders from reopening it, showed a disposition to accommodate their Creek troubles occasioned by the Arkansas Post raid, Alabamas, Abeikas, and Tallapooses came readily to Fort Toulouse. They asserted their friendship and disavowed the raid as the act of irresponsible young men. Rum, presents, and anti-English sentiments promoted French prestige.[1] Malatchi even visited Mobile and made arrangements for the French to visit Coweta.[2]

[1] Paris Arch. Nat. Col., C13 A34, pp. 261–69.
[2] Candler, *Ga. Col. Rec.*, XXI, 465–66.

At this juncture war broke out anew with the Cherokees.[3] Governor Glen regarded it as part of the French machination; however, it seems to have commenced accidentally, though basically its cause lay in the Cherokee violation of the 1749 treaty of Charlestown by failing to prevent northern Senecas from coming into their towns on the way to attack the Creeks. It may be that the French at Niagara inspired the Senecas to foray southward, but there is no evidence of the Louisiana French having caused the war. In the late fall or early winter, rumors reached the Upper Creek country that, contrary to treaty, a Cherokee and northern Indian party had attacked a Lower Towns hunting party, had killed the hunters, and had taken their women and children prisoners. Immediately an Upper Towns war party went into the neutral ground and killed fourteen Lower Cherokees. On news of this the Lower Cherokees assembled a large force of northern Indians and Cherokee warriors and went out to look for Creek hunters. Nevertheless, mixed parties of Creeks and Cherokees, believing the clashes accidental, continued to hunt together. The Gun Merchant of the Okchais blamed the Creeks for renewing the war, saying it was due to a misunderstanding.[4] Glen's immediate efforts to halt the fighting failed, but the Gun Merchant held off the Upper Creeks and worked out a non-aggression agreement between the Upper Creeks and the Upper Cherokees. The Lower Creeks under Malatchi attacked the Lower Cherokees in force. Five hundred warriors, the largest Creek war party since the Yamasee war, moved swiftly through the spring woods and fell on Lower Cherokee Echoi and Estatoe. They killed many Cherokees, looted and burned the two towns. At Estatoe they vented spite on the English by pulling down the trader's store which supplied the Cherokees with ammunition and carried off some of the trader's horses. The attack was one of the greatest Creek military successes and frightened the Cherokees into talk of abandoning all their lower towns and moving over the hills. Malatchi's reputation as a warrior stood high.

Convinced that the Creeks were at fault, Glen warned the

3 Jenkins, S.C. Commons House Journal, 1749–50, p. 467.
4 Gun Merchant to Glen, Apr. 5, 1750, S.C. Council Journal.

Upper and Lower Towns that under the treaty he must punish the aggressors and therefore, unless the Creeks made immediate peace, he would cut off their entire trade. The Upper Creeks promptly reported their negotiations with the Upper Cherokees, and the Gun Merchant went down to Coweta to induce Malatchi to make peace. But Malatchi was recalcitrant. After the spring raids he had gone to Mobile to sing his glories, receive presents, and to prepare the way for a French mission to come to Coweta.[5] All spring he had received anti-Georgia talks from Mary, who had by-passed Savannah to go from Charlestown to the forks of the Altamaha. By runners, Mary had detailed her difficulties with Savannah, and peddled the story that Oglethorpe and Georgia intended to take the Creek lands.[6] She reported that only by obtaining as much land as he did had Oglethorpe escaped Crown censure for his behavior in Georgia and that with the war's end Oglethorpe intended to send large numbers of English paupers to settle on Creek lands. Already, she said, the Georgians had invaded the Creek lands, for the trader Clement in violation of treaties had established a store on the Oconee River deep in the Creek country.[7] Mary's talks fitted in neatly with French propaganda that the English were the real enemies of the Creeks since they were the land grabbers.

Early in July, 1750, a French mission consisting of a lieutenant, ensign, and engineer came into Coweta square. For days the English traders were barred from the square where the French flag was raised and anti-English talks progressed.[8] George Galphin, who brought Glen's talk threatening embargo, had to deliver his talk outside the square. Malatchi answered that since the Cherokees were the aggressors, he would not make peace until Cherokee deputies appeared at Coweta with definite promises to drive the Senecas from their towns.[9]

Glen feared the rising French influence and understood that Georgia, which profited from the wartime trade in munitions,

[5] Candler, *Ga. Col. Rec.*, XXVI, 43.

[6] *Ibid.*, XXXI, 465–66.

[7] *Ibid.*, VI, 357.

[8] *Ibid.*, 342; McDowell, *Indian Affairs Documents*, I, 5.

[9] Candler, *Ga. Col. Rec.*, VI, 342.

would not honor his embargo. He hesitated. Yet the Upper Creek–Upper Cherokee peace remained inviolate for a year. Some said this was because the Gun Merchant had found that by covert arrangements with the English traders in the Upper Cherokee country who did not want the deerskin trade disrupted by the war, he could obtain goods more cheaply in the Cherokee woods or towns than he could on the Tallapoosa River. Malatchi's war with the Lower Cherokees continued in unabated fury, much to the dismay of the Cherokees, who blamed Glen's failure to invoke the embargo and combed the northern Indian tribes for allies.

The major check to French influence in the Lower Towns in the summer of 1750 came from an unforeseen source. Mary Bosomworth appeared in the Creeks towns and let it be known that to avoid their creditors she and Thomas would settle there, probably at Tuckabatchee where Mary's clan was strong.[10] Bosomworth, who stopped at St. Catherine's Island, would drive up his cattle herd and bring his goods and chattels to safety from Georgia constables and would operate from the nation to protect his interests. Since the Bosomworth land claims could only be made good under English title, the Bosomworth enmity toward Georgia did not extend to the Crown to whom Thomas planned a direct appeal. Creek-English amity was a necessity. Therefore Mary talked with Malatchi during the August Busk when all the Lower Towns headmen met in conclave. As a result the French flag over Coweta square came down and the English flag went up. Mary had proposed that she go directly to the Crown in England and present all Creek complaints against Georgia as well as her own land claims.[11] The headmen, who did not want a break with the English in time of war with the Cherokees, embraced the idea. They set their marks to a statement composed by Thomas Bosomworth which empowered Mary to speak to the Crown as the voice of the nation and to arrange all matters relating to lands. The English traders, who had feared that the French at any time might spirit up the Creeks to murder them, breathed more easily when the red banner waved

[10] *Ibid.*, XXVI, 43.
[11] *Ibid.*, XXVII, 274.

anew. About this time, Creek and Yuchi Indians, wishing to avoid the hazards of the Cherokee war, had moved down toward the seacoast near Darien. Game was scarce but they felt themselves entitled by the prevailing anti-Georgia sentiment in the Lower Towns to help themselves to settlers' cattle and corn and to indulge in a little pilfering at outlying plantations. They sold stolen horses at St. Augustine.[12]

In September, fears of Mary's machinations, the covert French influence, and the disturbance around Darien caused Georgia to decide to send Patrick Graham up to the nation with presents and instructions to counteract Mary. But Graham's departure was delayed. The Bosomworths went down to St. Simon's Island to take ship for England, while their creditors swore out new warrants against them.

At the time of Graham's projected visit, the Creeks had no overt intentions toward the English. Malatchi was on good behavior. From the Upper Towns, where trade prospered, came word that the Wolf of the Muccolossus would soon visit Savannah. In October the Gun Merchant had gone to visit the Upper Cherokees,[13] and the Upper Creeks had become embroiled with the Choctaws. The Choctaws, having made peace with the French, had renewed their quarrel with the Chickasaws and had attacked Chickasaws in the Upper Creek country and in so doing had killed Creeks. Upper Creek war parties assailed the Choctaws and the Choctaws retaliated.[14] Under the circumstances, hostility toward the English was out of the question. The French, perceiving this, maneuvered to bring about a Creek-Choctaw peace.

The winter of 1750–51 passed with everyone who could do so in safety out hunting. Graham was delayed in getting off to the nation, the Wolf did not go down to Charlestown, and the Bosomworths failed to obtain passage to England. To resolve some of their difficulties the Bosomworths petitioned the Georgia Board for a portion of the Crown Indian presents and that Adam be

12 *Ibid.*, XXVI, 38–39.
13 McDowell, *Indian Affairs Documents*, I, 1.
14 *Ibid.*, 7.

licensed as trader at the forks of Altamaha.[15] As usual the petitions were denied on the grounds that all the Bosomworth proceedings were "illegal and treasonable."

In the spring of 1751, the Creek-Cherokee war flamed afresh, but with complications which forced Governor Glen to act. Creek war parties hovered on the outskirts of the Cherokee Lower Towns, where Cherokees and Senecas caught one and killed nine warriors. The victors pursued the fleeing survivors to Clement's trading post on the Oconee River, where, believing they had them trapped, they assaulted the store, killing two white men and some Chickasaws. This desperate act and subsequent Cherokee border disorders caused Glen to clamp an embargo on the Cherokee trade until the Cherokees should make reparation and give satisfaction for the murder of the two whites. The Cherokees heard rumors that the English would join the Creeks in war upon them and, nervously apprehensive, began attacks on the Upper Creeks. By autumn the war had reached a new pitch, and the Cherokees hastened deputies to Charlestown to make an adjustment with the English.

The Creeks rejoiced in Cherokee difficulties and made the most of overtures coming to their own nation from Savannah. In May, 1751, Patrick Graham arrived in the Upper Towns with the long-delayed Georgia present. His was more than a mission of good will. He had instructions to obtain a Georgia title from the Creeks for all the lands claimed by the Bosomworths,[16] in particular the old Yamacraw lands given to Mary by Tomochichi and the islands of Ossabo, St. Catherine's and Sapelo given to Mary by Malatchi in 1747. Addressing an assemblage of headmen at the Gun Merchant's town of Okchai, Graham made much of Creek-English friendship, blamed the French for the Cherokee war, and charged the Bosomworths with making unfounded accusations against Georgia and fraudulently claiming lands which belonged to the Creeks. The Gun Merchant gratefully accepted the presents, graciously referred to the traditional friendship of the Abeikas and English, disavowed the Bosomworths' claims, and asserted "we are

[15] Candler, *Ga. Col. Rec.*, XXVI, 182.
[16] *Ibid.*, XXXIII, 522–25.

willing and fully satisfied that our friends and brothers the English, should possess and occupy all the lands upon Savannah River commonly known by the name of Indian lands and also the three islands called Sapola, St. Catherine's, and Ossabow." In confirmation of this cession to Georgia, the headmen present set their marks to a paper deeding the lands to the colony of Georgia.[17]

Thus fortified in the Georgia claim, in June, Graham went down to Coweta to obtain Lower Towns consent to the transaction. But Malatchi refused to execute any such deed. He asserted that the Lower Towns could only lend the lands. According to Graham, he "utterly rejected and disowned any claim that Mr. and Mrs. Bosomworth pretended to have to the said lands and positively affirmed they never executed any deed concerning the same." If Malatchi made any such statement, it was utter equivocation or else ignorance of the paper he had set his mark to on December 14, 1747.[18] Graham stated that the Lower Towns headmen thought they had sent to Savannah by Mr. Bosomworth a paper demanding redress for the Cherokee raid on the trespassing Clement's Oconee store and the death of Creeks in that raid, which paper, said Graham, "appeared to be the deed of gift the Bosomworths pretended to have of the aforesaid lands."[19] In referring to this paper, George Galphin asserts that it was never interpreted to the Indians.[20]

From this tangle of statements, everyone—Graham, Galphin, Malatchi, the Bosomworths—stands suspect. Obtaining Indian marks on dubious documents of land cession was not an unfamiliar practice in other colonies and was to become more frequent in the south as time went on. Later Creek testimony was to the effect that even the Upper Towns headmen did not know what was in the paper they signed for Graham.[21] One gets the impression that Creeks were ready signers and convenient forgetters, especially when abundant presents were in sight or rum flowed freely. Gal-

[17] McDowell, *S.C. B.P.R.O. Records*, XXIV, 335–38.
[18] Candler, *Ga. Col. Rec.*, XXVI, 396–97.
[19] McDowell, *S.C. B.P.R.O. Records*, XXIV, 329–40.
[20] Candler, *Ga. Col. Rec.*, VI, 355.
[21] McDowell, *S.C. B.P.R.O. Records*, XXV, 337–38.

phin told the Georgia Board that if they would send him an annulment of the Bosomworth grant, he could get more headmen to sign it than Mary had to sign her paper, presents being "a shure method to gain an Indian's interest."[22] However, the Bosomworths still had one title, and Georgia had another. The main flaw in both was that some Indians asserted that no land could be given "without all the nation was willing."[23] Just what this meant—whether all the people or all the headmen—was never cleared up in colonial times. Neither Graham's nor the Bosomworths' "deeds" had all the headmen's marks. Graham's deed had the particular weakness that it had none of the marks of the Lower Towns headmen whose title to the lands in question was more immediate than that of the Upper Towns headmen. Though, in 1751, Malatchi apparently denied to Graham the Bosomworth title, later, in 1753 in Charlestown, he affirmed it and stated that Graham's title constituted aggression on Creek territories.[24] Though Malatchi seems a reed bending in the winds of the moment, his behavior on the whole manifests more of a disposition to favor Mary's and the Creek titles to lands than to tolerate Georgia trespassing or pretentions. He seems fundamentally to have held the position that there should be no further European encroachment on Creek territory, for about the time he received Graham at Coweta he rejected a Spanish overture, accompanied by forty kegs of rum, to build a fort in the southernmost Creek territories at Pallachicola old town.[25]

By autumn of 1751, the Cherokee war had reached a new intensity, and the Upper Creeks were amenable to a French-negotiated peace with the Choctaws. In November or December, Vaudreuil invited deputies of the Upper and Lower Creeks to come to Mobile for presents and ratification of the Choctaw peace.[26] The Choctaws were rendered tractable by reports that northern Indians were offering their services to the Creeks.

[22] Candler, *Ga. Col. Rec.*, VI, 356.

[23] *Ibid.*

[24] McDowell, *Indian Affairs Documents*, I, 396–97.

[25] *Ibid.*, 268.

[26] Paris Arch. Nat. Col., C13 A36, pp. 36–47; McDowell, *Indian Affairs Documents*, I, 216.

About the same time, Glen, committed by his treaty of November, 1751, with the Cherokees, made overtures to the Creeks.[27] Glen's message arrived too late to prevent war parties going out against the Cherokees in the early spring of 1752.[28] The war licked furiously at the Cherokee towns from Hiwassee to Keowee, causing the Cherokees to arm their villages all along the line and even to consider abandoning their homeland to live in the north. Cherokee pleas for peace went to Charlestown and even to Okfuskee. In Charlestown, Glen was angry at the Cherokees for not fulfilling certain promises they had made at the November treaty, and hesitated to move rapidly. At Okfuskee the Cherokee deputies were spurned and had to make the best of their way home through a hostile wilderness.

But in April, 1752, an event occurred which forced Glen to pressure the Creeks to make a peace. Acorn Whistler of Ulchitchi, an Upper Creek headman who had served the French in 1746 by attempting to prevent the Creek-Cherokee peace of that year, murdered some Cherokee hunters who had sought protection in Charlestown. He had followed them into the town where Charlestown authorities had disarmed him and enjoined him to keep the peace. But when the Cherokees left, Acorn Whistler secretly sent word to a band of his countrymen outside the town. These ambushed the Cherokees almost at the city gates and killed several. To the outraged Carolinians the Whistler denied all knowledge of the affair and stole away to hurry back home.[29]

When the Cherokee nation heard of the affair, they accused Carolina of complicity and demanded that Carolina punish the Creeks. Needing to placate the mountaineers, Glen could no longer afford to be suspected of tolerating the Creek-Cherokee war. He determined to send a mission to the Creeks to demand the death of Acorn Whistler and an immediate Creek peace with the Cherokees on pain of a trade embargo. He chose as his agents Thomas and Mary Bosomworth, who were then in Charlestown awaiting a ship

---

[27] McDowell, *Indian Affairs Documents*, I, 204–207.

[28] *Ibid.*, 257.

[29] *Ibid.*, 211, 227–30.

for England where they intended to press all their money and land claims.[30]

Arriving at Coweta on July 24, the Bosomworths found that Malatchi had gone to war against the Cherokees to avenge the death of a friend. Old Chigelley greeted them cordially and lodged them in Malatchi's house to await the mico's return. The next day Chigelley satisfied public curiosity by convening the Lower Towns headmen. He told them that the Bosomworths had come from Carolina on important business, the nature of which he did not yet know; but, he said, since his relative, "their great beloved woman," Coosaponakeesa, had come such a fatiguing journey in such hot weather it must be of great consequence and could only be revealed when Malatchi came in. While the Bosomworths waited, the Creeks, uneasy in their awareness of Acorn Whistler's outrage near Charlestown, complained that they believed that the Carolinians favored the Cherokees. Indeed, frequently the traders in the nation informed the mountaineers when a raid impended. Furthermore the Creeks knew that Glen had not yet forced the Cherokees to deliver up the murderers of the two white men at Clement's store on the Oconee. The atmosphere did not augur well for the Bosomworth mission.[31]

On August 3, Malatchi came home triumphant. He welcomed his cousin but told her he could not listen to her message until he had physicked himself, related his exploits to the headmen, and had given orders for the annual busk to take place. These ritualistic matters consumed three days. On the sixth, purged and at peace, Malatchi with Chigelley listened in private as Bosomworth read his commission from Governor Glen. First it informed them that the business was so important that the governor had seen fit to entrust it to a near relation of theirs. It then set forth Glen's complaint against the Creeks for attacks upon Cherokee runners in Carolina territory and for the April murders near Charlestown. Citing the treaty of 1721 made by Ouletta, in which the Creeks promised to punish those of their nation who committed depredations or car-

---

[30] *Ibid.*, 264, 266–67; Jenkins, S.C. Upper House Journal, XXII, 42.

[31] McDowell, *Indian Affairs Documents*, I, 270–71.

ried on war in Carolina, Bosomworth read Glen's demand that the Cherokees taken prisoner in the specific episodes be delivered up and that the leaders of the guilty Creek parties be put to death. He further demanded that the Creeks make reparation for all robberies committed against whites in Creek raids on the Cherokees and that the Creeks make peace with the Cherokees. If the Creeks failed to meet any of these demands, Carolina would embargo the Creek trade until the Creeks complied.

Chigelley was aghast. He said he had never heard of such a demand as the lives of head warriors who had killed Indian enemies, even in the territories of friends of both parties. Previously Creeks had assassinated some of their own men guilty of peacetime murders of traders in the nation, but never before had such a request as this been made of them. Besides, he pointed out, some of those in the offending war parties were relatives of Mrs. Bosomworth. He forgot to mention that he knew that Acorn Whistler, who was not of Mary's clan, had ordered the Charlestown murders. With tears in her eyes Mary talked earnestly in Creek with the two headmen for a long time. They finally agreed that one or two of the offenders should suffer death but that they must first confer with all the Lower Towns headmen.

On August 10, the Lower Towns headmen sat all day and all night in council with Chigelley and Malatchi without coming to an agreement. Finally they summoned Mary to talk with them. Mary shamed them by telling them that she as a woman knew they should give satisfaction to the whites. Perceiving in the council one of the men who had participated in the Charlestown episode, she demanded of him on peril of his life that he tell the truth. The man described the whole incident and placed the blame squarely on Acorn Whistler. Mary then addressed the council, telling them they must think well on the matter, for some very important men must suffer death. The headmen, cowed and horrified, then agreed to abide by Malatchi's decision. While they were thus intimidated, Bosomworth spoke on the subject of horse stealing from whites by raiders against the Cherokees, and the headmen agreed to a public order that all such horses be returned. The meeting then adjourned, and the Bosomworths entered into a private session with Chigelley and Malatchi.

The two headmen demurred on passing death sentence on Acorn Whistler. Mary was adamant. Finally Malatchi sent for two of Acorn Whistler's near kinsmen, Este Paieche, the Warrior King of the Cussitas, and the Otassee King of the Upper Towns. To them he depicted Acorn Whistler as a bad man, who, returning from Carolina in anger because Glen had disarmed him, had threatened to kill some whites in order to plunge the Creeks into war and who had boasted to Malatchi that he had ordered the murder of the Cherokees. Both men admitted that Acorn Whistler had given bad talks in their towns. Malatchi then ordered the death of Acorn Whistler, but required that since the bad man had many friends, relatives, and warrior followers in both Upper and Lower Towns, he must not be informed lest he cause the killing of whites in the nation. He must be quietly put out of the way. Este Paieche and the Otassee King accepted the assignment. They went away, and, after much thought on the matter, sent an order to an Upper Towns nephew of the Whistler whom the Whistler had offended in a quarrel over a woman, to kill him and to give it out that he had killed his uncle because his uncle had threatened his life. The order was carried out. Then to keep the assassin's mouth shut, Este Paieche and the Otassee King had him killed, ostensibly in revenge for the murder of his uncle.[32]

While this plot was in process, Mary and Thomas went to the Upper Towns to make Glen's demand for peace with the Cherokees. Talk was rife in the towns that they had come to demand the lives of Creeks who had killed Cherokees in Carolina. Upper Towns traders, alarmed lest the talk result in their own deaths, gave it out that the Bosomworths had no commission from South Carolina, and that, if any lives of Indians were taken, the Bosomworths planned to take the credit in Carolina and demand money for it with which to pay their debts. In the Hitchiti town, feeling ran so intensely that the headmen openly insulted the Bosomworths. Chigelley and Malatchi, who had accompanied them ostensibly to

[32] *Ibid.*, 271–79.

be present at the Hitchiti busk, conscious of what was impending, drank themselves into a stupor. They were so drunk they did not hear the news of Acorn Whistler's death, which was secretly communicated to Mary in the dark of night along with the news that Este Paieche and the Otassee King had ordered the death of the assassin.

When the two headmen sobered, Mary reported the assassinations to them, and they all returned to the Lower Towns. But the affair was too sensational and became a matter of public and private talk with accusing fingers pointed toward the Bosomworths. Finally the Wolf King of the Okfuskees sent word down to Coweta that Mary had better come up to the Tuckabatchees, where she had sufficient kinsmen to protect her, and explain matters. On the way up, the Bosomworths met Acorn Whistler's son, who was demanding the life of a Cussita for the death of his father. At Cussita the fellow was quieted by a large reparation of presents. At Tuckabatchee a great conclave of headmen was convened to hear Mary speak. They listened intently as she presented the Carolina case, and finally the Otassee King came forward and told in detail how the headmen who were Acorn Whistler's relatives had agreed that he must die and had arranged to take his life. With matters thus explained, the Okfuskee Captain, a kinsman of the assassinated warrior, gave his assent, saying he hoped now with the blood of Acorn Whistler and his nephew, the Governor would be satisfied. The conclave gave thanks to the Whistler's clan "for the great regard they had shown to their nation" in giving this satisfaction to the English, and the episode of Acorn Whistler was closed.[33]

On September 22, Bosomworth talked to the Upper Creeks about peace with the Cherokees. After considering the proposal for several hours, the council agreed the matter should be left to Malatchi, since "the Cowetas was the great town of both nations" (Upper and Lower Creeks) and Malatchi the great king and son of the Emperor of both nations, and "whatever Malatchi agreed to, the whole Upper Creek nation would ratify and confirm." Bosomworth then spoke of the horses stolen from traders in the

[33] *Ibid.*, 280–91.

Lower Cherokees, and the Wolf of the Muccolossus followed him with a talk in favor of the English. Headmen of the Puckucholahassees in the Upper Towns stated that since the Creeks had taken the life of a headman who had offended Carolina, Carolina ought to ask the Cherokees to kill their warriors suspected of killing two white men on upper Coosa River. (These murders were never cleared up.) Old Brisket, the retired grand old headman of the Tuckabatchees, whose firm pro-English hand had always operated behind the scenes, put his weight to the English cause but took pains to ask that his past services to the English be not forgotten whenever presents were sent to the nation.[34]

Back in the Lower Towns, Bosomworth met with Malatchi's headmen, who for some time debated peace with the Cherokees. Finally, Malatchi consented that the Cherokees be informed by Governor Glen that peace could be confirmed in Charlestown in the spring. In the meantime, during the hunting season, raiding parties would be held in abeyance. The consensus again was that stolen horses should be returned, and steps were taken to carry it out.

Malatchi made it clear that he was dissatisfied with the English. He blamed the English for the disobedience of the young men to the elders; the English, said he, gave commissions to unqualified Indians, thus promoting them to a headship they had not earned from the elders of the nation. He was referring to Savannah's 1749 attempt to displace Malatchi as head of the Lower Towns by Weoffki, the Long Warrior of the Oconees. Weoffki, however, had had the good sense to decline the commission and to assert that Malatchi was king. It is true that some rose to undue prominence from English attentions. Such were Tomochichi and the half-blood Captain Allick of Cussita, whom Malatchi disliked for his catering to English claims. Also in 1752, Governor Glen, impressed by the pro-English sentiments of one Toluchea, an ordinary warrior, had commissioned him. Malatchi also complained of white people stealing Indian horses—a not unlikely occurrence—of traders who "debauched" the wives of Indian men; of traders who, when drunk,

34 *Ibid.*, 289–96.

beat Indians; and of free lance whites, beaver hunters on Indian territories, who decoyed Indians' wives and were therefore subject to "accidental" death in the wilderness. In these complaints he wished it intimated to Glen that if trouble with the Indians were to be avoided, the white governments must exercise better control over their subjects.[35]

One additional serious item of business remained to be handled. A Chickasaw had murdered a white packer in the refugee Breed Town of the Chickasaws among the Abeikas. These people, who had fled the French and Choctaw attacks on the Chickasaw towns, were now incorporated into the Creek confederacy with which their headmen sat in council. The murder, therefore, was a Creek responsibility, and Bosomworth demanded the life of the murderer. Malatchi went up to the Okchais and consulted the Gun Merchant, and the two went to the Chickasaw town to make the demand. The Chickasaws complied. By the murderer's uncle they sent word that he was to commit suicide or be put to death. The young warrior blanched with fear and hesitated. His uncle reasoned with him to no avail. Finally the uncle said, "You are young and afraid to die. I will show you I am not," and plunged a knife into his own heart. Thus the older man spared the young man's life and satisfied his clan's obligation to the confederacy.[36]

Thomas and Mary returned to Charlestown in December and, reporting the success of their mission, submitted a huge bill for expenses. As usual, the Bosomworths had been liberal with presents and with themselves. The bill was too much for the South Carolina Assembly, which, as ever, plaintively bemoaned Indian expenses, and the Bosomworths became almost as unwelcome in Charlestown as they were in Savannah. Carolina paid them but a fraction of what they claimed above the previously agreed-upon compensation. Nevertheless the Bosomworths had brought Carolina discipline to the Creeks and had paved the way for the ending of the Cherokee-Creek war. Fully conscious of this, they were to become more clamorous than ever for the recognition of their claims and rights.

35 *Ibid.*, 305–306.   36 *Ibid.*, 306.

9

Lowering Trade Prices
1753-56

T HE GUN MERCHANT'S EXCURSIONS to the Cherokee country to take advantage of lower prices of trade goods had major repercussions on Upper Creek politics and behavior. The Creeks discounted the fact that mountain deerskins were thicker and heavier than lowland skins and that the shorter haul from Carolina to the Cherokees was less expensive than the long haul to the Upper Creek country. They only saw that their mountain neighbors enjoyed a trade advantage over them and set about remedying the situation. Their efforts were to color the course of events for several years to come.

In late May of 1753, Malatchi, true to his promise to the Bosomworths, went to Charlestown to renew his friendship with the English and to terminate the Cherokee war. With him came a hundred Creeks including several important Upper Towns headmen. Among the latter were the Red Coat King of the Okfuskees, the Otassee King, who merited English good will for his hand in liquidating Acorn Whistler, Handsome Fellow (Hobbythacco), who as head warrior of the Okfuskees was to figure prominently in

Creek affairs for the next quarter century, and the Wolf of the Okchais. The Wolf of the Okchais or Yahatastanage, known as the Mortar, was a member of the Bear Clan and brother-in-law of the Gun Merchant. As an ardent nativist he was for years to head the anti-English faction in the Upper Towns. Though later to be suspected of being in French employ, it was at this period and on the matter of trade prices that he first manifested a grudge against the English.

At Charlestown, Malatchi shone at his best. Amiable, he impressed the whites with his good sense. He affirmed his friendship for the English, outlined the steps he had taken to meet Glen's demands, described calmly the assassination of Acorn Whistler and his method of obtaining satisfaction from the Chickasaws even before Glen had asked it, and stated that he had gone from town to town to obtain the surrender of property stolen from traders in the Cherokee country. While he accused the Cherokees of cowardice and double dealing in not coming to Charlestown to meet him, he indicated that he still desired peace and had withheld Creek war parties. He would leave the final negotiation of the peace in Glen's hands. As for peace with the Senecas, that must still be discussed in the councils of the nation. With Mary present in the role of interpreter, he brought up his disputes with Georgia over land claims and questioned the validity of Graham's deed from the Upper Towns but seemed content when Glen disclaimed authority in the matter.

The only discordant note in the conference occurred when Handsome Fellow protested trade prices and on Glen's demurrer withdrew from the council room for a day. Some headmen, hot on the subject, turned in their English commissions and numbers of young warriors stalked out of the conference. Malatchi smoothed over the difficulty and the next day brought the dissidents back to reaffirm their friendship for the English and gracefully apologized for them. Glen finally entrusted to him the distribution of presents, and even, on his urging, augmented them in order to assuage the irritation of those who had been rebuffed.[1]

[1] McDowell, *Indian Affairs Documents*, I, 389–408; *S.C. Gazette*, July 11, 23, 1753.

Events on Malatchi's return trip to the Lower Towns almost destroyed the Cherokee peace. Not far from Dorchester, just outside Charlestown, one of the Creeks was shot from ambush, scalped, and, most insultingly, part of his skull was carried away. Seneca tokens of an eagle's tail and some beads had been left by the body. A runner dispatched to Charlestown brought Glen and a party of horsemen to the scene to escort the Creeks safely from Carolina.[2] Near Fort Augusta the Creeks received a warning that enemy Indians skulked in the neighborhood. A war party went out, caught up with the strangers, and killed one, believed from a small wooden image hung at his neck to be a Seneca. They took his scalp with part of his head to avenge the death of their countryman. They also captured a warrior who spoke Cherokee. With scalp and prisoner, the Creeks led by Malatchi came into Augusta and raised the death whoop at the commander's house. They then gave their prisoner a vicious beating, stabbed him many times, and cut off his head.[3]

Returned to Coweta, Malatchi encountered opposition to peace with the Cherokees. Besides the episodes on the path, Cherokees had killed a score of Creeks during the winter and spring, and Creeks wanted vengeance.[4] Malatchi dispatched runners to Charlestown to inform Glen that unless the Cherokee deputies came soon, he could not hold his warriors. In July, warriors who were gathered in Upper Towns Okchai to assault the Cherokees heard the Gun Merchant plead for peace. The warriors demanded as the price that the Cherokee peace deputies bring two Senecas, one to be burned at Okfuskee and the other at Coweta.[5] However, by late autumn a Seneca deputy, in response to Glen's overture through New York colony, came safely into the nation and stayed, as the custom was for peace envoys, several months.[6] In the fall and winter there also developed a Creek-Cherokee exchange of deputies. Handsome Fellow of the Okfuskees and the Mortar of the Okchais, whose brother had married a Cherokee woman, went

[2] S.C. Gazette, June 12, 1753.
[3] Ibid., June 25, 1753.
[4] McDowell, Indian Affairs Documents, I, 381.
[5] Ibid., 389.
[6] Ibid., 509.

to the Overhill Cherokee towns to escort the Cherokee deputies to the Creek towns.[7] All that winter, Cherokee and Creek hunting parties operated together peacefully in the woods between the two nations, and in April, Cherokee deputies came into Coweta and satisfied Malatchi that the peace would stand firm. This peace lasted until well after the colonial period had ended.

While the protracted amenities were in process, war broke out between the Creeks and Choctaws. In February, 1754, Choctaws killed two Creeks at a hunting camp toward the Chickasaw nation, "mistaking" them for Chickasaws.[8] Encouraged by English traders, Tallapoose vengeance parties immediately went out. Louisiana Governor Kerlerec, who had succeeded Vaudreuil, fearing the English-sponsored alliance of Creeks with Chickasaws against the Choctaws because it would eventually involve the French, set in motion efforts to compose the quarrel. Duvall's Landlord, an important Upper Creek, opposed the French project,[9] but Malatchi was not prevented from appearing at Mobile with one hundred followers that spring to discuss the peace.[10] The Creeks set as the condition of a Choctaw peace the surrender of the murderers of the two Creeks. As usual the meeting had anti-English overtones, and traders heard gossip that a blow might be struck against them. Certainly there was no anti-English tone in the message Malatchi sent Glen in which, while reporting his visit to Fort Toulouse, he asked a pardon for a Carolina packhorseman whom he picked up at the French fort where he had fled after murdering a Carolinian.[11] Nevertheless Glen feared a Creek war.

The North American French, in 1754, were engaged in a strong reaction to the English efforts to penetrate the Mississippi Valley. In the south these efforts concentrated on raising up Creeks and Cherokees to oppose the English. To this end, breaking the English hold on the Abeika Upper Creeks was a necessity; to do this they

---

[7] W. S. Jenkins (ed.), South Carolina Book of Indian Affairs, 1710–1760, Vol. V, 1.

[8] Paris Arch. Nat. Col., C13 A38, pp. 205–206.

[9] McDowell, *Indian Affairs Documents*, I, 499, 502.

[10] *Ibid.*, 507–508.

[11] *Ibid.*

had to take advantage of every division of sentiment in the tribe. They found a willing ally in the Wolf Warrior of the Okchais, the Mortar, who, besides being an influential member of the largest clan in the nation, had through his brother's marriage to a Cherokee a powerful entry into the Cherokee nation.

Creeks and Cherokees were drawing close together, and to seal the peace, Cherokees were eager to have the Creeks join them in war on the Choctaws, against whom, as allies of the Chickasaws, the Cherokees had long been at war. Cherokees joined with a Creek war party under Duvall's Landlord going out against the Choctaws. The Mortar, perceiving a threat to peace with the French, declaimed against it; although opposed by the rest of the Abeika headmen, he sent out runners to warn all Creeks against going to war with the Choctaws. This did not deter Duvall's Landlord or the Cherokees. While the Landlord's party was out, Cherokee deputies came to the Okfuskees and addressed a meeting of headmen, accusing the French of wishing the Indians to destroy each other and intending, after the Choctaws had destroyed the Chickasaws, to turn the Choctaws on the Creeks. They urged the Creeks to support them, and the Gun Merchant assured them the Creeks would not listen to the French. The Cherokee deputies declared that French presents were few and poor and that the French were unable to compete with the English trade. Other Cherokees soon came to urge Creek co-operation in war against the French-allied northern Indians. Glen, apprised of this turn of events, saw an opportunity to form a great Indian coalition against the French and determined to invite the Creek headmen down to Charlestown in the fall for presents and talks.[12]

Aware of the Cherokee representations, the French reacted strongly. In August they summoned Handsome Fellow, Duvall's Landlord, the Mortar, and as many other headmen as would come to a meeting at Fort Toulouse to make peace with the Choctaws.[13] The Frenchmen made the meeting an occasion for an anti-English diatribe. They said the Cherokee peace was a decoy; and they fab-

[12] *Ibid.*, V, 1, 9–10.
[13] *Ibid.*, 61–62.

ricated a story that during the next winter, when the Creeks went out to hunt, the Cherokees and English would combine to devastate the Creek country. The Englishmen, they said, had even asked the French to join them against the Creeks, but the French, like a father protecting his child, had refused. The English, they darkly asserted, coveted the Creek lands and daily pressed in on them as the French did not.[14]

Creek opinion divided. Some headmen, mindful that in Georgia new settlers had encroached on Creek lands on Ogeechee River, believed the story of intended English attack.[15] Others did not. Many expressed doubts. Nevertheless the Creek-Cherokee *rapprochement* continued. In the fall of 1754 the Gun Merchant and a large following went up to the Cherokee nation to spend the winter near the Cherokee towns where they could profit by selling their deerskins to the English traders among the Cherokees. Indeed, Lachlan McGillivray, who since 1744 had traded among the Abeikas, asserted that the sole motive of the Creek-Cherokee peace was the trade, and that the Gun Merchant and the Mortar, his brother-in-law, aimed to use the peace to break traders' prices in the Creek country.[16]

Kerlerec did not perceive this subtlety of the Gun Merchant's venture to the Cherokees, and, fearing a Creek-Cherokee alliance against the French and Choctaws, he planned an October meeting of Creeks and Choctaws at Mobile. He invited Malatchi from Coweta; however, Malatchi, who had also received Glen's invitation to Charlestown, was ill and could not attend. To Glen the Coweta mico sent his regrets with an intimation that he would welcome presents as he had given away all his property to the "doctors" and had nothing left but his ailing body.[17] To Kerlerec he professed undying friendship and said as soon as he had recovered, he would bring his wife and children to Mobile.[18] Glen's Charlestown meeting did not transpire, because the Gun Merchant

---

[14] Candler, *Ga. Col. Rec.*, XXVII; Jenkins, Book of Indian Affairs, Vol. V, 30.
[15] Jenkins, Book of Indian Affairs, V, 60–61.
[16] *Ibid.*, 66, 69.
[17] *Ibid.*, 29.
[18] Paris Arch. Nat. Col., C13 A38, pp. 130–31.

had gone off to the mountains, and the Creeks were divided. The Mobile meeting did take place as planned, but it was an unhappy one. Dissatisfied with their quarters in the town, the headmen listened sourly to Kerlerec's anti-English tirade and caustically commented on the gifts the Frenchman had laid out. Old Peter Chartier, headman of the Shawnees who had moved into the Creek country in 1748, defended the French, but the headmen came away divided and confused.[19]

That winter the major concern in the nation was the trade. Some horse packers who traded in the nation on their own aggravated the discussion. These packers cut prices to take trade away from licensed trading stores, but soon perceiving that they lost money by it, raised them. The angry Creeks cried out against them, and they fled for their lives, screaming that the Creeks had gone over to the French and intended killing all the traders. The rumor had been disseminated, perhaps with the connivance of the regular traders, to scare them out of the country.[20]

The battle over the trade began early in 1755 when the Gun Merchant returned from the Cherokees laden with goods bartered for his winters' take of deerskins at lower-than-Creek prices. The Gun confronted Lachlan McGillivray, who had orders from Glen to fetch the headmen to Charlestown that spring, with a demand that Creek prices be lowered.

"At this time," wrote McGillivray, "we were surrounded in the Gun's house by all the headmen, vizt. Gun, Red Coat King, Oakfuskees Captain, Hillabee Captain, Duvall's Landlord, Wolf [the Mortar], several other headmen, and their head warriors and their visages prognosticated wrath and violence."[21] McGillivray told the Gun that for lowering the prices he must go to Charlestown and see the governor. The idea did not appeal. The Okfuskee Captain heatedly replied, "We have lost a great many headmen already in paying visits to your governor. It is high time to desist from that practice and to take a resolution to lose no more of the few that is

[19] Jenkins, Book of Indian Affairs, Vol. V, 62–63.
[20] *Ibid.*, 60.
[21] *Ibid.*, 67.

left." The truth was that the Creeks had been told by the Cherokees that the way to get prices lowered was to be bold with the traders, threaten them, and man-handle them if necessary; that was the way the Cherokees said they had used their traders to get favorable prices. The Gun refused to go to Charlestown until prices were lowered. McGillivray, as he proceeded with his spring trade, from time to time urged the headmen to go to Charlestown, but they were adamant. To add good measure to their show of hostility, they growled about white settlers on the Ogeechee River having invaded Creek territory.

About May 1, 1755, the French, capitalizing on the Creek disgust with the English, held a meeting at Fort Toulouse. Attending were Malatchi, the Red Coat King, Gun Merchant, Duvall's Landlord, Hillabee Captain, the Mortar, the Okfuskee Captain, innumerable other headmen, and two or three hundred of their followers. Brandy and presents abounded as the French captain held out the promise of opening up a great French trade. When the Indians demanded that he undersell the English, the captain glibly agreed. The meeting ratified a peace between the Creeks and the Choctaws, and in private conversations the Frenchman urged Malatchi to expel the English from Ogeechee. Malatchi said that if they didn't get out, he'd soon raise the war whoop.[22]

Although the meeting had tactical value for the Gun's and the Mortar's position on trade prices, it raised a great debate in the Upper Towns. The Gun announced that unless the English traders lowered their prices they must leave. Other headmen felt that the Gun should go to Charlestown to see what Glen had to offer. One of them, Yoakley's son, a head warrior of the Okchais, argued that to lose the English trade would be to put the Creeks at the mercy of the French, who in the long run could not supply them. The English should not be irritated into withdrawing the trade. The Mortar said that perhaps he had been too hasty in rejecting the governor's invitation; and Duvall's Landlord, angered at the French-sponsored Creek-Choctaw peace which Malatchi, the Gun, and the Mortar had approved, said he would go down to Charlestown. But

22 *Ibid.*, 70–72.

again the spectre of the summer sickness on the coast was raised. Everybody hesitated. The Gun then asserted that if the people would support him, he would bring everything off for the good of the nation. The final decision was to stand by the Gun. Duvall's Landlord took his warriors off to the Alabama town near Fort Toulouse for a ball game in which they got themselves severely banged and bruised by the French-loving Alabama, literally lost their shirts and everything else as stakes in the game, and then went into Fort Toulouse to recoup their losses with brandy and presents at the price of an anti-English talk.[23] McGillivray, having failed to induce any headmen to go to Charlestown, regarded the situation as favorable to the French. He went down to Charlestown convinced that prices must be lowered and that Glen must make an offer if he wished to see any Creek headmen in Charlestown.

In Charlestown Glen worried about the Creeks. Besides McGillivray's reports of Creek intransigence and French progress, he had George Galphin's reports from Coweta of renewed Spanish overtures to Malatchi. In the winter of 1754–55, a mission from Fort St. Marks, near the gulf east of Pensacola, had arrived at Cussita, opposite Coweta, with a sizeable rum present and an offer to buy the Apalachee old fields between that nation and the fort which the Lower Creeks had conquered in 1703–04. Though Malatchi had rejected the offer, the Spanish captain had issued an invitation to all the headmen to come down to St. Marks for presents and talks. Several hundred Creeks planned to go, but Galphin with two hundred pounds worth of presents from his own store caused many to change their minds. Only about a hundred, and among them no headmen of consequence, went.[24] From these events Glen wove a pattern of serious threat to English influence in the Creek nation, and in September he presented his council with proposals for lowering Creek prices, along with giving the Creek trade as a monopoly to a few traders.

Glen was an imperialist of major pretentions, eager to make a good record as royal governor. Aware of the Virginia thrust toward

<hr />

23 *Ibid.*, 72–75.
24 *Ibid.*, 59–60.

the upper Ohio Valley and desirous himself of extending Carolina's and England's domain to the Mississippi, in May he had obtained from the Cherokees a cession of all their lands to the Mississippi and Ohio. He thought now to obtain a similar cession from the Creeks.[25] He knew also that Braddock's defeat (July 9, 1755) at the forks of the Ohio foreshadowed an English war with the French, and he desired an English fort among the Creeks as a basing point for attacks upon Fort Toulouse and Mobile. He conceived that he could accomplish these ends at the price of a trade concession to the Creeks and, in September, sent off a message to the Gun Merchant that if he would come down, the prices of goods would be lowered.

Back in the nation during July, the French held a meeting of Creek headmen at Fort Toulouse, the substance of which was kept quiet. At that time, Malatchi placed himself under the care of the surgeon at the fort.[26] M. de Monberault, now commander at the fort, heard Creek complaints against the Georgia settlers building a block house at the Ogeechee River,[27] and the English traders reported the Creeks as very insolent,[28] with the Gun Merchant asserting that not a Creek should set foot in Carolina territory until trade prices had been lowered.[29] Nevertheless, division persisted, for Handsome Fellow went on his own to Augusta where he met McGillivray and carried back Glen's message to the Gun.[30]

The time was ripe for negotiation with the English. Creek-Choctaw hostilities had broken out anew with the Choctaws again the aggressors. Creek retaliation had taken place almost under the guns of French Fort Tombigbe. Vaudreuil, out of the necessity of keeping the peace, summoned the Creeks to Mobile; five hundred came, mostly friends of the French, who declared they would go to war whenever the French asked them. A few, however, protested Choctaw aggression. Thereupon Vaudreuil asserted that the Choctaws were friends of the French and that he would stand by them.

25 S.C. Council Journal, No. 6, p. 2.
26 *Ibid.*, 356.
27 Paris Arch. Nat. Col., C13 A39, pp. 60–62.
28 S.C. Council Journal, No. 6, Pt. 2, p. 356.
29 *Ibid.*, 365–66.
30 *Ibid.*, 356.

One headman urged that as the Choctaw war with the Chickasaws was the cause of all the trouble—for the Choctaws killed Creeks they mistook for Chickasaws—that the Choctaws ought to make peace with the Chickasaws. Committed to extermination of the Chickasaws and fearful that a Choctaw-Chickasaw peace would once again bring English traders into the Choctaws, Vaudreuil would not hear of it. The Mobile meeting indicates that once again a schism existed among the Creeks on the subject of the Choctaws, with the Alabamas, as usual, taking the French point of view. But large numbers of Creeks were upset that the French would support the Choctaws against them.[31] Malatchi, recovering, also appeared not to be as much of a Frenchman as the English feared. Early in November he promised to meet John Reynolds, the new royal governor of Georgia, at Augusta in the spring, and he would not support the Gun's stand on prices. He wanted no interruption or alteration in the trade.

In October, the Gun Merchant, having also received an invitation from Reynolds, sent word to Glen to meet him on December 7 at Fort More, in Carolina below Augusta, to talk about the trade;[32] since he feared a renewal of the Choctaw war, he said he could come no further. He also expected to meet Governor Reynolds at Augusta and receive the governor's presents. Arriving at Augusta a week late, he missed Reynolds, who had been forced to return to Savannah and had left the presents at Augusta with his deputy, William Little.

Three days of meetings ensued at which the main business concerned the Bosomworth claims. Mary and Thomas, having been rebuffed in England in 1754–55, had returned to Georgia to harass the Georgia council which finally had advised them to take their troubles to the courts. With Reynolds' connivance they had gone up to Augusta to obtain Indian help in convincing the governor that their titles were genuine. In England they had learned of a 1732 decision by the chief justice that certain Massachusetts land titles based on Indian deeds had been declared valid, and they had

---

[31] *Ibid.*, 484–86.
[32] Jenkins, Book of Indian Affairs, V, 98.

raised money by selling to one Levi half their land claims for one thousand pounds. At Augusta, Little put to the Gun Merchant the question of the validity of the Bosomworth titles. The Gun and his people debated one whole night and concluded that since Mary was an Indian, she had as much right to the land as any other Indian, and that specifically Malatchi's grant to Mary of the islands of Sapelo, Ossabo, and St. Catherine's and of the lands from Pipemaker's Creek to Savannah took precedence over the Upper Towns grant of the same lands to Georgia in the Patrick Graham deed. They intimated, however, that Mary being old and Malatchi on his death bed, as he was at the time, Mary's title was good only for her lifetime. But they did admit that Mary had the right to dispose of the lands in any way she pleased.[33] The general theory of land titles which they advanced was that all the headmen had a right to the land, that Malatchi being the superior headman of the Lower Towns and Coweta being "the head and most ancient" in the nation, Malatchi's action concerning the lands took precedence over any other. The doctrine, though permeated with Bosomworth logic, appears to have arisen from the right of the headmen to apportion crop lands. What influence Bosomworth presents and Mary's pressure had in this exposition, the record does not state, save to say that she prevailed on the Indians in private to discuss the lands.[34] When Reynolds later was called upon to defend his generous treatment of the Bosomworths, he implied that the Indians had left the matter of the lands up in the air by saying that they had agreed to take up the subject of who had the power to grant lands in a future meeting of all the nation. In this statement, Reynolds cited but part of the record which contains unequivocal Indian statements that Mary's title was good, at least as long as Mary lived. There is no record of a grand assembly of the Creeks in this period to debate the subject. The Georgia effort to discredit the Bosomworth claims had failed again, and the Bosomworths were to be treated with more respect by Georgia royal governors than they had been by the old Board and the defunct trusteeship.

[33] Candler, *Ga. Col. Rec.*, XXXVII, 451–56.
[34] *Ibid.*, Pt. 1-A, pp. 186, 196.

171

After the Augusta meeting, the Gun Merchant, Duvall's Land-lord, the Wolf of the Muccolossus, and the other headmen pro-ceeded to Charlestown to talk with Glen. Arriving at the capital in January, 1756, they displayed a truculent mood, always a good bargaining stance. Moreover, the Little Carpenter, Second Man of the Cherokees, was in town, and it was good face with him. Glen proposed to them three measures: that Carolina be allowed to build a fort in the Upper Towns; that the Creeks abstain from injuring Georgia settlers on Ogeechee River; and that the Creeks support the Chickasaws, either by forcing the Choctaws to make peace with them or by joining them and the Cherokees in war on the Choctaws.[35] After two days of debate among themselves, the head-men rejected the fort but consented that Carolina be permitted to build a house in the Upper Towns for storage of presents but with-out a garrison of soldiers. Concerning Georgia, they held to their treaty rights, that there be no more settlements west of the Savan-nah River, and asserted that their warriors would drive trespassers away. They declared the Chickasaws to be of no concern to them. However, these were apparently only bargaining positions, for in a few days time the Gun Merchant and the others set their marks to a treaty permitting the fort and stating that they would go to the aid of the Chickasaws. Carolina agreed to new prices based on weights and measures to be sent to the headmen by Glen.

The headmen came away from Charlestown very much pleased with their presents and their new treaty. Glen wrote of the treaty, "Never was any treaty better understood or more approved of by any Indians . . . for by it their peace with the Cherokees is con-firmed and strengthened. The Chickasaw nation is saved and their bids for the French so entirely altered that we can depend on their declaring war either against them or the Choctaws."[36]

For the Gun Merchant it was a triumph. He had won his battle for lower trade prices. The price, however, was high, and it re-mained to be seen whether the nation would accept his treaty.

Early in 1756, Malatchi died. The micoship of Coweta passed

[35] McDowell, *S.C. B.P.R.O. Records*, XXVII, 56–57.
[36] *Ibid.*, 56.

to Ishenpoaphe (Sempyoffee), whose brother Stumpe was appointed guardian of Malatchi's sixteen year old son, Togulki, now being groomed as his father's successor. The relationship of Ishenpoaphe and Stumpe to Malatchi is not clear; possibly they were younger half brothers of Malatchi by another wife of Brims. Though Togulki was never to amount to much, the English and French would attach great importance to him. Stumpe, as his guardian, also enjoyed a prestigious position, particularly with the French, who gave him a commission.[37] At French behest, Stumpe warned a party of English against settling within the Lower Towns claim and then sent to Mobile for a reward for his services.[38] This settlement appears to have been that of Edmund Gray on Saltilla River outside the Georgia bounds. A party of fifty or sixty Creek gunmen warned him off, but Gray sent for Mary Bosomworth, then probably at the forks of Altamaha or on St. Catherine's island, and she mollified the Indians.[39] Thus it appears that even when Malatchi had passed, Mary's influence with the Creeks was still strong.

[37] *Ibid.*, 72.
[38] Paris Arch. Nat. Col., C13 A39, pp. 149–54.
[39] Jenkins, Book of Indian Affairs, V, 218.

10

Rejection of the Treaty:
Ogeechee Incident
1756

T HE TREATY OF JANUARY, 1756, though a triumph for the Gun Merchant's drive to lower trade prices, also represented a triumph for Glen's imperialistic designs, for it promised to extend Carolina's military frontier to the Tallapoosa River. Herein lay its weakness. It would bring a British military post into the heart of the Upper Creek country and threaten to force the Creeks to take sides in the impending French-English war. However welcome the trade concession in the Upper Towns—and it was received with rejoicing—a division of sentiment occurred on the fort building provision. The treaty was not ratified.

The major stimuli to dissent were two. One was Louisiana Governor Kerlerec, who with war again erupting between England and France hoped for alliances with Creeks and Cherokees. In April at Mobile, Kerlerec held a conference with many Creeks. Present were Stumpe and his ward, "Emperor" Togulki, both of whom agreed to oppose English designs.[1] Shortly after, opposition to the Creek-Cherokee alliance developed, for this alliance pointed the

[1] Paris Arch. Nat. Col., C13 A39, pp. 149–54, 170–72.

way to a break with the French. As a result, two Cherokees were killed in the woods. The other source of dissent was nativist distrust of more European influence in the nation. In February the Mortar had gone to the mountains to sound out the Cherokees.[2] Late in June he returned with stories of nativist Cherokee opposition to a new fort Governor Glen planned to build in the Overhill Cherokee country. Many Cherokees asserted that the new fort would enslave them, that the cattle of the whites would overrun the Indian cornfields, and that the soldiers would seduce the Cherokee women.[3] Other Creeks brought back reports of Cherokee dismay at the westward advance of the Carolina frontier into the Long Canes Creek area just below the Cherokee Lower Towns, and of Cherokee dissatisfaction over treatment they had received from the Virginia frontiersmen as a result of their co-operating in defending the Virginia frontier against the French and their Indians. These stories aggravated the strong Creek nativist opposition to the building of an English fort in the Upper Creeks and the expansion of the Georgia frontier.[4] The French could play upon this sentiment at will and support it by hearty entertainment and presents for the headmen who espoused it. Nativist sentiment and pro-French attitudes were frequently one and the same, for Fort Toulouse, never aggressively expansionist, furnished a rallying place for anti-English personages and was regarded hopefully as a source of ammunition if a break with the English became necessary. Thus the Mortar on his return from the Cherokees took Cherokee deputies to Fort Toulouse where they voiced dissatisfaction with Glen's projected fort in their country and talked of war with the English. A pro-French, pro-Cherokee, nativist alignment was thus developing.

With his advocacy of the unpopular English fort, the Gun Merchant suffered a serious setback. In July, when William Henry Lyttelton replaced Glen as Governor of South Carolina, he sent up an invitation to the Gun to come down to see him. The Gun,

[2] S.C. Council Journal, No. XXV, 346.

[3] Jenkins, Book of Indian Affairs, Vol. V, 132–33.

[4] James Germany to Lyttelton, June 19, 1756, Sir William Lyttelton Papers, 1756–60 [hereinafter referred to as Lytt. Pap.].

still hoping to obtain ratification of his treaty over his brother-in-law's and nativist opposition, replied that he could not come until he had fulfilled his treaty obligations, which he said he was very hopeful of doing. Significantly, the opposition was so strong that he sent his messengers, Handsome Fellow and the Okfuskee Captain, by a roundabout route through the Cherokee nation, where they ostensibly countered anti-English talk.[5] Lyttelton had hardly read this message when he received another directly from the Upper Creek Towns composed by the nativist Mortar and his supporters. It repudiated the Gun Merchant's treaty and leadership. Referring to the Gun Merchant as one whom the English called "the great king of the Oachoys" but who actually did not rule the Upper Towns, it stated that not a single headman in the nation would support his treaty. The message accused the Gun of having made the treaty solely for the presents Glen had given him, objected to the fort, protested the traders' horses cropping Indian cornfields, complained of English settlers invading the Creek country on Ogeechee River, repudiated alliance with the Chickasaws against the Choctaws, asked that the trade be kept on the old basis, and concluded with an assertion of friendship for the English.[6] About the same time Lyttelton received messages from the Lower Creeks expressing a desire for friendship but for trade on the old basis.

Though the Gun's treaty had been sabotaged, the prevailing critical and monitory temper was not one of fundamental hostility to the English. Actually the nativist Creek-Cherokee coalition had not yet crystallized beyond opposition to English forts. No one, not even the Mortar, was as yet willing to forego the English trade. However, now that France and England were in formal war, Lyttelton, ignorant of Indian politics, concluded that the French point of view had made such headway that Carolina should send up an agent, Captain Dan Pepper, former commander of Fort More, to reside among the Creeks for an extended period. Pepper was instructed to push the English point of view and to get the Gun

[5] McDowell, *S.C. B.P.R.O. Records*, XXVII, 1555; Jenkins, Book of Indian Affairs, Vol. V, 177.

[6] Jenkins, Book of Indian Affairs, Vol. V, 176.

Merchant to come to Charlestown. The move was unnecessary save for occult English military ends. Had there been any real Creek disposition to break with the English, the Ogeechee incident of September 3, 1756, would have sparked it. Tuckabatchee warriors hovered about the settlement and stole horses. Settler pursuit of the horse thieves resulted in a gun fight in which three Creeks and no English died. Report of the clash caused settlers to run to the shelter of Forts Augusta and More.[7] Yet the affair brought no onslaught of Creek warriors. Instead it was peacefully handled through diplomatic channels before Pepper arrived in the Creek towns.

Georgia, the weakest and least belligerent of the English colonies, did not want war, nor did the Creeks. On news of the frontier incident, Governor Reynolds, acting on provisions of the Creek treaties which required the whites to punish settlers who injured Indians, issued warrants for the arrest of the Ogeechee men involved.[8] Though this action treated the settlers as at fault, Reynolds dispatched a message to Togulki at Coweta which diplomatically omitted mention of Indian casualties and treated the affair as an Indian depredation for which he expected redress. He also indicated that he and Governor Lyttelton would remove the Ogeechee settlers. Yet with rumors that French and Spaniards planned an attack on Georgia out of St. Augustine and that the Upper and Lower Towns would begin raids, he hysterically wrote the Board of Trade that an Indian war threatened, and he raised a troop of seventy rangers to patrol the frontier.[9]

No attack threatened. At the time, French Governor Kerlerec was writing despondent letters home concerning Creek complaints of French deficiencies in goods for trade and presents.[10] Coweta had had news of the Ogeechee affair independently of Reynolds. There, as the headmen sat in the square quietly discussing Lyttelton's pre-Ogeechee invitation to come to Charlestown and traders played at "nine holes" nearby, an Indian horseman frantically

[7] *Ibid.*, 207.
[8] Dan Pepper to Lyttelton, Sept. 22, 1756, Lytt. Pap.
[9] McDowell, *S.C. B.P.R.O. Records*, XXVII, 216–17.
[10] Paris Arch. Nat. Col., C13 A39, pp. 190–91.

rode up to the square to report the fight and the death of Indians. There was no beating of war drums and rushing to arms. Although alarmed, the headmen called the traders in for their advice and then sent for the battered horse thieves to come to town and tell the truth. This the culprits did, and the headmen concluded that the Indians had been the aggressors. Dispatching a runner to the Upper Towns, they sat several days discussing the problem. Finally on September 17, before any Carolina or Georgia messages reached them, they composed a conciliatory message to Reynolds. They blamed the affair on the Upper Creeks and suggested that, since they understood (erroneously) that whites had been killed, the matter be forgotten. They requested that whites withdraw from Ogeechee, "for their living so far up spoils our hunting ground and frightens away the deer." They said that because the hunting season was so nigh they could not come down. However, they hinted that the stresses they labored under had bred a thirst which might redound in favor of the French and Spaniards unless rum were sent, "as we are all much troubled by the accident" and "we have been used to have rum from children and it causes our people to go to the French and Spaniards to get some rum which they would not do if we had some from our friends the English.[11]

In the more immediately involved Upper Towns, the reaction was sharper but no more violent in result. Fortunately, when the panicked settlers poured into Augusta with woeful cries, Handsome Fellow and the Okfuskee Captain, homeward bound from Charlestown, were at the fort. The Augusta traders, Douglas, Rae, and Campbell, anxious that the trade be not interrupted, composed a tactful message to the Upper Towns headmen and sent it off by the trader Thomas Ross under the protection of the two Indians. Already the bad news had come by the Coweta runner into the Upper Towns. Startled and angered by the death of kinsmen, some demanded satisfaction and talked wildly of killing traders. A nativist and pro-French deputation of Lower Towns headmen on their way to the Cherokee towns to discuss ways of preventing the English from building forts in the Indian country,

---

[11] Jenkins, Book of Indian Affairs, Vol. V, 215, 217–18.

talked of a Creek-Cherokee war against the English. Pro-English Creeks proclaimed that if any traders were killed, they would attack the French at Fort Toulouse. But when the headmen met on the affair, they concluded it to have been an accident and that no more be expected than that Governor Reynolds give satisfaction for the slain.[12]

However, rough talk did not die down. The French chimed in with anti-English propaganda and, referring to the many French-fathered half-bloods in the Upper Towns, dwelt on the oneness of Creek and French blood. In certain segments of the Upper Towns, the threat of war looked more serious when a small anti-English delegation of Cherokees from Great Tellico came into the nation. They had stopped at the Shawnee town on the Upper Coosa and had joined the Shawnees in war talk. Then the Mortar had summoned them to Okchai and led them to Fort Toulouse where Montberault made a strong and unsuccessful effort to precipitate the war of which they had so glibly talked. The Cherokees were merely exploring potentialities.[13] Hearing the ominous note, the pro-English Wolf of the Muccolossus, despite the fact that one of the Indians slain at Ogeechee was his kinsman, threatened to lead his Creeks against the French. When a council of headmen at Tucka-batchee debated the question of war or peace, the gray and bent patriarch, Old Brisket, reputedly one hundred and twenty years old, and a defender of the English, stuck his hair full of turkey buzzard feathers, limped into the square, and delivered such a strong talk against war that the anti-English quailed and war talk ceased.[14] The original proposal to settle the affair by diplomacy prevailed, but not before the Wolf of the Muccolossus had taken affairs into his own hands and set out for Augusta to seek a peaceful solution. He was soon followed by Handsome Fellow of the Okfus-kees, who headed toward Savannah to present to Reynolds the headmen's proposals.

At Augusta, the Wolf informed Lieutenant White Outerbridge

[12] *Ibid.*, VI, 228–29.
[13] *Ibid.*, V, 229.
[14] *Ibid.*, 285.

that his nation desired peace; then, learning that Captain Dan Pepper of Carolina had already left Augusta for Coweta with Lyttelton's peace message, he returned to the Upper Towns.[15] Handsome Fellow arrived in Savannah in November and boldly confronted Reynolds with a demand for blood satisfaction for the slain Tallapooses. Reynolds calmed him with an account of how he had had the white offenders arrested, and how two of them had died as a result of the affair. Actually no whites had died in the Ogeechee action—one was missing, one had died in jail, and the others had been freed to Governor Lyttelton's jurisdiction—but Reynolds gave the Indians the impression that whites had fallen in the skirmish. Handsome Fellow agreed to call the blood score even and asked that presents, particularly rum, be sent the relatives of the slain Tuckabatchees. Reynolds complied and warmed Handsome Fellow with a personal present of a fine suit of clothes and a captain's commission.[16]

Back on the Tallapoosa, Dan Pepper, supported by the Wolf of the Muccolossus, pushed the English line. Pepper had received a warm welcome at Coweta, and when on November 3 he arrived at Tuckabatchee, Old Brisket greeted him with ceremony. On November 5 the Gun Merchant came out from Okchai with English colors flying, drums beating, and the firing of salutes to meet him. On the twelfth, after hearing Pepper's talk to the headmen assembled in the square, the Gun expressed pleasure that Lyttelton's message was so friendly. The Wolf of the Muccolossus rose and declaimed that at Ogeechee the whites had acted in self defense, that the Tallapooses had no official authorization to be there, and their deaths were their own fault. He challenged all to speak now or forever hold their peace, for the affair must be forgotten. The Gun seconded him, and no one else spoke. At Okchai, Pepper received Choctaw deputies who complained of French trade deficiencies and asked for an English trade. He discovered, however, that the Creeks had no disposition to break with the French, that indeed they seemed to hold the English with one hand and the

[15] *Ibid.*, VI, 228–29.
[16] Reynolds to Lyttelton, Nov. 26, 1756, Lytt. Pap.

French with the other. According to his instructions, he pressed the Gun to ratify the January treaty with Glen and to make another visit to Charlestown. The Gun was evasive, saying the matter couldn't be discussed till spring when everyone came in from the winter hunts and that not till then could he go to Charlestown. Hearts still burned in opposition to an English fort, but the Gun asserted that the Indians did expect the trade concession to hold.[17] Pepper later learned that the Gun had wife trouble on the subject of the treaty because his wife was the Mortar's sister and shared her brother's opposition. Evidently much prestigial power at Okchai lay on the distaff side and in the Mortar's Bear clan.

As for the Chickasaws, the Gun and the Wolf of the Muccolossus hoped in accordance with the treaty to negotiate a peace for them with the Choctaws, now restive with the French.[18] The Gun even expressed concern that the French were now building a fort at the mouth of the Tennessee River. To him, since he was being indoctrinated on the subject of white encroachments, this indicated a further European invasion of the Indian country, and he intimated to the Chickasaws that Creeks and Chickasaws might join to destroy it. This point of view was countered by sentiment building up under the influence of Peter Chartier, French half-blood headman of the Upper Coosa Shawnees, which, with some justice, regarded French forts as protective of Indian independence and English forts as projections of English expansionism. He strongly urged the Cherokees to resist the English building of Fort Loudoun in the Overhill Cherokee country and to the Creeks he preached driving the English traders from their towns. His positions were too extreme for the majority of Creek headmen, who opposed his bringing any more Shawnees from the French-dominated Ohio valley into their country.

From the peaceful resolution of the Ogeechee incident, it is clear that in 1756 the mass of the Creeks had no serious disposition to go to war with the English. True, the episode strengthened the French faction, increased the influence of the anti-English Shaw-

---

[17] Jenkins, Book of Indian Affairs, Vol. V, 284–85.
[18] *Ibid.*, 336–37.

nees and Cherokees, and spurred the Mortar's nativism. But all these were ineffective minorities. The testimony of Governors Lyttelton and Reynolds and of the South Carolina commissioners of Indian affairs grew somewhat out of wartime hysteria. It is suspect as largely designed for export to influence the Crown to send troops to the south where their support by gold currency would contribute to the prosperity of the southern economy. As Pepper discovered, neutralism dominated the Creeks. Partisanship existed, but strong patriarchal voices, which in the long run dominated the squares, held to traditionalism and advocated the retention of both Fort Toulouse and the English trade in order to obtain for the nation the benefits of both. The result, despite a loosely local self-determination, was one of the most effective feats of Indian statecraft on the American continent.

11

The Mortar's Conspiracy
1757

THROUGHOUT 1757, though in the northern colonies the English suffered severe reverses at the hands of the French and their Indians, English prestige among the Creeks remained high. It is true that the nativist Mortar prostituted to the French his opposition to English transmontane forts and caused the southern royal governors great doubts and fears for continued Creek neutrality, which they hysterically reported to the home government, but the noise and fury were out of proportion to the event. The main forces operating in the Creek mind led the headmen to frown on the Mortar's opposition and hold fast to the English trade.

In the late winter of 1756–57 and in the early spring of 1757, the situation for the headmen in the Creek nation was complex. The Mortar of the Okchais advocated and promoted an all-Indian alliance of Shawnees, Cherokees, Creeks, Chickasaws and Catawbas to eliminate the English forts in the Indian country, particularly Fort Loudoun among the Overhill Cherokees. To this end he had his private emissaries working in the various tribes.[1] He

1 Outerbridge to Lyttelton, Mar. 24, 1757, Lytt. Pap.

drew heavily for support upon the French, who at this time entertained a Cherokee exploratory mission at New Orleans. The French
contemplated a great conspiracy including the Choctaws which
would throw the English from the Creek country. In the light of
French resources, severely cramped by the English command of the
sea, this was almost totally visionary. The French lacked sufficient
goods to keep even the Choctaws happy, to say nothing of supplying the Creeks and the Cherokees. Moreover, early in January,
Choctaws, still pursuing their French-inspired vendetta against the
Chickasaws, threatened to bring down on themselves a Shawnee-
Creek coalition, when, again mistaking Creek-residing Shawnees
for Chickasaws, they killed two Shawnees, and the Shawnees
called on the Creeks to help them retaliate.[2] This episode summoned the French to soothe the Shawnees, vexed the Gun Merchant's English-inspired Choctaw diplomacy by raising up the
anti-Choctaw party of the Creeks, and disturbed the Mortar's
designs.

The Gun Merchant's behavior appeared somewhat vacillating.
Persuaded by Pepper to open negotiations with the Choctaws for
a Chickasaw peace pointing toward an eventual Creek-Choctaw-
Chickasaw alliance under English auspices, he nevertheless was
under pressure from his wife to countenance the nativist program
of his brother-in-law, the Mortar. He seems to have been feeling
his way but with an awareness of the validity of the nativist position. He could not halt the Mortar anyway, and at Charlestown he
had committed himself by treaty to bring about a Chickasaw-
Choctaw peace. If he succeeded, the Mortar's designs would wither.
Under any circumstances, the Mortar, however just his cause, was
under the necessity of proving, which seemed unlikely, that the
French could throw enough goods into the nation to convince the
headmen an anti-English position could be supported.

Pepper's position was also anomalous. While a Creek-Choctaw-
Chickasaw alignment in English favor was desirable, as long as
the Choctaws adhered to the French, a Creek-Choctaw war should
be fomented as the best way to keep the Creeks from the French

2 Jenkins, Book of Indian Affairs, Vol. VI, 12, 36.

orbit. In private discussions with the Wolf of the Muccolossus, Pepper held out the promise of English rewards for Choctaw scalps. The Wolf seized on the murder of two Shawnees as an excuse to raise war parties against the Choctaws.[3] But the French at Fort Toulouse deftly aroused their friends the Alabamas to head these off and hold a peace meeting of Creeks and Choctaws. The scheme backfired on the French, for the way was cleared for Choctaw deputies, responding to the Gun's overture, to come to the Creeks in May and to make it clear that the French were unable to supply them, that they desired an English trade, and that they would halt the Chickasaw war.[4]

Meeting the Choctaws in secret, the Gun Merchant spoke cogently of the Europeans' quarrel over lands which belonged to the Indians. For the purpose of his negotiation, he gave his talk an anti-French slant by warning the Choctaws not to allow French expansion in their country and promising that the Creeks would join the Choctaws to resist French expansion if it were attempted.[5] It thus appears that the Gun sought Indian interests above all else and was giving all circumstances and occasions a hard look and try. All ends stemmed from the middle: Creek concepts of Indian welfare.

Under these circumstances, official Creek deputies, plying the Mortar's line, could accompany the Cherokee deputies returning from New Orleans to Chota, the Cherokee capital. There publicly, for the benefit of the English officers at nearby Fort Loudoun, they could assert their mission as Creek-Cherokee friendship, while privately with Old Hop, the Cherokee Uku, they could assess the chances of driving the English out. The real block to concerted nativist action at this time was that the Cherokees had discovered at New Orleans what the Choctaws had proclaimed in the Okchai square—that the French were unable to supply the trade.[6]

The Mortar, now leader of a discredited small faction, yet having the license of a great headman, pursued his independent

[3] *Ibid.*, 29–30.
[4] *Ibid.*, 45–47.
[5] *Ibid.*
[6] *Ibid.*, 56; Paris Arch. Nat. Col., C13 A39, pp. 264–65.

course. Near the end of May he insisted that the Okchais receive nativist Cherokee deputies on their way to Fort Toulouse. The deputies then went to the fort, where, received with presents, they enjoyed an extended debauch on French brandy. On June 1 at Okchai the Mortar denounced the trade concessions of the Charlestown treaty of January, 1756, reminded of the Ogeechee trespass, and behaved rudely toward Pepper. But his belligerent anti-English utterances drew no significant support. Everyone seemed satisfied with Lyttelton and Reynold's handling of the Ogeechee matter.[7] The Choctaw willingness to defect from the French echoed loudly around the towns, and the vast majority of Creeks, Upper and Lower, smiled on the English. The Creek anti-English talks heard in July by Captain Raymond Demere at Fort Loudoun in the Cherokee country emanated from the Mortar's cabal, and, while they contained hints of French and Spanish overtures and the truth of Creek opposition to any English fort in the Mississippi valley, they were largely the muted voice of nativist gossip rather than the will of the Creek headmen in council.[8] Indeed the weight of Creek sentiment was so hostile to the continuing agitation of Peter Chartier's Shawnees for war against the English that the Shawnees talked of moving north to join their countrymen on the Ohio, who had made an outright commitment to the French.

With the Creek disposition so strongly for peace with the English, Pepper, accompanied by a few Indians, among them Handsome Fellow, left the Upper Towns in June and went down to Charlestown by way of Coweta. At Coweta, Togulki, the adolescent "emperor," joined him, and he picked up a Creek warrior who was demanding blood satisfaction for his brother killed at Ogeechee. At Charlestown, Lyttelton lavishly entertained the Creeks and gave the offended man a handsome present as compensation for his brother's death.[9] Creek-English relations were never better. In the light of these events the seaboard and frontier alarm over the Mortar's conspiracy seems to have arisen from hysterical exaggeration

---

[7] Jenkins, Book of Indian Affairs, Vol. VI, 58–59.

[8] *Ibid.*, V, 159.

[9] S.C. Gazette, July 21, 1757.

promoted to the end of obtaining a substantial British garrison and the consequent disbursement of large sums of needed British gold in the south.

That summer whatever headway the Spaniards had made in the Lower Towns received a rude check. Soldiers at the Spanish fort of St. Mark's committed some "indecencies" against women of the far Lower Creeks.[10] In early August a Creek war party under the Long Warrior (probably Weoffki, the Long Warrior of Latchoway) going against the Florida Indians, hearing of these, turned aside to attack a remote Spanish plantation. In the assault a Creek headman was killed, and the enraged Indians raided other plantations, slaughtering cattle and taking four Spaniards prisoner. They carried their prisoners to Alexander Gray's settlement of New Hanover on the Saltilla River. Spanish Governor de Heiride, indignant that in time of peace between Spain and England attacks should have been made from English territory, protested to Governor Ellis of Georgia. Sending apologies, Ellis strove to effect the release of the prisoners, which he accomplished through the Cowkeeper, headman of Latchoway, at a ransom of one hundred pounds apiece. He also cautioned the Creeks against making war on the Spaniards. Nevertheless, well aware of the advantage the attacks gave the English, he secretly operated to keep the Creeks suspicious of the Spaniards.[11]

In August, further to cement English-Creek relations, the Wolf of the Muccolossus sent a delegation to Charlestown with friendly talks, and Handsome Fellow again visited Savannah. The Wolf was now hailed by the English as "King" of the Upper Creeks in place of the Gun Merchant.[12]

In the spring and summer the English position in the Upper Creeks was so strong that to interpret, as some have done, Governor Henry Ellis' conference with the Creeks at Savannah in the fall of 1757 as marking the favorable turning point in Creek-English relations is uncritically to accept Ellis' evaluation of him-

[10] Ellis to Lyttelton, Jan. 21, 1758, Lytt. Pap.
[11] Candler, *Ga. Col. Rec.*, Pt. 1-A, pp. 95–100; McDowell, *S.C. B.P.R.O. Records*, XXVII, 295; Ellis to Lyttelton, July 21, Sept. 24, 1757, Lytt. Pap.
[12] Candler, *Ga. Col. Rec.*, XXVIII, Pt. 1-A, pp. 51–54.

self. That event, the most gaudy Indian reception ever produced in Georgia, arose partly to demonstrate English strength, but primarily, it seems, to lay at rest the Bosomworth claims.[13]

In July, Ellis had sent Joseph Wright to the Lower and Upper Creek Towns to invite the Indians down to Savannah, ostensibly to meet himself, as the new governor of Georgia, and to receive presents.[14] Georgia traders in the nation, jealous of Pepper's South Carolina successes, ably seconded Wright's endeavors with the result that 150 Creeks, representing 21 towns, came to Savannah at the end of October. Among them were the Wolf of the Muccolossus and Togulki of Coweta with his guardian, Stumpe. Colonel Henri Bouquet, commander of the regular garrison now established at Charlestown, had come down to impress the Creeks with British power and to dispel any illusions the Mortar's conspiracy had evoked.

On October 29 the Creeks were met in Ellis' name in an open field a mile west of Savannah by Captain Milledge with his troop of seventy rangers and by Captain Bryon with some of the leading citizens. Escorted to a huge tent erected for the purpose, they all sat down to an elaborate feast. After dinner, with the mounted citizens at their head and the rangers bringing up the rear, the Indians marched to the edge of town where they were saluted by cannon fire from the bastions. At the town gate, Captain Bryon and his horsemen filed to right and left, forming two lines through which the Indians advanced into the town. There, at the head of the foot militia, Captain Jones received them and conducted them toward the council chamber. As they passed the governor's house, seven cannons from a battery fired salutes. Cannons at the waterside and on ships in the river took up the tribute. Just short of the council house the foot militia divided to right and left and the Indians marched between the ranks to be received by a company of Virginia Blues drawn up in ranks which fired a volley in the air. The Blues then formed two lines to the Council house through which the Indians passed to be conducted to the governor.

[13] *Ibid.*, 96–101, 118, 123.
[14] *Ibid.*, VII, 643–44; Ellis to Wright, Aug. 7, 1757, Lytt. Pap.

Governor Ellis, a man of considerable histrionic talents, advanced toward the Indians with out-stretched hand declaiming, "My friends and brothers, behold my hands and arms! Our common enemies the French have told you they are red to the elbows. View them! so they speak truth let your own eyes witness! You see they are white, and could you see my heart, you would find it as pure, but very warm and true to you, my friends. The French tell you that whoever shakes my hand will immediately be struck with disease and die. If you believe this lying, foolish talk, don't touch me. If you do not, I am ready to embrace you!"

On translation of this message, the Indians, who had not come all this way to miss any of the pageantry or presents, responded through their spokesman, that the French had lied, and pressed forward to grasp Ellis' hand. The Governor then commiserated with the Indians for their lack of provisions on their way down and asserted that it was proof that no English occupied their lands; for if any had, there would have been provisions, since the English only wanted outsettlements to supply their Indian friends on their way down from the forests. He told them to rest a day or two before business began and have their guns and saddles repaired at colony expense. The Wolf of the Muccolossus and Togulki each replied with courteous remarks of general satisfaction. Ellis then invited the headmen to dine with him that evening, and the formal meeting adjourned for the day.

In private conversations between the governor and the headmen, the Bosomworth claims came under discussion, for Thomas Bosomworth's pretentions at that time still occupied the Georgia assembly. A strong Bosomworth party was building up, composed of Bosomworth creditors and those who believed in Bosomworth influence with the Creeks. Ellis, under instructions from the Board of Trade to assert Crown prerogatives over land grants and well aware of Mary's influence at Coweta, was eager for a settlement which would end the controversy without giving offense to the Indians. He therefore apparently had crucial discussions with Togulki and his guardian, Stumpe, which were to bear fruit in a few days when the treaty produced by the meetings was concluded.

When, on November 3, the Indians and colonials met in final conference, Ellis delivered another grandiose speech which he palmed off on the Indians as the words of the great King George over the water. Incidentally, it blamed the French-English war on the French, who in time of peace ordered "the murdering and scalping of some of my children and friends, the red men of the north." Stumpe, as spokesman for Togulki, replied to Ellis' fabrication with a speech which not only approved the "king's" sentiments but went to the heart of the Bosomworth matter:

"We have heard the great king's words with great satisfaction. We have heard yours, also, they are strong and good. There is nothing we desire more than to employ this opportunity towards confirming and renewing our antient friendship with our brothers the English, and as you have desired us to acquaint you with all our grievances we will open our hearts—— Our fathers were poor, but you have made us rich. This we often tell our young people. We desire them to hold you fast by the hand as the surest means to continue secure in their present happiness. When the great squire [Oglethorpe] came first here we made a treaty of friendship with him and his people to whom we gave sundry lands on the seaside that they might live upon them, reserving to ourselves three islands called Sapelo, St. Catherine's and Ossabow. These we left in the hands of an old woman [meaning Mrs. Bosomworth] to keep for us, which she pretending to have bought and that they belonged to her occasioned great animosities and disturbances between us and the white people. We now declare that we did not sell them to her and we desire that your honor will take them under your care in trust, to put an end to all future disputes concerning them."[15]

Having thus handed over Mary's holdings, Stumpe went on to dispose of the Gun Merchant's 1756 treaty by asking that no changes be made in the trade. He showed complacency about English settlers above the tide marks and requested that Ellis send a smith up to the towns to repair the Indians' guns. Finally he demanded the punishment of a white man who had behaved rudely toward him on the way down. Ellis replied that the projected

[15] Candler, *Ga. Col. Rec.*, VII, 657–61; Ellis to Lyttelton, Nov. 3, 1757, Lytt. Pap.

changes in the trade were Carolina's problem and Georgia would abide by Carolina decision. He could not send the smith, he said, for the colony lacked the money. He excused the white man's bad behavior on grounds of drunkenness. He then read and explained in detail the treaty drawn up as the result of the discussions. It provided that all former treaties be ratified and confirmed; that all former grievances be forgot; that in the future irregular acts of individuals should not be regarded as acts of the nations or causes of war, but should be treated on an individual basis by the authorities of both peoples; that no sale or grant of land had ever been made to the Bosomworths, but that the lands in question should be granted in trust to the governor of Georgia, as representative of the great king; and, finally, that the enemies of either party to the treaty be regarded as the enemies of the other.[16]

It was a glib treaty, probably entered into under the force of the abundance of presents and the generosity of the entertainment. With it Stumpe fades from the scene, whether from death or from repudiation the record does not state. Certainly the Creek nation did not carry out the provisions which would have required them to go to war with the French. Indeed Togulki would soon be visiting the French. Moreover, the Bosomworths were not to be so lightly divested of their claims. Mary, on learning of the treaty, informed Togulki that his father, Malatchi, had two hundred head of cattle on St. Catherine's island that Togulki would lose if the treaty went into effect.[17] Ellis had reason to believe that Mary kept up a constant agitation at Coweta, which raised doubts in many Indians' minds of Georgia's sincerity in dealings with the Creeks and led Indians into harassing frontier settlers' crops and cattle. Togulki repudiated the land clauses of the treaty; he also failed to set his mark to the treaty of April 22, 1758, made at the Muccolossus and the one made at Apalachicola in the Lower Towns on May 1, 1758, by which all the disputed lands in Georgia were assigned to the Crown. Moreover, Ellis realized that if England and Spain went to war, as they seemed likely to do before the French conflict ended,

---

16 Candler, *Ga. Col. Rec.*, VII, 665–70.
17 *Ibid.*, XXVII, Pt. 1-A, pp. 118–20.

he would need Mary's influence to undercut Spanish efforts to win the Lower Creeks. Mary's hold on Coweta, despite his treaties, was too strong to permit him to ride roughshod over the Bosomworths. He therefore proposed a compromise agreement with them by which they were to receive St. Catherine's island, and the islands of Ossabo and Sapelo were to be sold at public auction from the proceeds of which the Bosomworths were to receive two thousand pounds. The Bosomworths were to be released from any claims under their grants to Levi.[18]

[18] *Ibid.*, XXVIII, Pt. 1-A, pp. 209–11, 215.

12

Edmund Atkin's Mission
1758-60

I N THE YEAR 1758 the English hold on the Creek nation was firm; nevertheless, the Mortar, now operating as an ally of the French, sought secretly to fan the developing Cherokee animosity toward the English into a war which would eliminate Fort Loudoun once and for all. His conspiracy, though always that of a small minority, reached out to embrace the discontented at Coweta and other towns and by the spring of 1759 had become a formidable factor in neighboring Cherokee affairs. It embraced Togulki and his uncle Ishenpoaphe, king of Coweta, and even tarnished in English eyes the Gun Merchant who was now at odds with the Wolf of the Muccolossus whom the English hailed as "King" of the Upper Creeks in the Gun's place.

The abundance of presents which Ellis had given out in November of 1757 proved a stimulus to Creeks who had not come down to the treaty conference to descend on Savannah in begging swarms. Throughout the late winter and early spring of 1758 they came in parties of from twenty to seventy, their headmen bluntly stating that they had no official mission but came because they were poor and wanted goods as gifts. They all glibly affirmed their approval of the November treaty, and Ellis, under diplomatic necessity in wartime, was lavish.[1]

With such a bonanza it is not surprising that, in the light of French shortages, Creek good will toward the English ran high in the spring of 1758. But in the matter of goods, Creeks had catholic tastes. When the Spaniards at Pensacola obtained a large supply of contraband English goods from speculating New England sea captains and undercut the prices of Georgia and Carolina traders, Spanish prestige rose.[2] The French, who shared in the illicit Spanish abundance, also gained attention. This was neutrality as the Creeks loved to play it, with gifts and goods from all sides, though, with true nativist instinct, they were careful not to succumb to Spanish overtures for lands north of Pensacola and to French requests to be allowed to re-enforce Fort Toulouse.[3]

In the early spring the Mortar's hopes received a severe check. Cherokee deputies from Chota, which had been swamped with English largess, came to the Upper Creeks. They asserted official friendship for the English, approved of English forts in their nation, and stated a determination to fight as allies of the English if the Creeks ever broke out war against them.[4] Nevertheless, the conspiracy was to gain a recruit in mid-summer, when the discontented Togulki of Coweta went to Mobile and promised to join a French attempt to take Fort Loudoun.[5]

Matters of primary concern in the Lower Creeks in this period were the trade and the encroachment of settlers in the Ogeechee region. Increasing numbers of frontier settlers engaged in the trade at their homes, undercutting the licensed traders in the nation.[6] Most notable of these was John Smith, established on the Savannah River halfway between Savannah and Augusta. Smith's practice of purchasing skins in bulk packs instead of by the single hide as the regular traders did won him many Creek friends who came

[1] Candler, *Ga. Col. Rec.*, VII, 703, 733, 734, 765.
[2] Alexander to Ellis, Aug. 5, 1758, in Ellis to Lyttelton, Lytt. Pap.
[3] Lachlan McGillivray to Lyttelton, July 14, 1758, Lytt. Pap.
[4] David Douglas to John McQueen, Apr. 26, 1758, Lytt. Pap.
[5] Lachlan McGillivray to Lyttelton, Mar. 12, 1759, Lytt. Pap.
[6] Ellis to Lyttelton, Mar. 17, 1758, Lytt. Pap.

miles to trade with him, for in effect he lowered the price of trade goods. The licensed traders in the Creek towns made their profits by buying single hides by pound weight, disregarding the extra quarter and half pounds. By this method a pack of twenty skins could be bought by the trader for from half to three-quarters of its actual value in goods. Smith, by bulk weight per pack, gave more to the Indians. He was enabled to do this because he did not have the expense of the 250-mile carry to the Creek country. The Indians, who did not value time and trouble, were disturbed by the discrepancies between Smith's prices and those charged in the nation. In 1756, Glen had sought to cut prices by presenting the headmen in each town with a set of steelyards by which they could check traders' weights. But this had been tied to his fort proposal and consequently was rejected, though the matter of steelyards had bobbed in and out of Indian affairs ever since. The problem of the frontier trader was to remain a vexing one for years to come. The frontier trader took skins which Creeks owed their in-nation traders who had staked them to their hunts, with the result that quarrels between creditor traders and Indian debtors were frequent in the towns and were always potential sources of anti-English feeling. In 1758 Georgia attempted to remedy this situation by a law subjecting the frontier traders to the same controls as those in the nation. But Carolina would not co-operate and the law was ineffective.[7]

Settlers' invasion of Creek lands in the Upper Ogeechee area provided irritation but never a threat of open hostilities.[8] It lent substance to French statements that the English intended to take the Creek lands,[9] and became the subject of discussion between English and Creeks at Savannah. But when in the spring of 1758, warriors of the Yuchi town of the Lower Creeks took scalps of an English family which had settled across the line near Oconee River, the Lower Creeks repudiated the act and promised execution of the guilty Yuchis.[10] When Shawnee Indians came into the towns

[7] *Ibid.*
[8] Candler, *Ga. Col. Rec.*, VII, 763.
[9] Lachlan McGillivray to Lyttelton, July 24, 1758, Lytt. Pap.
[10] Joseph Wright's Journal, in Ellis to Lyttelton, Sept. 8, 1758, Lytt. Pap.

with English scalps taken in the north, they were widely repudiated, though at Coweta the rejection was not as strong as in the Upper Towns, and the southernmost of the Lower Creek Towns, Apalachicola, near the Spaniards, seemed to welcome them.[11]

Despite the officially maintained neutrality of the Creek headmen,[12] there was a slight tendency of Creek warriors to join Cherokee and Catawba war parties against the French in the Ohio valley. Forty Creeks were said to have been among the Catawbas who joined General John Forbes's 1758 Pennsylvania expedition against French Fort Duquesne (Pittsburgh).[13] In the Upper Towns the pro-English Wolf of the Muccolossus actually prepared a Creek expedition to go against French Fort de l'Assomption at the mouth of the Tennessee River.[14] However, both movements received checks. In April and May when horse-stealing, English-allied Cherokees in Virginia had armed encounters with Virginia frontiersmen, south-to-north Indian movements east of the mountains ceased. Machinations from Fort Toulouse frustrated the Wolf's designs on Fort de l'Assomption.[15]

When in the late summer the Cherokees, meditating war against the Virginia frontier, sounded out the Creek towns to see what vitality there was in the Mortar's following, the official answer was not reassuring. It blamed the Cherokees for the Virginia troubles and flatly refused to join the Cherokees against the English.[16] Indeed so delicate did Creek-Cherokee relations become that fear of war with the Creeks seems to have been an important factor in preventing the Cherokees from taking vengeance upon the Virginians in the fall of 1758.[17] This turn of events came about quite fortuitously. Two Okfuskee warriors visiting Little Estatoe in the Lower Cherokees were beaten up in a drunken frolic. They took vengeance by ambushing two Estatoes whom they killed and

---

[11] Wm. Bull to Lyttelton, June 20, 1758; J. Wright to Ellis, July 4, 1758, Lytt. Pap.

[12] McDowell, *S.C. B.P.R.O. Records*, XXVII, 104.

[13] Lachlan McGillivray to Lyttelton, Oct. 17, 1758, Lytt. Pap.

[14] Jenkins, Book of Indian Affairs, Vol. VI, 167.

[15] Jerome Courtonne to Lyttelton, Oct. 17, 1758, Lytt. Pap.

[16] Lachlan McGillivray to Lyttelton, Oct. 17, 1758, Lytt. Pap.

[17] *Ibid.*, Oct. 21, 1758, Lytt. Pap.

scalped. Shock ran through the entire Cherokee nation and emissaries were sent to Okfuskee to assure the Creeks that the Cherokees would not make an issue of the murders. But the emissaries feared for their lives and turned back. The Creeks made no apology.[18]

Nevertheless it is doubtful that in the spring of 1759 the Cherokees would have sought vengeance on the English for their losses in skirmishes with the Virginia frontiersmen had it not been for the Mortar. While the Mortar's movements in the fall of 1758 are obscure, his brother had a Cherokee wife from the clan most affected by the losses in Virginia. Through this channel the Mortar had access to the councils of the Cherokee town of Settico. In the Virginia frontier hostilities he saw an opening for the expulsion of the English from the Cherokee country west of the mountains which he and the French wanted to see. In the late fall of 1758 he went up to the mouth of Coosawaitee Creek (near present-day Resaca, Georgia) to establish a village to serve as a base from which he could readily fire up the Cherokees. In the background of his move was the implication that the French could supply the Cherokees. His support among the Creeks was still limited, but it included some Lower Creeks who had Cherokee wives and lived in the Lower Cherokee Towns, particularly Estatoe, which had suffered severely at the hands of the Virginians. It also included Togulki and his uncle, Ishenpoaphe, Mico of Coweta. At Mobile in the summer, Togulki had promised the French he would join them in the effort to take Fort Loudoun.[19] Publicly, Ishenpoaphe repudiated the plan, but, secretly, as he later admitted, he sympathized with the Cherokees.

At this juncture, Edmund Atkin, His Majesty's Superintendent of Indian Affairs in the Southern District, who for the past year had been preoccupied with Indian affairs in Virginia, entered the scene. With an apparent underestimation of the rising hostility of the Cherokees, he projected an extended visit to the heart of the

---

[18] Lachlan McGillivray to Ellis, Oct. 24, 1758, Lytt. Pap.; Atkin to Lyttelton, Nov. 24, 1758, Lytt. Pap.

[19] McDowell, *S.C. B.P.R.O. Records*, XXVII, 181.

Creek country where he intended to put an end to trade abuses, bring the Creeks into close offensive and defensive alliance with the English, choke the Mortar's activity, and force the French out of the lower Mississippi valley by tying the Choctaws to the English in a trade alliance. But these objectives were to be pursued at a leisurely pace.

Arriving at Augusta in October, 1758, he settled down to reorganizing the trade, much to the distress of the entrenched traders. On November 2 he issued a proclamation that prohibited the traders from carrying rum to the nation and unlicensed traders from doing business.[20] He restrained all the traders from going to the nation until he was ready to go with them. Then he sent up to the towns to prohibit the traders remaining there from doing business until he arrived. He informed the Cherokees that if they did not behave, he would bring the Creeks down upon them.

All his measures created unrest among the Indians. In effect he had declared an unprovoked embargo. Rum had been a staple in the Indian trade for nearly half a century, and the Indians demanded it. The unlicensed traders in the woods had always attracted the Indians because of their convenience and sometimes lower prices; moreover, they offered an escape from debts by giving on the spot goods instead of demanding payment in skins for goods long since consumed. The suspension of the trade and the delay in the arrival of the traders, though designed to cause the Indians to accept Atkin's mission as a condition for the continuance of the trade, caused doubts, fears, and uneasiness. This was augmented by the traders' anger at Atkin, and by the French, who from Fort Toulouse circulated rumors that Atkin intended to come with a large army to force the Indians to allow him to build forts.[21] Though the Wolf of the Muccolossus asserted the falsity of these rumors, they furnished ammunition to the conspiratorial elements.

Atkin remained at Augusta for six months, raising a small company of guards to accompany him, bringing up supplies and gift goods, and negotiating with Lyttelton and Ellis for their re-

[20] Atkin's Proclamation, Nov. 2, 1758, Lytt. Pap.
[21] Atkin to Lyttelton, Dec. 10, 1758, Lytt. Pap.

luctant support of his measures. Ellis, jealous of Atkin's vigorous assertion of control over trade and Indian affairs, and alarmed for fear his design of bringing the Creeks into active alliance with the English would cause the French to loose the Choctaws on the Georgia frontier, held back.[22]

While Atkin lingered at Augusta, the French-fostered intrigue of Ishenpoaphe and Togulki of Coweta and the Mortar of the Okchais to precipitate the Cherokees into war with the English made great strides. Ishenpoaphe visited the Lower Cherokee town of Keowee and assured the Cherokees that Atkin would not be able to induce the Creeks to attack them if they went to war with the English.[23] Beyond the mountains at Overhill Cherokee Settico, the Mortar's insistent hammering on the vengeance theme incited the Setticoes late in March to raise up a party to go secretly against the settlers on the North Carolina frontier.[24] In early April, Ishenpoaphe, Togulki, and Escochabey (the Young Lieutenant of Coweta) set off for Fort Toulouse where the arrival of rum and goods through the English blockade warranted hopes of affluence sufficient to back a Creek-Cherokee uprising against the English.[25]

As the cabal schemed darkly and restless sentiments went the rounds of the nation, the dominant headmen continued to work in harmony with the English. In February a large party of Upper Creeks under the Wolf of the Muccolossus visited Charlestown and worked out an agreement on weights and measures to be used in the skin trade.[26] In March, Lower Townsmen led by the Hitchiti king went to Savannah for presents and inconsequential talk. A feature of this visit was a pair of ball games, one by the men and one by the women, to entertain the Georgians.[27] As if to re-enforce Atkin's threat to bring the Creeks down on the Cherokees, who were at odds with the Catawbas, Lower Creeks met Catawbas at Fort More under Atkin's supervision. In February an unexpected

[22] Ellis to Lyttelton, Mar. 13, 1759, Lytt. Pap.
[23] McIntosh to Lyttelton, Mar. 31, 1759, Lytt. Pap.
[24] P. Demere to Lyttelton, May 12, 1759, Lytt. Pap.
[25] Bossu, *Travels*, 152–58.
[26] McDowell, *S.C. B.P.R.O. Records*, XXVIII, 148.
[27] *S. C. Gazette*, Mar. 31, 1759.

bonus for the English was a clash between Spanish horsemen and Creeks near Picolata on the St. Johns River.[28] In March, Choctaws, eager for the coming of an English trade, visited the Upper Towns and were held there by the Wolf of the Muccolossus to await Atkin's arrival. Shawnees, disgusted with the dominant pro-English sentiment, deserted the nation to go to Fort de l'Assomption on the Ohio from which they threatened to attack the English traders.[29] Disapproval of Ishenpoaphe and Togulki's scheme led to a split between Coweta and Cussita where Captain Allick and other headmen held the people in line for the English. When rumor circulated that strange Indians intended to attack Coweta trader George Galphin, Allick proclaimed that if any Englishman was killed, he would kill a Frenchman

Early in April, Atkin set out from Augusta for the Lower Towns. Escorted by a guard of a dozen men dressed in the green uniforms he had devised, he led a long convoy of traders with goods and presents. He had sent no messenger ahead to advise that he was on the way and desired to meet the headmen, so no formal greeting awaited him. Arriving in the Lower Towns just after Ishenpoaphe and Togulki had returned from Fort Toulouse and had circulated hostile rumors concerning his intentions, he made his headquarters at more friendly Cussita. There, biding his time, he made no formal talks, but held private conversations with Captain Allick and other friendly headmen. Ishenpoaphe had already gone off to the Cherokees to discuss his French-inspired schemes, and Togulki, ignored by Atkin, nervously talked over with the Coweta headmen the portent of Atkin's visit. Finally the Cowetas decided to go over to Cussita to shake Atkin's hand. But the Superintendent spurned them and accused Togulki of being a Frenchman whose hand he did not deign to touch. Abashed and angered, Togulki stole away into the woods toward the Cherokee country. When Escochabey, the Young Lieutenant, head warrior of Coweta, received English scalps taken by the Cherokees in their North Carolina raid, Atkin interdicted the Coweta trade. The Superintendent

---

28 Ellis to Lyttelton, Feb. 24, 1759, Lytt. Pap.
29 Lachlan McGillivray to Lyttelton, Apr. 25, 1759, Lytt. Pap.

now collected all the French and Spanish commissions of various headmen and caused the English flag to be run up in the squares. Nevertheless he handed out no presents. When a delegation of Choctaws came down from the Upper Towns, he made a great demonstration over them and sent them back to their towns to bring deputies to meet him in July in the Upper Towns to make a trade treaty. From Captain Allick he obtained a promise of assistance in frustrating the Mortar, who had returned from the Cherokees to the Okchais. He also refuted the Tomathley King of the Alabamas, who had arrived at the Lower Towns to repeat the French talk that Atkin had come to ask for lands and to build forts.[30]

By late June when Atkin made ready to go to the Upper Towns, anti-English agitation there led by the Mortar and tolerated by the Gun Merchant had generated force. Not only was the French story of Atkin's designs listened to, but the Mortar and Cherokees bearing English scalps taken in North Carolina had come into the towns. There were daily secret meetings to hear the Mortar and the Cherokees plead for the Creeks to join the Cherokees in war against the English. Rumors ran that if the Wolf of the Muccolossus persisted in friendship for the English, he would be assassinated.[31] Ishenpoaphe and Togulki were in the Lower Cherokee Towns, ostensibly assuring the Cherokees that the Creeks would be neutral but in reality concerting plans to bring on the war and holding out the possibility that the Creeks would join.[32]

From Cussita, Captain Allick sent the Cussita warrior, the Scotchman, who was the Mortar's uncle, to the Okchais to insist that Atkin be received with ceremony and without insult or untoward incident.[33] But Atkin had decided to by-pass Okchai, and, as a punishment for the Mortar's reception there, interdicted the trade of the town. He also halted the English trade to the pro-

[30] Galphin to Lyttelton, June 11, 1759, Lytt. Pap.; Atkin to Lyttelton, June 17, 1759, Lytt. Pap.; *S.C. Gazette*, June 30, 1759; Atkin to Lyttelton, Feb. 16, 1760; Lytt. Pap.; Candler, *Ga. Col. Rec.*, VIII, 161–63.
[31] Gertrude Selwyn Kimball (ed.), *Correspondence of William Pitt When Secretary of State with Colonial Governors and Military and Naval Commissioners in America*, II, 268.
[32] P. Demere to Lyttelton, Aug. 28, 1759, Lytt. Pap.
[33] Atkin to Lyttelton, June 17, 1759, Lytt. Pap.

French Alabama near Fort Toulouse, now rich with rum and presents. He went directly to the Tuckabatchee town to be near the friendly Wolf of the Muccolossus. The Mortar withdrew from the Okchais with the Cherokees and went to Fort Toulouse. Atkin was received at Tuckabatchee with great ceremony. There he set up his elaborate headquarters tent, guarded by his uniformed escort, and proceeded to hold conferences with various headmen. He discredited stories that he had come to take lands and establish forts. He had come, he said, merely to listen to Creek grievances, to remedy abuses in the trade, and to make a treaty with the Choctaws. A few miles away at Fort Toulouse, the Mortar glowered, drank copiously of French rum, and listened to commandant Aubert's boast of a great supply of French goods and ammunition to come which would enable the French, Creeks, and Cherokees to throw the English from the country.

But the cold fact of the Choctaw defection somewhat belied the French assertions. On July 18 at the Muccolossus under the friendly auspices of the Wolf, Atkin signed with the Choctaws a treaty of trade and alliance. From the French fort, the Mortar, Aubert, and the Cherokees could see that the sands were running out on the French in the southeast and they sought to nullify the treaty. To provoke a Creek-Choctaw war they sent a Creek to murder a Choctaw. But the Choctaw headmen, too poor to carry on a war, and too wise to be deterred from the English, suspected the slaying to have been French-inspired, ignored it, and presented the Wolf and the pro-English headmen with peace tokens.[34] The Choctaw headmen, laden with Atkin's presents, returned to their country ready when the time came to co-operate with the English against the French. There was a certain amount of Creek unhappiness over the English-Choctaw treaty, for Atkin, who had not yet given presents to the Creeks, had given abundant presents to his newly-found friends the Choctaws. Some professed that the English, now having won the Choctaws, would pay less attention to their old friends the Creeks.[35] Nevertheless the Creeks were in the same bind as the

34 *S.C. Gazette*, Sept. 1, 1759.
35 *Ibid.*

Choctaws, for lacking a French trade they needed an English trade. They could only await Atkin's will and hope that the Mortar would not precipitate a crisis.

With the Mortar balefully eyeing Atkin from Fort Toulouse, the French conspiracy with the Cherokees moved forward behind the forest screen. The Cherokee Prince of Chota bore from Fort Toulouse to the Overhills French anti-English propaganda and tales of help to come.[36] Ishenpoaphe and Togulki, now supported by Nehalachko, King of the Apalachicolas, who were near the French-sympathizing Spaniards, held talks with the Cherokees in the woods on the upper Savannah River and occasionally went into the Cherokee towns.[37] Late in July, rumors, bolstered by French rum, circulated in the Lower Cherokee Towns that at the Cherokee Green Corn dance toward the end of August there would be a rising of Creeks and Cherokees against the English.[38] Runners and deputies shuttled between the Lower Creek and the Lower Cherokee Towns, and on July 28 and 30 at Cherokee Keowee, secret meetings were held between Creeks and Cherokees. Conflicting accounts exist of what transpired. Coytmore, commander of Fort Prince George in the Lower Cherokee Towns, heard that the Creeks asked the Cherokees to join them and the French and that Wahatchie, the Lower Cherokee head warrior, agreed, provided the Creeks would commence by killing the traders in the Creek towns.[39] On September 11, Ishenpoaphe reported to Outerbridge, commander at Augusta, that the Cherokees had urged Nehalatchko to raise the Creeks, but that Nehalatchko had asserted Creek neutrality.[40] Tistoe of Keowee told Coytmore on August 28 that the Creeks had proposed war with the English and that Nehalatchko had offered to strike the first blow, but that the Cherokees rejected the proposal.[41] Later, at Savannah, Ishenpoaphe admitted that he had

---

[36] P. Demere to Lyttelton, Aug. 28, 1759, Lytt. Pap.

[37] *S.C. Gazette*, Sept. 22, 1759; Outerbridge to Lyttelton, Sept. 11, 1759, Lytt. Pap.

[38] Coytmore to Lyttelton, July 23, 1759, Lytt. Pap.

[39] *Ibid.*, Aug. 3.

[40] Outerbridge to Lyttelton, Sept. 11, 1759, Lytt. Pap.

[41] Coytmore to Lyttelton, Sept. 28, 1759, Lytt. Pap.

been privy to the Cherokee designs and had offered to join them.[42]

On August 3, Creek runners set off from Keowee to the Lower Towns. On August 10 a Creek runner raced into Coweta raising the death whoop and bearing the tokens of war, a red stick and a hatchet.[43] On August 23, Nehalatchko entered Apalachicola with the war whoop and guns firing[44] and went into secret meeting with his headmen. Already Captain Allick of Cussita had sent his daughter to warn the Lower Creek traders that something bad was being concocted and would soon break.[45] All the evidence points toward a plot of Ishenpoaphe, Togulki, and Nehalatchko with the Lower Cherokees to strike the English traders in the two nations on August 24, the date suspected by Coytmore in July.

Coytmore hurried off news of his August 3 discoveries to Lyttelton at Charlestown and to Outerbridge at Augusta, with advice to warn the traders and to tell the Creeks the plot had been exposed. Outerbridge dispatched a hard-riding courier to Atkin at Tuckabatchee, and Atkin at once informed the Upper Towns headmen. They disclaimed all knowledge of the plot or sympathy with it and, along with Atkin, sent runners to warn the Lower Towns to have none of it. With the threat of exposure the Coweta and Apalachicola headmen deftly covered the evidence. Ishenpoaphe and Togulki deserted the Cherokee country to go to Augusta to proclaim their innocence and solemnly to declare that in event of Cherokee-English war the Creeks would defend the English frontier.[46]

Meanwhile the Cherokee end of the affair had also fizzled. Round O, a pro-English headman from the Cherokee Middle Settlements, had heard of the plot. He went down to Keowee and sternly warned the headmen there that if they did not cease their scheming, he would provoke a Cherokee-Creek war by killing all the Creeks

[42] Ellis to Lyttelton, Oct. 16, 1759, Lytt. Pap.

[43] S.C. Gazette, Sept. 8, 1759.

[44] Outerbridge to Lyttelton, Sept. 11, 1759, Lytt. Pap.

[45] S.C. Gazette, Sept. 8, 1759.

[46] Ellis to Lyttelton, Sept. 8, 1759, Lytt. Pap.; Outerbridge to Lyttelton, Sept. 11, 1759, Lytt. Pap.

in the Cherokee country. Wahatchie and the conspirators quailed and belted their hatchets.[47]

At Augusta, Ishenpoaphe received an invitation from Mary Bosomworth to come down to Savannah and see Governor Ellis. Ellis, in the midst of effecting the Bosomworth compromise, had conceived the idea of having Mary invite her wayward Coweta relatives, Ishenpoaphe, Togulki, and Escochabey, to Savannah.[48] Reassured by Mary of good will and kind treatment, they washed their hands of the Cherokee intrigue and with a large following trekked serenely to the festival of love on the seaboard.

Meeting the Indians on October 10, Ellis sternly charged them with having conspired with the Cherokees against the English. Ishenpoaphe, as spokesman for his underage nephew, Togulki, brazenly denied all, asserting that "our people did not heed their talk, nor has a man of our nation ever been concerned with the Cherokees."[49] Ishenpoaphe expressed ill will toward Atkin for his behavior—his delay, his suspending the trade, his insult to Togulki, his disregard of the chief towns of Coweta and Okchai, and his taking away of the commissions—greatly pleasing Ellis, who disliked Atkin and spared no pains to belittle his mission and achievements. Ishenpoaphe asked that Atkin be withdrawn from the nation. All this was self-righteous defense of injured "innocence," as behooved a headman in Ishenpoaphe's dubious circumstances. Ellis apologized for Atkin and promised that for whatever wrong the Superintendent did, the great king over the water would punish him. He then expressed pleasure that the Creeks would hold to their old friendship for the English and pointedly emphasized the importance of the English trade to the Creeks, the poverty of those whom the French had befriended, and asked Ishenpoaphe to state to him any grievance he had against the English. Ishenpoaphe then complained of settlers from Virginia who, running away from the French war on the Virginia frontier, had begun to settle on the hitherto peaceful Georgia and Carolina frontiers, whence they

[47] Beamer to Lyttelton, Sept. 10, 1759, Lytt. Pap.

[48] Ellis to Lyttelton, Aug. 27, 1759, Lytt. Pap.

[49] Candler, *Ga. Col. Rec.*, VIII, 161–63.

hunted on the Indian lands, and he asked Ellis to halt their trespasses. On this note the day's conference ended. The next morning the Indians received a shock.

In the Upper Towns on September 28, Atkin had assembled the headmen in the Tuckabatchee square to hear his long-delayed grand talk to the Creeks. All the dissident Upper Towns headmen, including the Mortar, were present. As the peace pipe circled the assemblage, Atkin, in an unprecedented action, refused to allow it to be presented to the Mortar. Then in discussing the attitudes of the towns toward the English, he singled out the Alabama town of Cussita, near Fort Toulouse and friendly to the French, and announced that its trade would be withdrawn. At that moment, Totscadeter, the Tobacco Eater, a warrior, sprang up and brought his hatchet down on Atkin's head. The Superintendent fell. Traders and Indians started up from the cabins around the square and fled in all directions. However, men about Atkin friendly to the English, among them the headman Tupulgi or Molten, leaped upon the wildly flailing Totscadeter, flung him down and bound him. By then Atkin, bleeding profusely, had staggered to his feet. Fortunately for the Superintendent, the warrior's hatchet had struck a beam over his head before it hit him and the wound was superficial. His guard rallied round and escorted him to his tent. No Indian rising followed. In fact many headmen came to Atkin's headquarters with apologies. That night Atkin sent a courier riding toward Augusta to overtake fleeing traders before they panicked the frontier. Wisely he had chosen to regard the assault as the act of a single madman, though there is a strong probability that it was premeditated as part of the Mortar's conspiracy, which had planned a rising in the Cherokees for about the same date. Had Atkin been killed, the traders would have been massacred and the Creeks would have been committed to war against the English.[50]

Ellis at Savannah heard the news on October 10, the first day of his meeting with the Cowetas, but did not announce it to them until the morning of the eleventh. The startled headmen froze in fear, like guilty persons entrapped. Only as Ellis reported Atkin's

[50] *S.C. Gazette*, Oct. 13, 1759; Adair, *History of the American Indians*, 268–69.

survival, and the failure of the Indians to rise, did they relax. Togulki said his only concern in the matter was that Atkin bore the king's commission: "I should have rejoiced," he said, "at his disaster, if it had gone worse for him. I would have served him so myself long ago had not I been prevented by other Indians." Ellis, now more concerned about the possibility of a Cherokee war with the English, advised the Creeks to stay away from Carolina and the Cherokee country lest they be mistaken for hostile Cherokees. Ishenpoaphe promised to send runners to the Lower Towns to advise the Creeks, who, he said, would do no injury to Georgia. Further to placate the Creeks, Ellis informed them of the proclamation he would issue forbidding the frontiersmen to hunt on Creek lands. He also lifted Atkin's trade ban on Coweta. He then brought the conference to a close by distributing great piles of presents. That evening he entertained the headmen at a dinner at his home. Perhaps it was then that Ishenpoaphe acknowledged "they were privy to and disposed to act a part in the designs of the Cherokees" but were happy that they had not and had been induced to come to Savannah.[51]

The Creeks left town in a good mood, as well they might, for they had come through a tortuous intrigue unscathed. Ellis, too, had cause for satisfaction. He had ammunition to support his case against Atkin as a fomenter of more trouble than he prevented. He had kept a scheming, discontented crew out of the danger zone at a crucial time. And he believed he had won the Creeks to the English side.

However, the conference at Savannah had not entirely dissipated the Lower Creek anti-English sentiment; while Ishenpoaphe, Escochabey and Togulki talked with Ellis, Ufylegy, the brother of Escochabey, had attended Atkin's talk at Tuckahatchee and then had gone to Mobile and New Orleans, not to return until November.[52] Isfulgey of Apalachicola had brought beads and a warlike message from the Cherokee towns to Apalachicola. The Wolf of the Muccolossus sent orders for the beads to be returned. Isful-

51 Ellis to Lyttelton, Oct. 16, 1759, Lytt. Pap.
52 Atkin to Lyttelton, Feb. 13, 1760, Lytt. Pap.

gey, who had worn the beads about his neck, conveniently lost them. Since protocol required that the same beads that had been received must either be retained as approval of the message they spoke, or returned as a rejection, the Apalachicolas were in difficulties. The Cherokees would believe them allies till they returned the lost beads. The matter was not resolved until late in January when Captain Allick of Cussita took it upon himself to forward a message to the Cherokees explaining the trouble. This was too late to prevent the Cherokees from rising against the English in hopes they would have Creek aid.[53]

The day after the assault upon him at Tuckabatchee, Atkin reconvened the conference and took up his grand speech at the point where he had been interrupted by Totscadeter's hatchet. He remained in the Upper Towns six more weeks. He set up a system whereby Creek relations with the English could be controlled. Selecting certain Creek headmen to whom he presented gorgets, he assigned them the duty of protecting the traders and being the mouths of the talks he planned to send to the nation from time to time.[54] He attempted to reconcile the disputing factions by bringing the Gun Merchant and the Wolf of the Muccolossus together, and thereby brought the Gun Merchant back into a more friendly disposition toward the English. He won from the French-dominated Alabama towns a treaty by which they promised not to interfere with the English-Choctaw trade. He obtained the promises of a number of headmen to move against Fort Toulouse when an English fleet should appear off Mobile. He obtained an order from the headmen prohibiting the Mortar from going to the Cherokees. They sent the Gun Merchant instead with a peace message. Atkin, however, made a mistake when, believing he had won the Mortar over, he sent him to the Lower Cherokees to warn them not to attack the Carolina army now approaching the Cherokee country with Cherokee hostages to force the mountaineers to a peaceful settlement with Carolina. The Mortar delivered the message but also delivered one of his own to the effect that if the English attacked the Cherokees, the Creeks would join the Cherokees. But

[53] *Ibid.*, Jan. 25.   [54] *Ibid.*, Feb. 5.

for the moment the Mortar's voice seemed to be the muttering of a retreating storm. Atkin, with reason to believe he had stifled a threatened Creek-Cherokee conspiracy and had brought the Creeks together in friendship for the English, returned to Augusta in December. There he heard of Governor Lyttelton's peace treaty with the Cherokees and communicated its content to the Okfuskee Captain who had accompanied him. The Okfuskee Captain, impressed by the Carolina show of force against the Cherokees, pronounced the treaty just and good. He intimated that the Cherokees had brought their troubles upon themselves by listening to the French talks, and he expressed pleasure that the Creeks had not joined them, which, he said, they would have done had it not been for Atkin's talks in the nation. Atkin then sent the Okfuskee Captain back to the Upper Towns to call attention to that provision of the new Cherokee-Carolina treaty whereby the Cherokees agreed to apprehend any man or Indian bringing French talks to the Cherokee country.[55]

When late in January the Cherokees, incensed by Carolina's holding Cherokee hostages in Fort Prince George, broke out war, Atkin, then at Fort More, attempted to persuade Captain Allick of Cussita to fight against the Cherokees. Allick, who had come to Fort More to complain of Georgia Captain Carr's trespass on Creek lands at the forks of Altamaha, replied that before going to war he must go back to the towns to talk with the micos and get his war medicine which he had left at home. But instead of going to Cussita, Allick went to Savannah. Atkin dispatched a message to the Upper Creek headmen urging them to join the war on the side of the English, promising if they did so to reduce trade prices.[56] He held a conference with Lower Creeks under Escochabey, the Lieutenant, who after the October Savannah conference had gone from the nation into the woods on the Cherokee side of the Savannah River, to induce them to fight the mountaineers. But the Indians asserted that they would be neutral for the present.[57]

[55] *Ibid.*, Jan. 9; *S.C. Gazette*, Jan. 26, 1760.

[56] Atkin to Lyttelton, Feb. 5, 1760, Feb. 12, 1760, Lytt. Pap.

[57] *Ibid.*, Feb. 13.

After assisting in strengthening Fort More, the Superintendent, having run out of money and presents, withdrew to Charlestown. Because of ill health he was no longer to be a factor in Creek affairs. In appraising his mission, one must be mindful that traders and royal governors were hostile to this first attempt of the Crown to take direct control of Creek affairs. In many respects Atkin's presence in the Creek country was the equivalent of an English fort to counter French intrigue. Although he made the Creeks nervous, his strong presence overawed them, and he certainly lent strength to the pro-English and neutralist forces.

13

Holding Fast in the Storm
1760-61

THE OPENING of the Cherokee-Carolina war in January of 1760 caused division among the Creeks and very nearly led to civil war. While the Lower Creeks had been quieted by Governor Ellis, the Upper Creeks broke into three parties: a pro-Cherokee faction, led by the Mortar, who, aligned with the French at Fort Toulouse, saw an opportunity to throw back the English frontier; a pro-English faction, headed by the Tallapoose Wolf of the Muccolossus, who wished to join the English in disciplining the Cherokees; and, by far the most powerful, though perhaps not the largest, a neutralist faction headed by the Gun Merchant of the Okchais. Weighting this third group were the influential patriarchs dominated by Old Brisket of Tallapoose Tuckabatchee, who wanted peace and prosperity with a good trade.

When the war broke out, the English regarded the Creeks with suspicion, for certain Creeks had been in the Cherokee towns and were believed to have fomented Cherokee demands for satisfaction for the hostages held by the English.[1] Also that winter some of the

[1] *S.C. Gazette,* Feb. 9, 1760.

Lower Creeks headed by Ishenpoaphe and Escochabey, the Young Lieutenant, who at Savannah in the early fall had promised Ellis to stay away from the troubled area, hunted in the Little River region on the west bank of the Savannah River near the Lower Cherokee Towns. When, in January, Cherokees raided on the west side of the Savannah River, they were suspected of having joined the raiders. Nevertheless they came peaceably to Augusta, and when accused by White Outerbridge, the commander of the fort, protested their neutrality. They even went out and brought in lost settlers who had fled their homes, persuaded the Cherokees to surrender a few of their captives, and advised Outerbridge of the movements of Cherokee war parties.

Actually the presence of the Lower Creeks on the Upper Savannah diverted the brunt of the war away from the Georgia frontier. They warned the Cherokees not to commit further depredations there, lest the whites mistake Creeks for enemies, and not to molest traders bound for the Creek country unless they wished the Creeks to join the war against them. Shortly most of the Creeks deserted the region and went home.

Finally forced out of neutrality by the war talk of his son and nephew, Ishenpoaphe remembered his October pledge and went with twenty warriors to Savannah to promise to make war on the Cherokees.[2] Yet his son, co-operating with Carolina rangers, opposed an attack on Cherokee Estatoe, saying that Cowetas were visiting the town.[3] But it soon developed that the consensus at Coweta opposed war on the Cherokees, and Ishenpoaphe never became actively hostile.

Ellis at Savannah, much visited by straggling Creeks, enlisted Mary Bosomworth to engage them to go to war. By playing upon their cupidity, he hoped he could thrust some of them into a position to be killed and thus plunge the Creeks into the war. The Georgia council announced a generous reward for Cherokee scalps, and late in February, Ellis induced Seminole Lower Creek hunting parties under Weoffki, the Long Warrior of Latchoway, and Tu-

[2] *Ibid.*, May 10.
[3] *Ibid.*, May 17.

pahtke or White Cabin, to go with English guides against the Lower Cherokee towns. These, lying in ambush near Cherokee Keowee, took three scalps and returned to Savannah for a triumphal fete, presents, and the scalp bounties. The startled Cherokees, finding the bodies of the slain with Creek war tokens nearby, wisely overlooked the attack. They wanted no war with the Creeks at that time. Weoffki and Tupahtke went home to learn that they were frowned upon by all the Lower Towns and went no more to war against the Cherokees. This, however, did not prevent a few individual stray Creeks from joining the Lower Chickasaws in raids on the Cherokees.

Ellis, again using Mary Bosomworth, sent a war message to Coweta, and, disregarding Atkin's suspension of John Spencer's trading license for Muccolossus, Ellis allowed Spencer to take trading goods and a war talk to the Upper Creeks. When Ellis' message arrived at Coweta, the Lower Towns' answer had already been debated and determined. There Atkin's war message of February 13 had been received simultaneously with a Cherokee mission demanding Creek aid. The Cherokees proclaimed that they had captured large stores of English ammunition and goods. They also said that the English had insulted the Creeks by imprisoning two Cherokee headmen, whom to seal the Creek-Cherokee peace of 1753, the Creeks had installed as honorary Creek micos. On February 26, Togulki hoisted the French colors in Coweta square, the English colors outside, and summoned the Lower Creek headmen to a meeting. Few came, but among them was Hoyabney, headman of the Chehaw town, who presented the statement that "the Cherokees were mad and had spoiled the best friend they had," that they (the Creeks) would not help them. He warned the Cherokees not to "spoil" the Creek trading path, that the Creeks would guard their traders, and that, if any traders to the Creeks were killed, the Creeks would instantly war on the Cherokees. He reminded the mountaineers of the long and bitter Creek-Cherokee war early in the decade past, of what to expect if the Cherokees killed any Creeks.[4] On March 6 the headmen assembled at Cussita to reply

4 *Ibid.*, Apr. 7.

to Atkin. Togulki, who had just returned from Fort Toulouse with rum and presents, attended, protesting that decision should be deferred until an expected French talk arrived. The headmen decided that, though they knew the benefits of peace with the English and intended to keep them, the English had been at such pains to make peace for them with the Cherokees in 1753 that they did not now intend to break that either. However, they would provide guards for the traders' convoys, and if the Cherokees interfered with the trade, they would take up arms against them.[5] Nevertheless voices of certain Lower Townsmen who took seriously Atkin's suggestion of lower trade prices in return for going to war, urged that it be discussed and promised to force a meeting on the subject at a later date.

In the Upper Towns, where opinion divided more sharply, debate on Atkin's message proceeded on similar lines. In the absence of the Mortar, who was visiting the Cherokee towns, an undercurrent of opinion held that if the French could supply goods, war against the English would follow. Some traders believed this to be the prevailing attitude, for Cherokees bearing English scalps were allowed to pass unmolested through the Creek country to Fort Toulouse. Yet the Muccolossus headmen, of whom the Wolf was chief, hinted that if the English would send a large army against the Cherokees and ammunition to the Creeks, the Creeks would attack the Cherokees. The Gun Merchant demanded that a neutral course be followed, and in the end his point of view, mirroring that of the old men, prevailed. At a meeting of head warriors the Captain of the Pukantahassees summed up Indian sentiment with a statement that "the English are our friends and we love them greatly— we desire that goods may continue amongst us and your friendship as formerly. The Cherokees are what you called your greatest friends and we are sorry that you should be hurted by them. But the Abeikas, Tallapooses, Cowetas and Coosadas are resolved to have no hand in the war betwixt you—. It is our intent that our path shall not be spoiled, either to this place or to the Choctaws and Chickasaws. Some of the Cherokees may come to our towns; no

[5] *Ibid.*

doubt we shall have talks, if good, it's well, if bad, we shall give no ear to them. The day shall never come that the knot of friendship between us shall be loosed, it is not a slippery knot but tied very fast."[6]

On March 29 the Gun Merchant answered Governor Ellis' war talk by declaring that the Creeks neither had nor would have any concern in the present war between English and Cherokees, "alleging that he was some years ago in Charlestown when Governor Glen laboured hard to effect a reconciliation between the Creeks and Cherokees, that they yielded to his advice and had so well experienced the sweets of peace—that they want to avoid war by all possible means."[7]

In the face of Creek decision for neutrality, the meeting of Creeks and Cherokees at Fort Toulouse in mid- April effected little. Cherokees, accompanied by the Mortar's brother, exhibited English scalps, but the French were unable to supply them with trade goods. The Creeks bluntly informed them of their decision for neutrality and warned them to leave the Creek traders alone. The Creeks arranged for ransoming to traders captive Englishmen the Cherokees had brought with them.[8] The Mortar did not come down to Fort Toulouse. He remained at his Coosawaitees settlement where he could keep in touch with the Overhill Cherokees. Mountaineers returning from the meeting paraded English scalps in the Creek towns to incite the envious young Creeks to emulate them, much to the distress of neutralist headmen. Yet as of late April the vociferous pro-Cherokee faction appeared to have made little headway.

The French conspiracy had not yet played its ace.[9] Though it had succeeded in instigating war between the Cherokees and English, it still hoped to provoke Creek participation. Indeed in late April the conspirators had every incentive to force the situation. Their credit was low, but the Creek will to neutrality had been only tenuously achieved after bitter debate. A new English army ad-

[6] *Ibid.*, Mar. 28.
[7] *Ibid.*, May 24.
[8] *Ibid.*
[9] Paris Arch. Nat. Col., C13 A42, pp. 48–53.

vanced on the Cherokees, and the Cherokees needed Creek help. Word had reached the Upper Towns that stray Lower Creeks had taken Cherokee scalps and that some important Lower Towns headmen, lured by Atkin's promise of lower trade prices, considered making the war general. Ishenpoaphe, his sons, and even Togulki, perhaps encouraged by Mary Bosomworth, now seemed inclined toward the English. The conspirators had already threatened that if any Creeks warred on the Cherokees, they would make the English suffer.

In this crisis the conspiracy struck with bitter force. On May 16 in the Abeika town of Sugatspoges, fiercely-painted young warriors led by Handsome Fellow stormed into trader John Ross's store and murdered him and his two Negro servants. In their fury they quartered Ross's body, looted the store and swarmed with barbaric yells southward to Okchai and Okfuskee for more killing and looting. Before the day ended, at Sugatspoges, Okfuskee, Okchai, and Calailegies, eleven traders had been killed and their stores sacked. Other traders, valiantly defended by their Indian wives, escaped into the woods and sloughs to hide in thickets or under fallen logs until their wives, to whom the law of clan gave immunity, could bring them horses to escape to Augusta. Some warned by friends of the descending holocaust fled to the Wolf's town of Muccolossus. The Wolf, startled by the news as he unsuspectingly watched a ball game, armed and hid the refugees in a swamp. A few, alerted by the approaching furor and reading doom in the dark conspiratorial faces that suddenly loomed before them, raced out of their stores and stumbled in panic through forests and morasses to Pensacola, 150 miles away. In the Abeika town for one grim night the war spirit leaped in lurid flame. At Okfuskee under the approving eyes of the English-baiting Red Coat King, exultant warriors danced the war and scalp dance all night, and throughout the Upper Towns the excitable painted for war as they rejoiced in the bloody harvest to come.[10]

Strangely, the conspiracy did not get off the ground. The mas-

[10] Candler, *Ga. Col. Rec.*, VIII, 316; Adair, *History of the American Indians*, 278–83; *S.C. Gazette*, June 21, 1760.

sacre was the work of a few. At the sound of the rip in the painfully wrought fabric of neutrality, responsible headmen everywhere recoiled in shock. The Gun Merchant, the Wolf of the Muccolossus, Duvall's Landlord, the Okfuskee Captain and many others confronted the mutineers with violent disapproval. They took the surviving traders under their protection and began the task of requiring their turbulent people to quiet down and return the goods stolen from the traders. However, in the disturbed condition of the nation, punishment of the murderers proved impossible, for the Mortar's sympathizers were everywhere and threatened civil war. Finally, as passions cooled, on May 26 the headmen held a meeting at the town of the Muccolossus and decided that peace must be maintained. To Governor Ellis the Gun Merchant sped the headmen's talk stating that the massacre was the work of but a mad few and should not be regarded as "a concerted thing of the nation," that all the headmen wanted peace and trade, but for the sake of peace the punishment of the offenders must not be demanded "lest the desperate fellows be pushed to greater lengths."[11] When it became apparent that the Mortar might inflict further damage after a meeting of the headmen which he called for Fort Toulouse in June, the neutralists sent most of the surviving traders under Indian guard to Fort Augusta with a message that the trade should be reopened as soon as it was safe.

In the Lower Towns, on news of the massacre, the headmen gathered their traders together for safety and held a meeting attended by, among others, Escochabey of Coweta, Hoyabney of the Chehaws, and the warrior Saleetchie. They drew up a talk disclaiming all responsibility for the murders and sent it with the surviving traders under guard to Savannah.

On May 21 the fleeing packhorseman, Robert French, rode wildly into Augusta with the first news of the massacre. In the town were visiting Okfuskees who had set out before the disaster as guards for a traders' packtrain. Fortunately French bore a message from the friendly Okfuskee Captain to Milledge, the commandant of the garrison, stating that the massacre had been an

[11] *S.C. Gazette*, June 21, 1760; Candler, *Ga. Col. Rec.*, VIII, 327.

accident and requesting that the lives of the visiting Indian pack-train guards be spared. Milledge saw to it that the guards went safely back to the nation. The bad news spread swiftly over the frontier and in panic hundreds of Georgia settlers who had not been molested by the Cherokees fled into Augusta and Fort More, some, terrified at the hazards of backwoods living, to leave the colony forever.

At Savannah, Ellis was entertaining a few Lower Creek head-men who had come down before the outbreak. They had brought messages of friendship and of Lower Creek distress that Cherokees had been allowed to display English scalps in the Upper Towns. They also had come to explore Atkin's proposal for a reduction in trade prices in return for Creek aid against the Cherokees.[12] On May 26 a courier rode in from Augusta with the bad news. Unaware that the headmen in the Upper Towns already had the situation under control and fearing that the massacre presaged war, Ellis composed a peace talk and sent it by one of the visiting chiefs to the Lower Towns. He then called in Mary Bosomworth and, giving her a copy of the message, asked her to compose one of her own, and send both to her relatives at Coweta.[13] Expressing his shock at the murders, the governor dismissed his visitors with presents and expressions of good will. Soon Hoyabney of the Chehaws came into Savannah escorting the Lower Towns traders and bringing the Lower Towns' peace message. His arrival was followed by the Gun Merchant's message from the Upper Towns, and Ellis perceived that he had made the right moves. Peace could be had. His problems were whether to demand satisfaction and how soon to reopen the trade.

In mid-June the Mortar made his last effort to strike down the peace. Returning from his settlement at Coosawaitees, he loudly proclaimed that the Cherokees had won a great victory over British Colonel Montgomery with even the Cherokee old women striking down the red coated soldiers.[14] This was a bare-faced lie, either of

---

[12] Candler, *Ga. Col. Rec.*, VIII, 310.

[13] *Ibid.*, 316.

[14] *S.C. Gazette*, July 5, 1760.

the Mortar's or of Cherokee manufacture, for Montgomery, far from being defeated, had just burned several Lower Cherokee Towns and the Lower Cherokees had fled en masse into the mountains. Accompanied by Cherokees with English scalps taken on the Carolina frontier, the Mortar went to Fort Toulouse and summoned the Creek headmen to meet him. Few came, but among those who did was his neutralist brother-in-law, the Gun Merchant. Undeterred, the Mortar spoke to the assemblage of Cherokee invulnerability and the inevitability of Creek war with the English: "as several white men had been killed in their towns, they must never expect to be forgiven unless they delivered up all the murderers which he said could not be done and therefore temporizing was needless."[15] The Gun Merchant, who by then must have heard of Ellis' peaceful disposition, rebuked him, saying he was criminal to attempt to force the Creeks into war and that matters were now progressing toward an accommodation with the English. The truth was that the French could not supply the Creek trade, and the Creeks were greatly impressed that an English army could successfully enter the Cherokee country.

At a meeting of headmen shortly thereafter it was unanimously agreed to hold fast to the English. Upper Towns Duvall's Landlord, and Lower Towns Ishenpoaphe and Half-Breed Abraham of Coweta were dispatched to Augusta to urge that the trade be reopened as soon as possible lest the Creeks assume that the English no longer wished them as friends.[16] The Augusta traders, awaiting orders from the governors of South Carolina and Georgia, stalled, alleging that in the late alarms they had sent all their goods to Savannah and Charlestown for safety and that it would take time to get them back again. Actually belligerent South Carolina talked of an embargo on all Creek trade.

Ellis and the South Carolina council agreed that punishment of the murderers should be left to the Creeks themselves, but South Carolina felt that until it was accomplished the trade should be withheld. Ellis demurred. He thought that such a policy would

---

15 *Ibid.*, June 26.
16 *Ibid.*, July 12.

throw the Creeks into French hands, "the trade being the only tye we had on these savages."[17] He sent the trader, Joseph Wright, as ambassador to the Creeks to urge that the murderers be put to death lest "your wise men—will not loose all authority but all respect and for want of control your people will at length degenerate into wild beasts everyone preying upon another." Wright was to tell them that Ellis intended to reopen the trade but expected before he did it, as Atkin had proposed, the headmen of every town should meet and choose some powerful person to take charge of the traders and to answer to Ellis for their persons and effects. For this service the traders would pay the selected officials annually. The governor also hinted that he would invite two headmen from every town to come down to him in two months' time when presents should arrive from England.[18] Ellis even proposed that the Mortar be sent to urge the Cherokees to make peace with the English.[19]

Ellis then turned to a settlement with the Bosomworths. Mary's services to the colony in the spring had been great as usual, and it was highly desirable in the present delicate state of Creek affairs that she be made happy. A figure of twenty-one hundred pounds was set to recompense her for sixteen and one-half years of service at one hundred pounds a year, and for four hundred fifty pounds of losses in 1747–48. In addition the Crown granted her the twenty-two thousand acres of St. Catherine's Island. In return the Bosomworths surrendered their claims to the islands of Ossabow and Sapelo, along with four thousand acres of old Indian lands near Savannah. The sums to compensate her were to come from the sale of the islands of Ossabow and Sapelo. The Bosomworths became the largest landholders in Georgia and among the richest of colonists.[20] Thus ended fifteen years of acrimonious debate.

In the nation, Upper and Lower Towns headmen held repeated meetings to consider Ellis' various peace talks. The first of these, held at Okfuskee in early July and attended by the Mortar and the Gun Merchant, found the Gun Merchant's appeal, "to quiet the

[17] Candler, *Ga. Col. Rec.*, VIII, 329.
[18] *Ibid.*, 329–34.
[19] *S.C. Gazette*, July 26, 1760.
[20] Candler, *Ga. Col. Rec.*, XXVIII, Pt. 1-A, p. 360.

fires while it is yet in their power," successful. The villagers collected the bones of the slain traders, wrapped them in white deerskins, and ceremonially buried them.[21] Handsome Fellow, the ringleader of the murderers, went out in an expiatory mood to take a Cherokee scalp,[22] and carried it to the commandant at Augusta.[23] However, the Mortar, unmoved, set off for the Cherokee nation, where he arrived just as the Cherokees were rejoicing in their "victory" over Colonel Montgomery's British force, which had retreated from the Cherokee Middle Settlements without damaging them. The Mortar relayed this news to the Upper Creeks with war sticks. The Upper Creeks had just informed the French that since the French could not supply them, they would not fight the British. They treated the Cherokee news with disdain and threw the war sticks into the river. Already they were paying for their contacts with the Cherokees, for the smallpox epidemic Lyttelton had brought to the Cherokees in December had penetrated the Creek nation.[24]

Favorable reports of the Creek meetings reached Charlestown and Savannah as trade-hungry Creeks came down from the nation. Eager traders without authorization began to send small convoys of goods into the Creek towns. Both Carolina and Georgia held back, waiting for formal answer to Ellis' grand talk sent by Wright. Not until August 10 did Wright deliver the talk at Talassee before most of the greatest warriors and beloved men. The Gun Merchant spoke for all the Creeks when he said that "all past grievances must be forgot and never more thought about." In other words no satisfaction was to be given; but he went on to say, "this day we have agreed and given out in public that if there is ever an Englishman killed hereafter, the man that does it shall dye immediately."[25] Concerning the Cherokee talks he said they were never encouraged, for it was not in the Creek interest "to take part either of one side

21 *Ibid.*, VIII, 349.
22 *S.C. Gazette*, Sept. 13, 1760.
23 *Ibid.*, Sept. 27.
24 *Ibid.*
25 Candler, *Ga. Col. Rec.*, VIII, 421.

or the other, but to be at peace with both."[26] Privately he sent word to Ellis that Cherokee intrigue continued, that Cherokee spirits were high with victory, and that the Creek young men excitedly listened, that it was now impossible to put any of the murderers to death, but that perhaps later it could be done. He gave the impression the headmen were sitting on a powder keg, maintaining with difficulty a precarious neutrality, "for the people are all mad."

In mid-August on news of the Cherokee capture of English Fort Loudoun in the Overhill Cherokee country, the Mortar went up to Cherokee Chota to witness the dance of two hundred captives, the most extravagant display of Indian triumph in the English colonial period. Then he joined the Cherokees who were marching to take, as they hoped, English Fort Prince George in the Lower Cherokee country. He talked loudly of Creek participation in the war, promising four hundred warriors and sent inflammatory talks into the Upper Creek Towns. There, however furious the young men, the headmen held fast in their determination for peace and neutrality and awaited an explicit invitation to go down to Savannah to seal the peace.

When, in mid-October, Ellis' formal invitation reached the Upper Towns, widespread illness and the delicate state of affairs prevented men of consequence from leaving. The Mortar's reports of Cherokee successes had roused enthusiasm and a meeting of great numbers of Creeks and Cherokees in the woods near Oconee River was projected for the winter. Moreover, Creek relations with the French threatened to deteriorate. The French at Fort Toulouse had corrupted a Creek messenger sent to reassure the Choctaws of Creek intentions of peace with the English and he had falsified his message. Suspicious Choctaws came to the Creeks to learn the truth. The French, bent on destroying the English-Choctaw trade, then induced a Choctaw to kill an English packer. In retaliation, Creeks under Duvall's Landlord had joined pro-English Choctaws to kill a Frenchman near Fort Tombigbe. The French in the fort had fired on the Creeks and Choctaws. Duvall's Landlord came off with the Frenchman's scalp and set off for Savannah with a Choctaw

[26] *Ibid.*

headman to seal the English-Choctaw peace. A Creek-French war coupled with an anomalous Creek-Cherokee alliance seemed possibilities. The Gun Merchant sat tight, hoping to produce a formula of emollients for the crises.[27]

On November 7 at Savannah, where newly-arrived Governor James Wright had succeeded Henry Ellis, Duvall's Landlord found a party of Lower Creeks under Wehanny of Cussita and Toopahatchee delivering a peace talk from the Gun Merchant and Tomathly-hoy, headman of the Okfuskees. Wright received the French scalp and welcomed the Upper Creeks and Choctaws. The Lower Creeks, confessing that they could not speak for the nation, requested the reopening of the trade in time to outfit the winter hunts. Wright, green to the situation, gave a generalized peace talk, demanded guarantees of protection for the traders, and reiterated Ellis' invitation for leading headmen to come down.

Then events took a new twist. As Creeks and Choctaws returned to the wilderness, a French-inspired Creek killed one of the Choctaw emissaries. Choctaws in retaliation killed two Creeks. French machinations had thus brought the Creeks and Choctaws to the brink of war. Though this would hinder English-Choctaw trade, such as it was, it held out to the English the advantage of preventing a Creek-Cherokee alliance against the English. However, wise men on both sides, aided by the French, who now desired to channel the Choctaws into a war with the English-allied Chickasaws, who had attacked the Cherokees, patched up a Creek-Choctaw peace.[28] The Creek-Cherokee *rapprochement* continued; nevertheless, it did not develop into an anti-English alliance. Creeks merely mingled with the Cherokees in the Appalachian foothills enabling the latter to hunt without molestation from the English and furnishing a cover for illegal dealings with bootleg Georgia traders. Creeks even brought packs of Cherokee deerskins into Augusta to trade for goods and ammunition for the Cherokees. But the woodland meetings did serve the English well in that they drove home on the Creeks the Cherokee misery for lack of English

27 *Ibid.*, 394–98, 415.
28 *S.C. Gazette*, Feb. 21, 1761.

trading goods. In the Upper Creek Towns, however, pro-Cherokee Creeks protected Cherokees who plundered some of the traders' stores. In the absence of many warriors on their winter hunts, the neutralist headmen were unable to restrain or punish the marauders. Certain Creek elements showed an anti-English truculence which could not be quieted, and on the frontier, free-lancing bands of young Creeks ran off settlers' horses and slaughtered their cattle. Rumors persisted in the frontier forts that the Creeks planned to join the Cherokees in the spring.[29] Creeks of the Mortar's persuasion demanded that the Chickasaws give up their English-inspired war on the Cherokees and join the Creeks against the English. And in the Lower Towns, visiting Cherokees prophesied that the English would attack the Creeks after they had defeated the Cherokees. But as events revealed, the dominant voices in the Creek nation drew the line at anything beyond a friendly neutrality toward the mountaineers.

While Ishenpoaphe and Escochabey of Coweta now displayed partiality toward the Cherokees, the principal Upper Creek headmen staunchly demonstrated their friendship toward the English. With the outburst of Cherokee plundering of traders' stores in the Upper Towns, the Gun Merchant took English traders under his protection,[30] and Creek women in the affected towns hid most of the traders' goods in order to return them after the disorders had subsided.

In January and February the Wolf of the Muccolossus visited Savannah and Charlestown. To Governor Wright at Savannah he protested his friendship to the English and asserted that his Tallapooses would never join the Cherokees. He did, however, complain that the guards he had sent with the traders' convoys had never received compensation.[31] Wright declared that the traders must see to that, gave him presents, and sent him to Charlestown. In the Carolina capital, Lieutenant Governor Bull, who had succeeded the hapless Lyttelton, entertained him in his own home and impressed

29 *Ibid.*, Jan. 21.
30 Candler, *Ga. Col. Rec.*, VIII, 514.
31 *Ibid.*, 470.

him with a review of the array of regular troops intending to march
with Mohawk Indians from the north against the Cherokees in the
spring.[32] The excursion gave the Wolf strong talking points for
the English when he returned to the nation. Fruits of these were
that Ishenpoaphe and Escochabey, strongest Lower Creek friends
of the Cherokees, immediately sent down to Wright firm talks of
friendship;[33] and in late March the Okfuskee Captain and the now
converted Handsome Fellow, at the behest of the Gun Merchant,
arrived at Savannah with apologies for the plundering of the traders
in their region.[34]

On March 11 a grand meeting of Creeks and Cherokees at Fort
Toulouse under the Mortar's auspices succeeded only in confirming the opinion of the neutralist headmen, for the French again had
to confess that they were unable to supply the Creek nation with
goods. Under the circumstances even the Mortar admitted that a
Creek break with the English was out of the question. Much as he
desired to dam English expansionism with a war, he knew that resistance was impossible without a French supply.[35] In April, though
Togulki went off to Fort Toulouse, the White King of the Cussitas
and Escochabey of Coweta, impressed by English-Mohawk solidarity, again sent to Wright to tell him they would never join the
Cherokees.[36] On April 30 at a meeting of headmen at the Muccolossus, the Gun Merchant and the Wolf composed a talk for Governor
Wright telling him to disregard the winter rumors on the frontier,
that the winter turbulence in the nation had subsided, and that the
traders should come again. "We desire plenty of goods," said the
Gun Merchant, "and paint, as our young men paint much of late
years; and silver arm plates and gorgets and plenty of ammunition
to hunt with."[37] Apparently the pursuit of vanity and of the deer
was to be the main Creek preoccupation. He announced that headmen had been appointed to guard the traders in each town, that

[32] McDowell, *S.C. B.P.R.O. Records*, XXIX, 61–63.
[33] Candler, *Ga. Col. Rec.*, VIII, 512.
[34] *S.C. Gazette*, Apr. 4, 1761.
[35] *Ibid.*, May 16.
[36] *Ibid.*, May 30.
[37] Candler, *Ga. Col. Rec.*, VII, 543.

some had been faithful to their charge and some had not, but that the faithful ought to be rewarded. He noted that English failure to reward the young fellows sent to guard convoys had rendered the young men indifferent about such service in the future and had led them to compensate themselves by stealing traders' horses, which nevertheless the headmen would force them to return.[38] Wright answered the Lower Towns talk by reminding the Creeks of Cherokee misery, saying that he did not want the Creeks to fight against the Cherokees and that as long as the Creeks held fast to the English they should have a trade.[39]

In June, Togulki came back to Coweta from New Orleans, where he had become convinced that nothing was to be had from the French. At the insistence of Half-Breed Abraham he went down to Charlestown and assured Lieutenant Governor Bull of his undying friendship. Bull had received news that a trader going up to the Creek country had been murdered, presumably by Cherokees. He attempted to persuade Togulki to keep the promise he had once made of going to war against the Cherokees if they harmed a trader on the Creek path. The Creek blandly said he would talk it over when he got back to the nation and that, of course, the Creeks would keep their treaties.[40] On his return path he encountered three Cherokees, escaped prisoners of the Carolinians, and seized and returned them to Charlestown.[41] However, in the nation it developed that the murderer of the trader on the Creek path was Togulki's older half-brother (by an "extra wife of Malatchi").[42] The murder had arisen from vengeance: Togulki's brother, suspected of having stolen a horse from trader Rae at Augusta, had attempted to return it to Rae for a reward. Indignant, Rae took the horse and refused to reward the Indian. The angry Indian went up the path and overtook a trader, whom he robbed and killed. Then he came to Coweta to boast. Ishenpoaphe and Escochabey did not dare put so highly rated a warrior to death. They sent a

---

[38] *Ibid.*, VIII, 544.
[39] *S. C. Gazette*, June 6, 1761.
[40] McDowell, *S.C. B.P.R.O. Records*, XXIX, 61–63; *S.C. Gazette*, June 13, 1761.
[41] *S.C. Gazette*, June 20, 1761.
[42] *Ibid.*, July 11.

message to Wright promising to restore the goods and asked him to excuse the murder as done in drunkenness. They begged him not to embargo the trade "for we are so used to the white people and their clothing that we should be very poor without them."[43] Togulki at Augusta, hearing that the murder had been committed by a Creek, but unaware of which Creek, sent word ahead to Coweta to have the murderer killed.[44] No action was taken. Creeks were not putting Creeks to death on anybody's account and Togulki's influence was beginning to decline; he had been on the wrong side at the wrong time. Only brought to treat with the English by Half-Breed Abraham, his true feelings lay with the French, and he could not be trusted as an English ally. A friend of the Cherokees at the beginning of the war, he had turned against them at the end. Always a satellite to older men, he at no time exhibited strength of character as the Indians regarded such strength. Too young to have gained battle fame in the old Creek-Cherokee war, he was not mature enough to have influence in the stresses of this period.

By the beginning of August the British army under Colonel James Grant had forced the routed Cherokees to beg for peace. Governor Wright now felt he could take a bolder line with the Creeks. He sent strong talks to both Upper and Lower Creeks reminding them of their treaty agreements to kill their countrymen who killed whites and demanding the death of the murderer of Thompson.[45]

By this time the Mortar, having seen the collapse of French projects in a total paucity of goods, munitions, and presents, and aware of the Cherokee inability to halt the English invasion, did an about-face. He appeared at Little Tallassee, an Abeika town a few miles above Fort Toulouse on Coosa River, and to William Struthers, the trader there, vehemently denied the charge against him of being in the French interest. Perhaps the agent of this denial was the rising pro-British warrior, Emisteseguo, who was Struthers' "landlord." Struthers sent down to Wright and Bull the Mor-

[43] Candler, *Ga. Col. Rec.*, VIII, 553.
[44] *S.C. Gazette*, July 11, 1761.
[45] Candler, *Ga. Col. Rec.*, VIII, 557.

tar's message denying complicity with the French and encouragement of the Cherokees to fight the English. He declared himself a firm friend of the English and said he would be pleased to receive a small present. The Georgia Board, hastening to profit by the seeming penance, sent up a silver gorget and a silver arm plate.[46] Nevertheless, rumors had the pro-French faction of the Creeks bent on punishing the pro-English Chickasaws for warring on the Cherokees. While stories circulated that vengeful Creeks had waylaid Chickasaws returning from Charlestown with English presents, Chickasaws sought to ambush the Mortar. Instead, they caught and killed his brother, whereupon the Mortar went out with a war party to take vengeance.[47] This Creek break with the Chickasaws led to a Creek-Choctaw alliance under French auspices, with an anti-English undertone which the Mortar was to cultivate in the years of English ascendancy to come.[48]

[46] *Ibid.*, 539.
[47] *S.C. Gazette*, Sept. 19, 1761.
[48] McDowell, *S.C. B.P.R.O. Records*, XXIX, 187.

14

The British Encirclement *1761-65*

WITH THE FRENCH going down to defeat and all the southeast including Florida about to fall into British hands, the British Board of Trade pressed Governor Wright to obtain from the Creeks land cessions above the tide marks in Georgia.[1] Since Wright was having no success in his demands for satisfaction for various murders, he did not think the time ripe. It was clear, however, that once the British had definitely defeated the French they would move to set aside the boundary restrictions of the old Georgia treaties.

That this could be achieved without rousing Creek bitterness seemed doubtful since the Creeks were already displaying restiveness over the frontiersmen's invasions of Indian lands. On December 27, 1761, Creeks who lived among the now defeated Cherokees killed fourteen settlers in the Carolina Long Canes region above Augusta. Creeks visiting Savannah and headmen in the nation disavowed the murderers who they said had straggled long ago from their nation. Since the Long Canes settlers were anathema to the

[1] Candler, *Ga. Col. Rec.*, XXVIII, Pt. 1-B, p. 713.

Cherokees, who resented the Carolina peace treaty which had forced them to cede lands to the settlers, the ex-patriate Creeks apparently had done what Cherokees themselves wanted but feared to do. The murders were also symptomatic of bad feelings between the Creeks and the frontier settlers. For years the Creeks had protested the invasion of their hunting grounds by "Virginians," as they called the frontiersmen. The murders also indicated what the plundering of the traders' stores had pointed to: the young men's contempt of the English, who had not succeeded in obtaining the punishment of the perpetrators of the May, 1760, massacres and other murders. In their peace-making the beaten Cherokees had complained that although armies had marched against them for the frontier murders they had committed, none had marched against the Creeks, who since May of 1760 had killed at least thirty whites. It was true. The English had leaned so far backward to keep the Creeks from involvement in the Cherokee war that many Creeks had grown contemptuous of them. The Creek headmen appeared to have developed a formula of non-compliance with English demands. With the French war drawing to a close and a strong English distaste for further Indian wars fully developed, it remained to be seen how the English would decide to handle the Creeks.

The English hoped that Creek involvement in a war with Spanish Florida would force them to be more tractable. In July, 1761, skirmishing between Creeks and Spaniards had occurred near St. Augustine and Pensacola. By January, 1762, nine Creeks had been killed, and large parties of Lower Townsmen prepared to go against Florida.[2] A ship bearing Spaniards of note from Havana to St. Augustine, stopping at the Florida keys, was fired upon by Creeks who took a Spanish gentleman and held him for ten thousand pounds ransom. Cardenas, Spanish governor of Florida, then applied to Wright to accommodate matters.[3] Creek war parties working along the Florida coasts drove Spanish-allied Indians inland and occupied the coast, where they lay in wait for Spanish vessels.

[2] *S.C. Gazette*, Mar. 20, 1762.
[3] *Ibid.*, Apr. 10.

One party had great good luck. Two Dutch schooners laden with goods bound from St. Eustacia to Mobile and New Orleans touched the Florida shore, where they were stormed and plundered of goods, rum, and ammunition, and the crews killed. Cardenas, obtaining no help from Wright as the English had now declared war on the Spaniards, sought other channels for making peace with the Creeks. He persuaded one Samuel Piles, who from the neighborhood of Edmund Gray's settlement on the Saltilla River south of Georgia traded illegally with St. Augustine, to go to the Lower Creeks with a peace message. Other forces also operated for peace. The French at Mobile, apprehensive of English attack from the sea, fed the Upper Creeks rumors and stories that once the English had taken St. Augustine and Mobile they would send armies into the Creek nation to punish them for their crimes. The Upper Creek headmen held many meetings to discuss the grim situation and decided the Lower Creeks should make peace with the Spaniards. In the Lower Creeks, Escochabey, the Young Lieutenant, influenced by Piles, the French, and the Upper Creeks, dissuaded the Chehaws and the Latchoways under the Cowkeeper from attacking St. Augustine. Taking the classic position that the Europeans should be left to solve their own problems, Escochabey went himself to St. Augustine, made a peace, and brought home to the Lower Towns a large present of Spanish rum.[4]

Though as a result of these maneuvers the English traders apprehended trouble, the Creek headmen maintained a very docile attitude toward Carolina and Georgia. They had been too profoundly impressed by what British armies had done to the Cherokees, and they were alive to rumors of great British successes against the French in the north. Numerous Creeks visited Savannah with professions of peace but no promises of satisfaction. Nevertheless, many young Creeks, perceiving that as an aftermath of war with the English the Cherokees had obtained a cheaper trade, recklessly declaimed that the Creeks, too, might benefit from an English war and that perhaps killing a few more white people

<hr />

[4] Candler, *Ga. Col. Rec.*, VIII, 688–90; XVIII, Pt. 1-B, pp. 564, 635; *S.C. Gazette*, May 15, 29, July 24, 1762.

might turn the trick. In this ticklish situation, Creek headmen healed the Creek-Chickasaw break and looked nervously into the future.

In the prevailing atmosphere of suspicion, Wright sought a conference with leading headmen. As a result, in December, 1762, the Gun Merchant, who had struggled so mightily to maintain Creek neutrality, the Okfuskee Captain, who had sided with him, and Handsome Fellow, who had been on both sides, came down to Savannah.[5] The meeting did not accomplish much except to assure the continuance of the status quo. Wright attempted to take a strong line. Recalling the treaties, he reminded the headmen that they should curb their young men or they would have English armies to contend with, that the great and numerous nation of English could get along well without the Creeks but that the Creeks could not survive without the English trade. He reminded them that according to treaty Creeks who killed Englishmen had forfeited their lives. The Gun Merchant dodged the issue. Acknowledging the treaties, he promised that the headmen would do all in their power to enforce them, but stated that he had not come empowered to talk about past mischief. He intimated that the English were at fault. The English should not permit stray Indians to come among them, for those who came were generally Indians who had left the nation for crime or at least to avoid control. The English should prevent free-lance trading, which lured Indians down to the settlements. He recalled his own service of staying home during the troubled times to obstruct the schemes of the Cherokees.[6] In private conversations with the Gun, Wright learned that there was disquiet among the Creeks over the fact that the Cherokees after two years of bitter warfare had been accorded a much cheaper trade than the Creeks had.[7] Apparently the Creek was pointing toward a bargaining position. The meeting ended in professions of mutual friendship, a renewal of old treaties, and the distribution of presents.

[5] *Ibid.*, VIII, 777.
[6] *Ibid.*, IX, 12–17.
[7] *Ibid.*, XXVII, Pt. 1-A, pp. 584, 662.

Back in the towns a new cloud had appeared. The Gun Merchant arrived at Okchai in February, 1763, just in time to meet the Mortar. The nativist had come down from his settlement at Coosawaitees with Cherokees discontented over their English peace treaty and perhaps restless from the influence of Pontiac's developing conspiracy north of the Ohio to drive the English back over the mountains. At Okchai, dark meetings of headmen ensued. A great conference of Creeks, Choctaws, and Cherokees was held at Fort Toulouse, where the commander, Chevalier de Lanoue, stimulated anti-English talk. In the towns, talks unfriendly to the traders gained ground, and rumors circulated that the Upper Creeks would attack the English in the spring. Traders fled to the Chickasaws for protection.[8]

The Gun Merchant and his friends, true to their professions at Savannah, refused to allow the Creeks to be drawn into the conspiracy. In the face of this stand, the best the Mortar could do was at a meeting at Okchai on April 8 to obtain a protest to Wright against the encroachment of English settlers on Creek lands near the Georgia frontier above Augusta. The Virginians, he said, "had settled all over the woods with people cattle and horses, which had prevented them [the Creeks] for some time from being able to supply their women and children with provisions as they could formerly, their buffalo, deer and bear being drove off the land and killed" with the result that "Creeks kill cattle wandering in these lands to fill their bellies."[9] The Mortar demanded that the governor remove these people as he had in the past promised. Handsome Fellow pointed out that Englishmen had settled on lands never granted, as at Saltilla, Ogeechee, and above Augusta.

A month later, with rumors prevalent that the French had ceded the Creek lands to the English, the Mortar's voice grew stronger. At Okchai on May 8 the Mortar drew up a talk to Governor Wright bitterly stating the Creek case. "The red people," he said, "are poor and dependent upon the whites but the whites appear to believe that the red people have no lands"; he had heard that the

8 Stuart to Amherst, Mar. 15, 1763, Amherst Papers, Vol. III.

9 Candler, *Ga. Col. Rec.*, IX, 71.

white people "were going to take all the lands which they [the Creeks] lent the French and Spanish and they are surprised how people can give away land that does not belong to them." The Creeks as friends to the English had allowed them some lands to settle on "but now the white people intend to take all their lands and throw away the old talks entirely . . . that it made their hearts cross to see their lands taken without their liberty." War was possible, for though "the white people's physic is strong for war—their [the Creeks] head warriors have strong physic also." English and French, he said, had urged Indians to use weapons on the other, but now these two might be cut by the very same weapons. "We are cross and love our lands—the wood is our fire, and the grass is our bed and our physic when we are sick"; the Creeks "know no master but the Master of Breath," but "the white people intend to stop all their breaths by settling all around them."[10]

In mid-May, rumors reached the Lower Creeks that the British troops had landed at Mobile and Pensacola. Immediately they bridled. Meeting at the Apalachicola square to protest the request of trader Wilson to settle on Indian lands with cattle and a store, the headmen sent a message to Wright pointing out that white people had been killed and a house burned in that neighborhood the year before. They demanded that Wright order Wilson out of there "before further mischief was done." Noting other irregular settlers, they demanded that all unlicensed traders be removed from Indian lands. They observed that such stores dealing in rum and buying deerskins that belonged to regularly licensed traders caused disturbances between the regular traders and the Indians. Loftily they concluded their demands with requests that large supplies of guns and ammunition be sent each town and greatcoats be sent each beloved man. Privately their runner informed Wright of the report that English troops had landed at Pensacola and Mobile and that they had heard that the English intended to punish them for their misdeeds. The headmen, he said, wanted to know "if it was to be peace or war."

10 *Ibid.*, 73–74.

When early in May a Creek killed trader John Spencer on his way down from the Upper Towns with his leather, the headmen went through the motions of resolving to punish the murderer but allowed him to escape into the woods. The headmen hinted that they did not think the English would spoil the trading path for the death of one man.[11] The murder of trader Pierce at Okchai brought a similar response. Creeks waylaid traders on the path from Augusta to the Cherokees and robbed them of goods, rum, and leather, alleging that traders had stolen horses from them.

With Creeks strongly protesting the English right to occupy lands without their consent, a situation built up in which a clash seemed probable. The English intended to establish themselves in their newly-won French and Spanish territories without let or leave of the Creeks and had determined to clear the way for the expansion of Georgia. They further felt that the Creeks and other restive southern Indians must be disciplined and that old treaties must go. Yet with Pontiac's war in the north taxing every resource of the British North American army and with a drive on in England to end the expenses of the now terminating French war, a new war in the south must be avoided. In this situation the Crown ordered Captain John Stuart, newly appointed Superintendent of Indians in the Southern District, to call a conference of southern governors and southern Indians to meet in the fall.[12] This order reached the governors in early May. Wright now sought to reassure the Creeks by asking them in reply to their talks to hold fast to all past agreements until all differences could be settled in the fall. In July, to allay Indian distress over encroachments on their lands, he ordered his council not to certify any grants of land above Augusta or Buckhead Creek until further notice.[13] At the same time, to hold the Creeks in bargaining position, the council determined not to permit the Creeks to have large amounts of presents or goods until after the congress at Augusta. In England, Lord Shelburne was pre-

11 *S.C. Gazette*, June 24, 1763.
12 Stuart to Amherst, May 31, 1763, Amherst Papers, VIII.
13 Candler, *Ga. Col. Rec.*, IX, 77.

paring to issue a proclamation regulating Indian trade and prohibiting settlement west of the mountains.[14] To counter the influence of Pontiac's rebellion, repercussions of which had reached the
Creeks and Cherokees, Stuart dispatched messages to the headmen
of the southern Indian nations not to listen to the seductive words
of the northern tribes.

These moves were too late to prevent the Mortar from acting.
The great nativist, now convinced that the English traders among
the Chickasaws had caused the death of his brother, waylaid traders in the remote transmontane forests and killed two and distributed their goods among his people. Likewise in the Hillabees, far
up the Tallapoosa toward the Appalachian foothills, a trader was
killed and his goods seized. War was prevented only by the determination of the bulk of the Creeks to avoid it. To keep the out-
rages from spreading further, the Okfuskees halted an eighty-horse
pack train of traders' goods bound for the Chickasaws and Choctaws and hid the goods in their homes.[15] Cussita Captain Allick,
the best friend the English had among the Lower Creeks, hastened
down messages of friendship to Wright.[16]

The Mortar meanwhile had sent to dissident Cherokees to come
and share the goods he had taken from the murdered traders and
to inform them that when the French garrison left Fort Toulouse
all their ammunition would be given to the Creeks and Cherokees
to wage war against the English. But any possibility of a Creek-
Cherokee anti-English coalition collapsed when Emisteseguo, of
Little Tallassee, whose father had told him on his deathbed to hold
fast to the English, killed two Cherokees. Incensed, official Cherokees had captured a Creek who had murdered a white man and
turned him over to Carolina authorities. The Mortar, as yet unaware of these developments, while waiting for a Cherokee answer
to his message, threatened to cut off English traders bound for the
Choctaw country.[17]

[14] Shelburne to Stuart, Aug. 5, 1763, Gage Papers [hereinafter referred to as
G.P.], Vol. XI.
[15] S.C. Gazette, Sept. 21, 1763.
[16] Stuart to Amherst, Oct. 4, 1763, Amherst Papers, Vol. III.
[17] S.C. Gazette, Sept. 24, 1763.

The Creek young men, impressed by the Mortar's activism, broke into virulent unrest. With the English occupying Mobile and Pensacola, the French about to evacuate Fort Toulouse, and rumors that the Georgians would take more land, the young warriors talked resistance. In October, belligerent Creeks visiting the new British garrison at Pensacola menacingly showed their tomahawks to the soldiers on parade and came back to the Upper Towns demanding war. Following the Mortar's line, Creek war talks entered the Cherokee country.[18] In the Upper Towns even headmen ostensibly friendly to the English refused to accept Stuart's invitation to the Augusta meeting.

Finally, when the French had evacuated Fort Toulouse, the old Wolf of the Muccolossus, longtime staunch friend of the English, called a meeting of the Upper Towns headmen and won their approval of his going down to Pensacola to spy out the true situation. Two minor figures, Emisteseguo of Little Tallassee, who was neither a war captain nor a beloved man, and the second man of Tuckabatchee either volunteered or were appointed to go to Augusta without plenary powers.

Emisteseguo, ambitious and of high birth, during the next twenty years was to be the foremost friend of the English and eventually to succeed to the "kingship" of the Upper Towns. Evidently he had the confidence of the Mortar and for some time had been playing for more notice from the English by intimating that he could bring the Mortar around. At this time he must have been in his mid-forties, as he had been born since the French had built Fort Toulouse in 1716.[19] His attendance at the congress of Augusta was to help his rise to power. However, his influence with the Mortar did not prevent that belligerent from going off to the Cherokee country to push his anti-English alliance of Creeks and Cherokees and to observe the Augusta meeting from a near but safe vantage point.

The congress at Augusta, delayed by the unsuccessful attempt of the southern governors to have the meeting held nearer Charles-

18 *Ibid.*, Oct. 22.
19 Emisteseguo to Stuart, Apr. 10, 1764, G.P., Vol. XVIII.

town, convened early in November. Present were Governors
Fauquier of Virginia, Dobbs of North Carolina, Boone of South
Carolina, and Wright of Georgia, Indian superintendent John
Stuart, and six hundred Indians—Creeks, Choctaws, Chickasaws,
and Cherokees. Of the Indians about one hundred and fifty were
Creeks, equally divided between Upper and Lower. Emisteseguo
led the Upper Creeks; Youwilliewianne or Captain Allick of Cussita, White Cabin of Cussita, Tallichea of Okmulgee, now head
beloved man of the Lower Creeks,[20] Ishenpoaphe, and Togulki led
the Lower Creeks. The Upper Creeks were nervous because of the
recent murders perpetrated by the Mortar and were the principal
reason why the congress was held at Augusta instead of nearer
Charlestown; they had alleged fear of going farther toward Carolina, lest they like the Cherokee ambassadors to Carolina in 1759
be seized and held hostage for the good behavior of their countrymen. The Lower Creeks, arriving later, had been inveigled into the
meeting by George Galphin, who had been drafted for that service
by Governor Wright. Galphin had entertained the headmen at his
establishment at Silver Bluff on the Savannah River some miles
below Augusta and had put them in a more cheerful frame of mind
about the congress. In discussions preliminary to the opening of
formal meetings Wright and Stuart discovered that the Lower
Creeks were willing to make a land cession in return for forgiveness
of past offenses. In the formal conferences beginning November 3,
boundaries of the land cession to Georgia were determined and a
discussion was held on the topics of horse stealing by the whites
and Indians, the rum trade, the extra-legal trade in the woods, and
the punishment of trespassers on the Indian lands. The Indians
made clear their intention to seize the cattle and horses of trespassers and the goods of illegal traders. However, in the treaty
which was concluded the Indians agreed that complaints of illegal
trade and trespass would be made to colonial governors before
action was taken. They renewed the old provision which had been
in every treaty since the beginning of Creek-English relations, that
Indians who killed whites would in turn be killed by Indians in

[20] Stuart to Gage, Jan. 16, 1766, G.P., Vol. XLVII.

the presence of whites, while whites who killed Indians would be tried under colony law and punished in the presence of Indians. It was agreed that neither Indians nor whites should trespass upon the lands of the other. The treaty defined the boundary of the new cession as "extending up Savannah to Little River and back to the fork of Little River and from the fork of Little River to the ends of the south branch of Briar Creek and down that branch to the Lower Creek path to the main stream of Ogeechee River and down the mainstream of that river just below the path leading from Mount Pleasant and from there in a strait line cross to Santa Seville on the Altamaha river and from thence to the southward as far as Georgia extends or may be extended to remain to be regulated agreeable to former treaties and His Majesty's royal instructions." The boundaries of Spanish-ceded Florida were to be determined by future treaties.[21]

In Creek affairs this land cession was the most important aspect of the congress. It did away with the outmoded limitation of Georgia settlement to the heads of tidewater. The lands ceded were those most subject to trespass, and by ceding them the Creeks hoped to eliminate the recent causes of friction on that score. But it was the first great English bite into Creek territory since 1733. In the minds of suspicious and fearful Creeks it seemed to confirm the French prophecy of what the Creek fate would be after the English had conquered the French. Interestingly, the Upper Creeks at the congress did not set their marks to the cession. It was the work of Lower Creeks and seems to have been the idea of Captain Allick who may have been prevailed upon by George Galphin to see it as a way out of a demand for satisfaction for past murders.

The Lower Creek representation and the speech-making at the congress demonstrate the great decline in Coweta's power. Tallichea, headman of Okmulgee, appeared as "the first beloved man of the nation"; Captain Allick of Cussita was a prominent speaker; Ishenpoaphe of Coweta said little; and Togulki, the heir of Malatchi, confessing youth and weakness, publicly resigned the commission as "Emperor" which Georgia governors had given him. The

[21] McDowell, *S.C. B.P.R.O. Records,* XXX, 108–12.

old Coweta "regal" line of Emperor Brims had finally dissipated. The war town of Cussita became from this time forward the most influential town of the Lower Creeks. This change was primarily due to the fact that since the hereditary "kings" of the Lower Creeks were very young men, the elder patriarchal voices had taken over.

Emisteseguo, the Upper Creek deputy, did not speak at the formal meetings, nor did he set his mark to the treaty. Alden, the historian of Stuart's superintendency, does not think he attended. But he is on record as attending under the name "Mistisequa,"[22] and his own statements in "Talk of Emisteseguo," July 15, 1764, Gage Papers, Vol. XXVII, make such references as, "when he was at Augusta . . . he was told at the Congress . . . ." He apparently had several private conferences with Stuart in which he accepted promises of rum and ammunition for the Upper Creek headmen and for himself made promises to report the congress to the Mortar and other headmen.[23] At the congress he demonstrated himself to be a discreet agent of the headmen who had sent him and was accepted on his return to the nation as an authority on relations with the English. He is an instance of hereditary ascendance to power, for his father had been a headman of some importance who had held a commission from South Carolina.[24]

As the Congress of Augusta was assembled, the Wolf of the Muccolossus visited Pensacola and Mobile. At Pensacola, without knowledge of what the Lower Creeks intended at Augusta with reference to boundaries, he told Major Forbes the English could have only the land upon which the fort was situated and threatened war if the English attempted to settle inland from Florida.[25] At Mobile he warned Major Farmer not to occupy Fort Toulouse until the Indians living near it had been consulted.[26] In these statements he only reflected what he knew to be Upper Towns sentiment. Though truculent and demanding, he was soothed by presents and departed in a good mood. For the moment, Major Farmer decided

---

[22] Stuart to Boone, Oct. 15, 1763, McDowell, *S.C. B.P.R.O. Records*, XXX, 33–34.

[23] Candler, *Ga. Col. Rec.*, XXVIII, Pt. 2-A, pp. 72, 73, 86, 87.

[24] Emisteseguo, June 26, 1767, G.P., Vol. CXXXVII.

[25] Rowland, *Miss. Provincial Archives*, 142–43.

Hopothle Mico. Probably Opeitly Mico of Tallassee. From a 1790
sketch now in the Fordham University Library.

Long Warrior. Pro-British "King of the Seminoles."

to use Fort Toulouse merely as a depot for traders and instructed James Germany, trader at Fushatchee on the Tallapoosa, to move in. The Alabamas, however, had decided to use the fort as a residence and took over.[27]

Though the Lower Creeks regarded the new treaty of Augusta, November 10, 1763, as establishing relations with the English on a firm footing, confusion of councils prevailed in the Upper Towns, where repercussions of the fierce Indian war in the north agitated the headmen. Since the Cherokees had rejected northern overtures and, at English behest, had actually undertaken war against the northerners, Creeks talked of war against the Cherokees, whom the Mortar still labored to win over to renewed war against the English. Yet Upper Creeks clearly recognized that with the departure of the French, their base for war against the English had been removed. The Upper Creeks helplessly deferred decision until after the winter hunts.

In December a situation arose in which it appeared their hand might be forced. On December 24, seven Creeks who lived among the Lower Cherokees murdered fourteen whites in the Long Canes area. An unprovoked assault, it seemed aimed at undoing the Congress of Augusta. Settlers fled the frontier and traders, unnerved by constant rumor and counter rumor, deserted their stores and ran for Pensacola. In Charlestown and Savannah, reports that the Mortar had been giving bad talks in the Cherokee towns and that in Cherokee Toogaloo other Creek headmen had been urging joint attack on the frontier made war seem imminent.[28]

But far from inspiring war spirit in the Lower Towns, the Long Canes incident brought dismay. There was fear the trade would be interrupted. On news of the incident Togulki disavowed official responsibility. He identified the murderers as ex-patriates who had lived long in the Cherokee country with Cherokee wives. He blamed Seroweh, the Young warrior of Cherokee Estatoe, for inspiring the act and said that Seroweh should be required to put the guilty

[26] *Ibid.*, 12.
[27] *Ibid.*, 18.
[28] Prevost to Gage, Apr. 5, 1764, G.P., Vol. XVI; Stuart to Gage, May 20, 1764, G.P., Vol. XVIII.

Creeks to death.[29] The Cussita White King dispatched a message expressing distress that two of his sons had been involved and stated that he had taken all the Lower Towns traders under his protection.[30] Even in the Upper Towns voices decried the murders. The Wolf of the Muccolossus informed Wright that no Upper Townsmen had been involved, that it was primarily a matter for the Lower Creeks to handle.[31] From the Abeikas the Gun Merchant sent Handsome Fellow and the Okfuskee Captain to Augusta to assure the English of friendship and to ask that there be no embargo on the trade: "We are in great want of goods and desire that we may have our old traders back among us."[32]

While responsible Creeks endeavored to stave off embargo and war, the suave Cherokee, Seroweh of Estatoe, disavowing all complicity, suggested to Prevost, British commander at Charlestown, that the Creek nation ought to be chastised as the Cherokees had been for their repeated murders of whites. He remembered bitterly that Creeks had egged him into the disastrous war with the English and then had failed to come to his aid.[33]

But war was as far from the official English mind as it was from the official Creek. Wright and Stuart under orders from Gage to abstain from a southern Indian war,[34] sought only by peaceful means to obtain satisfaction by the death of those Creeks guilty of murder. For fear of provoking a war they even eschewed a trade embargo.[35] But with the recent Creek history of non-compliance with any demand to put guilty Creeks to death and the pervasive bitterness among the Creeks against frontier settlers, satisfaction by diplomacy was to prove a protracted and next to impossible business. Aware of a fundamental sympathy with their acts, the offending Creeks had come into the Lower Towns with scalps to boast. Two of them were sons of the White King of Cussita. Headmen deplored and responsible persons frowned, but the murderers

29 Togulki to Stuart in Stuart to Gage, Jan. 16, 1764, G.P., Vol. XII.
30 Stuart to Gage, Apr. 11, 1764, G.P., Vol. XVII.
31 Candler, *Ga. Col. Rec.*, IX, 148.
32 Prevost to Gage, Apr. 9, 1764, G.P., XVI.
33 *Ibid.*, Apr. 5.
34 Gage to Stuart, May 1, 1764, G.P., XVIII.
35 Stuart to Gage, Apr. 11, 1764, G.P., Vol. XVII.

were allowed to escape into the woods.[36] English armies did not come, and, though Stuart sought to pressure the nation by threat of a Choctaw war, the traders returned to the towns. To the Creeks the practices of official obsequiousness, delay, and evasion seemed once again justified.

With the winter crisis apparently evaded, the Upper Creeks turned in the spring to considering the treaty of Augusta. On April 10, 1764, a meeting of Upper Creeks at Little Tallassee on the Coosa River signalized the new importance of Emisteseguo as a man who had talked business with Stuart and Wright and had received messages from them. It was he who summarized the consensus of the meeting in a message to Governor Wright. In essence, while it belittled the Lower Creeks for ceding territory, it ratified the treaty. The test, it said, would be whether for four years the English settlers could keep their slaves and cattle from wandering across the new boundary line. It agreed that the Upper Creeks would surrender horses stolen from the whites in return for white delivery of horses stolen from the Indians. It blamed the Long Canes murders on the Lower Towns but promised, as so frequently in the past, to prevent such episodes in the future. Finally it advised that Fort Toulouse, which had become an Indian town, should not be garrisoned and that the English never in the future should build a fort in the Creek nation.

To supplement the increasingly influential Emisteseguo's talk, the Gun Merchant, as befitted the head beloved man of the Abeikas, sent a talk of his own to Stuart at Pensacola, where he was soon expected. He spoke of the historic trade and friendship of the Abeikas and the English, of his many past visits to the colonial capitals. He noted that times had changed from those days and that the English now surrounded the Creeks and insisted that there should not be English encroachment on Creek lands, and that the settlements at Pensacola and Mobile should be limited to the lands that the French and Spaniards had actually used. Mindful of rumors that Stuart sought to spirit up the Choctaws against his people, he quietly mentioned that the Creeks had peace ambassa-

[36] John Mullins in Stuart to Gage, Apr. 11, 1764, G.P., Vol. XVII.

dors among the Choctaws. He suggested that better relations between the traders and the Indians could be had if the traders and their help would be less free with the Indian women. And he not too subtly intimated that the communications of Wright and Stuart ought to be addressed to him and not to the upstart Emisteseguo.[37]

In the background sat his brother-in-law, the Mortar, now returned after having been rebuffed by the Cherokees. Recognizing that he could not force a break with the English, the Mortar confined himself to insisting that the Creeks take a strong line against further English encroachments.

Although Emisteseguo's rise turned on Stuart's recognition, it also depended on the good will of the Mortar and the Gun Merchant. In July, receiving a letter from Stuart indicating the peaceful disposition of the English, Emisteseguo called a meeting of minor headmen and composed a reply in which he pointed out that he was not a "captain or a beloved man" and spoke for the nation only as a "kind warrior." He intimated his usefulness by stating that though some of the headmen were hostile to the English, he was friendly. Then he presented a case for the Mortar who, he said, now stood for peace. He took it upon himself to say that an English trade from Mobile to Pensacola would be welcome, but reflecting nativist sentiment, he announced that settlement in the two areas should not extend beyond the posts themselves. He decried English efforts arising from the Pontiac rebellion in the north, to set Indian upon Indian, and protested the rumored English plan to build a fort among the Chickasaws.[38]

The Mortar, whom Stuart was also cultivating, and the Gun Merchant, jealous of Emisteseguo's growing authority and disapproving of the idea of an English trade from Pensacola and Mobile, called a meeting at Little Tallassee in which they framed a talk supplementing and amending Emisteseguo's. They rejected Emisteseguo's enthusiasm for trade from Mobile and Pensacola, the development and expansion of which they opposed. While asserting his disposition to peace, the Mortar uttered his fears that

[37] Stuart to Gage, May 20, 1764, G.P., Vol. XVI.
[38] Emisteseguo to Stuart, July 15, 1764, G.P., Vol. XXVIII.

the English intended to seal off the Gulf coast from the Upper Creeks. Any attempt, he said, to enlarge the Mobile area by settlements across Alabama River would result in the death of the settlers. He was emphatic that English trade be limited to the Augusta route. Belittling Emisteseguo, he desired the English to listen to no talks from minor figures. The Gun Merchant seconded the talk, and Emisteseguo, rebuked, diplomatically chimed in with praise of the Mortar.[39]

The Gun Merchant, seeking to undercut the English-Choctaw *rapprochement*, added a few words of his own in which he warned that the Choctaws were not as heartily in the English interest as Stuart supposed, that, indeed, undercover talk had Choctaws conspiring with young Creeks to the disadvantage of the English.[40]

These talks sped toward Pensacola; the Mortar made an overture to Wright at Savannah. He sent Handsome Fellow to Augusta with a white wing, a string of white beads, and a talk in which he acknowledged past errors, asked forgiveness, and demanded that the trading path to Augusta and no other be kept white and clean. Wright responded with a promise to keep the path open if the Creeks behaved.[41]

Stuart had not yet arrived at Pensacola. Major Farmer reacted to the Mortar's talk by inviting the headmen to come down and advising them that a trade from the south would be greatly to their advantage. He protested the limiting of settlement to Mobile but denied that the English came to take lands. However, they were, he said, entitled to every bit as much land as the French and Spaniards had held and would be glad to purchase any more the Creeks would sell. He scoffed at the idea of Choctaw discontent, saying that the English used them much better than the French had.[42]

Meanwhile at St. Augustine in early July, Stuart was reaching for the Creeks from the southeast in order to try the pulse of the nation. Seventy miles northwest of St. Augustine at a town called

---

[39] Mortar, etc., to Stuart, July 22, 1764, in Stuart to Gage, Nov. 30, 1764, G.P., Vol. XXVIII.

[40] *Ibid.*

[41] Wright to Gage, Aug. 28, 1764, G.P., Vol. XXIII.

[42] Farmer to Gage, Aug. 18, 1764, G.P., Vol. XXVIII.

Latchaway, lived the nucleus of the future Seminoles or outlaw Creeks. Their headmen were Ahaye, or the Cowkeeper, and Weoffki or the Long Warrior, who in 1760 had acted independently of Lower Creek councils in going to war against the Cherokees. Stuart invited them down, and, flattered by such importance, they came to express pleasure that the English had superseded the Spaniards with whom they had warred at St. Augustine. But being outside the main stream of Creek affairs, since they were over two hundred miles from the Lower Creeks, they could report little but gossip that certain Creeks conspired with the Choctaws against the English.[43]

Arriving in Pensacola in September, Stuart met chiefs of the semi-Creek Apalachee towns from below the forks of the Chattahoochee. These chiefs expressed fear of the English land hunger, but after learning from Stuart of the October 1763 Crown proclamation forbidding further invasion of the Indian lands and ignoring or having no knowledge of the strict limitations on land occupancy held by the Abeikas, they confirmed the English in the lands the Spaniards had formerly held.

Nor were the Tallapooses as rigid in their attitude toward land cessions and trade routes as the Gun Merchant and the Mortar. Indeed they seemed to welcome the opportunity of breaking the Carolina and Georgia monopolies. Early in September, three hundred Tallapooses under the leadership of the Wolf of Fushatchee (probably the Wolf of Muccolossus) came to Pensacola just before Stuart's arrival. In conference with Captain McKinnon, the commander of the post but who had no authority to treat, in total disregard of the Apalachee claims, they granted the English a strip of land ten miles in depth extending from Pensacola to Mobile Bay.[44] Stuart repudiated the treaty on his arrival and sent up to the Abeikas for the Mortar and Emisteseguo to come down and renegotiate it in March.[45] He sent for the Lower Creeks also to be

---

[43] Stuart to Gage, July 19, 1764, G.P., Vol. XXI; Ogilvie to Gage, July 20, 1764, G.P., Vol. XXII.

[44] McKinnon to Gage, Sept. 20, 1764, G.P., Vol. XXIV.

[45] Stuart to Emisteseguo, Nov. 19, 1764, G.P., Vol. XXVIII.

present at the conference, and envisioned a whole nation's approval of a more extensive cession.[46]

The Tallapoose cession had upset the Mortar. The Mortar had never closed his ears to the French, and, encouraged by the British-employed French interpreter, Louis Surnam, to believe that French aid might be available through New Orleans, he went to the Cherokee country to agitate against the English, who, he said, were surrounding the Indians. For a time he had a sympathetic listener in Oconostota, the Cherokee Great Warrior, who remembered French support in his war against Carolina. But Oconostota could not stand up against Attakullakulla, the great proponent of peace with the English, and the Mortar's mission failed. Leaving the Cherokees with a promise to return for another try the next August, he returned to the Okchai.[47]

As the new conference approached, Stuart, unaware of the Mortar's activities, employed Monberaut, former French commander of Fort Toulouse who now lived at Mobile, as a special agent to urge the Mortar to attend. The Mortar felt guilty apprehensions for his own safety and did not want to come. Furthermore his suspicions of the sinister intentions of Stuart had been augmented by the whisperings of Carolina and Georgia traders who feared the development of trade from Pensacola and Mobile would ruin their Charlestown and Savannah based operations. Monberaut sent his son to the Mortar and in the name of their old association finally prevailed upon him to change his mind.

The Congress of Pensacola, May 12–28, 1765, assembled five hundred Creeks led by the Mortar, Emisteseguo, the Wolf of the Muccolossus, and Duvall's Landlord for the Upper Creeks and by Captain Allick and White Cabin of Cussita, and Escochabey of Coweta for the Lower Creeks to meet Stuart and Governor Johnstone of West Florida. Convinced by Monberaut that he could expect no help from the French, and charmed by Stuart's flattery and intimation of lower trade prices if the crown approved, the Mortar dropped his opposition to the Wolf's land cession. On May 28 in

---

[46] *Ibid.*
[47] Cochrane to Gage, Apr. 26, 1764; Apr. 26, June 3, 1765; G.P., Vol. XXXVII.

a treaty signed by thirty headmen, including the Mortar, the nation ceded all lands granted by the Wolf in September and somewhat more, creating a continuous boundary about ten miles inland from Pensacola to Mobile. The Indians agreed to the death of all Creeks who murdered white men, and the English agreed to maintain a trade from Pensacola and Mobile with a schedule of set prices, presumably lower than Carolina and Georgia prices.[48]

The winning of the Mortar, though due in part to Monberaut's firmness and address, displays Stuart's Indian diplomacy in its most artful aspects. Much impressed by the inveterate, who he perceived to be "a sensible manly Indian—actuated in his opposition—more by principles of love of his country and jealousy on account of their lands than by love of the French who he adhered to for purposes of his own," Stuart set out to conquer him with blandishments, presents, sedulous attention, and promises of recognizing him as a power in the nation. It was too much for the Mortar, who had a long history of disappointments. The dominant headmen in his nation had been against him for a decade; the Cherokees were unwilling now to follow his lead; his former French ally, Monberaut, sided with the English; and, finally, the Choctaws, from whom he had sought help in his anti-Europeanism, had succombed to the new masters of the southeast. Recognizing that his people were abjectly dependent upon the English from whom he expected at least lower trade prices, the great nativist fell into line. He accepted designation as one of the four English Great Medal Chiefs of the Creek nation.

Stuart gives a vivid picture of his seduction: "The first time he visited me, I received him with the French commissions, medals, and gorgets given up by the Choctaws strewed under my feet and chair; they soon attracted his attention; he seemed struck at the sight and formed conceptions of our influence with that nation superior to any I could otherwise have conveyed to him which contributed greatly to facilitate our negotiations. I was minute in explaining the privileges and power conferred upon medal chiefs which seemed extremely agreeable to him, and altho I could per-

48 Rowland, *Miss. Provincial Archives*, 211–24.

ceive that he had a strong inclination for a great medal, yet I allowed myself to be solicited many days before I consented to confer one upon him. He was with four other chiefs (Emisteseguo, Duvall's Landlord and the Gun Merchant)[49] and as many small medals, installed with great parade on the King's birthday at the instant that the great guns and musquetry were firing to solemnize that anniversary."[50]

The Mortar also accepted Stuart's plan for a British commissary or deputy Indian agent to serve in the Upper Creek country: "He was at first startled at the proposal of sending a commissary into the nation, as a novelty which might affect their independency. But when I explained to him privately and shewed him the mutual dependence and connection between that officer and the medal chiefs he was charmed with it and pitched upon a particular person who is to be in that character."[51]

The establishment of medal chiefs and commissary was theoretically to set up a new order among the Creeks, a chain of influence from Stuart through to the nation in a tightening of government. Though it led to the ascendancy of Emisteseguo and eventually much more firmly to the "kingship" of the half-blood, Alexander McGillivray, actually because of traditional Creek institutions of local autonomy in the squares, the system brought about no such immediate centralization as was envisioned. The medal chiefs, except for Emisteseguo, were Creeks first and went their ways in Creek outlooks and interests, and gave to the British only sparingly and reluctantly.

The elevation of Emisteseguo to a great medalship was his making. The other great medal chiefs were old men and he was relatively young. He probably would not have gone far in national councils but for the confidence of the British, but he outlived the other great medals and eventually became the most important man in the nation. Increasingly from this time forward his home town of Little Tallassee became a major center of influence.

---

[49] Perhaps the Wolf of the Muccolossus was the unmentioned fourth medal chief.
[50] Stuart to Gage, Aug. 6, 1765, G.P., Vol. XL.
[51] *Ibid.*

The Mortar was a disappointment as a medal chief. Opportunistic in accepting the office, he, as Stuart had perceived, was a nativist at heart. Late in July, Cherokees came to him at Okchai to tell him he had been right all along: in Carolina settlers trespassed over Cherokee boundaries, and in Virginia whites had killed Cherokees. The Mortar accused Stuart of double dealing in talking of inviolable boundaries and the white man's intention of fair dealing with the Indians. He set off for the Cherokee country with a band of one hundred young men to stoke up the smouldering fires of resentment toward the English.[52]

At Pensacola, Stuart had invited the Lower Towns headmen to meet him at St. Augustine in the fall in order to fix the boundaries of East Florida. Accordingly, on November 15, 1765, thirty-one Lower Towns headmen arrived at Picolata, on the St. Johns River a few miles west of St. Augustine. They were led by Tallachea of Okmulgee, who as white chief of the white towns was now the principal beloved man of the Lower Creeks. Others present were Captain Allick of Cussita, Ishenpoaphe and Estime of Coweta, and Weoffki, the Long Warrior of Latchaway. Absent were Escochabey, the Young Lieutenant of Coweta, who, alleging the sickness of his wife, remained away in opposition to any land cession, and Togulki, who then sank from sight for a few years.

The conference opened with an unctuous greeting by Stuart, which was immediately followed by Ishenpoaphe's presentation of the Young Lieutenant's excuses for his absence. They were that English settlers had passed the line set at the treaty of Augusta in 1763 and that Stuart had failed to lower the trade prices as he had promised at Pensacola. His message ran: "The rates were too high and that if all the country were settled up to their towns they would find nothing but rats and rabbits to kill for their skins for which the white people would not give them goods, that deer are turning very scarce and that white people sold goods very dear." Stuart, on the defensive, replied that it was not in his power to force the traders to lower prices, and sophistically, as it seems, said that he had never promised to do it. Thus rebuffed in an opening gambit

[52] Stuart to Gage, Aug. 30, 1765, G.P., Vol. XL.

designed to obtain trade concessions, the Indians, through their mouthpiece Tallachea, stated that they could cede but little land and that they would kill settlers or cattle straying beyond the new boundary line. When Stuart indicated his dislike of the limited cession and the threatening tone, Captain Allick seconded Tallachea and then indicated that Stuart could have more land by lowering the trade prices. Stuart became angry, for he wanted more land, and regardless of the impression he had given at Pensacola, he was powerless to lower trade prices. He determined to pressure the Indians. Neglecting to invite the headmen to the customary formal dinner of welcome, he abruptly adjourned the meeting. That night he privately sent word to Tallachea and Captain Allick that unless they enlarged their land grant, there would be no presents and very likely a great deal of unpleasantness with settlers in the disputed area. He instructed the veteran interpreter, Stephen Forster, to show the headmen a map on which he had marked the boundary he wished. Thus frowned on and shown what they must do, the Indians spent a day in earnest discussion, and weakly, for the sake of a few presents, decided to yield. In a reconvened meeting on November 17 they agreed on Stuart's line. Westward it ran considerably back from the head of the tides, and it extended from the mouth of Latchoway Creek (Ochlawaha River) in the St. Johns on the south to the mouth of Turkey Creek in the Altamaha on the north, adding two million acres to His Majesty's territories in Georgia and Florida. The treaty as finally concluded gave assurances that settlers' cattle which transgressed the line would not be molested, and the usual provision that whites who killed Indians and Indians who killed whites would be punished by their respective peoples.

In a showy ceremony, Stuart installed Tallechea, Captain Allick, and Estime as great medal chiefs, and Ishenpoaphe, Weoffki, Lachige, and Clayhage as small medal chiefs. To Ahaye, the Cowkeeper of Latchoway, Stuart sent a great medal. Captain Allick's elevation was a signal honor, the product of years of unswerving loyalty to the English.[53]

[53] *Ibid.*, Jan. 21, Vol. XLVII.

In the two years since the expulsion of the French, the Creeks, encircled by the English, had surrendered several million acres of territory. The Lower Creeks, bankrupt in leadership, were the prime losers. With the decline of the great Brims line they had no rugged nativists to oppose the tide of English settlement. Hungry for trade and without the Spanish and French threats with which to bludgeon the English, the spineless Tallachea and subservient Allick were unable even to make advantageous bargains. Conscious of being in a losing position and fearful of outright war with the English power, henceforth the Creeks could only vent their spite in vicious little frontier incidents.

15

Troubled Frontiers
1765-68

M AKING TREATIES was easy and pleasant for the Creeks. They
enjoyed English attention, the ceremony, the glib oratory,
the bargaining, the rum drinking, and, above all, the presents.
Implementing treaties was something else, particularly in a situation where patriarchs and headmen had become weak and the
young men had grown bold in the knowledge that the English
lacked the will and power to enforce sanctions. Unrest with the
British encirclement and the British-inspired Choctaw war smoul-
dered, and the advancing frontier threatened. Undercover intrigue
with the Spaniards in Cuba flourished, fomented by discredited and
rancorous Coweta. The situation invited incidents which the headmen could neither prevent nor punish. Stuart and Wright could
only try amelioration, negotiation and hope.

In October, 1765, while the Picolata conference assembled,
Ishenpoaphe's son with a party of Creeks murdered three white
hunters, the Pyne brothers and one Hogg, whom they caught trespassing in the Creek hunting grounds above the Little River. Conscious of the justness of their act, the murderers came boldly into

Coweta to boast and exhibit scalps and plunder. A posse of frontier whites pursued them into the town and seized them, but their kinsmen rallied and freed them without injury to the whites, who hastily retired to the Carolina frontier. The headmen, once again faced by treaty obligations but powerless before inflamed sentiment and clan loyalties to take the murderers' lives, banished the offenders, who fled into the woods. Escochabey followed them and informed the commanders of the British frontier garrisons of their whereabouts, but they were not taken.

The first test of the medal chiefs was at hand. Wright, consulting Stuart, sent messages to the Upper and Lower Towns demanding the lives of the murderers and calling attention to the fact that the English had honored their treaties by executing three runaway Negroes who had murdered a Creek on the Saltilla River. The time was not auspicious. In the Upper Towns, most of the headmen were absent on their winter hunts. The Mortar, discontented that his demands for lower trade prices had not been met either at Pensacola or Picolata, had roused his following with angry talk. The arrival in March of Stuart and Wright's demands created an uproar. The murderers' fellow clansmen would not tolerate punishment, and they disregarded the admonitions of the headmen concerning robberies and murders. The Wolf of the Muccolossus looked on in dismay. His message to Stuart and Wright in April disgustedly stated "there is nothing but deceit and lies in the red people for many years past."[1] He recommended that the English discipline the nation by stopping the trade for two years.

The situation was further complicated by Creek suspicions that the English had roused the Choctaws against them. This in fact had occurred. Ostensibly Choctaw attacks upon the Creeks arose from a sequence of killings and counter-killings which had begun well before the conference at Pensacola, which had been preceded by Stuart's peace with the Choctaws. The English had muffled these only to decide early in 1766 that a Choctaw attack on the Creeks might be useful in curbing the renewed anti-English feeling generated by the Mortar. When on March 15 Creeks near English-

[1] Candler, *Ga. Col. Rec.*, XXXIII, 157–58.

occupied Fort Tombigbe killed a Choctaw, the English trader Colbert arrived in the Choctaw nation to stir the Choctaws to reprisal, presumably acting on orders of Charles Stuart, brother of John and commissary to the Choctaws. Late in April near Pensacola, Choctaws attacked a party of Creeks while the Wolf King's brother, Old Warrior, visited the English garrison. Drunken Choctaws leaked the word that the English had set them on. The Old Warrior confronted Charles Stuart, then at Pensacola, who denied complicity, and lavished presents upon him and sent him off toward the Tallapoosa apparently satisfied. Yet the story persisted, and on the Pensacola path, Creeks killed an English trader.[2]

The Mortar, who had been at Coosawaitees sending talks into the Cherokees to rouse them to take vengeance for the murders of Indians in Virginia, returned to Little Tallassee in May just as the story of English double dealing permeated the towns.[3] He sent an indignant message to Governor Johnstone at Pensacola resigning his great medal, accusing the English, and demanding lower trade prices. Old Neahlatchko, Second Man of Little Tallassee, hoping the situation could be smoothed over, persuaded the Mortar to take back his resignation, but the Mortar persisted in his demand for lower trade prices.[4] Emisteseguo, conscious that the murder of the trader would call for reprisal which could not be tolerated, sent down to Johnstone a request that since in the attack on the trader two Creeks had been killed the matter be considered closed. As for the satisfaction for the Pynes and Hogg murders, the Upper Creeks left these to Lower Towns decision.

In the Lower Towns, Wright and Stuart's demands met evasion. Tallachea, Ishenpoaphe, and Escochabey replied that because the murderers were not in the towns, no action could be taken. They even suggested that since the guilty had gone to avenge alleged murders of whites by northern Indians in the country between the Creeks and the Cherokees, the episode be forgotten. Ishenpoaphe protested English trespasses beyond the line set at Picolata and

---

[2] Charles Stuart to John Stuart, May 17, 1766, G.P., Vol. LV; Emisteseguo to Johnstone, May, 1766, *Miss. Provincial Archives*, 528–29.

[3] Phillips to Gage, June 14, 1766, G.P., Vol. LII.

[4] Rowland, *Miss. Provincial Archives*, 529–30.

said that cattle of such trespassers would be killed.[5] Wright, lacking news of any such murders as Tallachea and the others described and knowing of no trespasses, rejected the talk. There the matter rested.

Now English counsel as to the course of action was divided. At Pensacola, Governor Johnstone and Colonel Taylor, the commander of the garrison, confronted by stories of the Mortar's activities, Creek unrest, the murder of the trader, and Creek failures to give satisfaction for any murders, became obsessed with the thought that the Creeks intended war. They urged Stuart and Gage to form a coalition of Choctaws, Chickasaws, Cherokees, and English to attack the Creeks. Preparing the way for this action, Colonel Taylor sent a stiff warning to the Upper Creeks that the murder of the trader had violated the treaty of Pensacola.[6]

Wright sought more pacific solutions. He was very much annoyed because the Royal Proclamation of October, 1763, had taken control of the Indian trade from the colonial governors. To the English authorities he alleged that Indian insolence arose from too many traders and an overstock of trade goods and that to remedy the situation control of the trade should be returned to the governors. Following the suggestion that trade abuses lay at the base of the Indian troubles, the Crown authorized Stuart to remedy trade conditions.

When General Gage frowned on Johnstone and Taylor's aggressiveness, it became clear that English force would not be used against the Creeks. The Creeks, however, were unaware of this and stirred themselves into a crisis that soon forced them into less belligerent attitudes. Rumors of impending English attack fired an intensity of anti-English sentiment which in September resulted in the murder of two English traders by a Creek head warrior on the Choctaw path. These were the fifth and sixth murders of Englishmen within a year and were so flagrant that the peace-minded of the Upper Towns headmen could see no way to condone them. Rumored war was on the verge of becoming horrid fact. At this

[5] Candler, *Ga. Col. Rec.*, XXXVII, Pt. 1, pp. 159–61.
[6] Rowland, *Miss. Provincial Archives*, 518–19.

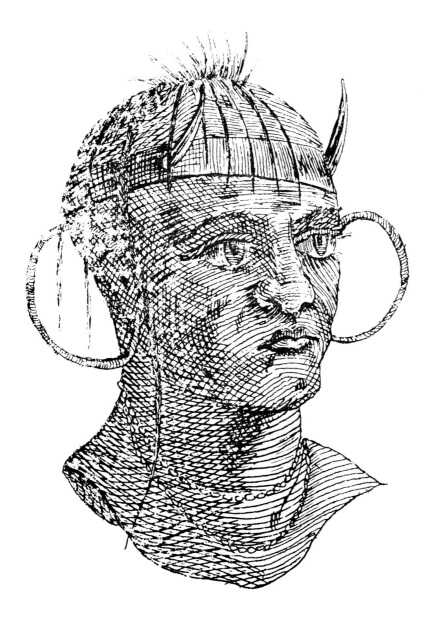

Characteristic head of a Creek war chief

Courtesy of Smithsonian Office of Anthropology, B.A.E. Collection

Pictograph made by a Creek war party,
c. 1775

very moment Major Field of the Pensacola garrison arrived on the Tallapoosa with a stern warning from Johnstone and Taylor, who had not yet heard of Gage's disapproval of their program, that unless the Creeks gave satisfaction for all the recent murders, the English would supply the Choctaws with arms and cut off the Creek trade. The warning had a powerful effect. Emisteseguo summoned the headmen of fourteen Tallapoosa towns and two Lower Towns into a secret night conclave and decided on the assassination of the head warrior who had killed the Choctaw traders. They sent orders to Otaseky, the old head warrior of the town of White Ground, a relative of the murderer, to dispose of him at once and show his dead body to an Englishman. Otaseky carried out the orders. The body was displayed and the dead man's relatives were publicly forbidden to bury it. This was the first time in thirteen years that any Creek had been put to death for the murder of Englishmen. Emisteseguo sent the news to Johnstone and begged that the trade be not stopped.[7] The Choctaw war flared into sudden intensity.

Emisteseguo decided to go down to Pensacola to treat in person with Johnstone and Taylor. With the Creek disposition to peace apparent after such a resolute satisfaction given, the talks took place in a cordial atmosphere. When Emisteseguo departed with assurances there would be no trade embargo, he left behind in the council room a strong token of peace, "a wing—so perfectly white that there was not the least shade on any of its feathers."[8] Delighted in their success and perceiving that in the Choctaws they had a strong weapon, Taylor and Johnstone continued to stoke the Choctaw war fire in order to remind the Creeks of their dependence upon the English for goods and ammunition.

Stuart had now been empowered by the Crown to make a regulation of the trade. Assured of the peaceable disposition of the Creeks, early in 1767 he sent Roderick McIntosh to act as commissary in the nation with powers to adjust trade matters and supply the headmen with standard weights and measures by which they

[7] Phillips to Gage, Nov. 27, 1766, G.P., Vol. LIX.

[8] Taylor to Gage, Nov. 30, 1766, G.P., Vol. LX.

could check on the traders. He also was to invite the headmen to meet Stuart at Augusta in May to concert a new regulation of the trade and set a new scale of prices. From Tallachea at Ocmulgee, McIntosh accepted in good faith a promise of giving satisfaction at a later date for the Pynes and Hogg murders. To Ishenpoaphe at Coweta McIntosh asserted that there had been no boundary violations and that if any should occur, he must inform the commissary, who would take proper steps. With McIntosh, Wright sent a message that he had dispatched rangers to march along the boundary in search of violators and that they had found none. They had, however, found a newly-established Creek village near the line, which Wright urged Ishenpoaphe to remove before it caused trouble arising from Indian or white drunkenness.[9]

McIntosh delivered messages to Emisteseguo and the Mortar asserting that the English had not broken the treaty of Pensacola in the matter of trade and that no violations of the boundaries set at Pensacola and Picolata had occurred. For the Mortar's benefit Stuart recalled how the two together had held eagles' tails at Pensacola, and that while he recommended that the Creeks and Choctaws make peace, it was not the business of the English to interfere in their quarrel. On the subject of past murders, McIntosh produced a string of white beads ending in seven black ones, symbolic of Englishmen killed by Creeks in recent months, and told the headmen that when satisfaction was given for each murder, the black beads would be removed and thrown into the river.[10]

When on March 13 at the Chehaws, McIntosh presented Ishenpoaphe with a pipe sent up by Wright and a demand that the murderers of the Pynes and Hogg be killed, Ishenpoaphe was dismayed. His own son was one of the murderers. Returning the pipe to McIntosh, he declared he would die in place of his son. However, he did not die, and the matter continued to be troublesome.

On April 20, McIntosh talked to the Upper Creek headmen assembled in Emisteseguo's square at Little Tallassee. They approved of much of the talk and agreed to send deputies to the

[9] Candler, *Ga. Col. Rec.*, XXXVII, Pt. 1-A, pp. 171–73.
[10] Stuart to Upper and Lower Creeks, Dec. 17, 1766, G.P., Vol. LX.

meeting at Augusta. Confronted by the black beads, they remonstrated that they had already atoned for their own misdeeds and declared that satisfaction for the Pynes and Hogg murders was a Lower Towns affair: "We wash'd our spot white," they said, "and as we look upon the Lower Creeks to be a different nation from us we cannot intermeddle with them."

After McIntosh's departure the Lower Towns debated their course of action. Division cut deep. A substantial number of headmen believed that the Cussitas, as chief warriors in the nation, should be commanded to put the guilty to death, but the murderer's kinsmen asserted that if the Cussitas acted they would kill all the traders in the Lower Towns. Unable to give the demanded satisfaction, the Lower Towns headmen decided that they could not go to the Augusta meeting.

A new complication suddenly developed in the Upper Towns. An Abeika murdered a packhorseman, one Thomas, at the Hillabees. Emisteseguo, fearing all his good work for harmony with the English would be undone, went himself to the Hillabees to demand the death of the murderer. The man had fled. Emisteseguo then took up the matter with old Otaseky of White Ground, who had engineered the assassination of the murderer of the Choctaw traders in the fall. Otaseky sent his best runner to pursue and kill the guilty man. Emisteseguo then sent Tupulga, a little medal chief who had protected Atkin in 1759, down to Stuart to inform him he could not come to the Augusta meeting until he was sure that satisfaction had been given for the Thomas murder. The Mortar, who had set out for the Augusta meeting to which he looked forward in hopes of obtaining the reduction of trade prices he had so long demanded, hearing on the path of the Thomas murder, turned back to see that satisfaction was given.

Stuart, determined to go ahead with his meeting, sent for the headmen regardless. On May 28, 1767, the Indians, mostly Lower Townsmen, had assembled at Augusta. The principal headmen present were Captain Allick of Cussita, Salleche, headman of the Eusitchees, and Mad Dog of the Eutassies. Stuart, having obtained the traders' agreement to a lower price scale in return for his promise to limit the number of traders, thus restoring the monopoly of the old line traders, addressed the meeting to the effect that it had been called to establish the abatement of prices asked by the Mortar at Pensacola. He had George Galphin read the new schedule of prices which was greeted with great satisfaction. Then Stuart took up the matter of a specific marking of the boundary line. He asked the headmen to set a date when their representatives could go with English representatives to do this. He promised that when the line was marked, all transgressors would be removed or punished. He then urged them to keep their promises of killing murderers and presented them with a string of white beads ending in three black representing the dead Pynes and Hogg. "When you do justice," he said "we will remove the three black beads and throw them into the river." He also demanded the return of runaway Negroes.

Salleche, speaking for the Indians, asked an explanation of the boundary lines, saying that the headmen who had agreed to them had always kept them a secret. Stuart responded with a detailed description of the line. Then Salleche, displaying a piece of white cloth given him years before by Governor Ellis, spoke of peace and harmony, and promised that Ishenpoaphe's son would be killed and that runaway Negroes would be returned. He spoke of disturbances in the towns caused by many new traders who "in order to ingratiate themselves with our young people give them credit and many of them never pay which causes quarrels and much uneasiness." Another cause of disorders was the practice of traders' going into the woods and buying skins from the Indians before they returned to their towns, thereby defrauding the licensed town trader of his just debts. Mad Dog of the Eutassies complained of free lance traders who had set up an establishment at a place called Buzzard's Roost on the Chattahoochee sixty miles above Coweta. He announced that he would seize them and their goods. It appeared from the talks that Stuart's new trade dispensation would be a great success. The Lower Townsmen went home happy in the trade regulation but much troubled by the matter of Ishenpoaphe's son.[11]

Relying on Stuart's reassurances, Emisteseguo arrived with a following at Augusta on June 5. Stuart gave him much the same talk he had given the Lower Creeks with the added admonition that unless satisfaction were given for the murder of Thomas, the trade would be stopped. Presenting Stuart with a pipe as pledge, Emisteseguo promised the murderer's death. He then spoke eloquently of his friendship for the English. Displaying a faded Carolina commission, he said: "Before my father died he gave me this piece of paper which he received from the governor of Charlestown. He desired that I would keep it as a memorial of his attachment to the white people. He ordered me to continue firm in my friendship for the white people as he had always before me. He enjoined me that I keep the path between Charlestown and the Creek nation clear and straight for his sake and advised me to keep peace with the Chickasaws and all the surrounding tribes. I have not forgot my father's injunction and advice; I shall follow his example in keeping the path clear and white." He then recalled Stuart's talks to him and the Mortar at Pensacola: "He and I answered that we would embrace you as a vine does a tree. We still adhere to the agreements we entered into at Pensacola and our engagements in regard to the land shall be confirmed as soon as circumstances will permit by marking the boundary line." As usual, lofty utterances were followed by trivia. Emisteseguo reminded Stuart that he had promised to send up wine and rum with all his talks.

After the Okfuskee Captain had seconded Emisteseguo's talk, Stuart explained the new trade regulations by which types of persons to be employed in the trade were defined: credit was limited to thirty pounds of leather for each Indian, standard weights and measures would be lodged with the commissary as a check on traders' scales, and traders would be confined in their trade to the towns for which they were licensed. There were numerous other provisions, but these struck at the principal defects in the unsuccessful Crown system of the past four years.[12] Stuart then read the

---

[11] Journal of the Superintendent's Proceedings, Apr. 21–June 5, 1767, G.P., Vol. CXXXVII.

[12] Stuart to Gage, Mar. 10, 1767, G.P., Vol. LXII.

newly lowered scale of prices. The Indians approved enthusiastically.

Other matters taken up in the conference were the boundary line and the Choctaw war. Creek bitterness against the Choctaws led Emisteseguo to reject Stuart's offer of mediation. He did, however, agree that Upper Towns deputies would join the Lower Towns deputies in marking the boundary. In private conversation with Stuart on the Lower Towns' failure to give satisfaction for the Pynes and Hogg murders, Emisteseguo advised a trade embargo against the Lower Towns.

In July, Stuart's hope of creating happy Indians and an orderly frontier received a rough shock which indicated that the difficulties of the region were deeper than trade troubles. Virulent frontier antagonisms and weak Crown and Indian authority figured fundamentally in an explosive area. On the Oconee River, not far from the newly decided boundary, one Houmahta had set up a village of seven houses from which vagabond Creeks raided the frontier to steal settlers' horses, which they profitably sold to the Cherokees. A band of exasperated settlers went to the village to reclaim horses and was fired upon. Retreating, they soon returned in augmented numbers, stormed into the place, and, finding it deserted, burned it to the ground and carried off some clothing and packs of deerskins. Houmahta, indignant, went down to George Galphin's at Silver Bluff to seek redress. Galphin soothed him, the two talked the matter over, and finally Houmahta admitted that his people had provoked the incident. To forestall Lower Towns retaliation on the whites, on Galphin's advice he hurried off a runner to Escochabey, the Young Lieutenant of Coweta, admitting his people's guilt in provoking the trouble and then sent to Wright asking for compensation for his losses. Stuart and Wright, with no sympathy for the frontiersmen's taking matters into their own hands, ordered the seizure of the whites involved in this violation of their treaties. To Houmahta they sent goods equal in value to his people's losses.[13]

The two English officials then sent messages to the Upper and

[13] Wright to Gage, Aug. 6, 1767, G.P., Vol. LXVIII; Wright to Shelburne, Aug. 14, 1767, Candler, *Ga. Col. Rec.*, XXXVII, Pt. 1, p. 232.

Lower Creeks setting forth the measures they had taken and advising them to discipline and call in all such outsettlements, for only thus could the treaties be maintained. Since no lives had been lost, the tribesmen expressed satisfaction with Wright's action. However, Tallachea of Okmulgee admitted that disciplining vagabond peoples would be difficult: "Our kings are but young and they cannot behave as they formerly did, but they will do their endeavors to do it."[14] Thus he confessed the weakness of the patriarchs and the incompetence of the rising generation. Nevertheless he saw weakness in Stuart and Wright's control over the frontiersmen. Of the Virginians (as the Creeks called the frontiersmen) he said, "When our people tell the Virginians they are over the line and if they don't keep in bounds they [the Creeks] will burn their houses, they make answer they will burn the governor's house over his head. If the governor cannot keep these Virginia people under how can we keep our people under?"[15]

Blue Salt of Cussita and Escochabey of Coweta professed helplessness but suggested that officials of both sides should not be too much concerned if Indian hot heads and wild frontiersmen settled their differences after their own fashion. Said the Young Lieutenant, "If the Virginia people and them [the Indians] shall fall out with one another I hope you will not trouble yourselves but let them alone." Blue Salt added, "if they hurt one another it is not our fault. I hope there will be no misunderstanding between us."[16]

Wright inclined to much the same attitude. When at about the time the Creek headmen composed their talks, Latchoway Creeks, to satisfy a private grudge, killed two white men near Saltilla River, he decided not to make an issue of it. Investigation showed him that perhaps the Creeks had been justified.[17]

By October it appeared that the promises made by the Creeks at Augusta would not be kept. Satisfaction for the Pynes and Hogg and the Thomas murders had not been given. Known runaway

14 Stuart to Gage, Nov. 27, 1767, G.P., Vol. LXXII.
15 Talk in the Chehaw square, Sept. 19, 1767, in Stuart to Gage, Nov. 27, 1767, G.P., Vol. LXXII.
16 Ibid.
17 Candler, Ga. Col. Rec., XXVIII, Pt. 2-B, p. 445.

Negroes in the nation had not been delivered. No Indians had come down to participate in the boundary marking. Stuart sent McIntosh, who had come down for the May meetings, back up to the towns with peremptory demands.

The Upper Towns were preoccupied with the Choctaw war. Early in October the most violent engagement of the conflict had taken place. A huge party of Choctaws under Red Captain, English great medal chief of the Choctaws, had approached Little Tallassee with intent to burn it. But most had turned back leaving Red Captain and forty-two men to carry out the design. Warned of the larger party, Emisteseguo, Duvall's Landlord, and Tupulga set an ambush. It was sprung on the smaller party. A fierce little woods fight ensued in which Red Captain and twenty-four of his men died before the survivors fled. But Tupulga had been killed and the Creeks went on the offensive to avenge him. The war took on a dimension very satisfying to Johnstone and Taylor at Pensacola, but both sides now had a grudge against the English. The Creeks suspected that Red Captain had been spirited up by the English traders to the Choctaws and in grim satisfaction presented the dead Red Captain's English medal and commission to one of the Choctaw traders who passed through their towns. The Choctaws, on their part, suspected that their plan of attack had been betrayed by a trader who had seen them assembling.

McIntosh arrived with Stuart's message just as Emisteseguo returned from his success against the Choctaws and had to wait till the days of purification and mourning had passed before a meeting could be called to hear him. As usual the headmen were evasive on the satisfaction, promising only that eventually it would be given. However, the Mortar, who seemed much pleased that he had won the reduction in trade prices, set off to the Cherokee country to demand that the Cherokees who sheltered the Thomas murderer put him to death.[18]

Emisteseguo then accompanied McIntosh to the Lower Towns to use his influence in persuading the Lower Towns headmen to fulfill their promises. Tallachea, Ishenpoaphe and Salleche met

[18] McIntosh to Stuart, Nov. 16, 1767, in Stuart to Gage, Dec. 16, 1767, G.P., Vol. LXXIII.

with them. Escochabey had gone off to Picolata for a meeting with Governor Grant of East Florida, who had a penchant for conducting Indian affairs independently of Wright's and Stuart's objectives. The responses of the headmen were lame. Despite the fact that, at Augusta in May, Stuart had explained the boundary to him, Salleche said that since he did not know where the boundary was, he could not go to the marking. Concerning the runaway Negroes the headmen were obliging. They rounded up all but five, who had Indian protectors who refused to surrender them. They talked compliantly on the matter of satisfaction for murders and even volunteered to punish the Saltilla River murderers. But McIntosh gained the impression they were powerless old men. To Stuart he wrote, "their young men are become so boistrous and wanton that without a hearty drubbing such as the Cherokees had they will never be a tractable people."[19]

While McIntosh groped for firm commitments in the Lower Towns, Grant at St. Augustine, disregarding the Saltilla murders, convivially entertained Escochabey and his confederates, the Pumpkin King of the Eusitchees, the Chehaw King, a couple of deputies from Latchoway, and seventy others. There were speeches, parades of eagles' tails, firing of cannon at the fort, rum drinking, pipe smoking, and easy promises of satisfaction for all murders. Grant's idea of Indian diplomacy comprised much good will mixed with high entertainment. Wright and Stuart thought him soft, but no more Indian disorders occurred on his frontier in his time.[20]

Returned to the Upper Towns, McIntosh enjoyed greater successes than he had had in the Lower Towns. There, Emisteseguo's influence and the posture of events favored co-operation with the commissary. In January the Chickasaws joined the Choctaw war, assaulting Creek hunting parties. Placating the English seemed desirable. Wright's demand that all runaway slaves be delivered was complied with.[21] Much to the distress of the Lower Towns,

[19] *Ibid.*

[20] Stuart to Gage, Dec. 26, 1767, G.P., Vol. LXXIII; Russell to Stuart, Dec. 10, 1767, G.P., Vol. LXXIII.

[21] McIntosh to Wright, Feb. 8, 1768, in Wright to Hillsborough, July 4, 1768, *Ga. Col. Rec.*, XXXVII, Pt. 1.

Emisteseguo co-operated with McIntosh in the suppression of illegal trading. The principal target was the Buzzard's Roost trading establishment on the Chattahoochee of which Mad Dog had complained at Augusta. Here Edmund Barnard, a nephew of George Galphin and legal trader at Lower Towns Chewalie, had an outpost in the woods which intercepted Upper Towns hunters and traded for their deerskins at the expense of their home town traders. Barnard, however, was a favorite of Ishenpoaphe and Escochabey of Coweta, who winked at his illegal operation and privately made the most of it. Emisteseguo, obtaining a written authorization from McIntosh, led a party which looted the place and carried off deerskins and goods to the Upper Towns as legal forfeits to the plunderers. Among the goods they took were quantities intended for the legal store at Chewalie. There was heart burning in the Lower Towns. Ishenpoaphe and Escochabey indignantly complained that McIntosh "did very wrong in sending Indians [on] such an errand—it was a very bad example for their young men who of themselves were ready enough to rob white people without encouragement and they did not see any occasion for the young people to go hunt if they could get goods for nothing."[22]

After this show of vigor, McIntosh went down to the Lower Towns to press again for the boundary marking, return of runaway Negroes, and satisfaction for past murders. For the boundary marking the headmen promised deputies would go to Augusta in May. More runaway Negroes were rounded up, though a fortunate nine, forewarned by Indian friends, escaped into the swamps. Pursuit produced one scalp, which was turned over to McIntosh. The matter of satisfaction for murders still proved difficult. No one was ready to assassinate Ishenpoaphe's son for the Pynes and Hogg murders. Finally McIntosh persuaded the headmen to kill one of the Saltilla River murderers.[23]

Pushed as they were by the English, underlying dissatisfaction encouraged the Cowetas in developing a Spanish intrigue sponsored

[22] Affidavit of William Frasier, Mar. 16, 1768, in Stuart to Gage, July 2, 1768, G.P., Vol. LXXVIII.
[23] McIntosh to Stuart, Apr. 18, 1768, in Stuart to Gage, July 2, 1768, G.P., Vol. LXXVIII.

by Escochabey and carried on by his son and Togulki. Creeks ranging down the Florida peninsula had made contact with Spanish trading vessels. Venturesome Creeks had gone to Havana and returned to the nation gaudily outfitted in Spanish clothing. There was talk of a permanent Spanish supply to be obtained through a proposed Creek grant to the Spaniards of a trading concession on the Lower Appalachicola River. This would be a possible source of ammunition if the Creeks chose to do anything about the colonial frontiersmen.[24] Renegade, vagabond, and perhaps official Creeks talked blackly that spring in the Cherokee townhouses of joint action against the frontier. They asserted that the failure of the English to punish Creek murderers displayed a weakness which ought to be taken advantage of.[25]

It was against this background and that of Emisteseguo's looting of the Buzzard's Roost establishment that Escochabey, without McIntosh's authorization, plundered an illegal trading store within the Georgia boundary on Ogeechee near the trading path. The bootleg trader, Carter, raged that he had been robbed of his private property and sought to raise a party of whites to go to Coweta to retake his goods. However George Galphin intervened from Silver Bluff with messages to his friend, Escochabey, that trouble brewed and that he had better send the plunder down to Silver Bluff. Such was Galphin's persuasiveness that Escochabey sent the goods, which, however, Galphin held for Wright's officers as evidence of Carter's illegal trade.[26] The Ogeechee settlement became a center of strong anti-Indian sentiment.

In June the boundary-marking encountered difficulties. Salleche and Escochabey represented the Lower Towns. All went smoothly until the party blazing trees reached the junction of Penhollaway Creek and the Altamaha. There a dispute broke out. The Georgia authorities wished a variation from the agreed-upon line to include some natural grazing lands in the meadows about

[24] Sinnott to Stuart, Mar. 2, 1768, in Stuart to Gage, Mar. 30, 1768, G.P., Vol. LXXV.
[25] Ensign Keough to Capt. Fuser, Apr. 28, 1768, in Fuser to Gage, May 10, 1768, G.P., Vol. LXXVII.
[26] G. Galphin to Stuart, June 2, 1768, G.P., Vol. LXXVIII.

the ponds of the area. Salleche protested. The operation halted while all went down to Savannah where Wright suavely entertained and feasted the Indians and presented them with a fine array of goods. Finally the matter seemed adjusted to Georgia satisfaction and the party went back to work at the new ceded area. But there the temperamental Salleche balked again, alleging that the presents were insufficient, as they undoubtedly were, and stalked off to the nation. For a few months the line from Penhollaway to St. Mary's River remained unmarked. Under constant pressure from other headmen and from Wright, Salleche finally gave in and in the autumn the line was finished.[27]

The Upper Creeks that spring and summer had other concerns than friction on the Georgia frontier. At war with the Choctaw and Chickasaw, they sought peace. Stuart held that good British policy was to permit no peace except under British auspices. He attempted to discourage the Choctaws and Chickasaws from receiving Creek overtures which he had not sanctioned. But the Creeks, restraining their war parties, sent out covert deputies to their enemies. Wright and Stuart looked on apprehensively, for they feared the real Creek objective was to raise up a coalition of southeastern Indians against the English.[28] It is probable that their influence through traders among the Choctaw and Chickasaw frustrated the Creeks, for in the autumn the Creeks sought Stuart's mediation.

In July, 1768, Stuart's short-lived control over the Indian trade was terminated by Lord Hillsborough. The pressure of the colonial governors had been too great, and they were again empowered to license traders. Wright still was not satisfied, for the new dispensation portended a return to chaos in the Creek country. Each governor was permitted to license whatever traders he pleased for

[27] Stuart to Gage, July 2, 1768, G.P., Vol. LXXVIII; Candler, *Ga. Col. Rec.*, XXXVII, Pt. 1, p. 329; Stuart to Gage, Aug. 22, 1768, G.P., Vol. LXX; Cander, *Ga. Col. Rec.*, XXXVII, Pt. 2, pp. 347–50.

[28] Phillips to Gage, July 20, 1768, G.P., Vol. LXXIX; Stuart to Gage, Sept. 12, 1768, G.P., Vol. LXXX; Stuart to Gage, July 2, 1768, G.P., Vol. LXXVIII; Candler, *Ga. Col. Rec.*, XXXVII, Pt. 2, pp. 371–72.

any Indian towns he desired, resulting in an over-lapping of licenses and cut-throat competition.

When Emisteseguo paid his first visit to Savannah in early September, Wright welcomed him as providing a reliable Indian witness of the conditions he deplored. Describing the Indian as a man of clarity and great good sense, he retailed Emisteseguo's testimony to Hillsborough.[29]

With the necessity of explaining to the Indians the change in trade regulation Stuart called a conference of Creeks and Cherokees for Augusta in November. He had, of course, other matters to take up: frontier frictions, the unauthorized Creek attempts to make peace with the Choctaws and Chickasaws, murders for which no satisfaction had been given, and the rumored Spanish overtures of the Lower Creeks. About three hundred and fifty Indians assembled, mostly Lower Creeks led by Tallachea of Okmulgee, Captain Allick and Blue Salt of Cussita, Escochabey and Ishenpoaphe of Coweta, and the Pumpkin King. Only one Upper Creek headman, the Second man of Little Tallassee, was present. After the black drink and the pipe had been passed around, Stuart opened the council. Piously he invoked the Supreme Being and renewed all Creek-English treaties. He spoke of the King's will that no Indian lands be taken without Indian consent. He read the boundary description as set forth in the Augusta treaty of 1763 and referred to the boundary marking then in progress. He called attention to horse stealing and robberies inflicted on the whites. Then he announced that the trade had been returned to the supervision of the colonial governors and that he had dismissed his commissary, Roderick McIntosh.

Ishenpoaphe, knowing that the meeting would not adjourn without treating of the Pynes and Hogg murders, made a moving plea for his guilty son's life: "At Picolata I met you and Governor Grant in the woods. I then said that if any of my people should spoil the path by spilling blood in it I would contribute all in my power

[29] Stuart to Gage, Aug. 21, 1768, G.P., Vol. LXXX; Candler, *Ga. Col. Rec.*, XXXVII, Pt. 2, p. 338.

to make it streight and wash it clean. Malatchi who governed my nation for many years was a good man and was a friend of the English—with his last breath he recommended to his people to hold the English fast. He is dead. He left a son [Togulki] who has forgot the advice of his father. He resembles a snake in his coil spreading the poison of his breath all around him. It is he who makes the young people mad. I am now an old man and I give public testimony that the English have always been our best friends— You know, my father, that at Picolata Governor Grant made me his friend and I engaged for the good behaviour of my people. I then heard nothing but good talks, but since that time my son's behaviour has covered me with shame; and I have never appeared at any public meeting till now that you have sent for me. I am grieved that my blood should be capable of hurting my friends the English and my grief is daily augmented by the reproaches of my own people. Yet he is my son and I feel for him like a father. You are advanced in years and have children. Judge then of my feelings by your own. If he can be forgiven I will answer for his behaviour in [the] future. I engage that while he breathes he will be a firm friend of the English, that he will no more listen to bad counsellors. Father, I hope you and Governor Grant will intercede with the great king for my son's pardon. If that can be obtained it will remove the cloud which hangs over my aged head and I shall again with confidence attend public meetings and listen to the word of my father. The medal and commission that you gave me that I might serve the great king I have been unlucky with them. I take them off and bestow them on one more worthy."

Stuart responded to this plea by promising to lay the matter before the Crown. He returned to Ishenpoaphe his medal and commission, saying, "I am convinced that none of your countrymen deserves it better." It is to be presumed that Ishenpoaphe's plea was granted, for there is no further reference to Ishenpoaphe's son in the record.

With Stuart softened, Captain Allick rose to defend Creek horse stealing. He blamed the settlers, saying the Creeks "learned to be thieves and rogues from these back settlers— the Virginians are very bad people. They pay no regard to your laws. Yet you expect that we who have no laws can govern our young men. They are corrupted and made rogues by the example of these back settlers who give them rum for stolen horses. I and my warriors present have had many horses stolen by white people—"

Escochabey continued the attack on the back settlers, but he had admiring words for the Quakers among them: "When the line was marked I then saw a number of people settling near the line who I liked very much. They are good and peaceable and do not take a pride in riding about with rifle guns in their hands, drinking and swearing like the Virginians. They offend nobody but cultivate the fields. I am told they will not even resent an injury or return a blow— I wish that a great number of them may be encouraged to come and settle near the line by which means the Virginians may be kept back from settling near us."

The Second Man of Little Tallassee demanded that Stuart invoke an embargo on the Choctaw trade if the Choctaws did not cease their war against the Creeks. Stuart replied that, while he would forward Creek peace talks to the Choctaws, he would not interfere in the war. Stuart then demanded to know what the Lower Creeks intended with the Spaniards. Eschochabey blandly denied any contact with the Spaniards. Stuart confronted him with his own past admissions on the subject. Caught out, Escochabey then asserted that he had abandoned the project: "I do not want the Spaniards amongst us and I know of no chief who wants them," he said. Tallechea and the Pumpkin King seconded the sentiment, saying that if Spaniards came among the Lower Creeks they would take their scalps. Escochabey urged Stuart to think no more of the matter. Thus the headmen sought to cover up the unpleasantly exposed affair.

However, a Lower Cherokee headman, Tistoe of Keowee, who was present and heard the colloquy, refused to allow the intrigue to be so easily disposed of. He pulled from his pouch a string of white beads ending in one black and reminded Escochabey of the bad talks from renegade Creeks and others in the winter and spring. "If what they say is false," he said, "and your intentions are good and peaceable, throw away the black bead." Escochabey, facing out the challenge, took the black bead from the string and threw it away. Thereupon Tistoe asked him to recall all vagabond and other Creeks who had married into the Cherokee nation. Escochabey promised that he would. With this seeming exposure and burial of an abortive intrigue, the conference ended. Nevertheless, though certain headmen had frowned, the Spanish contact was not broken off. In 1769 a faction at Coweta and Hitchiti continued to urge permission for Spanish settlement on the lower Chattahoochee. With the old animosity for Spanish St. Augustine in mind, the majority of headmen disapproved.

16

Indian Counterpoint
1769-74

IN THE UPPER TOWNS during the year 1769 the primary concern was to liquidate the Choctaw war. The Indians were becoming acutely aware of increasing frontier pressures on all the tribes. Cherokees complained bitterly to the Creeks of Virginian invasion of Cherokee hunting grounds. In the upper Ohio valley the Shawnees, angry at Iroquois cession of Shawnee hunting grounds to the English by the 1768 treaty of Fort Stanwix, once again began to consider an all-Indian coalition against the English and in the fall of 1769 sent emissaries to sound out the Cherokees and the Creeks. In January, 1770, these deputies had a receptive audience among the Upper Creeks. The Mortar revived his earlier hopes and began to scheme and plot. For the Creeks to be effective in the developing pattern of alliances, they must have peace with the Choctaws. In certain quarters peace talk became more pervasive. While Governor Wright, who distrusted the Creeks, wrung his hands apprehensively, Stuart, unaware of behind-the-scenes developments, offered to mediate a Creek-Choctaw settlement.[1]

[1] Stuart to Gage, May 24, 1770, G.P., Vol. XCII.

The mediation was not achieved without obstruction from the English traders, who either profiting from ammunition or sensing the deeper Creek mood, encouraged young Creeks to continue the Choctaw war. Stuart, however, induced the Choctaws not to retaliate, and in June, Emisteseguo went to Pensacola and accepted from Stuart the white wing of peace which the Choctaws had left with the superintendent. At the conference, Stuart probed Emisteseguo for the meaning of the Shawnee winter visits, but the medal chief was evasive. In 1770 the secretive enterprises of the Shawnees, the lakes Indians, and the Ohio Valley Indians led to a great meeting at the Shawnee capital of Scioto above the Ohio at which all agreed to oppose the Iroquois cession and to accept a peace with the southern Indians, with whom, particularly the Cherokees, they had been at sporadic war. The Shawnees had achieved what Gage called a "notable piece of policy" in "creating a general confederacy of western and southern Indians" to oppose the English expansionism which the Iroquois had aided.[2] Actually the southern alliance had not yet been accomplished, but it was the next objective of the Shawnees.

Along the Georgia-Creek frontier, frequent incidents generated friction. Escochabey had a brush with taproom louts. In order to allay his countrymen's suspicions of dishonesty in the recently marked boundary line in the Little River area, he had gone down to inspect the blazes. Stopping at a tavern to refresh himself, he got into an altercation with local tipplers and was shot at. Outraged, he went down to Augusta to complain and threaten revenge. Though dissuaded by the commandant, he went back to Coweta in an ugly mood. In April, Cowetas infected by his resentment staged a horse stealing raid on the Little River people. A posse of settlers pursued them and ineffective shots flew. The posse then went down to Augusta determined to prevent ammunition from reaching the nation. They unloaded the packs from the horses of a traders' convoy and threatened to kill the packers. Indians who had witnessed the episode went up to the towns in alarm to spread the story that the English intended war. However, Wright stepped in and ordered

2 Gage to Stuart, Oct. 16, 1770, G.P., Vol. XCIV.

the punishment of the posse and sent reassurances to the Creeks.[3]

In August, Okfuskee horse stealers raided the Little River region with some success. Wright sent the frontier militia after them. The militia pursued as far as Houmahta's Oconee River hamlet which they again burned. Shortly thereafter the militia ran into an ambush and lost two men. No Indians were killed. Tallachea and Escochabey, learning of the incident and fearing a trade embargo, hastened off a message to Wright blaming the clash on the Upper Creeks. Wright replied with a demand for satisfaction. This time the Lower Creeks had to put pressure on the Upper Creeks. As usual, the guilty had fled to the Cherokees. The Mortar and other headmen discussed putting them to death. The clans of two of the raiders consented, but the clan of the third, the powerful Tyger clan, refused. The Okfuskees then sent word to Wright that at present no satisfaction was possible. Angered by the recurrent pattern of evasion and delay, Wright meditated war and lamented that Stuart had negotiated a Creek-Choctaw peace.[4]

Stuart's Creek-Choctaw peace did not stand up. By January, 1771, the two tribes were again clawing at each other.[5] What caused the renewal of the conflict the records do not state, but how little these things depended on policies of the leading men and how precarious was the balance between peace and war is indicated by an episode in July which nearly caused war between the Creeks and the Cherokees. In a drunken brawl at Augusta a half-blood Cherokee killed a Creek headman and fled to the Cherokee nation. With great difficulty the local whites restrained other Creeks from killing the great Cherokee headman Attakullakulla, who was then visiting the town. Talk of a Creek-Cherokee war boiled up, but, somehow, good sense prevailed.[6] More dangerous to Creek peace was the killing by persons unknown of two English traders on the path between Tallapoosa and Pensacola.

In the winter of 1770–71 the Mortar had become active in the

---

[3] Candler, *Ga. Col. Rec.*, XXXVII, Pt. 2, pp. 458–59; Stuart to Gage, May 24, 1770, G.P., Vol. LXXXX.

[4] Candler, *Ga. Col. Rec.*, XXXVII, Pt. 2, pp. 489–91.

[5] Stuart to Gage, Feb. 8, 1771, G.P., Vol. LXXXXIX.

[6] *Ibid.*, Aug. 6, 1770, Vol. LXXXXIV.

complex of transmontane Indian negotiations pointed toward a break with the English. In February he visited the Chickasaws in an effort to obtain Chickasaw mediation for a Creek-Choctaw peace.[7] In March he sent messages to the Cherokees with a white belt and a string of black and white beads. Ostensibly he sought the investiture of a Creek as an honorary Cherokee beloved man to symbolize the peace between Creeks and Cherokees. However, Cameron, Stuart's deputy among the Cherokees, diagnosed the message as aimed to cement the two tribes in hostility toward the English.[8] In April, Andrew Hamton, who had settled east of the Alabama River above Mobile, was run off his place by Tallapooses who had told him that he was over the line and that if he returned they would kill him.[9]

When in April the Upper Creeks heard that one of their number had been killed by a white man near Augusta, their attitudes toward the English stiffened. On May 1 at the Okchai square a meeting of headmen including Emisteseguo and the old Gun Merchant convened to consider the repeated demands of Governor Wright for satisfaction for past murders, English invasions of Creek lands, and the talk of a great Cherokee cession of upper Savannah River lands to the English in payment of Cherokee trading debts. Concerning the Hamton affair, they were adamant that they had acted within their native right.[10] They protested settlers' cattle crossing the line. On the subject of satisfaction for murders, they agreed that the death of the Creek at Augusta should be considered as satisfaction in place of the life of a member of the Tyger clan which Wright had been demanding. They insisted on knowing the details of the rumored Cherokee cession since it involved lands claimed by the Creeks. These determinations with many professions of friendship they sent down to Wright in messages from Emisteseguo and the Gun Merchant, accompanied by the suggestion that to keep the

[7] Haldimand to Gage, Apr. 14, 1717, G.P., Vol. CII.

[8] Cameron to Stuart, Mar. 19, 1717, in Stuart to Gage, Apr. 29, 1771, G.P., Vol. C.

[9] Affidavit of Andrew Hamton, Apr. 12, 1771, in Haldimand to Gage, Apr. 14, 1771, G.P., Vol. CII.

[10] Stuart to Gage, Aug. 31, 1771, G.P., Vol. CVIII.

young Creeks in line the governor should send up much ammunition and plenty of goods.

Wright, who felt that the Creeks were getting overbearingly insolent, regarded the messages as ridiculous. He answered stiffly that the Creek who died near Augusta actually had drowned while being helped by two white men to escape from trouble. His death certainly could not be regarded as satisfaction for the numerous whites killed by the Creeks since the Congress of Augusta in 1763. He became somewhat threatening: "We cannot allow your mad people to rob our settlers of their horses and murder them when they please. This is not the way to keep the path straight and white and to be well supplied with ammunition and goods."[11] As for the Cherokee land cession, he said he had heard of it, that he had told the Cherokees they must obtain Creek consent, and that he had written the Crown for approval if the Creeks and Cherokees could come to an agreement. He protested ignorance of any whites settling beyond the line but said he would investigate.

That summer the problem of the integrity of their lands was uppermost in Creek minds. In July, Emisteseguo sent Stuart a message that he would soon come down to mark definitively the boundary between West Florida and the Creek country, which boundary he said was to be "like a stone wall never to be broke." He then went down to the Lower Towns to discuss the proposed Cherokee grant. There the consensus was that the Creeks should make no more land cessions, and that the proposed Cherokee cession did them great injury. "It is most certain," said the Lower Creek headmen, "our nation is much in debt. They intend to discharge their debts in skins and don't mean to give up their lands at all as the skins is the produce of the lands."[12] Emisteseguo went back to present this decision to "the great king of the Cherokees," who had come to Okchai to negotiate Creek consent for the cession.[13]

Despite all the issues, dominant Creek headmen opposed the

[11] Candler, *Ga. Col. Rec.*, XXVIII, Pt. 2-B, pp. 684–91.
[12] *Ibid.*, Pt. 2, pp. 559–60.
[13] *Ibid.*

Mortar's warlike sentiments. When in mid-summer Ohio River Shawnee deputies secretly brought belts to Emisteseguo and the Gun Merchant soliciting their consent to Creek membership in the transmontane confederacy, after much discussion they decided in the negative. Emisteseguo said the decision arose out of friendship for the English, for the Shawnees had admitted that their confederacy was forming without the consent of Sir William Johnson, Superintendent of Indians of the northern district.[14]

On November 2, 1771, when Emisteseguo met Stuart at Pensacola to define the boundaries of West Florida, he discovered that the English wanted more land in the area. Far from being an English pawn on the subject, he strongly reflected Creek sentiment. When Stuart pointed out the areas on the Escambia River he wanted, Emisteseguo, who was surprised by the demand, said he was powerless to grant them. He asserted the doctrine that the lands belonged to all the tribe. "My nation is numerous and every child in it has an equal property in the land with the first warriors, making any alteration in the boundary without the consent of the whole was improper."[15] This was the most extreme doctrine of Indian land title and one on which the Creek headmen in the past seem never to have acted, and must be regarded as a statement of position for negotiation. That evening, Emisteseguo consulted the other headmen, and these, taking on themselves the power Creek headmen had always exercised, decided that some concession could be made. In the morning they told Stuart he could have a little more land on the Escambia River. But the areas they defined were worthless for agriculture, and Stuart rejected them, saying he wanted tillable lands up to the line of the former Spanish holding. Emisteseguo then argued that he had come empowered from the nation only to mark the tidewater boundary, that Stuart had not informed him that a major land grant was wanted. That evening the headmen discussed the day's problems and decided to stand firm. The next day, Emisteseguo launched an attack upon a cession the Choctaws had made to the English on Mobile bay and river,

[14] Stuart to Gage, Dec. 14, 1771, G.P., Vol. CVIII.
[15] Treaty of Pensacola, Nov. 2, 1771, G.P., Vol. CXXXVII.

saying the Choctaws had ceded Creek lands. He accused the English of violating all Stuart's promises: "We have no other method of subsisting but by hunting for which that land is well calculated and at every meeting you have always promised that no encroachments should be made for the future. I have always upon my return home from such meetings repeated these promises but they have always been broken and new encroachments made. You have always told us as well as the governors that you wanted land for planting and not for hunting and that the deer belonged to us, notwithstanding which there are white people who tell us that they intend hunting on our lands in spite of us. You ordered that there be no trading in the woods but I understand that it is in agitation to fix stores in the woods. So I find that you and I have talked to no purpose and that our agreements have fallen to the ground."

Stuart parried the thrusts as well as he could. He explained that he no longer had control of the trade, but he asserted that the Indians still had the right to take the deerskins and guns of white people who illegally entered the Creek country and to force trespassing settlers to remove out of the Indian country. He denied that he had broken any promises.

The next day the Indians signed a treaty defining boundaries. They made a small cession of a little room for plantations between Mobile River and Tensa River and said they would discuss the Escambia River area in a great council of the nation. In private conferences with Stuart, Emisteseguo told of Creek summer rejection of Shawnee overtures and of Lower Creek Spanish contacts.[16] Stuart complained of the lawlessness of the Seminoles who marauded in the neighborhood of Mobile Bay stealing settlers' cattle. But this was outside Upper Creek jurisdiction, and the Superintendent had to send an emissary to the Lower Creeks on the subject.

For the Lower Creeks the fall of 1771 again brought a delicate situation. Upper Towns Okfuskees engaged in a horse-stealing raid on the Georgia frontier. Pursuing whites killed "a young beloved man." The incident was reported back to Okfuskee as an unpro-

[16] Stuart to Gage, Dec. 14, 1771, G.P., Vol. CVIII.

voked assault, and the victim's kinsmen talked vengeance. Lower Creek headmen, seeing in this situation trouble for the Lower Towns, investigated the affair and, deciding it arose from Creek misbehavior, sent runners to Emisteseguo urging restraint. Then they sent word to George Galphin at Silver Bluff that the matter would be settled peacefully. Emisteseguo called a meeting of the offended Tyger clan at which, though the young warriors were hot for satisfaction, reason finally prevailed. An uncle of the slain Okfuskee announced that since a member of the clan had killed two whites on the Oconee River two years before and had not been put to death as the treaties required, the recent slaying of the young beloved man should be regarded as satisfaction to the whites for past murders. However unsatisfactory from the Georgia point of view, this reasoning carried weight with the Tyger clan, and no retaliation on the Georgia border occurred.[17]

Lower Creek determination to keep the peace was more force-fully displayed when a Lower Creek killed one Carey near Queens-borough in Georgia. The excited frontier demanded retaliation. When Galphin and acting president Habersham, impressed by the frontier excitement, pushed the matter, the Lower Creeks assassi-nated the murderer and showed his body to the traders.[18]

Maintaining peace with the English appeared to be the main concern in the Creek nation during the spring and summer of 1772. To some extent this turned on the Choctaw war, which the Mortar in the interests of the all-Indian confederacy was attempting to end. For a brief period the Mortar's prospects seemed good. When Cherokees killed six trespassing whites on Holston's River, the Mortar again agitated a Creek-Choctaw-Chickasaw anti-English alliance. Support developed in the Lower Towns, where Salleche sponsored war talk in the midst of which a white man, one Inman, was killed on the trading path. Yet the Gun Merchant and Emiste-seguo stood fast in opposition to the Mortar's projected alliance, and the Choctaw war went on. Disgusted and war weary, a majority of the old friends of the French, the Alabamas, responding to the

[17] Candler, *Ga. Col. Rec.*, XII, 148–50; XXXVII, Pt. 2, p. 558.
[18] *Ibid.*, XII, 318; XXXVII, Pt. 2, pp. 592–94.

overtures of a French trader from New Orleans, seceded from the nation and went to live beyond the Mississippi.[19]

Distrustful of the undercurrents of Creek restlessness and sympathizing with the Creek traders who had joined the Cherokee traders in promoting an Indian land cession to pay off accumulated Indian trading debts, in September, Stuart sent David Taitt as his deputy into the nation to keep an eye on events and to negotiate. On September 19, Taitt assembled a large number of Lower Towns headmen at the Apalachicolas to discuss the cession. Salleche, who had long shown more jealousy on the subject of lands than any other Lower Creek, strongly opposed. But Escochabey of Coweta, a friend of Galphin who traded heavily at Coweta and had large Indian debts there, supported the cession, and it was tentatively agreed to. Since the cession involved the Cherokees, Escochabey insisted that the English send certain Cherokee headmen to him to discuss the relative land claims of the two nations in the area to be ceded. Opposition boiled up in the Upper Towns, but the Gun Merchant decreed the cession was entirely a Lower Creek matter.[20]

The cession was completed at Augusta on June 1, 1773. The tract of 2,100,000 acres extended from the Altamaha River to the Ogeechee River and up the latter river to the headwaters of the Oconee River and thence to the Savannah River almost to the Cherokee towns. It brought under Georgia control most of the west bank of the Savannah River for a depth of thirty or forty miles in the region where Creeks and frontiersmen had most frequently clashed. It gave the English frontier a huge forward thrust, and though many Lower Creeks had benefitted by the forgiveness of their trading debts, ill feeling about it was widespread in the nation.

The year 1773 was one of great restlessness among the transmontane tribes. As the northern Shawnees became more determined to attack the English invaders of their old hunting grounds ceded by the Iroquois, the tempo of intertribal diplomacy picked up. To counter the growing movement toward solidarity, English

[19] Forster to Stuart, Sept. 7, 1772, G.P., Vol. CXIV.

[20] Talk of Lower Creeks to Stuart, Sept. 19, 1772, in Stuart to Gage, Nov. 24, 1772; Taitt to Stuart, Oct. 19, 1772, in Stuart to Gage, Nov. 24, 1772, G.P., Vol. CXV.

agents everywhere probed into the councils of the nations and sought by every means possible to turn the tribes against each other. In the south, Cameron, Stuart's agent to the Cherokees, worked to prevent Cherokees and Creeks from getting together and to turn the Cherokees against the northern Indians. Charles Stuart, agent to the Choctaws, warned the Choctaws against making peace with the untrustworthy Creeks,[21] with the result that the Choctaw war sputtered on, and in November the best friend of the English, Emisteseguo, was wounded in an ambush. At Coweta, among the Lower Creeks, interest in the Spaniards increased.[22]

As always, though official Creek and English policy eschewed war, the inflammatory moods of the young warriors were a constant threat. In December, 1773, their festering resentment toward the "Virginians" who had moved into the new ceded lands broke into the wildest violence since 1763. In a series of episodes on the Upper Savannah, thirteen settlers and four militia men were killed. It was a *casus belli* if there ever was one, yet both the Creeks and Wright refused to regard it as such. The massacres had ostensibly arisen from a quarrel between two Indians in which one, Ogulki, a kinsman of Escochabey (possibly "Togulki," son of Malatchi), murdered the other and, to avoid the vengeance of the victim's kinsmen and perhaps intentionally to incite a border war, left a trail which pointed from the dead man's body to the cabin of a settler, one White. The murdered man's kin fell on the White family, killing all six members. When no retaliation ensued, Ogulki's band struck again, killing the entire Sherrill family. The frontier fled. Militia went out to punish the Indians, fell into an ambush in which four were killed, and retreated. But the Creek nation did not flood out to war. The triumphant warriors returned to Coweta where they strutted about insolently displaying the scalps they had taken and boasting their prowess while headmen frowned and nervously considered action against them. Ogulki belonged to the powerful Tyger clan, which in the past had resisted all demands for satisfaction. The headmen feared to touch him, but sent down to Wright

[21] Charles Stuart to John Stuart, Mar. 17, 1773, G.P., Vol. CXVII.
[22] Stuart to Gage, Dec. 25, 1772, G.P., Vol. CXIX.

a message disavowing the massacres. Stimulated by Taitt, the Upper Creeks, deeply involved in the Choctaw war and fearing an English embargo, sent down to the Lower Creeks asking them to take Ogulki's life. At Coweta, relatives of Ogulki threatened to cut off the Upper Towns trade by closing the path if their kinsman was assassinated. Emisteseguo warned Ishenpoaphe that civil war impended, and the matter stood at a stalemate.

Wright, lacking regular troops and fearful of an Indian war, had already sized up the massacres as an individualistic act for which satisfaction must be demanded. He sent to the nation for deputies to come down to Savannah under his protection.[23] After some hesitation, Captain Allick for the Lower Towns and Emisteseguo for the Upper went down to negotiate.

So general was the Creek disposition to avoid war that when the Cowkeeper of Latchoway visited St. Augustine for the investiture of Patrick Tonyn as the new governor of East Florida, he and his Indians behaved in exemplary fashion throughout the festive week. The hundred Indians, though drunk most of the time, "were cautious so as to avoid offence; they did not pluck an orange from the orchards without first asking leave."[24]

In Savannah on April 14, Captain Allick and Emisteseguo were told the bad news that the trade would be cut off until the Creeks put the ring leaders in the attacks to death. Wright's position, however, had been somewhat weakened by news from the frontier that two Indians had just been killed by whites. One of the killings appeared to be justifiable; the Creek had murdered a white man, fled to the Cherokee country, and there had been killed by whites. But the other killing was an outright murder of an innocent man by an Indian-hating white. Mad Turkey, who had come in to Augusta from the Upper Towns escorting a trader's pack train, was attacked in the streets by Thomas Fee, who, claiming vengeance for a relative slain by Indians, hit him on the head with an iron bar. Wright ordered Fee seized, but Fee escaped. At Savannah, Wright reported the murder to his Indian guests, and as a conciliatory con-

---

[23] Candler, *Ga. Col. Rec.*, XXXVIII, Pt. 1-A, pp. 163–70, 186–88, 256.
[24] B.P.R.O., C.O.5/554, No. 2, p. 38.

cession, he said that the giving of satisfaction for the White and Sherrill murders would be regarded as satisfaction for all murders since 1763. Emisteseguo felt that the Upper Towns should not suffer for Coweta misbehavior and argued that the trade embargo should be against the Lower Towns alone. He further blamed the irresponsibility of the young Indians upon the condition of the trade. Once again, he said, there were too many traders trading in the woods and wherever a house could be found, that under these circumstances the headmen could no longer control the young Indians as they formerly had when there were but few traders assigned to specific towns. Wright would not accept these propositions as reasons for mitigating his embargo. The whole nation must suffer until it brought pressure on Coweta to give the required satisfaction.[25] The trade from Carolina and from East and West Florida would also be stopped. Emisteseguo and Captain Allick left Savannah determined to obtain the required satisfaction, but the murder of the two Indians that spring complicated their task.

While the deputies were in Savannah, heat built up in the nation. From Mobile, Charles Stuart urged on the Choctaws. Creek idlers about Augusta talked vengeance for Mad Turkey, and Escochabey of Coweta corresponded with the Spaniards in Cuba for ammunition. Feelers were sent out to the Cherokees. Yet responsible headmen knew that resistance was impossible. Whatever hope there lay in Cherokee help died when Oconostota, the Great Warrior of the Cherokees, informed the Wolf of the Muccolossus and the Gun Merchant of Cherokee neutrality. Even the Mortar grew cold to war, for the Creeks would stand alone confronted by the Choctaws on one side and the English on the other. He sent a pacific message to Stuart.[26] When on their return the deputies reached the Lower Towns, the guilty ringleaders fled into the woods.

On May 23 a great meeting of headmen of twenty-six Upper Creek Towns decided that despite the bitterness over the death of Mad Turkey the Lower Towns must give satisfaction. The requi-

---

[25] Candler, *Ga. Col. Rec.*, XXXVIII, Pt. 1-A, pp. 254–59.
[26] Stuart to Gage, May 12, 1774, G.P., Vol. CXIX.

site pressures were brought to bear, and a June 23 meeting of Lower Towns Hitchitis, Apalachicolas, Oconees, and Okmulgees, but not of Coweta, decided on the deaths of Ogulki of Coweta, and Sophia and Houmacha,[27] the ringleaders in the White and Sherrill massacres. The Cussitas assassinated Ogulki, who in his dying words commanded vengeance on the "Virginians." Sophia and Houmacha had fled. Two warriors who had killed white men in Florida recently were also assassinated. So stern was the order for execution that a Cussita headman, the father of one of these, went after his son to kill him; however, weakening, he brought him in for others to kill.[28] Coweta kinsmen of the executed were angry. The death of Ogulki alienated his Tyger clan kinsman, Escochabey, further from Stuart and Wright, and in the Cherokee country, Creek conspirators sought to kill Stuart's deputy, Cameron.[29]

With Houmacha and Sophia still at large the trade embargo was not lifted, and by mid-summer the avenging headmen lost their ardor. George Galphin seems to have let it be known that perhaps Wright and Stuart would be placated with the satisfaction already given. But this was far from Stuart and Wright's mood. They continued to press for and succeeded in obtaining the death of two more of the murderers in the Upper Towns.

But forces were operating against continued pressure. Wright had word from England that in case of war he could have no regular troops, which were all needed in New England Boston, where colonial insurrection impended. For Georgia, an Indian war without regulars seemed impossible. Wright had a restless frontier where lawless settlers had freed Mad Turkey's murderer, Fee, from the sheriff's posse. News of a Shawnee attack in the north on the Virginia frontier had seeped into the Creek country strengthening the hands of the intransigent.[30] But the Creeks suffered from a shortage of ammunition with which to fight the Choctaws and

[27] Probably Houmacha, whose border town had been burned by whites in 1767.

[28] Taitt to Stuart, July 18, 1774; Talk of the Pumpkin King to Stuart and Wright, June 23, 1774, in Stuart to Gage, Aug. 8, 1774, G.P., Vol. CXII.

[29] Wilkinson to Cameron, June 26, 1774, in Obilby to Haldimand, July 18, 1774, G.P., Vol. CXXXI.

[30] Wright to Gage, Sept. 9, 1774, G.P., Vol. CXXIII.

needed to have the embargo lifted. Wright therefore sent for deputies again to come to Savannah.

Present to make the new treaty of Savannah on October 20, 1774, were Emisteseguo with twelve Upper Towns headmen and for the Lower Towns, Tallachea of Ocmulgee, the Pumpkin King of the Eusitchees, LeCoffe of Coweta and five others. In essence the treaty was a compromise way out for Wright. By it the headmen agreed to put Houmacha and Sophia to death in return for an immediate reopening of the trade. They also agreed to return goods and cattle stolen from settlers and to deliver up runaway slaves and to prevent future damage. The Creeks were not to allow Indians to settle on the Ocmulgee or Oconee rivers near the boundary line.[31]

Implementation of the treaty, as always, proved difficult. Though thirteen runaway Negroes were delivered, the assassination of Houmacha and Sophia could not be carried out. Dissidents at Coweta threatened trader McQueen, who ran for his life. Outlawed Houmacha, protected by his kinsmen, proclaimed his intention to kill traders on the path. Escochabey, seeking ammunition, went down the Chattahoochee to meet Spanish agents.[32] Finally the headmen became grimly determined to carry out the treaty. Warned, Houmacha and Sophia fled to the Cherokees. Executioners were sent after them but were unsuccessful.[33]

At the Savannah conference, Wright had undertaken to frustrate the land-grabbing scheme promoted by the trader and staunch American patriot, Jonathan Bryon. Sometime in 1774, Bryon, who was popular with the Lower Creeks, by one means or another had obtained the marks of a number of prominent Lower Creek headmen to a paper making what the Indians thought to be a small grant of land for a trading establishment in the Seminole country of lower Georgia and upper Florida. Actually the deed was to a domain of several hundred thousand acres. Wright explained to

[31] Candler, *Ga. Col. Rec.*, Vol. XXXVIII, Pt. 1-A, pp. 337–44; G.P., Vol. CXXXVII.

[32] Taitt to Stuart, Dec. 10, 1774, in Stuart to Gage, Jan. 18, 1775, G.P., Vol. CXXV.

[33] Wright to Stuart, July 6, 1775, G.P., Vol. CXXXII.

the Lower Townsmen at Savannah who had signed Bryon's deed that they had been deceived and that anyway under colony and Crown regulations such a cession to a private individual would not be tolerated. The headmen promptly tore their marks from the deed and repudiated it. But on their way home Bryon intercepted them, made them drunk, and obtained their marks to a new cession of the same lands. Later the headmen denied that they had marked any such paper, but Bryon continued to flaunt his paper and, despite the opposition of Wright and Stuart, was determined to survey the land. The complications of the Revolutionary period finally prevented Bryon from executing his deed, but his popularity with the Lower Creeks seems in no way to have been impaired.[34]

A powerful influence in Creek affairs at the end of 1774 was the English-maintained Choctaw war. It engendered two points of view: Emisteseguo and the majority of Creek headmen saw the necessity of peace at any price with the English; the nativist opposition held that the Creeks must raise up allies with which to fight the English, and they therefore sought French and Spanish aid. Escochabey of Coweta went to Cuba; the Mortar looked to Spanish-held New Orleans. He dreamed of getting the Spaniards and French to intercede with the Choctaws for a peace and then to erect a protectorate over the Creeks. In November, when the pinch of the embargo was most severe, he raised up a large party of Upper Creeks who were to be joined by Lower Creeks to go to New Orleans to promote his scheme. It proved to be his last venture in a history of ill-fated nativist anti-English intrigue and diplomacy. On his way down the Alabama River he was ambushed and killed by Choctaws.[35]

[34] Stuart to Gage, Jan. 18, 1775, G.P., Vol. CXXV.
[35] *Ibid.*

17

The American Revolution:
Struggle for Neutrality
1775-78

T HE COMING of the American Revolution brought new problems
to the Creeks. In the years 1765–74 the Indians had no awareness of the conflict between the colonies and the Crown, but in the
winter of 1774–75, inklings of seaboard confusion and division of
sentiment and authority began to reach them. Despite Wright's
lifting of the trade embargo as a result of the treaty of October,
1774, only limited quantites of goods and ammunition entered
the nation. The goods failure was caused by the disturbed condition
of the colonial overseas trade, attendant upon non-importation
agreements enforced in opposition to the Boston Port Bill of 1774.
Among the Indian traders most active in rebellion against the
Crown were two of the largest suppliers of the Creeks, Robert Rae
of Augusta, who traded with the Upper Towns, and George Galphin of Silver Bluff, who traded with the Lower Towns. Their
packers and agents seemed to have discussed with some of the
headmen the mounting troubles with the Crown, because in April,
1775, when the headmen of the Eufalees and Cussitas assembled

at the Apalachicolas for the Acorn Dance, Stuart's deputy, Taitt, was assured that they would not listen to any bad talks.[1]

The real struggle between the patriot and loyalist forces for ascendancy in the Creeks did not begin until June, 1775, when, at Charlestown, Stuart was accused of encouraging the Cherokees to rise against the frontier. The South Carolina patriot council of Safety appointed George Galphin, David Zulby, and Leroy Hammond as commissioners of Indian affairs. Galphin immediately informed the Cussita king that Stuart and the Great King over the water had misbehaved and that he would take the place of Stuart as Superintendent of Indian Affairs until a good governor was sent to Savannah. No doubt troubled at this surprising announcement, the Cussita King affirmed his loyalty to Stuart and declared to Taitt that he would receive no talks but from him.[2] About this time, Thomas Gray, a half-blood with important connections, was at Seminole Latchoway pressing with speeches and bribes the patriot Jonathan Bryon's land claim and urging co-operation with the rebellious forces.[3]

Driven from Charlestown to St. Augustine, Stuart, on receiving word of the appointment of the rebel Indian commissioners and of the rebels' having seized a shipload of ammunition intended for the Indian trade, set about counteracting the rebel influence in the Creek nation. His objective at this time was not so much to enlist the Indians against the frontier, where an Indian war would unite loyalist and patriot in a common cause, as to keep his influence with the Creeks intact. Gathering together a few packs of presents from the limited supply of Crown goods at St. Augustine, he sent them to Taitt with instructions to explain the new turn of events in the colonies. Taitt summoned a meeting of headmen at Little Tallassee, where, to be next to Emisteseguo's ear, he made his headquarters. He outlined the current difficult position of the Superintendent and the confusion in the colonies, with heavy emphasis upon the British

[1] Stuart to Dartmouth, July 21, 1775, B.P.R.O., C.O.5/76, No. 28, p. 307.

[2] *Ibid.*, Sept. 17, 1775, B.P.R.O., C.O.5/75, No. 30, p. 357.

[3] Tonyn to Dartmouth, Sept. 20, 1775, B.P.R.O., C.O.5/55, No. 11, p. 387.

point of view. He strongly denounced the rebel contempt of Stuart and of the Great King and blamed the Indians' shortage of ammunition upon the rebels, who he said had seized the ammunition for their own use. Aware that the restless young men saw only that ammunition for hunting the deer and for fighting the Choctaws was denied them and talked of reprisals on the frontier, Taitt advised the headmen to warn their young men to stay away from the frontier where they might get into trouble with lawless mobs.[4] The headmen responded with expressions of loyalty to the Great King. To relieve the ammunition shortage the deputy sent down to Mobile for military supplies.

In the Lower Towns, Taitt found that sentiment toward Stuart and the Crown had cooled since April. Whether this was due to rebel talks or Spanish influence he could not discover. Old Ishenpoaphe at Coweta, where Galphin's influence was traditionally strong and where Escochabey had recently returned from Havana, refused to meet him. The Pumpkin King of the Eusitchees was evasive, and an undercurrent of uneasiness became apparent. There was talk of war, for the combination of rallying and counterrallying of frontier forces, which the Indians did not realize related to the quarrel with the Crown, and the continuing ammunition shortage, were interpreted as intended hostility toward the Indians.[5]

At St. Augustine, Stuart, on reading Taitt's report, sought a supply of Crown ammunition to quiet the Indians on that score. He even hoped the rebel commissioners would also send ammunition. He instructed Taitt to tell the headmen to remain neutral and allow the white people to settle their own dispute.[6] Wright at Savannah, knowing that the patriots had already begun to woo the Creeks, sent up a message urging them not to listen to bad talk. But before Stuart and Wright's talks could arrive in the Lower Towns, Galphin's nephew, David Holmes, came into Coweta with a large convoy of ammunition sent from Augusta by the Georgia Council of Safety. Holmes brought a talk from Galphin the purport

---

[4] Taitt to Stuart, Aug. 1, 1775, B.P.R.O., C.O.5/76, p. 361.

[5] *Ibid.*

[6] Stuart to Creeks, Aug. 15, 1775, B.P.R.O., C.O.5/76, p. 369.

of which was to urge neutrality, indicating that the quarrel between the King and his subjects was but temporary. Galphin also stated that he had turned his trade over to his son and to Holmes and that the Indians would be supplied as usual. The Coweta headmen, especially Escochabey, seemed impressed.

On September 7, Taitt, having received Stuart and Wright's talks, confronted Holmes at Eusitchee before the assembled headmen. A heated debate ensued between the two, after which the headmen divided into pro-Wright and pro-Galphin factions. Finally they agreed that though they would listen only to the talks of the Crown authorities, they would not take sides in the white men's quarrel. Said Tese Mico of Eusitchee, "We hope the path between us and you will remain white and clear, and as we are a poor people we hope you will help us with as much ammunition as you possibly can and we are determined to lye quiet and not meddle with the quarrel." This reply was sent to both Wright and Galphin.[7]

For the moment, having quieted the Lower Towns, Taitt returned to Upper Towns Tuckabatchee to counter the patriot Augusta traders, Robert Rae and Joseph Cornell, who had arrived among the Abeikas with a present of ammunition from the Georgia Council of Safety. There he met with confusion and division, for when Emisteseguo and the Mad Dog called a meeting to listen to him, Handsome Fellow of the Okfuskees, Rae's friend, called a meeting to hear Rae. Emisteseguo's meeting declared its displeasure with the Georgia Council's present and asked for goods in the regular way of trade. Handsome Fellow's meeting decided that a deputation should go down to Savannah and talk with the Council of Safety.[8] Thence forward Handsome Fellow and the Okfuskees were to be the center of pro-American or neutralist sentiment in the Upper Towns.

Toward the end of September a slight shift in the Lower Towns position occurred. Whereas, at the Eusitchee meeting, Tese Mico had declared that only talks from the Crown authorities would be

[7] Talk to Gov. Wright given at Usitchee town, Sept. 7, 1775, Candler, *Ga. Col. Rec.*, XXXVIII, Pt. 2, p. 18.

[8] Taitt to Stuart, Sept. 20, 1775, B.P.R.O., C.O.5/77, p. 119.

received, on September 29 in the Cussita square, old Ishenpoaphe of Coweta, Blue Salt, the King of Cussita, Pumpkin King of the Eusitchees, and the headman of the Chehaws declared they liked both the talk from the liberty people and that from Stuart, and, since they were not desired to join either party, they all wanted the old trading path to be kept "white and clear."[9] Though they agreed to go down to St. Augustine to talk with Stuart, this talk indicated that the "liberty people" had gained more stature at Cussita, and that the Lower Creek headmen had decided to accept the favors of both parties and to join neither.

Nevertheless, the Creeks were confused and dissatisfied because the Crown's and the liberty people's gifts of ammunition together were not sufficient for the fall hunts and the war against the Choctaws.[10]

Events, however, soon created a situation in which both the Creeks and Stuart were to find neutrality difficult to maintain. The liberty people had intercepted a British convoy of ammunition sent up from East Florida by Governor Tonyn, and they had taken an English ship off Savannah with six and a half tons of ammunition designed for the southern Indians. On July 12 the Continental Congress, intent on weaning the Indians from the British, had established three Indian departments, the Northern, the Middle, and the Southern, and soon appointed commissioners for each. For the Southern District the commissioners were George Galphin, Robert Rae, John Walker, Willie Jones, and Edward Wilkinson. Their appointment meant an active pro-American program for the Creeks. On September 12, General Gage, beseiged in Boston where his sentinels were fired upon by Stockbridge Indians enlisted in the American cause, wrote Stuart commanding him "when opportunity offers" to rouse the southern Indians "to take arms against His Majesty's enemies."[11]

Stuart undertook negotiations to accomplish Gage's desires. Before the Creeks could be used effectively against the rebels, the

[9] Taitt to Stuart from Cussita square, Sept. 29, 1775, Clinton Papers.
[10] Galphin to Council of Safety, Oct. 15, 1775, Laurens Papers; S. Thomas to Stuart, Oct. 2, 1775, B.P.R.O., C.O.5/77, p. 105.
[11] Gage to Stuart, Sept. 12, 1775, G.P., Vol. CXXXV.

Choctaw war had to be ended.[12] This was in line with Upper Creek thinking, for while the strongly pro-British Emisteseguo, under Taitt's influence, considered going to the aid of the British, his Second Man, Neahlatchko, sent to Stuart asking that he make a peace with the Choctaws.[13] About the same time Stuart ordered his younger brother, Henry, to go to Little Tallassee, seek out Taitt, and give him Gage's orders to enlist the Indians against the liberty forces. From there, Henry Stuart was to proceed on the same mission to the Cherokees.[14] With his supply of Crown ammunition cut off by the rebels, the Superintendent contracted with private merchants for ammunition with which to support the intended Creek assault.[15] There was thus shaping up a British plan to use the Creeks against the colonial back country.

With Emisteseguo's influence working to keep the Upper Creeks firmly on the British side, Stuart's problem was to swing the Lower Creeks away from their disposition to neutrality. To this end, from December 4 to December 16 at Cowford near St. Augustine he met with pro-British elements of the Lower Creeks. These were led at this time by the wavering Pumpkin King of the Eusitchees and Weoffki, the Seminole Long Warrior of Latchoway, who appears not to have succumbed to Bryon's influence. They met Stuart and Governor Tonyn with great friendliness and a ceremonial display of the eagle dance. Stuart's speeches took a hostile line toward the rebels. He declaimed that bad people in Savannah and Charlestown had caused the interruption of the trade. They had stolen the ammunition the Great King over the water intended for the Creeks and then, as a little gesture, had sent the Creeks a small part of it. But their real intention was to make the Creeks poor by stopping the trade. These same thieves, he said, were the so-called beloved men of Savannah who sent the Creeks beguiling talks. Actually, said Stuart, there would be no trade until these rebels were crushed. Privately he prevailed on the Pumpkin King

---

[12] Stuart to Dartmouth, Oct., 1775, B.P.R.O., C.O.5/76, No. 31, p. 373.

[13] Talk of Neahalko, Oct. 20, 1775, in Stuart to Dartmouth, Jan. 6, 1776, B.P.R.O., C.O.5/77, No. 33, pp. 79, 95.

[14] J. Stuart to H. Stuart, Oct. 24, 1775, B.P.R.O., C.O.5/76, p. 385.

[15] *Ibid.*

to endeavor to influence the Cussita council to agree with whatever measures the Upper Towns, who, he said, were loyal to the Crown, took.[16] Tonyn also talked privately to the Pumpkin King to undermine the influence of the rebel Jonathan Bryon by stressing the cheating nature of his land grabbing. The Pumpkin King asserted his loyalty to the Crown and indicated that the Lower Creeks were ready to come to the assistance of the Great King's friends.[17]

With the tide running, as he thought, strongly his way, Stuart acted to obtain a large shipment of Indian goods and ammunition from England with which to establish a powerful British trading base at Pensacola and support an Indian war. However, he was troubled by the thought that a Creek war would hurt loyalists as well as rebels on the frontiers and worried about how to solve this problem.[18] Then suddenly the situation altered. He received orders from Gage to hold everything in abeyance; Gage had been supplanted by Sir William Howe, who would give new orders. Stuart informed Taitt at Little Tallassee that he must hold the Indians in readiness to attack when the time was ripe.[19] His idea was that the time would be ripe when a British fleet and army made an attack upon either Charlestown or Savannah.

Stuart's optimism had also failed to reckon with habitual Creek divisiveness. Currently this turned on the genuinely neutral disposition of many headmen. The rebels had developed a channel of influence in the Upper Towns through Handsome Fellow of the Okfuskees, who had gone on his own to Savannah in November, where he had astutely listened to both sides. Talking with Wright he won a promise of pardon for the murderer Houmacha in return for the assured death of Sophia, Houmacha's accomplice. Then calling on the rebel Council of Safety, he emerged with abundance of presents. Thus he effectively practiced the doctrine of neutrality to which Rae had counselled him in the late summer.

About the time Handsome Fellow visited Savannah, the American southern Indian commissioners meeting at Salisbury, North

[16] Stuart to Dartmouth, Dec. 17, 1775, B.P.R.O., C.O.5/77, No. 32, p. 47.
[17] Tonyn to Dartmouth, Dec. 18, 1775, B.P.R.O., C.O.5/56, No. 18, pp. 141–46.
[18] Stuart to Dartmouth, Dec. 17, 1775, B.P.R.O., C.O.5/77, No. 32, p. 47.
[19] Stuart to Clinton, Mar. 15, 1776, B.P.R.O., C.O.5/77.

Carolina, sent a message to the Upper and Lower Towns urging neutrality and inviting them to send deputies to a meeting at Augusta on May 1, 1776. They assured the Creeks that the dispute between Great Britain and America was "like a dispute between a father and his child" in which the Creeks should have no concern. The commissioner warned against Stuart's war talk and advised them to listen only to the American Commissioners, who would keep the trading path open.[20]

In the Upper Towns, as could be expected, Emisteseguo rejected the American commissioners' talks and asserted his loyalty to Stuart and the Great King.[21] However, in the Lower Towns they seem to have made an impression on the Cussita King and others; on March 23, 1776, in the Cussita square the headmen of all the Lower Towns except the Euchees and Hitchitis phrased a talk to Stuart in which, distressed at the great interruption of the trade, they recommended that the white men heal their quarrel: " We are now going to speak to our eldest brothers, the white people; we have heard all your talks to the red people and hope that you will hear ours. We thought that all the English people were as one people but now we hear that they have a difference amongst themselves. It is our desire that they drop their disputes and not spoil one another; as all the red people are living in friendship with one another we desire that the white people will do the same. It is the custom with the red people when they send such a talk and these tokens to prevent any of our warriors from going to war. They agree and we hope that the white people will do the same and agree to our talk— We send this wing and tobacco as a token of friendship and desire that the beloved men will smoak the tobacco and look at the wing and agree to each others talks."[22]

When, in April, Governor Tonyn of East Florida sought the active cooperation of the Latchoway Seminoles against the Georgia frontier, they told him they were reluctant to act in the King's cause "until the sentiments of the nation are signified to them."[23]

[20] B.P.R.O., C.O.5/94, p. 145.
[21] Emisteseguo to Stuart, Mar. 2, 1776, B.P.R.O., C.O.5/94, p. 117.
[22] B.P.R.O., C.O.5/77, p. 255.
[23] Tonyn to Taitt, Apr. 20, 1776, B.P.R.O., C.O.5/56, p. 631.

Though Taitt came down from Little Tallassee to the Lower Towns to urge the Lower Towns headmen to order the Seminoles to co-operate with Tonyn, and Thomas Brown, passing through the Lower Towns with a convoy of ammunition from St. Augustine to the Loyalists of the Carolina back country, talked to the headmen about co-operating with a planned British attack on the south, no Indians appeared at St. Augustine that spring to help repel a threatened American attack.[24] Some of the Lower Towns Chehaw people had gone down to Savannah, from which Wright had fled, to talk with the rebels, and a large delegation from Coweta and Cussita had appeared at Augusta for the May 1 conference with the American commissioners.

The headmen who met George Galphin, Robert Rae, and the other Continental commissioners were largely Upper Towns Okfuskees under Handsome Fellow and Lower Towns Cowetas led by Ishenpoaphe. They represented the elements in the Upper Towns which had opposed Emisteseguo and in Handsome Fellow perpetuated some elements of the Mortar's old conspiracy. The Cowetas, who included Escochabey, had had for the past fifteen years a certain independence of and truculence toward the British, especially Stuart and Wright. Escochabey was a representative of the Tyger clan, which had suffered the most from Stuart and Wright's demands for satisfaction for frontier assaults. Escochabey for years had been a good friend of Galphin, and Handsome Fellow had long been associated in the trade with Rae's Augusta house and its Okfuskee branch. Other prominent headmen were Blue Salt of Cussita, the Upper Towns Chevulkey Warrior, who was a spy for Taitt, LeCoffe of Coweta, and the long-outlawed Houmacha, recently pardoned by Wright but apparently still harboring grudges and also possessing loyalty to Handsome Fellow, who had obtained his pardon.

They heard a strong anti-English talk. Hamilton, the spokesman for the commissioners, described Stuart as a man who feared the truth and who intended after the Choctaw peace to get many

[24] Taitt to Tonyn, May 3, 1776, B.P.R.O., C.O.5/56, p. 639; Brown to Tonyn, May 8, 1776, B.P.R.O., C.O.5/56, pp. 643–54.

Creeks killed by sending them against the frontier. He blamed the King for the stoppage of the trade, saying the King intended to impoverish the traders but said that the colonists would soon be able to manufacture their own trade goods. He intimated that Spain and France would give the colonists huge supplies of ammunition, and he declared that colonial troops everywhere had beaten the British, referring, of course, to the forced British evacuation of Boston. He said colonial ships would attack St. Augustine and Pensacola and stop the supply of goods to the nation from there. He accused Taitt of causing all the trouble and demanded that he be driven out. Finally he asked that no British troops be allowed to pass through the nation to attack the frontier and that the Indians remain neutral.

The only dissident voice raised at the conference was that of the Chevulkey Warrior who demanded satisfaction for the death of an Indian on the frontier. This Galphin promised and asked that two of the Indians remain after the conference to see the murderer executed.[25] The Americans had relatively few goods to give out as presents, but they did have large quantities of rum, the Cowetas alone carrying ninety kegs back to their town. The Lower Townsmen went home convinced of the generosity of their hosts and thoroughly impregnated with the doctrine of neutrality. At Coweta they celebrated with the American rum and threatened the lives of traders from St. Augustine and Pensacola.[26] Pro-American feeling ran high, and large numbers of Upper Townsmen and Cussitas under Blue Salt prepared to go down to Savannah to attend a talk to be given by Georgia commissioner Bullock. Taitt pressed Emisteseguo into service to try to halt them.

But the great surge of pro-American feeling generated at Augusta was dashed by other forces. Despite ties of friendship with Galphin, Coweta was fundamentally hostile to the frontier which Augusta represented. This hostility suddenly flared anew when that inveterate frontier Indian baiter, Thomas Fee, who some years before had murdered Mad Turkey, killed a Coweta warrior on Ogee-

---

25 Talks at Augusta, B.P.R.O., C.O.5/94, p. 121.
26 Taitt to Stuart, July 7, 1776, B.P.R.O., C.O.5/77, pp. 323ff.

chee River. Coweta demanded vengeance. Although the Georgia Council of Safety ordered the seizure of Fee, Ishenpoaphe and Escochabey began to listen to Taitt's talks. In the Upper Towns the Chevulkey Warrior fanned hostility when representatives he had sent to see justice done for the murder of his kinsman returned to report that they had been deceived, that the man they saw hanged had actually been executed for the murder of his own wife. Lower Creek checks on the Seminoles were removed. When in July of 1776 a small American force raided toward St. Mary's River in East Florida, the Cowkeeper of Latchoway went to Tonyn's aid. Cowetas took their own satisfaction for the death of their fellow townsman by killing a frontiersman on the Ogeechee River. From this time on, Coweta was largely anti-American. Had not the British attack on Charlestown in June been repulsed, and had not the Cherokees been almost destroyed by the frontiersmen, most of the Creeks certainly would have approved war against the Americans.

The result of the Second Cherokee War, which broke out in July, 1776, had a profound effect upon the Creeks. This war was waged independently of Stuart's grand plan for a united Indian attack upon the frontier should the British make a successful lodgement in the South. The Cherokees, incensed at the invasion of their lands by settlers on Holston's and Nolichukey rivers, and spirited up by the war talk of the northern Indians, swept out to war all along the frontiers of the two Carolinas, despite the efforts of Stuart's deputy, Cameron, to hold them back until the British had landed in South Carolina. They killed patriot and tory alike. Cherokee deputies approached the Creeks for an alliance, but Emisteseguo, held back by Stuart and Taitt, rejected the overture, saying the Cherokee war was not authorized by Stuart. His was a fortunate decision for the Creeks, for frontier vengeance on the Cherokees was swift and terrible. Armies of several thousand frontiersmen, both tory and patriot, stormed into the Cherokee country, overwhelmed feeble resistance, destroyed many towns, and devastated the crops. On the frontier, "Virginians," flushed with their success over the Cherokees and mindful of Stuart's war talk to the Creeks, talked boldly of turning their forces upon the Creeks.

Galphin seized onto the Cherokee defeat and the frontier anti-Creek fervor to send a warning by Houmacha to the Lower Creeks to hold fast to neutrality lest they suffer the fate of the Cherokees.[27] American General Arthur Lee sent to Blue Salt of Cussita, the Pumpkin King of Eusitchee, and Ishenpoaphe of Coweta an invitation to meet him in Savannah along with a warning that if the Creeks started a war, they would be destroyed as the Cherokees had been.[28] Already the Lower Towns had again decided to leave the white man's war alone. The Creeks who had gone to Tonyn's aid in East Florida left for home.[29]

Nevertheless the full extent of the Cherokee disaster was slow to make an impact upon the Creeks. Strong animosities operated against the frontiersmen. The Chevulkey Warrior's kinsmen skulked about Augusta seeking a favorable moment to take revenge for the death of his relative, for whom the frontiersmen had failed to give satisfaction. In the early autumn of 1776, the liberty party having as yet failed to produce goods for trade, the British effort to pull the Creeks entirely back into loyalist allegiance enjoyed a temporary success. Stuart planned a meeting of Creeks and Choctaws for Pensacola in October to cement a Creek-Choctaw peace and form a definitive military alliance with the Creeks. Concerning Emisteseguo and his following he had no doubts. Only in the Lower Towns where neutrality talk had been the strongest was there question. And here he was aided by the fortuitous circumstance that Ishenpoaphe and the other headmen had their latent anti-Americanism stimulated by the death of a Cussita warrior on the frontier. Ishenpoaphe "threw away" Galphin's admonition to neutrality. Furthermore Galphin's strongest agent in the Lower Towns, his nephew David Holmes, had apparently defected to the British. Holmes, having taken over Galphin's trade and having found it impossible to obtain goods from Charlestown and Savannah, had shifted his base to Pensacola. He was now playing a

[27] Galphin to trader George Burgess, Aug. 28, 1776, B.P.R.O., C.O.5/78, p. 39; S. Thomas to Stuart, Sept. 19, 1776, B.P.R.O., C.O.5/78, p. 59.

[28] Jonathan Bryon to Headmen of the Lower Towns, Sept. 1, 1776, B.P.R.O., C.O.5/78, p. 51.

[29] Tonyn to Taitt, Sept. 3, 1776, B.P.R.O., C.O.5/78, p. 105.

double game. Taking advantage of Ishenpoaphe's vengeful mood, he induced the Coweta headman to send out a party to try to kill Jonathan Bryon's American agent, Thomas Gray, who, having already once saved his skin by going to St. Augustine and making a superficial oath of allegiance to the Crown, had again set out for the nation with American talks. Needless to say, Ishenpoaphe did not go down to Savannah as General Lee had requested. Instead he went to Pensacola to hear Stuart.[30]

Stuart's October, 1776, meeting at Pensacola gave every appearance of success. Though "the Indians were greatly dispirited by the unopposed success of the rebels in repulsing Clinton at Charlestown and the non-appearance of any support from government to His Majesty's distressed subjects in the interior parts of the provinces," Emisteseguo's Upper Creeks engaged to send assistance to the Cherokees. Both Upper Creeks and Choctaws "vied with each other in strong declarations of attachment to His Majesty and determined resolution to act in his cause whenever desired."[31] The Lower Creeks, who came to the meeting late, after much persuasion promised to defend St. Augustine against the rebels.[32]

The peace between Creeks and Choctaws was cemented in brilliant pageantry in the streets of Pensacola. Reported Stuart: "Both parties appointed to meet in the street before my door; each party had a white flag as an emblem of peace and were highly painted. They halted about three hundred yards distance from each other, their principal chiefs singing the peace song and waving eagles' tails and swans' wings over their heads. Then they began to advance slowly when at a signal given a number of young men sallied out from each party and made a sham fight in the space between them. At last the parties met and after saluting each other joined hands in my presence. Their chiefs then came into my house and delivered into my hands two war clubs painted red as the last ceremony of laying down their arms; which I promised to bury very

[30] D. Holmes to Stuart, Sept. 26, 1776, B.P.R.O., C.O. 5/78, p. 63.

[31] Stuart to Germaine, Oct. 26, 1776, B.P.R.O., C.O.5/78, No. 10, p. 29.

[32] B.P.R.O., C.O.5/57, p. 70.

deep in the earth and made them a short congratulatory speech . . . ."[33]

In the temporary pro-British mood of the Lower Towns, William McIntosh, Stuart's deputy to the Lower Creeks, even while most of the headmen were at Pensacola and the bulk of the young men out hunting, prevailed on a few of the Hitchitis under the warrior Hycut to go down to St. Augustine to be fitted out against the rebels.[34] These with small British parties fanned out from St. Augustine into lower Georgia and in January of 1777 ambushed and defeated an American detachment on Beard's Creek. After the Pensacola meeting, Latchoway Seminoles under the Cowkeeper joined the East Florida British forces, and on February 18, eighty Creeks under Cussappa with seventy British Florida rangers captured the American Fort McIntosh on Saltilla River.[35]

Despite this commitment, the great bulk of the Creeks hesitated to implement the grand promises made at Pensacola. The reasons were several. In the Lower Towns, George Galphin had succeeded in raising up dissention at Cussita. Even as the Pensacola meeting had convened, Galphin had inveigled a party of Cussitas to come down to Silver Bluff, where he told them stories of French and Spanish aid to come, of an American trade to be developed, and gave them substantial presents. Confronted by this news, the Cussita King on his return trom Pensacola, reconsidered his commitments to Stuart.[36] His decision was timely, for American scouting parties, sent out of Fort Augusta as a result of the Seminole action, probed toward the Lower Towns. About the same time, the American General William McIntosh sent into the Lower Towns a message that the British would soon be forced to leave all the country to the Americans. Against the background of the Cherokee disaster, fear of American retaliation mounted in the Lower Creeks and paralyzed action. As an aftermath of the Pensacola meeting large convoys of British trade goods arrived in the Lower Towns

[33] Stuart to Germaine, Oct. 26, 1776, B.P.R.O., C.O.5/78, No. 10, p. 29.
[34] McIntosh to [Stuart], Nov. 9, 1776, B.P.R.O., C.O.5/57, p. 93.
[35] Brown to Tonyn, Feb. 20, 1777, B.P.R.O., C.O.5/77, p. 345.
[36] Stuart to Knox, Mar. 10, 1777, B.P.R.O., C.O.5/78, p. 231.

and the Cussita King, Ishenpoaphe, and Escochabey sent a message to Stuart that "we are all of one opinion to hold you fast"; they said that "the Virginians are daily approaching our towns" and that they would assume a defensive stance.[37] However, American influence still exerted leverage by subterranean means. By April, 1777, Stuart was complaining, "the rebel agents have found means to keep up a party there, although not of any weight or consequence, yet sufficient to give much plague and trouble to my officers and by means of emissaries amongst the traders and packhorsemen (out of Pensacola . . . .) they disturb and distract the Indians with forgeries and stories calculated to excite their jealousy and give them distrust of all my measures."[38] It seems that Holmes had whispered around that the goods he brought from Pensacola were actually Galphin's.[39]

On his return to Little Tallassee from Pensacola, Emisteseguo found the Abeikas paralyzed with shock at their discovery of the extent of the Cherokee defeat. Stuart's agent to the Cherokees, Alexander Cameron, and a host of starving Cherokees were refugees in the Abeika towns. Emisteseguo apologetically informed Stuart: "When I was at Pensacola we all thought Scotchie [Cameron] was still in the Cherokee nation but it seems the Virginians were so hot upon him that he and all the Cherokees were obliged to run— I have sat quietly a long time without joining either party, but the Virginians are now come very near my nation and I do not want them to come any nearer. When I was down there [Pensacola] I told you that if the red warriors to the Northward would hold a red stick against the Virginians there, I would hold one against them here—I am in great hopes that the Great King will fight strong and not drop the hatchet, if he should we will be badly off when we have nobody to assist us but to be left to fight for ourselves . . . ." In short he awaited British troops to help the Creeks. Meanwhile he desired a little rum to bolster him in his worries and to wash away the fatigues of the hunt he was about to undertake.[40]

[37] B.P.R.O., C.O.5/78, p. 221.
[38] Stuart to Howe, Apr. 13, 1777, B.P.R.O., C.O.5/94, p. 567.
[39] Tonyn to Taitt, June 12, 1777, B.P.R.O., C.O.5/57, p. 615.
[40] Emisteseguo to Stuart, Nov. 19, 1776, B.P.R.O., C.O.5/78, No. 13, p. 151.

During the winter Taitt seems to have pried him out of his doubts, for in February or March he set out for the Cherokee country with three hundred warriors.[41]

It was an abortive move. Rumors of an intended attack by Americans from South Carolina on a backwoods British convoy of goods and ammunition from Pensacola to the Cherokees turned him back. Taitt informed Governor Tonyn, who under apprehension of American attack upon St. Augustine was crying for more Creek aid, "the fate of the Cherokees has struck the people of this nation with such a panic that, although they have a great aversion to the rebels yet they are afraid to go against them until they hear of His Majesty's troops being at Charlestown or Savannah."[42] Moreover, in the Upper Towns, Handsome Fellow's anti-Emisteseguo schism in the interest of a neutral course had considerable influence, and only awaited a strong move from Galphin to be encouraged to exert greater pressure against the pro-British faction.

In May, 1777, Galphin, whose main aim was to keep the Creeks neutral in spite of Stuart and his own difficult frontier, went on the offensive. He planned another conference with the Creeks for June, this time at Ogeechee Old Town on the Ogeechee River. The Lower Creek partisans of neutrality at Cussita, where kinsmen of Handsome Fellow were strong, had been prepared for this meeting by a message from Savannah, that the French and Spaniards would join the Americans to cut off St. Augustine, Pensacola, and Mobile, that there would be no more land fighting to trouble the Creeks. Soon after arrived George Galphin's invitation to the Ogeechee meeting coupled with an assurance that all Creek sins against Americans would be forgiven. The invitation was particularly welcome at this time because it was taken as a sign of peace from a quarter from which rumors of attack had been circulating,[43] and there was some basis for apprehension since Seminoles had taken a conspicuous part in the British repulse of Colonel Baker and

[41] B.P.R.O., C.O.5/78, p. 213.
[42] Taitt to Tonyn, May 22, 1777, B.P.R.O., C.O.5/77, p. 599.
[43] Ibid.

Colonel Elbert's American expedition against St. Augustine in May.[44] Despite British deputy William McIntosh's efforts to frustrate the Ogeechee meeting, the Cussita King, who had been so friendly to Stuart at Pensacola, decided to go. But Coweta, which had of recent months lent a surreptitious ear to American undercover talk and had again displayed some signs of joining the neutralist faction, once again was hostile. A head warrior of the Tyger clan and nephew of Ishenpoaphe had been killed in a horse stealing raid into the Ogeechee country and Cowetas talked of revenge.[45]

In the Upper Creeks, Handsome Fellow gathered a party from Okfuskee, Sugatspoges, and Big Tallassee to go down to meet Galphin. There was talk of assassinating Emisteseguo who opposed Handsome Fellow and labored conscientiously to commit all the Creeks to the British cause.[46] After Handsome Fellow's party set off, Emisteseguo promised Taitt to send a war party against Georgia late in the summer, and entered into negotiations with the northern Indians for an alliance against the Americans. Ishenpoaphe sent up from Coweta to the Upper Towns for his kinsman of the Tyger clan, the Mad Dog of Tuckabatchee, to raise up his relatives among the Okchais and among the Alabamas to come down and join him against Georgia. He had been roused to positivism by the arrival at Coweta of half-blood Alexander McGillivray, newly commissioned a British deputy by Stuart. This seems to have been McGillivray's first appearance among the Creeks during the revolution.[47]

[44] McCall, *History of Georgia*, 119-22.

[45] McIntosh to Tonyn, May 29, 1777, B.P.R.O., C.O.5/57, 607.

[46] Tonyn to Stuart, June 16, 1777, B.P.R.O., C.O.5/57, p. 626.

[47] Milfort, in the "Memoirs," says he accompanied McGillivray to the Creek nation in the spring of 1776 and there attended the spring national meeting of the Creeks. Neither British nor American records indicate McGillivray's presence in the nation in 1776, much less Milfort's. While it seems likely from the apparent authenticity of his accounts of Creek institutions that Milfort had at some time visited the Creek nation, his account of his having been raised to the position of head war chief of all the Creeks seems apochryphal. In this period there was no such position. Milfort's account of his leading eighty Creek Warriors on an eighteen months' trek through Arkansas, Missouri, and Illinois in the period 1780-82 likewise seems romantic. It is, of course, possible that he was a French secret agent in the Creek country. Considering the long association of the French with the Creeks, the sending of such an agent to the Creek country during the Revolution does not seem improbable. There is, however, no evidence of such an agent's having had any influence on the

He was speedily to rise to great influence. He was the son of trader Lachlan McGillivray and a highly placed woman of the prestigious Wind Clan, had been educated by his father as an Englishman, and had served as a clerk in a counting house in Charlestown. Creeks listened to him with interest.[48] However, at this time he was unable to prevent the Cussita King from going to meet Galphin.

On June 17 at Ogeechee Old Town, Handsome Fellow, Opeitley Mico of Tallassee (known as the Tallassee King's son), the Cussita King, and four or five hundred warriors (none of them Cowetas) met the continental commissioners George Galphin and Robert Rae, and the Georgia Indian commissioners, of whom Jonathan Bryon was one, at the riverside. Galphin opened the meeting by regretting the blood that had been spilled and asking for restraint lest the Creeks find themselves in the same plight as the Cherokees. He requested the return of two whites taken prisoner in frontier clashes and announced that he had goods to send to the nation provided the Indians would protect his traders and drive out Taitt and McIntosh. He invited some of them to go to Philadelphia to see the Continental armies and asked reparation for damages done in raids and that the Indians agree to punish future murderers.

Opeitley Mico replied, somewhat expansively, in the name of all the towns of the Chattahoochee, Tallapoosa, and Coosa rivers, and with full regalia of white pouch and white beads and an eagle's wing, that he was glad the trading path from Carolina and Georgia would now be open. He asked that to convince the opposition in the nation goods be sent immediately. Handsome Fellow then spoke. First invoking the Master of Breath, he sentimentally recalled the long history of the friendly trading path from Carolina and Georgia. Referring to Cussita and Tallassee as the largest towns in the nation, he spoke of their desire for peace and an open trading path. He had come, he said, despite the talk of Taitt and Emisteseguo, but he must take back plenty of presents if he were not to

course of Creek events in the Revolution. As yet unavailable French and Spanish cypher archives may someday solve the Milfort problem.

[48] Taitt to Stuart, June 5, 1777, B.P.R.O., C.O.5/78, p. 313; Milfort, *Memoirs*, 198.

be laughed at (which was true). He said he could not go to Philadelphia but he would go to Charlestown. He had been unable to bring prisoners down for release but would send for them, saying that unless they were surrendered the trade could not be renewed. The British, he said, had been unable to supply half the trade needs of his town, which would require fifteen or twenty horseloads of goods and four of ammunition. He then concluded by saying, "I have no view in private interest in what I have said but have consulted the good of our young people in general."[49]

Galphin was able to give out a large present of guns, ammunition, and rum, though not many goods, and the bulk of the Indians went back to their towns well pleased. Handsome Fellow with some of the Cussitas and Okfuskees visited Charlestown where they were shown the vast stores of ammunition and weapons with which the French had supplied the rebel state. They were treated to a parade of the militia and were entertained aboard French ships in the harbor. They were taken on a tour of the forts and told how the English fleet had been beaten off the year before. Received by the provincial council, they were told by Edmund Routeledge that Taitt and Stuart only wanted to involve them in a war of destruction so that the British could eventually destroy them, that the French and Spaniards would soon block the gulf ports to stop the British Indian trade. Mistaking the seaborne move of British general Howe from New York to the Chesapeake to attack Philadelphia as a British withdrawal, he told how in the north the British had been forced to take to their ships. He concluded with a demand that the Creeks either kill or drive away Taitt and McIntosh.[50]

With Handsome Fellow among the Americans the war party hesitated; if they went to war, his life would be threatened and his fellow clansmen would split the nation.[51] Another ground for hesitancy was the near famine in the towns caused by the partial failure of the corn crop the year before. The war party, however, did chase Murphy, Galphin's agent at the Okfuskees, from the Upper

49 Laurens Papers, June 17, 1777.
50 Stuart to Germaine, Oct. 6, 1777, B.P.R.O., C.O.5/79, p. 57.
51 Taitt to Stuart, Aug. 13, 1777, B.P.R.O., C.O.5/78, p. 431.

Towns with threats to his life. Okfuskees loyal to Handsome Fellow rallied to protect him and escorted him to their kinsmen at Cussita for safety. From the Lower Towns some Eufalees and Cowetas were out on horse stealing raids on the frontier. One of these parties massacred the Dilkes family on the Ogeechee River and another routed an American scouting party on the Broad River. The American-hating Tyger clan's Escochabey of Coweta, hearing from Cussita talk that there was a strong surge in the Upper Creeks to go over to the neutralist cause, went up to Little Tallassee to consult with Taitt and sound out sentiment.[52]

Escochabey had reason to worry, for Handsome Fellow's clan was determined that the fruits of the Ogeechee meeting with Galphin should not be lost, and that war talk and action in the nation must cease. On August 13 at Augusta, on his return from Charlestown, Handsome Fellow met the American Colonel Elbert, who had been sent up with troops to protect the frontier from such acts as those of the Cowetas. Elbert, eager to avoid war, told Handsome Fellow that the price of peace was the killing of Taitt, Cameron, and McIntosh.[53] The great neutralist apparently accepted these terms. However, Handsome Fellow died on the path to Okfuskee. Leadership in his projects then devolved upon his Cussita kinsmen, Nea Mico and Neaclucluckotico. When they arrived at Cussita, they found that McIntosh had gathered a mixed war party of Creeks, Cherokees, and refugee loyalists to proceed against Augusta and Galphin's home at Silver Bluff and that Cameron with one hundred horseloads of ammunition to support the assault had arrived with another party of refugee loyalists at the Upper Towns village of Hickory Ground. Apparently the two expeditions had only awaited the safe return out of American reach of the neutralist deputies before launching their attack, which was set for September 20.[54]

The returned Cussitas knew they must act quickly. They sent orders to their kinsmen at Okfuskee to kill Taitt and Cameron

[52] *Ibid.*, Aug. 3, p. 417.
[53] Talk of Col. Elbert, Aug. 13, 1777, B.P.R.O., C.O.5/57, p. 729.
[54] Talk from Headmen of the Upper and Lower Creeks, Oct. 13, 1777, Galphin Papers in Laurens Papers.

while they disposed of McIntosh. Some of the Chehaws and Cowetas, discovering the Cussita intent, set a guard over McIntosh. Frustrated in their designs on the British deputy, the Cussitas plundered the Pensacola traders in the Lower Towns. Traders and McIntosh fled to Pensacola. Great confusion prevailed as Cussitas and Cowetas angrily confronted each other on the brink of civil war. On September 19, in the Upper Towns, Okfuskees of Handsome Fellow's clan, crying that the British plan of action would bring an American attack on the Creek towns, rushed upon Little Tallassee to kill Taitt and Emisteseguo. At Hickory Ground, Tallapooses plundered Cameron and his men. All the British fled to Pensacola, and Emisteseguo, spared by the intervention of Alexander McGillivray, abdicated his role as the great proponent of the British.[55]

In this situation, McGillivray asserted his Creek heritage and came forward as leader of the pro-British faction. Apparently by birth and clan he enjoyed a prestige which rendered him immune to proscription. When the Okfuskees had stormed into Little Tallassee, he had stood between them and Taitt and Emisteseguo, whose lives he saved. The Okfuskees had probably feared to injure him lest they rouse the Wind clan against them, for Emisteseguo told McGillivray that since he belonged to a large, powerful clan who would support him, McGillivray must now take over the responsibility of resolving the crisis that had threatened civil war. McGillivray struck out boldly. He summoned a meeting of headmen to compose tribal differences and wrote Stuart that he thought he could eventually restore the British position.[56]

For the moment the neutralist faction had triumphed. Opeitley Mico of Little Tallassee sent belts to the Chickasaws and Choctaws announcing the rout of the British and urging these nations to follow his neutral line.[57]

---

[55] Stuart to Germaine, Oct. 6, 1777, B.P.R.O., C.O.5/79, p. 591.
[56] A. McGillivray to Stuart, Sept. 21, 1777, B.P.R.O., C.O.5/79, p. 65.
[57] Opeitly Mico to Galphin, Feb. 22, 1778, Galphin Papers in Laurens Papers.

18

The American Revolution: Choosing the Wrong Side 1778-83

I N THE WINTER OF 1777–78, the triumphant neutralists were confronted by the appalling fact that theirs was a hollow victory. With the winter hunts coming on, the nation was devoid of goods with which to equip the hunters or to purchase their deerskins, for Galphin had as yet been unable to fulfill his Ogeechee promises and the British traders had fled. Both factions knew that a trade must be obtained and that whichever side got there first would prevail.

In late October, ten pro-British Upper Towns sent deputies with large followings to Pensacola to declare their loyalty to the Crown and to assert that if the British trade was restored they would go against the Americans. Stuart feared that if Indians without British leadership attacked the frontier, many loyalists would suffer. He also feared that the neutralist faction would retaliate by attacking West Florida. He therefore rejected the Indian offer. He would reopen the trade only if the Indians could guarantee the safety of his deputies to the nation. This the pro-British party could not do. Stuart then encouraged them to go home, go out on their winter hunts and trust that differences in the nation could be cleared up by spring. Promising that after the winter hunts they would hold a meeting of all the headmen and bring the disaffected Okfuskees over, the unhappy Indians returned to their towns.[1]

Soon after, six hundred Lower Townsmen, including some Cussitas, appeared at Pensacola. Stuart gave them much the same answer. Lower Towns' deputies also visited St. Augustine on a similar mission. Governor Tonyn sent them back to "upbraid" the "disloyal" towns. According to Tonyn's information, on the deputies' return the pro-British townsmen surrounded the neutralist towns Apalachicola and Cussita, and "made them promise to relinquish their engagements with Galphin and took hostages from them for their fulfilling the promise." Lower Towns parties went out to scout the frontier.[2]

In December, McGillivray arrived at Pensacola to report that the Okfuskees repented their misbehavior and desired that the nation be not punished for their sins. They would welcome anybody except Taitt as Stuart's deputy. Stuart told McGillivray to invite the penitents down to see him.[3]

McGillivray either misrepresented the state of mind at Okfuskee or presented the point of view of some of the weaker townsmen. Actually in November at about the same time that the ten towns had gone to Pensacola, Handsome Fellow's successor, Tuskenahathka, or the White Lieutenant of Okfuskee, and Opeitley Mico of Tallassee with three hundred and fifty followers had gone down to Ogeechee Old Town to meet Galphin and Rae and had had a great success. They asked Galphin to send up trade goods immediately, and Galphin responded by fitting out a convoy of eighty horseloads of goods, rum, and ammunition. They also protested settlers' trespassing on Creek lands and heard Galphin lamely assert that the trespassers were actually agents of Stuart.[4]

The mid-winter arrival in the nation of goods sent by Galphin

[1] Stuart to Germaine, Jan. 23, 1778, B.P.R.O., C.O.5/79, p. 127.
[2] Tonyn to Germaine, Dec. 26, 1777, B.P.R.O., C.O.5/58, p. 20.
[3] Stuart to Germaine, Jan. 23, 1778, B.P.R.O., C.O.5/79, p. 127.
[4] Talk at Old Town on Ogeechee River, Nov. 6, 1777, Galphin Papers in Laurens Papers.

made a powerful impression. Anti-American Coweta, from which parties had killed two white land trespassers, divided, and the bulk of the Lower Towns people promptly espoused the neutralist cause.[5] In February, 1778, Fine Bones of Coweta, who had killed whites on the frontier, sent a message to Galphin stating: "I take your talk and will kill no more white people—the Virginia people first began by killing our people. As all the towns has taken your talk I will not be against it." He warned Galphin that a Coweta party was still out against the people of the ceded lands.[6]

The activity of this party undid all the good the White Lieutenant had accomplished at Ogeechee Old Town. They attacked a detachment of American rangers near the ceded lands and killed three. The flow of American goods all but ceased.[7]

With the goods shortage again acute the surge of pro-American feeling began to disintegrate. Deputies from both Upper and Lower Towns went to Pensacola to plead with Stuart. Hycut of Cussita, once strongly anti-British, and some of the former anti-British headmen of Okfuskee assured Stuart his deputies would be protected. His policy a success, with an abundance of trade goods pouring into Pensacola from London, Stuart early in March sent McIntosh under Hycut's protection back to the Lower Towns, Taitt under Indian escorts to the Upper Towns, and traders to all the towns. The British moved toward triumph.[8]

At the end of March, McIntosh summoned a meeting of all the Lower Towns headmen at the Hitchitis. Even the Fat King of the Cussitas came and, moved by McIntosh's talk of peace and plenty of goods, promised not to listen to Galphin. With the arrival of traders from Pensacola, the Cussita young hunters who had sold their deerskins to one of Galphin's agents on credit for goods to be delivered later, repossessed them in order to trade with the British. When Governor Tonyn sent up a request for Lower Creek aid in an expedition against Georgia, a large number of Hitchitis, Chehaws and Flint Rivers expressed a readiness to go to St. Augustine

[5] Patrick Carr to Galphin, Feb. 19, 1778, Galphin Papers in Laurens Papers.
[6] *Ibid.*
[7] Stuart to Germaine, Mar. 5, 1778, B.P.R.O., C.O.5/79, p. 223.
[8] *Ibid.*

in April.[9] Already Colonel Thomas Brown operating out of St. Augustine with British rangers and a few Seminoles had taken and burnt the American Fort Barrington on the Altamaha River.[10]

On March 30 at a big meeting called by Taitt, the Abeikas and Tallapooses agreed to protect the British traders. Taitt sent traders to the disaffected towns of Great Tallassee, Okfuskee, Sugatspoges, and Corn House, hoping to win them over. The Okfuskees invited him to visit them, but Taitt, thinking they only awaited goods from Galphin to become hostile again, refused. He wished to get them down to Pensacola to give their allegiance to the British cause, and told them to look him up at Little Tallassee if they wished to go to Pensacola.[11] Failing by mid-April to receive any more goods from Galphin, Red Shoes, the Mad Dog, and other headmen went down to Great Tallassee to win over Opeitley Mico and his pro-American confederates to making a trip to Pensacola in May.[12] But the neutralists had not entirely succumbed. Mad Dog of Tuck-abatchee prevented those Lower Creeks who had promised to go to Tonyn's aid from moving by sending word that Stuart wished them to be at peace. Die-hard Okfuskees announced that if Lower Townsmen went to St. Augustine to operate against the Americans, they would attack loyalist settlers near Pensacola and Mobile.[13] Of the seventeen hundred Creeks Tonyn expected, barely one hundred appeared, and these did not stay long. The only Indians Tonyn could count on were a few free-lance Seminoles from Latchoway.[14] Tonyn blamed this failure upon Stuart, whose theory it was that the Creeks should not make a major descent upon the Americans until the British army made a successful landing on the Carolina and Georgia coasts. Stuart denied he was to blame for Lower Towns failure to support Tonyn, which suggests the Indian factors to have been dominant in this situation. However, after the disastrous rout of the traders in September, 1777, following the aggressive British

[9] McIntosh to Stuart, Apr. 3, 1778, B.P.R.O., C.O.5/79, p. 299.

[10] Report on American Mss., Vol. VIII, No. 44.

[11] Taitt to Stuart, Apr. 7, 1778, B.P.R.O., C.O.5/79, p. 303.

[12] Ibid., Apr. 13, p. 307.

[13] Stuart to Tonyn, July 10, 1778, B.P.R.O., C.O.5/58, p. 279.

[14] Tonyn to Germaine, May 15, 1778, B.P.R.O., C.O.5/58, pp. 314–15; Tonyn to Taitt, May 16, 1778, B.P.R.O., C.O.5/80, p. 57.

efforts to organize the Creeks to go against the frontier, Stuart seems to have been cautiously determined on a less belligerent course until he had won over the dangerous anti-British elements.

This line of thinking lay behind the meeting at Pensacola on May 2, 1778, of four hundred Okfuskee, Tallassee, Cussita, Hitchiti, and Apalachicola Indians, many of them former dissidents. Stuart put on a showy display for them with bands playing and cannons firing as they made their ceremonial entrance into the town in the graceful maneuvers of the Eagle Tail dance. As a result of the talks, they gave "strongest assurances of good behavior" and promised to "drop all communication with the rebels, place their whole confidence in a trade from Pensacola; and would not hinder those who would go to help His Majesty's forces."[15]

Stuart's report of events was optimistic to say the least. He had not heard all the voices. Important neutralists had not yet given up. Even as the swing to the British appeared to be in full tide, the King of the Tuckabatchees and his following appeared at Savannah to see what the Americans had to offer. They probably complained of the same trespasses of which Galphin had been informed, for during their stay at Savannah the Georgia Provincial Council ordered a cessation of all grants of land on the upper Ogeechee. They also gave the Indians presents of ammunition and goods.[16] Indians who had attended the Pensacola meeting informed Galphin that they had forced Stuart to sanction their neutralism. They said they had threatened him that if any more Cowetas went against the frontier, they would lead war parties against Pensacola. They also said that they had forced him to withdraw Taitt and lower the trade prices.[17] During the Pensacola meeting up among the Abeikas there was a fracas demonstrating neutralist strength. Paddy Carr, one of Galphin's agents, had arrived with a small convoy of trade goods and a message for Richard Henderson in which Galphin asked him to urge the Indians to side with the Americans. British

[15] Stuart to Knox, May 18, 1778, B.P.R.O., C.O.5/79, p. 315.
[16] Allen D. Candler, *The Revolutionary Records of the State of Georgia*, Vol. II, pp. 66–67.
[17] Indian Talks to Galphin, Okfuskee, June 9, 1778, Galphin Papers in Laurens Papers.

traders in the region, interpreting the willingness of so many former neutralists to go to Pensacola as giving the British a free hand, attempted to seize Henderson as an enemy agent and either kill him or send him prisoner to Pensacola. But Okfuskees and Sugatspoges had rescued Henderson. Paddy Carr expressed the opinion to Galphin that the little of American goods would eventually be more effective than the muchness of British presents, if Galphin would continue to talk peace and neutrality.[18] The Tallassee King, who had heard via Coweta that the Spaniards would soon take St. Augustine and Pensacola, promised to kill Taitt if he did not get out of the nation.[19] All that spring Galphin was at Ogeechee receiving Creek visitors. In June he learned that many of those who had been at Pensacola, having heard that the French and Spaniards would soon repossess the gulf coast, planned to visit him. Galphin's post was so influential in sustaining anti-British sentiment that the British offered a reward of five hundred pounds sterling for him dead or alive.[20]

When, in June, Stuart received news of the planned American attack on East Florida, he called on his Creek friends to implement the promises of co-operation they had given him in May. He sent "the most pressing instruction" to Taitt and McIntosh to employ the Indians against the frontier and to go to the aid of St. Augustine. Most of the pro-British Creeks, oppressed by the shortage of food due to crop failures in 1777, deferred action until after the Green Corn dance in late July or early August. However, a few parties, including one from divided Okfuskee, went against the frontier.[21] Some Cowetas went out to make cattle raids on the ceded lands. The only help Tonyn had to turn back the American thrust was a party of Seminoles.[22]

The neutralist faction reacted characteristically. Okfuskees returning from meeting Galphin at Ogeechee Old Town in June called a council of headmen to propose an immediate attack on the British

[18] Patrick Carr to Galphin, June 10, 1778, Galphin Papers in Laurens Papers.
[19] Henderson to Galphin, June 12, 1778, Galphin Papers in Laurens Papers.
[20] Galphin to Henry Laurens, June 25, 1778, Galphin Papers in Laurens Papers.
[21] Stuart to Tonyn, July 10, 1778, B.P.R.O., C.O.5/58, p. 455.
[22] B.P.R.O., C.O.5/58, pp. 414–15.

traders in retaliation for the frontier assaults. Except for McGillivray, only neutralist headmen attended. Division of opinion developed. Will's Friend and the White Lieutenant of Okfuskee, while opposing Creek attacks upon South Carolina and Georgia, also opposed attacks on Pensacola or the British traders. They argued that all traders should be protected in their persons and properties. Thus effectively opposed, the belligerents had to acquiesce and agree to be quiet at least until the war parties returned from their forays. Will's Friend and the White Lieutenant did not trust their colleagues and hesitated to go down to Pensacola to treat with Stuart until they could see what developed on the raiding parties' return.[23] In the Lower Towns, where McGillivray's cousin, the half-blood McPherson, operated at Coweta to raise a large party to go even to the gates of Charlestown and Savannah, the Cussitas warned the Cowetas that if they went out the Cussitas would attack the loyalist settlers near Pensacola. They even threatened the life of McIntosh, who was raising a large party of Chehaws and Hitchitis to go to St. Augustine.[24] The Fat King of Cussita sent a runner down to Ogeechee Old Town to warn Galphin that Lower Creek parties intended to go against the frontier.[25]

In the long run, however, because of division and lack of a substantial American trade, the neutralist gestures proved ineffective. During July and August, 1778, several hundred Creeks operated on the perimeters of the Georgia frontier. Seminoles assisted Tonyn in repulsing the attack of American General Howe on East Florida. Galphin's nephews, Holmes and Barnard, suspected by Tonyn of actually being American agents, led parties from the Lower Chattahoochee towns of Red Ground and Miscaque toward St. Augustine, but after crossing the Suwannee River they turned back upon learning that the Americans had retreated. By stratagem a Creek party captured and burned an American fort on the Saltilla River and carried off forty horses.[26] One hundred and twenty warriors from Eufalees, Apalachee Old Fields, and other Lower Chatta-

[23] A. McGillivray to Stuart, Aug. 26, 1778, B.P.R.O., C.O.5/79, p. 387.
[24] Stuart to Germaine, Aug. 10, 1778, B.P.R.O., C.O.5/79, p. 367.
[25] Galphin to J. L. Gervaise, Aug. 10, 1778, Gervaise Papers in Laurens Papers.
[26] David Holmes Journal, July–Sept., 1778, B.P.R.O., C.O.5/80, pp. 67ff.

hoochee towns went down the Altamaha River. McIntosh esti-
mated that eight hundred Upper and Lower Creeks (two hundred,
according to neutralist Opeitley Mico of Tallassee) went against
the ceded lands above the Broad River.[27] There they massacred
twenty or thirty of the inhabitants, killed many cattle and hogs,
and laid waste the settlements on the Broad River.[28] The Creek
offensive broke up when Cherokees warned that Americans were
preparing a counterattack. The American offensive was not
mounted, but rumor of it caused many Upper Towns headmen to
complain to Stuart that the British forces at Pensacola were too
weak to help them.[29]

On the return of the war parties in September and October the
Creek nation again came to the verge of civil war. Okfuskees and
Cussitas, true to their earlier threat, went down toward Pensacola
and Mobile and killed several loyalist settlers. Opeitley Mico of
Tallassee and the Fat King of Cussita talked of assassinating Emisteseguo. The two neutralists even informed Galphin that they
would attack parties of their own countrymen assembling on the
Ocmulgee River for an assault upon the frontier.[30] Stuart, for his
part, was said to be urging the assassination of those who plotted
the death of Emisteseguo and fomented the killings in West Florida.
Some of the neutralists even talked of seceding from the nation.[31]
From the Cussitas, Paddy Carr wrote Galphin that if the Americans
could send up goods the neutralists would stand fast even to a
civil war and that if an American army came many Creeks would
join them against the pro-British forces. When British agent Barnard at Cussita demanded the return of property plundered from
West Florida, the Fat King refused, saying he would return nothing
until Stuart's friends ceased attacks on the Georgia frontier. The
Lower Towns neutralists looked increasingly to Spanish interven-

---

[27] A. McGillivray, Sept. 1, 1778, B.P.R.O., C.O.5/80, p. 93.

[28] Col. Williamson to Gervaise (n.d.), Gervaise Papers in Laurens Papers.

[29] Stuart to Knox, Oct. 9, 1778, B.P.R.O., C.O.5/80, p. 5.

[30] Telassee King's Talk to Galphin, Oct. 10, 1778, Galphin Papers in Laurens
Papers.

[31] Talk of Patuoy Mico to Galphin, Nov. 4, 1778, Galphin Papers in Laurens
Papers.

tion and sent an emissary to Havana in Cuba.[32] Many of the neutralists became strongly pro-American. Ten of them, including Patuoy Mico, the Cussita King, and Opeitley Mico, prepared to go down to see Galphin again. They were desperately impoverished for goods, for their towns were so hostile to the British that British traders feared to enter them, while the Americans, angry at the raids in the ceded lands, had halted their feeble trade. These headmen even pleaded for an American army to come and stated that nine towns—including the Yuchi, the Hitchiti, Swagliees, and Apalachicola in the Lower Towns and Great Tallassee in the Upper—would welcome the Americans. Barnard told Stuart that Upper Towns Calilgies, Otassies, half of Tuckabatchee, and half of Okfuskee would also join the Americans and that if an American army came many more headmen would defect.[33]

At Ogeechee Old Town, Galphin, who had struggled for four years to keep the Creeks neutral and prevent the holocaust of a large-scale Indian war on the Georgia frontier, awaited with bitterness the coming of the Creek headmen. The American frontier as well as the British establishment hated him, and the frontier now wanted to attack the Creeks. By demanding satisfaction for the frontier slain and invoking trade embargoes until it was given, Galphin had followed too pacific a course to satisfy the frontier. Now he only contemplated lifting the trade embargo in order to keep the Creeks divided until the Americans attacked them.[34] When the headmen arrived in December, he blandly talked of a great peace meeting to be held in the spring. In the inflamed condition of the frontier he had little hope that it could be held.[35] But time was against an American offensive, against Galphin, against the neutralists. In December, 1778, British land and sea forces captured Savannah and prepared to move upcountry, and Stuart began to rally his pro-British Creeks for his long-contemplated major offensive against the Georgia and Carolina frontiers. With

[32] Patrick Carr to Galphin, Nov. 4, 1778, Galphin Papers in Laurens Papers.
[33] T. Barnard to Stuart, Nov. 9, 1778, B.P.R.O., C.O.5/80, p. 101.
[34] Galphin to Laurens, Nov. 11, 1778, Galphin Papers in Laurens Papers.
[35] *Ibid.*, Dec. 29.

the arrival of strong British forces in the South the neutralists' was a lost cause.

After the fall of Savannah, British forces under Lieutenant Colonel Archibald Campbell moved upcountry toward Augusta to support the back-country loyalists. On February 1, 1779, at Pensacola, Stuart issued orders to Taitt to raise the Creeks and lead them under loyalist captains to join Campbell.[36] Taitt sent runners through the woods to bring the far-flung hunters into the towns. On the twenty-fourth he held a meeting of headmen who promised to set out for the frontier on March 5. The neutralists were too weak to oppose them. On March 23, 1779, McGillivray and Emisteseguo were on the path between Oconee and Ogeechee rivers moving with war parties toward Augusta. At abandoned Fulsom's Fort, Taitt received orders from British Colonel Prevost to proceed to Savannah. The Indians balked at this change of objective, and Taitt halted to await the coming up of a large war party following him. Ranging out from his camp, the Indians destroyed abandoned American Fort Rogers and reassembled to move against the ceded lands and an eventual junction with Campbell. In this latter objective they were blocked by a force of a thousand frontiersmen whom they did not dare to attack. For lack of provisions Campbell's force withdrew from Augusta toward Savannah. Taitt then gave orders for his followers to break up into small parties to act as they pleased. He, himself, turned back to join McIntosh, who was bringing up a large party from the Lower Towns, which Taitt determined to lead to Savannah. McGillivray went forward with a party of eighty Creeks and a few loyalists with the objective of raiding into South Carolina below Augusta.[37] Emisteseguo went off to operate in the ceded lands.

On April 2 on the Little River, a few miles beyond Fulsom's fort, McGillivray's party was surprised by two hundred Americans and dispersed with loss. When the fleeing Creeks reached Taitt's force, there was great dismay and confusion which resulted in most

---

[36] Stuart to Taitt, Feb. 1, 1779, B.P.R.O., C.O.5/80, p. 497.

[37] Taitt to Germaine, Aug. 6, 1779, B.P.R.O., C.O.5/80, pp. 473–74.

of Taitt's following returning to their towns.[38] Taitt and McGilli-vray, after being joined by a few Lower Townsmen, went down to Savannah. Stuart's great Indian attack upon the frontier was thus something of a fiasco.

Meanwhile the neutralists of Tallassee, Cussita, and Apalachi-cola, powerless to halt the stream of war parties against the Amer-ican frontier and stirred by rumors that the British drained off the warriors in order to bring up troops to occupy the Indian country, headed toward West Florida to ravage the loyalist settlements there.[39] Holmes, learning of the proposed attack on West Florida, sent runners to head it off and to urge the warriors to go to Pensa-cola for peace talks with the Board of Indian Commissioners which had been set up to handle Indian affairs on the death of John Stuart in early March. Though no Indians went to Pensacola, the hostile march faded. In late April, after its abortive move on Pensacola, the neutralist cause collapsed. This was due partly to the many war parties that went out as a result of the widespread Upper Towns demand for vengeance on the frontier for the death of Indians in McGillivray's debacle. A second factor was the arrival at Little Tallassee of Kessinqua, a Huron, with the northern In-dian declaration of all-out war against the whole colonial frontier. The third factor was the demise of American support. With the advance of British forces from Savannah, Galphin had fled from Ogeechee Old Town. The Creek attacks on the frontier terminated all possibility of further American overtures. The dissident neu-tralist Upper Creek Towns subsided, and even Opeitley Mico of Great Tallassee talked of taking the warpath against the Amer-icans. Deputies from Great Tallassee went to Pensacola and prom-ised the commissioners that in the future they would adhere to the British cause.[40]

On the seaboard, Taitt and McGillivray's seventy warriors ad-

[38] Taitt to Clinton, June 11, 1779, Clinton Papers; James Kuff to Holmes, Apr. 27, 1779, B.P.R.O., C.O.5/80, p. 411.

[39] C. Stuart to Germaine, Aug. 7, 1779, B.P.R.O., C.O.5/80, p. 521.

[40] Florida Board to Germaine, May 10, 1779, B.P.R.O., C.O.5/80, p. 375; *ibid.*, July 12, Vol. 81, p. 145.

vanced from Savannah with the British army into South Carolina. They plundered plantations of patriots and stole Negro slaves, but under Taitt's restraint they killed no women and children. From the Lower Towns, Holmes, now British commissary for the Lower Towns, led war parties against the frontier, where under loyalist guidance they raided selected objectives. In July he took one hundred and twenty Creeks to Savannah to join the British forces there.[41]

Though the British were everywhere successful, that autumn a faint note of doubt presaging events to come crept into the Lower Towns. From Havana in Cuba came rumors conveyed by Spanish ships to the gulf coast that the Spaniards and French would soon attack the British on the seacoast. The result was that the Lower Townsmen refused to sally forth to aid the British when the French fleet appeared off Savannah in September.[42] These doubts were not shared in the Upper Towns, which, when the Spaniards threatened Pensacola in April of 1780, responded to the British call for help with fifteen hundred warriors under McGillivray and McIntosh. But as the Spaniards failed to attack, these drifted off. Upper Creeks did, however, visit Mobile, which had fallen to the Spaniards in March, but disappointed in the presents they received, they did not enter into alliance with the invaders.[43]

The greatest Creek fight of the war was at Augusta in September, 1780. In mid-summer, Colonel Thomas Brown, then British superintendent of the Creek Indians, moved up from St. Augustine with a force of loyalists and two hundred and fifty Creeks and captured Augusta. From Augusta, Brown sent out a call to the Creeks and Cherokees to attend a great conference for which he had assembled an abundance of presents. On September 14, before the conference could assemble, the American Colonel Clarke attacked with six hundred men. A nasty little battle ensued in which the Creeks, fighting in the open fields like regulars, beat back the

---

[41] Journal of the Board of Commissioners, Pensacola, July 5, 1779, B.P.R.O., C.O.5/81, p. 657; Wright to Germaine, Aug. 1, 1779, Candler, *Ga. Col. Rec.*, XXXVIII, Pt. 2, p. 198.
[42] Cameron to Germaine, Dec. 18, 1779, B.P.R.O., C.O.5/81, p. 79.
[43] Shaw to Germaine, Aug. 25, 1780, B.P.R.O., C.O.5/81, p. 629.

Americans and made repeated assaults upon an American-held fortified house. Creek losses were heavy, but the Americans were forced to withdraw.[44] Because of their great losses the Creeks massacred Americans captured on this occasion.

The appointment of Brown as Superintendent of the Creeks had bad repercussions for Pensacola. With Creek-British relations now based on St. Augustine and Savannah and with Brown concentrating on the Georgia-Carolina front, Pensacola lacked funds, goods, and authority to supply presents to the Creeks. The Upper Creeks lost interest in the place. When in the spring of 1781 the Spaniards returned to the attack, only forty Creeks came to the aid of the British garrison. Pensacola fell on May 9, and with it fell the British trade which had sustained the Upper Creeks. Deeply committed to the war against the Americans, many Upper Creeks under Emisteseguo set off to join the Cherokees in attacks on the American frontier in Kentucky and Tennessee. On the Carolina frontier, Creeks participated in Colonel Brown's unsuccessful advance from Augusta toward Ninety-Six in South Carolina.[45]

The last acts of the Creek war against the Americans took place before Savannah when it was besieged by the Americans in the winter of 1781–82. In January of 1782, goods-starved Creeks, desperate to trade, tried to push a packtrain of ninety-three pack horses loaded with deerskins through the American lines, but were captured.[46] Since by this time the Americans wished to get the Creeks out of the war, which was rapidly drawing to a close in American victory, Anthony Wayne, commander of the siege, released his captive Creeks and sent them back to the nation with talks to the effect that peace could be had.[47] About this time Emisteseguo fought his last battle. Bitterly determined to hack his way into Savannah, he led a party of one hundred and fifty warriors against the besieging American lines. A fierce hand-to-hand struggle ensued, in which Emisteseguo was slain. The bulk of his warriors

---

[44] *Ibid.*, 633.

[45] Browne to Germaine, Aug. 9, 1781, B.P.R.O., C.O.5/82, p. 505.

[46] A. Wayne to Nathaniel Greene, Feb. 1, 1782, Greene Papers.

[47] A. Wayne to Joseph Cornell, Feb. 25, 1782, Greene Papers.

made it into Savannah.[48] The great leader of the pro-British faction thus died in the service of his allies.

With their trade blocked at all points save St. Augustine, and with little coming up from there, hundreds of Creeks—Brown said three thousand—pleading friendship and trade visited St. Augustine in the fall of 1782. Brown, knowing the war was lost and having little to offer, urged them to go back to the nation and go about their hunting.[49]

Among themselves the Creeks, considering their losses in the Choctaw and American wars and the fact that they now faced a hostile and successful American frontier, looked about for means of strengthening their confederacy. They began overtures to the despised Seminoles to come north and join the parent Creek towns. East Floridians learning of this saw an opportunity to acquire the Seminole lands which Jonathan Bryon once had coveted. But the Seminoles were not yet ready to move.[50]

The war itself was rapidly being extinguished. Since early 1782 the Americans had been sending peace talks to their old friends at Great Tallassee and Cussita. These increased in tempo until at the end of 1782 the Creeks were being told that the English meant to abandon them, that they should place no confidence in British promises, that actually the great council of the British nation had agreed there would be no more fighting.[51] Already Tallassee and Cussita had begun to return cattle and property plundered in frontier raids. They even brought cattle and horses of their own to Augusta for a feeble trade in goods with the reviving merchants there. Georgians informed the nation that as compensation for damages done by the Creeks during the war, Georgia expected a big land cession—all the area between Oconee River and Okmulgee.[52] In January, 1783, Cussitas and Tallassees waited on the Oconee River

---

48 Brown to Carleton, Oct. 9, 1782, Reports on American Mss., Vol. III.
49 Brown to Townshend, Jan. 12, 1783, B.P.R.O., C.O.5/82, p. 695.
50 Observations of P. Fatio, Dec. 14, 1782, B.P.R.O., C.O.5/60, pp. 911–12.
51 Brown to Townshend, Feb. 25, 1783, B.P.R.O., C.O.5/82, p. 711.
52 Ibid.
53 Candler, Revolutionary Records of Ga., II, 417.

for definitive arrangements to be made for a peace conference.[53] Later that month the Georgia Council sent up word that the peace meeting would take place at the Big Shoals on the Oconee River, May 1, and appointed a commission consisting of General William McIntosh, General Twiggs, Colonel Clarke, Colonel William Few, Edward Telfair, Esq., Colonel John Martin, and General Elbert. Galphin had died in 1780. However, the conference was delayed.

The pro-British faction, now led by McGillivray and supported by the northern Indians, refused to consider peace talks till they had heard directly from the Crown of England that the war was over.[54] When Georgia emissaries came into Coweta to invite head-men to come to Augusta to cede lands, they were told to get out of the country.[55]

But when reports that England intended to abandon Florida to Spain pervaded the nation, there was consternation. Many headmen went to St. Augustine to learn the truth. Fine Bones of Coweta on May 1, 1783, stated the dominant Creek sentiment: "The old be-loved men informed me that the warriors of my town first joined the English as men and friends—that they gave them lands and became one flesh—that they considered their enemies as our own—that in all the wars either against Indians, Spaniards or Virginians, they assisted them—that they often took prisoners whom the English redeemed and had children by them who live among us— Do the English mean to abandon their own children with their friends? Why will they turn their backs on us and forsake us? We never expected that men and warriors our friends would throw us into the hands of our enemies— Is it the great king's talk that we left in distress? I hope he will inform us—If the English mean to abandon the land we will accompany them—We cannot take a Virginian or Spaniard by the hand—we cannot look them in the face."[56] The King and head warrior of the Upper Creeks came down to St. Augustine on May 27 and demanded that the king's ships come and

54 McIntosh to Brown, Apr. 14, 1783, B.P.R.O., C.O.5/82, p. 649.
55 *Ibid.*, May 27, p. 539.
56 Talk of Fine Bones of Coweta, May 15, 1783, B.P.R.O., C.O.5/82, pp. 746–47.

take the Creeks away to new lands, saying that since they had constantly been in the king's service, they should not be sacrificed to their enemies.[57]

Although an atmosphere of defeatism began to pervade the nation, the general sentiment opposed land cessions to the Georgians. Some boldly declared that if the Americans wanted lands, they should come and take them if they could.[58] To Georgia they sent protests against trespassers in the American-coveted area. Georgia's governor began to fear renewed warfare if an accommodation could not soon be reached.[59] McGillivray, who, according to Brown, had now been elected chief and head warrior of all the nation, wrote Brown asking for aid if the Creeks went to war with Carolina and Georgia.[60] With a felicitous feeling for half truth, he reminded Brown that " 'twas not from a sense of any particular injuries received by us from those people that we waged war, but from principles of gratitude and friendship to the British nation whose repeated calls for assistance we cheerfully obeyed and after a nine years contest during which this nation gave proofs of unshaken fidelity and at the close of it to find ourselves betrayed to our enemies and divided between Spaniards and Americans is cruel and ungenerous."[61] Brown, who was merely waiting for information of the formal signing of the treaty of peace in Paris, advised McGillivray not to enter into any hostilities as yet but to apply to the Spaniards at Pensacola, who were jealous of the Americans, for arms and ammunition.[62] He thus pointed the way to the future.

At Augusta on November 1, 1783, a large party of Upper and Lower Towns headmen, primarily of the old neutralist and pro-American factions and led by the Fat King of Cussita and Opeitley Mico of Tallassee, met the Georgia commissioners for a formal signing of a peace. They agreed "that all differences between the said parties heretofore subsisting shall cease and be forgotten . . .

---

[57] Brown to Townshend, June 1, 1783, B.P.R.O., C.O.5/83, p. 735.
[58] Brown to North, July 30, 1783, B.P.R.O., C.O.5/82, p. 785.
[59] Candler, Revolutionary Records of Ga., Vol. II, pp. 510-11.
[60] Brown to North, Oct. 28, 1783, B.P.R.O., C.O.5/82, p. 807.
[61] A. McGillivray to Browne, Aug. 20, 1783, B.P.R.O., C.O.5/82, p. 811.
[62] Brown to North, Oct. 24, 1783, B.P.R.O., C.O.5/82, p. 807.

that all just Indian debts to the traders of Georgia shall be fairly and fully paid; that a trade shall be carried on by Georgia merchants and traders in the Creek towns." Finally the Creeks ceded the lands desired. They agreed that "a new line shall be drawn without delay between the present settlements in the said state and the said Indians to begin on Savannah River where the present line strikes it, thence up the said river to a place in the most northern branch of the same currently called Keowee [River] where a northeast line to be drawn from the top of Oconee Mountain shall intersect; thence along the said line in a southeast direction to Toogaloo River; thence to the top of Cunohe mountain; thence to the head and source of the most southern branch of Oconee River, including all the waters of the same, thence down the said river to the old line."[63] It was not all the land the Americans desired, but the cession was of some eight hundred square miles, the blood price of war which the Creeks had fought on the losing side. Though for all practical purposes the treaty ended the war, it had been made by a minority faction and was not acceptable to McGillivray and the pro-English. The Creeks thus entered the post colonial period divided into bitter factions.

[63] Candler, *Ga. Col. Rec.*, XXXVI, 503–504.

Bibliography

MANUSCRIPTS, PUBLISHED MANUSCRIPTS, COLLECTIONS, ETC.

Clements Library, Ann Arbor, Michigan:
  Amherst Papers.
  Sir William Clinton Papers.
  Papers of General Thomas Gage relating to his command in
    North America, 1762–76. 137 vols.
  General Nathaniel Greene Papers.
  Sir William Lyttelton Papers, 1756–60.
  Lord Shelburne Papers.
Georgia:
  Candler, Allen D., ed. *Colonial Records of the State of Georgia.*
    26 vols. Atlanta, 1904–16.
  ————. Additional Colonial Records of the State of Georgia.
    12 vols. [transcripts on microfilm].
  ————. *The Revolutionary Records of the State of Georgia.*
    3 vols. Atlanta, 1908.
  Georgia Historical Society. *Collections.* Savannah, 1840.

Library of Congress transcripts:
British Public Records Office: C.O.5/74–82, 94, 387–89, 555–61 (1715–61).
Paris Archives Nationales Colonies. B33, C13A, Vols. 26–39.
Mississippi and Alabama:
Rowland, Dunbar, ed. *Mississippi Provincial Archives, English Dominion, 1763–66*. Nashville, 1911.
——— and A. G. Saunders, eds. *Mississippi Provincial Archives*. 3 vols. Jackson, Miss., 1927–32.
South Carolina:
South Carolina Department of Archives and History. Council Journal. [Miscellaneous photostats.]
Easterby, J. H., ed. *The Journal of the Commons House of Assembly*. I–VI (Nov. 1736–June 1746). Columbia, Historical Commission of South Carolina, 1951.
Jenkins, W. S., ed. Journals of His Majesty's Honorable Council. Reels 1–8 [microfilm].
———. South Carolina Book of Indian Affairs, 1710–1760. 2 reels [microfilm].
———. South Carolina Journals of the Commons House of Assembly, 1692–1779. 20 reels [microfilm].
———. South Carolina Journals of the Upper House of Assembly, 1721–1783. 6 reels [microfilm].
Laurens Papers, South Carolina Historical Society, Charleston, South Carolina.
McDowell, W. L., Jr., ed. *Documents Relating to Indian Affairs*, May 21, 1750–Aug. 7, 1754. Columbia, South Carolina Archives Department, 1958.
———. *Journals of the Commissioners of the Indian Trade*, Sept. 20, 1710–Aug. 29, 1718. Columbia, South Carolina Archives Department, 1955.
———. *Records in the British Public Record Office Relating to South Carolina, 1663–1762*. [Microfilm.] Columbia, 1955.
Yearbook of the City of Charleston, 1894.

NEWSPAPERS AND MAGAZINES

Gentleman's Magazine, Vol. IV (1734).
London Magazine, Vol. III (1734).
South Carolina Gazette, 1733–63. [Microfilm, American Antiquarian Society.]

OTHER PRIMARY SOURCES

Adair, James. *The History of the American Indians*. London, 1775.
Barcia Carballido y Zuñiga, Andres Gonzalés de. *Historia general de la Florida*. Madrid, 1723.
Bartram, William. "Observations on the Creek and Cherokee Indians," *Transactions of the American Ethnological Society*, Vol. III, Pt. I. New York, 1853 (Reprint, 1909).
———. *Travels through North and South Carolina, Georgia, East and West Florida*. London, 1791.
Bossu, Jean-Bernard. *Travels in the Interior of North America, 1751–1762*, trans. and ed. by Seymour Feiler. Norman, 1962.
Bourne, Edward Gaylord. *Narratives of the Career of Hernando de Soto*. New York, 1904.
Campbell, Thomas. "Narrative of Visit to Creek Nation 1764–1765." [Ms.] Athell Papers, University of Aberdeen, Aberdeen, Scotland.
Carter, Clarence Edwin. *The Correspondence of General Thomas Gage with the Secretaries of State, 1763–1775*. 2 vols. New Haven, 1931.
Egmont, Earl of. *The Journal of the Earl of Egmont*, ed. by Robert G. McPherson. Athens, 1962.
Force Transcripts of Georgia Records. Library of Congress.
Fortescue, John, and Cecil Headlam. *Great Britain Public Records Office, Calendar of State Papers, American and West Indies, 1681–1685, 1701, 1708–1709, 1716–1720, 1722–1725, 1728–1730*. London, 1898–1937.
Great Britain Historical Manuscripts Commission. Report on American Manuscripts in the Royal Institution of Great Britain. 4 vols. London, Printed for His Majesty's Stationery Office, 1904–1909.

Kimball, Gertrude Selwyn, ed. *Correspondence of William Pitt When Secretary of State with Colonial Governors and Military and Naval Commissioners in America.* 2 vols. New York, 1905.

Mereness, Newton D. *Travels in the American Colonies.* New York, 1916.

Payne, John Howard. Cherokee Manuscripts. The Newberry Library, Chicago.

Serrano y Sanz, Manuel. *Documentos Historicos de la Florida y la Luisiana, siglos xvi al xvii.* Madrid, 1912.

Surrey, N. M. Miller, ed. *Calendar of Manuscripts in Paris Archives and Libraries Relating to the History of the Mississippi Valley to 1803.* 2 vols. Washington, 1928.

United States De Soto Expedition Commission, *Final Report.* Washington, 1939.

Wesley, John. *The Journal of the Rev. John Wesley, A.M.* 4 vols. London, 1903.

BOOKS AND ARTICLES

Alden, John R. *John Stuart and the Southern Colonial Frontier.* Ann Arbor, 1944.

Bolton, Herbert E. *Arrendo's Historical Proof of Spain's Title to Georgia.* Berkeley, 1925.

Boyd, Mark F. "Expedition of Marcus Delgado from Apalache to the Upper Creek Country in 1686," *The Florida Historical Quarterly,* Vols. XVI–XVII, No. I (July, 1937), 3–32.

Corry, John P. *Indian Affairs in Georgia 1732–1756.* Philadelphia, 1936.

Coulter, Ellis Merton. "Mary Musgrove, Queen of the Creeks," *Georgia Historical Quarterly,* Vol. XI (March, 1927).

———. *A Short History of Georgia.* Chapel Hill, 1933.

Crane, Verner W. *The Southern Frontier 1670–1732.* Durham, 1928.

Ford, Lawrence Carroll. *The Triangular Struggle for Spanish Pensacola 1689–1739.* Washington, 1939.

Hale, Richard Walden. *Guide to Photocopies of Historical Materials in the United States and Canada.* Ithaca, 1961.

Harris, Thaddeus Mason. *Biographical Memorials of James Ogle-thorpe*. Boston, 1841.

Hewatt, Alexander. *An Historical Account of the Rise and Progress of the Colonies of South Carolina and Georgia*. 2 vols. London, 1779.

Hodge, Frederick Webb. *Handbook of American Indians North of Mexico*. 2 vols. Washington, Gov't Printing Office, 1907–10.

Howard, Milo B., Jr. and Robert R. Rea. *The Memoir Justificatif of the Chevalier Montault de Monberaut: Indian Diplomacy in British West Florida, 1763–1765*. University, Alabama, 1965.

La Harpe, Bernard de. "Historical Journal of the Establishment of the French in Louisiana," *Historical Collections of Louisiana*, ed. by Benjamin F. French. New York, 1851.

McCall, Hugh. *The History of Georgia*. 2 vols. Savannah, 1811.

McCrady, Edward. *The History of South Carolina Under the Royal Government*. New York, 1901.

———. *The History of South Carolina in the Revolution*. New York, 1901.

Milfort, LeClerc. *Memoirs Or a Quick Glance at My Various Travels and My Sojourn in the Creek Nation*, ed. by Ben C. McCarey. Kennesaw, Ga., 1959.

Mohr, Walter H. *Federal Indian Relations, 1774–1788*. Philadelphia, 1933.

Mowat, Charles Loch. *East Florida As a British Province, 1763–1784*. Berkeley, 1943.

Pénicault, André. *Fleur de Lys and Calumet*. Baton Rouge, 1953.

Pickett, Albert James. *History of Alabama and Incidentally Georgia and Mississippi from the Earliest Period*. 2 vols. Charleston, 1851.

Ramsey, David. *History of South Carolina 1670–1808*. Charleston, 1809.

Reese, Trevor Richard. *Colonial Georgia*. Athens, 1963.

Shaw, Helen Louise. *British Administration of the Southern Indians, 1756–1783*. Lancaster, 1931.

Shea, John Gilmary. *History of the Catholic Missions among the*

Indian Tribes of the United States, 1529–1854. New York, 1881.

Swanton, John R. *Early History of the Creek Indians and Their Neighbors.* Washington, 1922.

———. *The Indians of the Southeastern United States.* Washington, 1946.

———. *Social Organization and Social Usages of the Indians of the Creek Confederacy.* Washington, 1928.

TePaske, John J. *The Governorship of Spanish Florida.* Durham, 1964.

Tyler, L. G., ed. *Narratives of Early Virginia.* New York, 1907.

Index

Abbeville, Ga.: 41
Abeika Indians: 5, 6, 31, 44, 62, 65, 72, 94, 100, 105, 108, 114, 116, 118, 122, 127, 242, 246, 259, 291, 302; dealings with English of, 74–76, 112, 113, 117, 121, 150, 216; dealings with French of, 129, 145, 163–65; neutralism of, 312, 313
Acorn Dance: 289
Acorn Whistler: 128–29; 153–57, 161
Adair, James: 3, 5, 10, 33, 34, 35, 117, 130
Ahaye: *see* Cowkeeper
Alabama (state): 4
Alabama Indians: 4, 6, 51, 206, 241, 304; friendship with French, 54–58, 106–108, 112, 113, 117, 118, 145, 168, 170, 185, 201, 208, 280
Albany, Ga.: 42
Alden, John: 240
Altamaca (town): 41, 42, 43
Altamaha River: 68, 70, 71, 77, 91, 96, 98, 100, 115, 121, 123, 125, 143, 147, 150, 209, 239, 251, 267, 281, 312, 316
Americans, defeat and expulsion of British by: 301–25

American Southern Indian Commissioners: 294
Apalachee (region): 4, 50, 51, 66, 82, 114, 246
Apalachee Indians: 59, 64; war with Lower Creeks, 51–56; attacks on English, 62–70
Apalachee missions: 52, 56
Apalachee Mountains: 6
Apalachee Old Fields: 100, 168, 315
Apalachee River: 6
Apalachicola (town): 7, 49, 51, 65, 82, 95, 110, 152, 191, 196, 204, 207, 234, 281, 310, 313, 317, 319
Apalachicola (region): 80
Apalachicola Indians: 78, 203, 285, 289
Apalachicola River: 100, 267
Arkansas Post raid: 145
Arkansas River: 129
Atkin, Edmund: 220; visit to Creeks, 197–209; advocate of lower trade prices, 213–18
Attakullakulla: 172, 247, 275
Aubert, ——— (French commandant): 202
Augusta, Ga.: establishment of, 93; as a

333

Ulchitchi (town): 153
Ulibahali (town): 45, 66
Umpyche: 85, 95

Vaudreuil (La. governor): 112, 118, 122, 152, 163, 169, 170
Vera Cruz: 62
Virginia: 48, 168, 175, 196, 197, 205, 238, 250, 255, 262, 285
Virginia Blues: 188
Virginians, friction between Creeks and: 230, 233, 263, 270, 271, 273, 282, 285, 298, 302, 311, 323

Wahatchie: 203, 205
Walker, John: 252
Watson, —— (trader): 90
Wayne, Gen. Anthony: 321
Weas Indians: 118
Wehanny: 223
Weoffki, the Long Warrior: 144, 158, 187, 212, 246, 250, 251, 293
Wesley, John: 13, 34, 97, 98
West Indies: 53
Westo Indians: 48, 49
White murder: 282, 284
White Cabin of Cussita: see Tupahtke
White Ground, Town: 257, 259
White King of the Cussitas: 225, 242
White Lieutenant of the Okfuskees: 311, 315
Wilkinson, Edward: 292
Willimico: 69
Will's Friend: 315
Wilson, —— (trader): 234
Wind Clan: 104, 305, 308
Windsor Castle: 88
Wolf King of the Okfuskees: 157
Wolf of Fushatchee: see Wolf of Muccolossus

Wolf of Muccolossus: 24, 26, 27, 107, 114, 121, 122, 129, 130, 149, 158, 172, 179–81, 207, 208, 214, 284; strong pro-British stand of, 185–202, 211, 214, 216, 217, 224, 225, 237, 240, 242, 247–49, 254
Wood, Captain: 102
Woodward, Henry: 49, 50, 51, 63
Wright, Governor James: 12, 26; first encounters with Creeks of, 223–27; attempts to control frontier disturbances, 229–38, 242–45, 253–58, 262–69, 273–77, 282–88; attempts to win Creeks to loyalist side, 290, 291, 294, 296
Wright, Joseph: 188, 220, 221

Yahatastanage: see the Mortar
Yahatastanage: 61
Yamacraw Bluff: 80, 82, 83
Yamacraws: 82, 84, 87, 90, 95, 96, 99, 101, 103, 104, 109, 114, 115, 119
Yamacraw lands: 120, 125, 126, 133, 138, 150, 151, 220
Yamasee Indians: 4, 57, 58, 59, 67–78, 81, 83, 95, 98, 110, 115, 127
Yamasee War, 52, 57, 61–78, 141, 144
Yoakley's Son, warrior: 167
Youfalas, town: 7 (see Eufalees)
Youholomico, headman: 65
Young Lieutenant of Coweta: see Escochabey
Young Twin: see Malatchi
Youhowlakee: 78, 79, 84, 91
Youwillieniane: see Captain Allick
Yuchi Indians: 4, 51, 80, 81, 104, 119, 120, 149, 195, 295, 317; see Eutchi

Zulby, David: 289

The text for *The Creek Frontier* was set on the Linotype in Old Style No. 7. An exceptionally legible, modernized face, Old Style has been one of the most popular book faces for years because of its even color, its uncommon legibility, and its compact fitting.

The paper on which the book is printed bears the watermark of the University of Oklahoma Press and has an effective life of at least three hundred years.